Economics for 'A' level

D J Browne B SC (Econ) ACE
Head of Economics
Upton Grammar School
Slough

Edward Arnold

© D J Browne 1983
First published 1983
by Edward Arnold (Publishers) Ltd
41 Bedford Square London WC1B 3DQ

Edward Arnold (Australia) Pty Ltd
80 Waverley Road
Caulfield East 3145
PO Box 234
Melbourne

British Library Cataloguing in Publication Data

Browne, D.J.
   Economics for 'A' level.
   1. Economics
   I. Title
   330   HB171.5

ISBN 0-7131-0866-5

All rights reserved. No part of this publication may be reproduced, stored in a retrieval system, or transmitted in any form or by any means, electronic, mechanical, photocopying, recording or otherwise, without the prior permission of Edward Arnold (Publishers) Ltd.

Text set in 10/11 pt Times Compugraphic by Colset Private Limited, Singapore
Printed and bound in Great Britain by Richard Clay (The Chaucer Press) Limited, Bungay, Suffolk.

Acknowledgements

The Publishers would like to thank the following organisations for permission to reproduce copyright material and photographs:

The Controller of Her Majesty's Stationery Office for the Treasury Bill (Crown Copyright) on page 149 and the National Westminster Bank PLC for the sterling certificate of deposit on page 148.

Contents

Foreword		viii
Introduction		1
Section one Production		9
1	**The search for efficiency**	9
	The basic ingredients of production	9
	Capitalist or centralized?	10
	Production – the macro-economic view	11
	Production – the micro-economic problem	12
	The law of diminishing returns	13
	Economies of scale	13
	Why small firms still exist	14
	Summary	17
	Appendix: The mathematical calculation of the optimum using isoquants and the iso-cost curves	19
2	**Types of firm and methods of financing them**	22
	Types of firm	22
	Stocks and shares	25
	How firms finance themselves	26
	Summary	29
3	**The labour supply**	31
	Division of labour	31
	Advantages of division of labour	31
	Disadvantages of division of labour	33
	The labour force	34
	Recent trends in UK working patterns	37
	The population base	40
	Recent trends in the UK population structure	40
	The consequences of a static population	44
	Summary	44
4	**Structural and regional unemployment**	46
	Location of industry	46
	Structural unemployment	48
	The regional problem	49
	Regional policy	51
	Regional policy in practice	52
	Major features of regional policy	52

	Regional policy in the 1980s	56
	Summary	57
5	**Cost and supply schedules**	58
	Costs	58
	The industry's supply curve	61
	The long run	64
	Joint supply	66
	Conclusion to Section one	66
	Summary	67

Section two Demand — **68**

6	**Individual demand**	68
	Utility	68
	Factors which influence demand	68
	The law of diminishing marginal utility	69
	The law of equi-marginal returns	71
	Indifference curve analysis	72
	Summary	78
7	**Market demand**	79
	The demand curve	79
	Price elasticity of demand	80
	Other elasticities of demand	83
	Perverse demand curves	85
	Elasticity of demand in the real world	86
	Summary	87

Section three The price system — **89**

8	**The free market in operation**	89
	The function of price	89
	Changes in demand and supply	90
	Special cases	96
	Summary	96
9	**Government intervention in the price system**	97
	Why and how governments intervene in free markets	97
	Summary	103

Section four Monopoly and competition — **104**

10	**The firm in equilibrium**	104
	The nature of equilibrium	104
	Types of market	106
	Summary	108
11	**Monopoly, oligopoly and restrictive practices**	109
	Monopoly	109
	Monopolies legislation in the UK	114
	Oligopoly	116
	Restrictive practices legislation	118
	Summary	119

12	**Imperfect and perfect competition**	120
	The argument for competition	120
	Imperfect competition	120
	Perfect competition	121
	Monopoly and competition	124
	Summary	125
13	**Nationalised industries**	126
	The state sector	126
	Finance of nationalised industries	128
	Criticisms of nationalised industries	130
	Conclusions	135
	Summary	135
	Appendix Performance targets	136

Section five   Money and banking — **137**

14	**Money**	137
	Introduction	137
	The functions of money	138
	Bank debt	139
	How bank deposits are created	139
	Summary	141
15	**The Bank of England and the commercial banks**	142
	Bank of England	142
	Commercial banks	145
	Asset structure of banks	146
	Summary	148
16	**The discount and secondary money markets**	150
	Discount houses	150
	Secondary money markets	151
	Other markets	152
	Summary	153
17	**The mechanisms of monetary policy**	154
	The money supply	154
	Aims of monetary policy	154
	Mechanisms of monetary policy	157
	The problems of monetary policy in the 1970s	159
	The August 1981 measures	163
	Summary	164

Section six   Index numbers — **165**

18	**Index numbers**	165
	Measuring trends in economics	165
	Index numbers	166
	The retail price index	168
	Problems of index numbers	170
	Uses of index numbers	171
	Summary	171

Section seven International economics	**172**
19 International trade	172
The law of comparative advantage	172
Free trade versus protection	177
The terms of trade	182
Summary	183
20 The balance of payments	184
Structure of the balance of payments	184
Methods of curing a current account deficit	190
The UK's balance of payments problems	192
Summary	195
21 Exchange rates	196
How exchange rates are determined	196
Possible types of exchange rate systems	199
Post-war developments in the world monetary system	200
Summary	204
22 The United Kingdom and the European Community	206
Evolution of the European Economic Community	206
The UK's attitude to the Community	208
Features of the common agricultural policy	210
The UK's problems concerning the Community	212
Summary	216
Section eight Income distribution	**217**
23 Wages – the marginal revenue product theory and its application to the real world	217
The demand for labour – the marginal revenue product theory	217
The supply of labour	219
Equilibrium in the labour market	221
Factors affecting wage determination in the real world	221
The government and wages	227
Summary	234
24 Trade unions and labour relations	236
The functions of trade unions	236
The structure of trade unions	238
The growth of the trade union movement	239
Criticisms of trade unions	241
Summary	243
25 Rent, interest and profits	244
Economic rent	244
Theory of the rate of interest	247
Profits	250
Summary	251
Section nine Macro-economics	**252**
26 The circular flow of income	252

Macro-economics	252
Types of unemployment	252
The circular flow of income	255
Summary	259

27 National income accounts — 260
The calculation of national income — 260
Interpretation and uses of national income accounts — 264
Summary — 267

28 The multiplier and the accelerator — 268
Equilibrium in the economy — 268
Consumption and savings — 268
Investment — 270
The trade multiplier — 277
The government multiplier — 280
Inflationary and deflationary gaps — 281
The multiplier in the real world — 284
Summary — 285

29 Inflation – causes and cures — 286
Inflation — 286
Possible causes of inflation — 287
The problems created by a high rate of inflation — 291
Controlling inflation – Keynes or Friedman? — 294
Stagflation — 302
Summary — 304
Appendix: the UK's taxation system — 307

30 Economic growth and the clash of macro-economic targets — 312
Economic growth — 312
Factors affecting economic growth — 313
The costs of economic growth — 315
The clash of macro-economic targets — 318
The UK in the 1980s — 319
Summary — 320

Bibliography — 322
Index — 324

Foreword

My brief was to produce a textbook which the average student taking GCE Advanced Level or similar examinations would find intelligible and straightforward. Clearly, the subject-matter cannot and should not be diluted for the benefit of those unwilling to apply themselves to the rigours of the syllabus, but the material can, perhaps, be presented in a slightly less daunting manner than in some of the textbooks which are available.

I have attempted to present an orthodox treatment of economic theory, illustrating with facts and figures from the real world. The chapters specifically devoted to the UK's economic problems are more freely written, discussing many of the views in vogue concerning contemporary issues. No economics teacher (and I have been teaching for eighteen years) will ever find an 'ideal' book; no doubt, many will question my 'order of events' in this somewhat circular subject. I hope that each section will stand on its own, however, and there are many cross-references in the text which may help students who tackle the various sections in a different order to that presented.

I am greatly indebted to Dr W K Norris, Reader in Economics at Brunel University, whose comments, suggestions and criticisms have been of inestimable value. Dr Norris was once a school teacher himself and is presently Chief Examiner at Advanced Level for the University of London Board, so his advice was invaluable[1]. In addition, the typing of Mrs Christine Newnham was as excellent as I was told it would be. Such errors, omissions and inadequacies as remain are, of course, my responsibility.

I believe that the writing of this book has assisted my own teaching. I hope that the average candidate will find the book comprehensible and clear and that the 'high-flier' will also find it of value as an introduction and base for further studies.

David Browne
May 1982

Dr Norris took up appointment as Professor of Economics at Murdoch University, Western Australia, 1983.

Introduction

Economics – not the 'dismal science'

Although the standard of living of most people has risen steadily in the industrialised world since the Second World War, economists are hardly the most admired body of academics in the modern world. Since the War, the UK seems to have stumbled through all sorts of economic crises – balance of payments problems, currency crises, poor labour relations, inflation, unemployment, unpopular government policies which raise taxes and interest rates or control income rises. Economists have pondered these problems and come up with various remedies, which have achieved limited success. George Bernard Shaw's famous gibe that 'if all the economists in the world were to be joined end-to-end, they still would not reach a conclusion' would appear to be borne out by many conflicts of opinion in the profession. Even when 364 university teachers of economics sent a letter to the Prime Minister early in 1981 criticizing government policies they were unable to offer an agreed alternative strategy.

Economic crises are not new. Between the wars there was widespread world depression and unemployment with no apparent agreement amongst economists of the time as to how to deal with the situation. Even in the nineteenth century when the Industrial Revolution was under way and Britain in particular was developing at an unprecedented rate, there were still poverty (even starvation in Ireland), trade restrictions, worsening labour relations and quarrels about the proper role of the state in economic affairs. Indeed, economics (or 'Political economy' as it was at first known) was known as the 'dismal science'.

Why do countries appear to lurch from one crisis to another? Why cannot economists cure a malfunctioning economy in the way that an engineer can mend a damaged machine? Why are there no magic formulae which can be applied to problems? Why do economists disagree? Many of the reasons for these matters lie in the nature of economics itself.

The broad setting

An economist does not study natural forces in the way a physicist studies energy or sound, or a chemist studies the nature and interaction of natural elements, because economics is not a 'natural science' but a '*social science*', a study of human behaviour. It is in the same field as subjects like psychology, sociology and political science. As all individuals differ from one another in aptitudes and attitudes, each individual has his own identity and follows his own behaviour pattern. Whereas a chemist knows that, under specified experimental conditions, when H_2O is added to SO_2, H_2SO_4 will *always* be produced, an economist can make no such predictions about the behaviour of the objects in his field. If, for example, two people have the same amount of money at the same time in the same place, an economist cannot predict how they will use this money. Although the money and even the environment may be the same, the other vital element, the people, are not. They have their own individual aims, ideas, preferences and priorities. No two people or groups of people can be guaranteed to act in the same way in any sphere of human activity when faced by similar circumstances.

The situation is not quite as desperate as it seems, however. Although everyone behaves in their own individual way, there are not 56 million random behaviour patterns for the 56 million inhabitants of the UK, for example. To take our example of the two people, although their behaviour cannot be anticipated, it can be said with some confidence that they will spend at least some of their money. If we have some details of their environment we can even anticipate how they might spend it. Social scientists are not groping around completely in the dark. A psychologist, who studies the human mind, finds out how most people react to certain environments, particularly stress environments like being alone, under threat, deprived of sleep, or even being unemployed. A sociologist, who studies the behaviour and interaction of groups can make statements about the behaviour of people in high-rise flats, prisons or football crowds. The rules or laws of behaviour which are discovered are true for the 'average person', or for 'most of the people, most of the time'. That is about as accurate as a social scientist can be when establishing rules about human behaviour. *Tendencies*, which most people will follow, can be identified, even though certain individuals will always deviate from the 'normal' pattern.

An economist's laws have exactly the same nature as those of other social scientists – they are general rules, to which there may be individual exceptions. For example, an economist may assume that most people aim to improve their standard of living, so that if they suddenly inherit a fortune they will spend widely on goods which they previously could not afford. Yet if the person inheriting the fortune were a monk, who has taken a vow of poverty, and thus does not wish (or is not allowed) to spend his inheritance, he may give all the money to his monastic order or to a religious charity. Nevertheless, the monk is an exception; most people will behave in a different way.

The specific sphere of economics

Economics is concerned with the study of human behaviour in three specific fields, those of *Production, Consumption*, and *Exchange* (or Trade).

In order to survive, everyone needs food and drink, shelter and (in most climates) clothing. For many countries all but the privileged few had to provide all these for themselves - or die. Throughout the last two hundred years or so, this pattern has changed, at least in the industrialised world. Few people now grow all their own food, make their clothes, build their shelter, attend to their ailments - ie exist in a completely self-sufficient manner. Most of us work only at one particular job (in fact, about 30 million people in the UK have *no* paid employment, as they are children, retired people, students or housewives). Yet we are *all* consumers. So, for us all to consume what others provide, there must be means of trading goods - a 'market'. Originally, this was literally 'exchange' - bartering of goods; now, money is usually used for buying, but the principle is the same.

In this book, we shall be studying the principles behind these functions of *production, consumption* and *exchange*, and some of their aspects in the modern world, particularly in the UK. Yet we cannot ignore other factors. Psychological factors enters into every individual's decision-making and subjects in the economic sphere cannot ignore psychology (for example, advertising and marketing). Sociology, ethics, morals and particularly politics are all relevant subjects. Economics cannot be studied in isolation from these other sciences because the economy does not exist in a vaccuum. Few decisions are made by producers, consumers, traders, or governments on purely economic grounds.

The economic problem

In making statements about human behaviour it has to be assumed that people have certain fundamental aims. These aims are assumed to be that human beings are rather an ambitious and self-seeking breed, wishing to improve the quality and happiness of their existence in some way. In the economic sphere, these assumptions are on the same lines. For example, we believe that consumers aim to maximise the benefits gained from the things they buy, and that producers seek to maximise the profits they receive from the goods or services they make and sell. There will always be exceptions, of course. For example, the providers of the state education service or the National Health Service do not aim to maximise their profits; indeed, the services they provide are virtually or entirely free to the consumers. Nevertheless, the assumptions of benefit-maximisation and profit-maximisation can be assumed to apply to most people.

If these aims are accepted, at least for the moment, it is clear that all those concerned, producers or consumers, have to make important decisions in order to achieve their objectives. A consumer has to decide how to dispose of his or her resources (spending power) in order to maximise his or her satisfaction; a producer must decide how to use his or her resources (labour force, machinery and raw materials) in order to make profits. Every decision, by definition, means that, as one course of action is chosen, others have to be rejected.

All these decisions are limited by the resources at the disposal of the decision-maker. No-one has unlimited assets or resources. If I, as a consumer, have to make a choice about where to take my summer holiday, I need not consider all those alternatives for which I have insufficient assets – for example a world cruise, for which I have neither the money nor the leisure time available. Yet even after these eliminations, many alternatives remain to me, and I must make my choice according to my tastes. Assets can only be used once, however. The choice, once made, means that other alternatives have been sacrificed. If I spend £x on a holiday to France, I have sacrificed all the other things I could have spent £x on – holidays elsewhere, new golf clubs, new carpets or an almost infinite variety of other things. This same principle of sacrifice applies to decisions made by producers, traders, or indeed the government.

This sacrifice principle is known in economics as *'opportunity-cost'*. The opportunity-cost of a decision is equal to the foregone alternatives on which the resources could have been used. For example, if a government decides to spent £100 million on a new guided-missile instead of on new machinery for the coal industry, the opportunity-cost of the missile is the coal machinery.

The economists' task

Economic decisions are clearly not made merely by economists; everyone is engaged in making such decisions in their functions as consumer or producer. The task of the economist is to shed light on these decisions and to assist them to be made in a more efficient or informed manner. The economist is concerned with the search for *efficiency*. When a person says that something (eg the performance of a new car) is or is not 'economical', what he or she means is that it is or is not 'efficient'. Efficiency really means 'gaining maximum benefit from the resources involved'. In the same sense as this, an economist advises on the most efficient way of using resources in order to achieve a stated aim. The search for the most efficient is known as *'Positive'* economics. If a government wants to build a new airport or prison, economists may be asked to advise on the 'best' or most efficient site. Economists have political and moral views like everyone else, and they may find that the 'best' site would have harmful effects on the local residents or environment. They might even be opposed to the whole idea of new airports or prisons anyway, but their job is not to question the aim or to stray outside their field. In other words, "Economics cannot (or should not) make value-judgements about society. What it can do is develop measures of the way society is functioning and of whether, given a particular set of objectives . . . it is functioning well".[1] Notice, the objectives are 'given', either by society (to improve the living standards) or the government (to build a new airport in the best place). Strictly speaking, the economist should not make value-judgements, but only 'efficiency-judgements'; he or she should stick to Positive economics and let others make the value-judgements. In a real world example, the Roskill Commission advised the government in 1971 to put its new airport in North Buckinghamshire; although this was the most efficient site, the government rejected the recommendation on non-economic grounds and picked an alternative, more expensive site on the Essex marshes – before dropping the idea of a new airport entirely.

Of course, economists have opinions about aims and they express them. JM Keynes, probably Britain's most famous economist, attacked the implications of the 1919 Peace Treaty with Germany. In more recent years the eminent American JK Galbraith has attacked the aim of constantly seeking to improve living standards at the expense of pollution and exhaustion of resources. When an economist makes a value-judgement he is indulging in what is called *Normative* economics. A normative statement, unlike a positive one, is a statement of opinion which cannot be resolved by an appeal to the facts.

An attempt has been made in recent years to try to combine Positive and Normative economics to some extent by a technique called *cost-benefit analysis*. This attempts to give a quantified value to the non-economic costs and advantages of proposed projects. It was first used in the UK in the 1950's on motorway planning and is still mainly used in transport projects. The technique is necessarily less than perfect, as it tries to express in monetary terms concepts like time, life and noise, but it is a start in the right direction.

The economists' techniques

The biggest problem an economist, or for that matter any social scientist, has is that he or she cannot easily conduct a controlled experiment in an isolated environment. This is in contrast, of course, to the way in which a natural scientist can work. Even if an economist can set up an experiment, the conditions of the experiment cannot be reproduced in a real world situation. As experiments are virtually impossible to set up, and probably of limited value because of their artificiality, the economist is reduced to two main methods of research – *deduction* and *induction*.

a) *Deduction*

This merely consists of observing real world events and identifying trends and tendencies in behaviour. Many problems must be faced, however.

(i) The behavioural trends observed may only apply to one particular set of circumstances; several similar environments must be studied over a period of time.

(ii) Behavioural patterns have an annoying habit of changing – for example, people tend not to save much when price rises are reducing the value of money, but in the late 1970's, savings rose in the UK despite high inflation – a new behavioural pattern.

(iii) The deductions made may not tell the whole truth, or, indeed, may be quite wrong. To take an example from an allied field, one of the most famous cases of a misleading conclusion is that of the Hawthorne Experiments in the USA between the wars. The workers in the Western Electric Company were told that their working conditions were going to be improved in stages over a period of time. When each successive improvement was made, output per worker rose. The experimenters concluded that good working conditions were conducive to higher output. Luckily, they decided to check by telling the workers that conditions would now be regularly worsened. The result was astonishing – productivity continued to rise. What the researchers had proved was something quite different – that productivity rises when workers are consulted, informed and made to feel important.

(iv) The direction of causality must be proved. Many people associate the economic problems of recent years with recent events – eg the UK's admission to the Common Market; a rise in trade union activity; an increase in immigration. Now it is possible that governments, trade unions, the EEC and other favourite targets *may* have some responsibility for problems like inflation and unemployment – but this must be proved. Merely because things exist simultaneously does not necessarily mean that they are related. Even if they are related, the *direction* of causality must be proved. For example, do rising wages cause inflation, because employers have to pass on their higher production costs to the consumer, or do rising prices lead to higher wage demands, which may thus perpetuate inflation but not actually cause it? This is a very simple question – but economists are not agreed on their answer; the direction of causality has not been undeniably proved.

(v) Situations are never identical. It is now known how to cure a worldwide slump like that of the 1930's – but that does not mean that the slump of the 1980's can be cured in the same way because other factors are not the same in the 1980's as they were in the 1930's (eg there was no significant inflation in the 1930's;

women were not so involved in the work force as they are now; North Sea Oil was not known about, never mind being exploited – and so on).

This last point is absolutely crucial – circumstances never remain static in the real world. Thus, all laws in economics are followed by the words *other things being equal* (or, in Latin, 'ceteris paribus'). The laws only applied in an 'equal' or unchanging set of circumstances. But laws are static, and the real world is dynamic – it changes. So we might say that, if prices rise, consumption will fall, other things being equal. But if when prices rise 10% incomes rise simultaneously, consumption may *rise*. This is because 'other things' (ie incomes) have not remained 'equal' (ie unchanged).

b) *Induction*

As well as observing events, economists may also construct theses about likely behaviour in certain imagined circumstances. These theses must then be tested in the real world. Sometimes this can be costly. In the 1950's and 1960's, the economic effects of supersonic air travel had to be calculated, without any direct evidence, because such travel for passengers did not then exist. The sad story of Concorde shows how wrong these exercises of induction were! Real-world testing of the hypothesis was very costly.

By a mixture of deduction and induction, perhaps with some limited help from experiments, economists construct simple *'models'* of human behaviour in certain carefully-described circumstances. These simple models then have to be applied to the real world and modified where necessary by collecting information and statistics and by indulging in the most difficult task of all – forecasting.

Thus, the economist has a daunting task, with all the limitations inherent in a volatile world. This book aims to try to shed light on these problems, albeit at an elementary level. Many ideal, simple models will have to be explained and then the real world problems illustrated. The over-simplifications of the one and the over-complications of the other may appear frustrating at times. Economics can be frustrating in its inability to give simple answers to complicated questions. Nevertheless, few economists would describe their discipline as the 'dismal science'.

Summary

1 Economics is a social science, so its chief problems is that human behaviour is unpredictable. Laws can only be tendencies, not absolute truths.
2 Economics is concerned with the functions of production, consumption and exchange.

3 The main economic problem is choice, involving the concept of opportunity-cost.
4 Positive economics is concerned with a disinterested search for efficiency: Normative economics involves value-judgements.
5 Economic method consists of a mixture of deduction and induction, with limited opportunities to experiment. Ideal models have first to be constructed.
6 There are no easy answers, but some basic principles of behaviour can be identified, explained and assisted by the economist.

References

1 'What About Welfare?', Economist 'Schools Brief', 18 December 1976, p 64.

Section one Production

1 The search for efficiency

The basic ingredients of production

Production consists of the making of any good or service. Growing food, driving a lorry, filling teeth or even writing books are all as valid examples of production as are making a suit of clothes, building a house or assembling a motor-car.

In order to produce a good or service, four ingredients are necessary – *Land, Labour, Capital* and *Enterprise*. Different products will require different amounts of each, but all will require at least some of each. These ingredients are known as *Factors of Production* or *Inputs*.

1 *Land*

This really means *natural resources* – land, water, the minerals and fuels contained therein (eg North Sea Oil), even birds, animals and plants. All production requires land – a place of work, even if it is just for an office or headquarters of some kind. The reward or income which owners of land receive for allowing their resource to be used is known in economics as *rent*.

2 *Labour*

This means *human resources*. All production requires some labour; even in highly-automated factories there must be supervisors, maintenance staff and cleaners. The owners of labour (ie the workers themselves) receive wages (paid weekly) or salaries (paid monthly) as their income. In economics this is usually just called '*wages*'.

3 *Capital*

This means *artificial resources* – machinery, tools, buildings, equipment, fixtures and fittings and, of course, money. All production requires this – even a lawyer or accountant needs a chair, desk, typewriter, ledgers, filing cabinets and so on. The owners of capital receive an income known to economists as '*interest*'. Capital which is durable, like buildings is called *fixed capital*; that which is used-up, like raw materials and components, is called *circulating capital*.

4 *Enterprise*

Every business requires an owner. This person is called the *'entrepreneur'* and his or her income is called *'profit'*. Income is the only one that could be negative (ie a 'loss') and it is the only one where the level is not negotiated or fixed in advance.

The entrepreneur's functions could be defined as:

a) Establishing the *aim* of the business (eg to maximise profits).
b) Organising and employing the other factors of production in order to achieve the aim. This includes obtaining the capital.
c) Making the fundamental decisions about production:
   WHAT to produce
   HOW to produce
   WHERE to produce
   and *FOR WHOM* to produce.
d) Taking the risk – the 'opportunity-cost' decisions which may bring success (profits) or failure (losses).

The entrepreneur may well be both owner and manager in small firms. A plumber or decorator might fulfil both functions (and be the labour factor as well). In a large business, however, the owners may employ salaried managers to carry out the organising functions – though the owners will almost certainly still set the aim. In a state-run business, the government carries out the entrepreneurial functions, and appoints salaried managers.

It would appear that the entrepreneur's profits or losses are obtained by a simple equation:

Profit = Income − Costs.

This would be wrong, however. Profit is entitled to be regarded as a cost, just as much as wages, rent and interest are costs. No entrepreneur will stay in business unless his profits are adequate. Every entrepreneur's view of what are 'adequate' profits will vary, but whatever the level is in each case economists call it *normal profit*. This 'normal profit' is considered to be a production cost.

Thus:

Excess (or Supernormal) Profit = Income − Costs

Costs are wages, rent, interest and normal profit.

Capitalist or centralised?

In the UK, a capitalist system still dominates, so we still have literally hundreds of thousands of entrepreneurs who are employers and seek to make profits. Most workers are employees in the private enterprise sector. Yet an economy can be organised on a centralised basis, as in Communist countries. There, the state owns and directs production; profits accrue to the state and not to individuals; everyone's employer is the state. The state makes all the fundamental decisions about *What, How, Where* and *For Whom* to produce.

Although the UK exists in the free enterprise sector of the world, there are considerable and growing centralised elements. Central and local government and similar regional authorities provide many services like defence, law enforcement, education, National Health Service and roads. There are also over 20 'nationalised industries', like steel, coal, railways, gas and electricity. Thus the UK operates a *'mixed economy'*, with about ⅓ of the capital and labour operating in the so-called 'public sector' of the economy.

Much of the economic theory we shall be studying is based on the free enterprise, profit-making principle, but due attention will be given to the public sector and the increasing economic role of the government.

Production – the macro-economic view

Even in a capitalist economy, the government is closely involved in economic problems and can, by use of financial aid and the operations of its own sector, influence the basic questions of 'What, How, Where and For Whom'. In emergencies like wartime a government will have to regulate the economy very closely.

Let us simplify the production problem by reducing production to just two headings, food and machinery. A country's factors of production could all produce food, all produce machines, or be split between the two products. A production possibility frontier AB shows the maximum quantities which the factors could produce. Diagram 1.1 shows such a frontier.

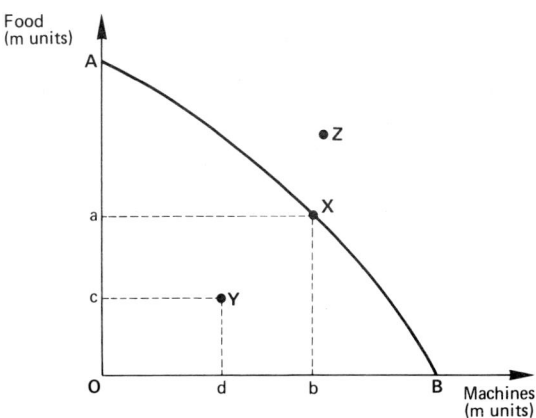

1.1 Production possibility frontier (1)

At OA, only food is produced: at OB, only machines: at point M, Oa food and Ob machines are produced. AB is curved convex to the origin, because near the middle the factors are relatively easily interchanged, but at or near OA and OB it is very costly to employ increasingly unsuitable factors (eg barren land for food production) in one industry at the expense of the other.

At any point inside the production possibility frontier (eg at point Y in Diagram 1.1), there must be unemployed factors – the country is below its production potential and is wasting idle resources. A government should aim to get its economy on the frontier, at a point it thinks most desirable.

To get to point beyond the frontier (eg Z) the frontier must be expanded beyond OA and OB. This can only be done by more efficient use of the factors of production, such as better machines, better-trained labour or management, or overall technological improvements. Clearly the frontier can also be moved outwards by obtaining more factors of production, for instance increasing the workforce or even 'conquering' some more land.

Production possibility analysis can be used employing several different categories of output on the axes, like public sector and private sector; goods and services; consumer goods and capital goods (ie machines). An analysis of the UK's current position would show production at a point like W an Diagram 1.2 – high production of consumer goods, too few capital goods (new equipment and machines) and unemployed resources.

Production – the micro-economic problem

Business units

We have replaced the term 'businessman' by 'entrepreneur'. Now, the

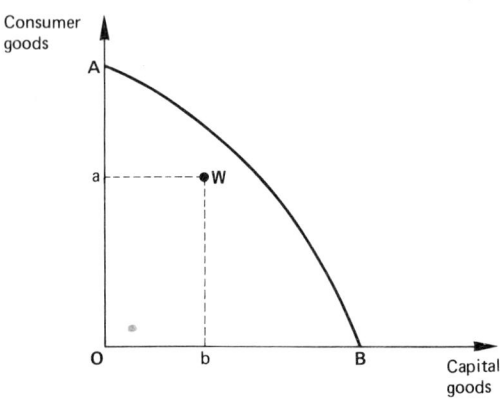

1.2 Production possibility frontier (2)

word 'business' will go. Two basic production units are identified in economics – the *firm* and the *industry*.

The firm is the unit of ownership. The entrepreneur owns a firm, which may be a one-man business or a large multi-factory unit employing thousands, like ICI or the Ford Motor Company. All the firms making the same product constitute the industry. This may seem simple, but an industry can be difficult to define in the real world. For instance is there a 'car industry' in which Rolls Royce is in competition with small family cars, or do different customers seek different types of car, thus creating several divisions of the 'car industry'?

There may be only one firm in an industry. A nationalised industry is run as one firm. Yet even they have to face some competition. Gas and electricity compete with each other; British Airways competes against foreign airlines; British Rail competes against road transport.

The law of diminishing returns

If firms seek profits, one thing they want to do is to be efficient. An entrepreneur's task is to make the most efficient use of the factors of production he or she employs.

In a short period of time an entrepreneur will not easily be able to increase the supply of all factors. Costly land and enterprise may be fixed whereas capital and labour may be more easily increased. Suppose a woman sets up as a florist. She may do all the work herself at first; later she may employ an assistant, who may only fetch and carry, clean up etc – but who will assist the firm's efficiency. Later still, she may employ some clerical assistance to deal with orders, invoices, purchase of stocks and so on. In the real world, economists have observed that this sort of process adds an increasing amount to output at first, then decreasing additions come later. In other words, *average production* per worker first rises by ever-increasing amounts, then rises by diminishing amounts. As each successive worker is employed, *marginal production* (ie the amount by which total production goes up each time another worker is employed) will rise at first, then fall.

Let us take an imaginary example where an entrepreneur has 1 acre of land and 2 machines, but decides gradually to increase the workforce. The results might be something like those of Table 1.1.

Efficiency rises greatly for the first four workers, then slower thereafter until nine get in each other's way and output actually falls. Maximum efficiency (highest average product) comes when four or five are employed, where MP = AP.

In fact, the most efficient points is really five workers. On a graph like Diagram 1.3, the marginal product figures are usually plotted half way between the number of workers – eg the extra product of the first (6) is plotted against half a worker; the extra product of the second (10) against one and a half worker and so on, this being a more accurate representation of the extra person's work.

Table 1.1

No of workers	Total production	Average production	Marginal production
1	6	6	6
2	16	8	10
3	27	9	11
4	40	10	13
5	50	10	10
6	54	9	4
7	56	8	2
8	56	7	0
9	54	6	-2

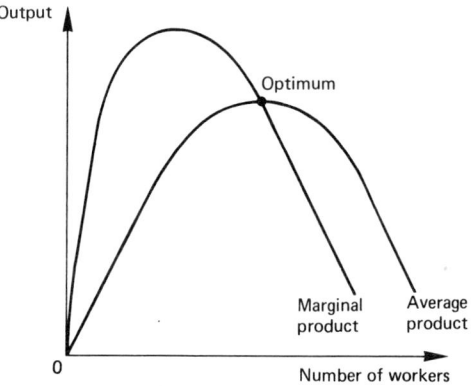

1.3 The optimum level of output

This point of maximum efficiency is called the *'optimum'*. It is reached soon after 'diminishing returns' set in. Diminishing returns start after the fourth worker: each worker up to the fourth adds more to output than the predecessor; thereafter, each worker adds less. The *law of diminishing returns* states that:

'As successive quantities of a variable factor of production are added to fixed quantities of other factors, the returns eventually become less than proportional' (ceteris paribus).

In our example labour is the variable factor and after the fourth worker, labour's returns (ie the extra production) become less than proportional (ie less than the previous worker added).

Economies of scale

In this example, the most efficient scale of output is where five people work with two machines and one acre. If, in the long-run, the entrepreneur can afford to employ more machines and land *as well as* more labour, he or she will decide to expand in this scale (eg ten workers plus four machines plus two acres; twenty workers with eight machines and four acres).

The results would, in fact, show exactly the same trend as in the short-run. For example, there would be *increasing returns to scale at first*, then *decreasing returns*. In other words as Table 1.2 shows:

Table 1.2

Acres	Machines	Workers	Total production	Average production per worker
1	2	5	40	8
2	4	10	100	10
3	6	15	300	20
4	8	20	480	24
5	10	25	500	20

Average production would rise to a *long-run optimum level*, then decline. Thus, in the long-run, where the supply of *all* factors increases in scale, there are *economies*, then *diseconomies of scale*.

Large firms enjoy many economies of scale, which should give them advantages over small competitors in the same industry. These economies can be divided into several groups:

1 *Technical*

a) Increased dimensions
   Large machines are more than proportionately efficient than small ones – eg a double-decker bus does not require twice as much fuel and labour as a single decker; a 1 million ton oil tanker is more efficient than ten 100,000 ton tankers.
b) Superior technique
   Some machinery cannot be reproduced on a smaller scale (eg giant motor-body press) – though the micro-processor revolution is changing this, for example computers being reproduced on a smaller scale as pocket calculators.
c) Linked processes
   This involves the use of assembly lines, wherein different processes in a firm can be linked in one chain of events, saving time and space. Car sssembly is the clearest example, though editing and printing a newspaper in the same building is an equally valid example.
   The problem with linked processes is that the machines and the labour force have to work at the same speed, regardless of their abilities; some may be over-worked, others may be wasting potential.
d) Research and development

Only large firms can afford facilities for research (much of which ends in failure) and for development of the results of successful research.

2 *Managerial*

Large firms can employ specialist managers, who are divided into departments, whereas a manager in a small firm may have to deal with sales, personnel, accounts, marketing, buying and all the other aspects of management. Although firms often switch managers to give them experience of several fields, most managers eventually become specialists in order to increase their expertise.

3 *Financial and marketing*

Large firms tend to raise money more easily, as they are usually a safer 'risk' to the investor or lender, because of their larger resources or proven history. Large-scale buyers and sellers also tend to gain marketing advantages, like priority, discounts, rebates or credit. This is because their custom is more valuable to the firm dealing with them than is the custom of a smaller firm.

4 *Diversification or risk-spreading*

These economies tend to contradict the others, but it is important to a firm to spread its risks by increasing the scope of its activities without of course losing the technical benefits of specialisation. The following may be diversified:

a) *Product*   to guard against a collapse in demand for its basic product – eg a confectionary firm produces several varieties of sweets and chocolates.
b) *Market*   to guard against problems which may arise in only one area – eg a firm develops and widens export markets.
c) *Source of supply of factors of production*   to guard against bottlenecks or interruptions to supply – eg Fords have at least two suppliers for every component, to guard against strikes or other problems in the component manufacturers.
d) *Manufacturing process*   to guard against breakdowns, which make assembly lines particular vulnerable.

    Many firms have become extremely large (for example ICI and Unilever) by spreading into many fields, serving many makets.

Despite all these economies of scale, there are in theory also diseconomies which set in beyond the optimum level of output. In the real world there is not much evidence of diseconomies in the technical field; new inventions and processes tend to push production on to ever-increasing levels of efficiency. Marketing and financial diseconomies are also difficult to find. The main diseconomy seems to be managerial. Despite sophisticated forms of delegation of responsibility and chains of command, and much research into managerial techniques, it seems clear that large firms are more difficult to administer than small ones. Multi-plant firms (even split-site schools), multinational firms (operating in several countries), nationalised industries and huge plants seems to breed problems. Managers, especially those at the top, seem remote from the workers; co-ordination of production and sales, especially where several products are involved, proves to be difficult, industrial relations are often worse.

Excessive diversification might also lead to diseconomies, partly because of managerial problems, and partly because the benefits of specialisation may be lost.

All these economies are *internal* economies. That is to say, they originate from *within* a firm and give that firm advantages over its rivals. *external* economies also exist. These originate from *outside* the firm and may benefit the whole industry. These can include the spreading of information via technical and trade publications; government aid; integration of firms into one area, such as the different spinning and weaving towns of the Lancashire cotton industry.

Why small firms still exist

Despite the obvious advantages brought by economies of scale, about a million small firms still exist in the UK. Why is this the case?

1 In many industries there are few economies of scale – the optimum level of the firm is at quite a low level of output. This can be true of small firms of craftsmen, like plumbers and decorators, panels of doctors or dentists, lawyers' practices or shops serving small communities.
2 Some firms, like the village shop, serve only small, local markets. A supermarket in a village would not be able to enjoy economies of scale and would not reach its optimum level – this is as bad as going beyond it. Firms making expensive goods (eg haute couture fashions) also have only small, albeit rich, markets.
3 Some entrepreneurs may have limited ambitions being content with a comfortable level of profits and not wish to gain extra worries by seeking always to expand and enter the 'big league'. By not challenging in this way, they may be left in peace and, for them, adequate prosperity.
4 At any moment in time new firms are being set up by would-be entrepreneurs. These will almost certain be small at first. Thus, several small firms are in the process of growing; many others will collapse.

Many of the small firms in existence do not make economic sense and will not survive. Yet others are efficient and well-run, and in the last few years governments have increased their aid to small firms, having become somewhat disenchanted with ideas of economies of scale. The biggest problems small firms have are raising the money to start up and then existing in the time between producing their product and being paid for it.

In the Budgets of 1980, 1981 and 1982, moves were made to benefit small firms in three ways, providing finance, easing their tax burden and reducing government interference.

Three schemes were introduced. The *Venture Capital Scheme* involved direct government aid to small firms. The *Loan Guarantee Scheme* provided state guarantess to financial institutions who lent to certain projects. The *Business Start-Up Scheme* provided tax relief for investors who put up to £10,000 into new companies for at least five years. Concessions on income tax, corporation tax and value-added tax were also made. and small firms were given exemption from providing some information and complying with various regulations concerning labour relations.

Small businesses laid off 800,000 workers in 1981. Although new firms also created jobs, it takes a great deal of small firms to create a significant number of new jobs. Finance, particularly cash flow, will always be a problem for small and new firms. The next chapter examines various types of firms and their financial problems.

Summary

1 In order to produce anything, *land, labour, capital and enterprise* are needed; this involves costs – *rents, wages, interest and normal profit.*
2 The entrepreneur in a capitalist system seeks to make profits in excess of normal profit. A centralised economy may have different aims. There, the State is the entrepreneur.
3 An economy should produce somewhere on its *production-possibility frontier.*
4 An entrepreneur, seeking maximum efficiency, should use the *law of diminishing returns* to find the *optimum* level of output.
5 A firm expanding in the long-run will enjoy technical, managerial, marketing and financial economies of scale, and will probably also wish to spread its risks by several forms of diversification.
6 Nevertheless, there is a place for the small firm in an economy.

Appendix
The mathematical calculation of the optimum, using isoquants and iso-cost curves

If we assume that entrepreneurs wish to produce a certain level of output, they can do this by employing their factors of production in various different combinations. If we assume that land and enterprise are fixed in the short-run, but capital and labour can be varied, we can draw an *isoquant* (QQ_1), showing all the different quantities of capital and labour which could be used to produce this desired output, for example Oa units of capital and Ob units of labour, or Oc units of capital in conjunction with Od units of labour. Diagram 1.4 shows an isoquant.

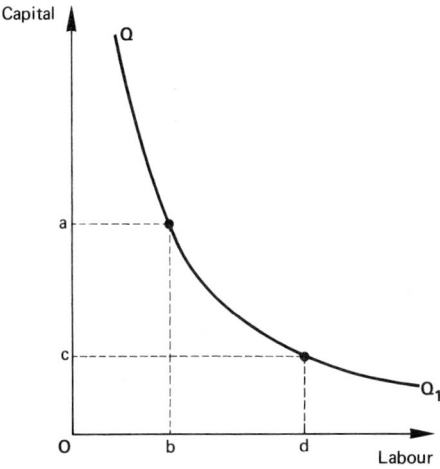

1.4 An isoquant

An isoquant is a curve joining points of equal quantity, or output. It is curved in a convex manner because of the *law of diminishing marginal productivity* – to employ a great deal of one factor and little of the other means sacrificing efficient units of the second factor for increasingly less suitable units of the first. The slope of the curve, in fact, reflects this ease or difficulty of substitution, called the *elasticity of substitution*.

The factors of production have costs, however. The relationship between the costs of the two factors can be shown by an *iso-cost* line (joining points of equal cost). For example, if a unit of capital costs twice as much as unit of labour, two units of labour could be employed at the same cost as one unit of capital. Diagram 1.5 illustrates an iso-cost line.

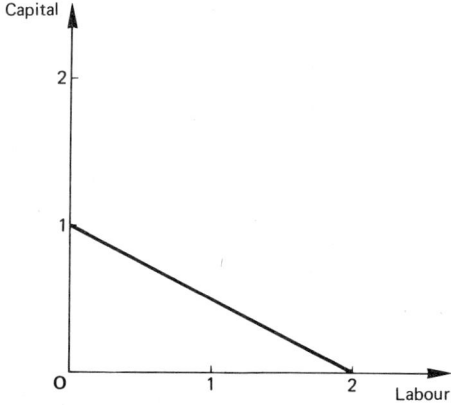

1.5 An iso-cost curve

If both isoquant and iso-cost are plotted on the same diagram (see Diagram 1.6), the *optimum* point will be found. This occurs at the point of tangency where isoquant QQ_1 and iso-cost AB touch, at point M. At this point the factors can be most efficiently employed to produce the required output: Ox units of capital and Oy labour will be employed.

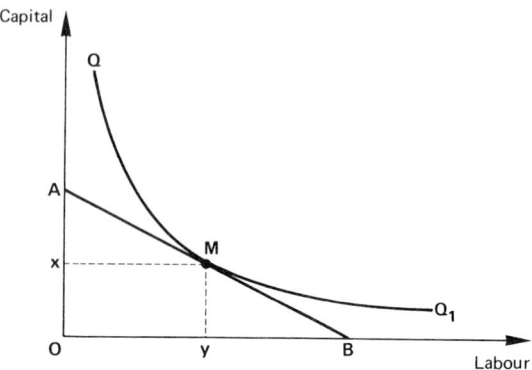

1.6 The optimum level of output

If the entrepreneur desires to raise output, there are two ways in which this can be achieved. First, the entrepreneur can employ more of the two factors by spending more, as shown in Diagram 1.7. A new iso-cost, CD, is thus introduced and isoquant Q_2 is reached at point N, the new optimum.

Alternatively, one of the factors could become cheaper. In Diagram 1.8 labour has become cheaper relative to capital, so iso-cost AC replaces AB: now OC units of labour can be employed for the equivalent of OA capital. Now, isoquant Q_2 is reached at a new optimum point, R.

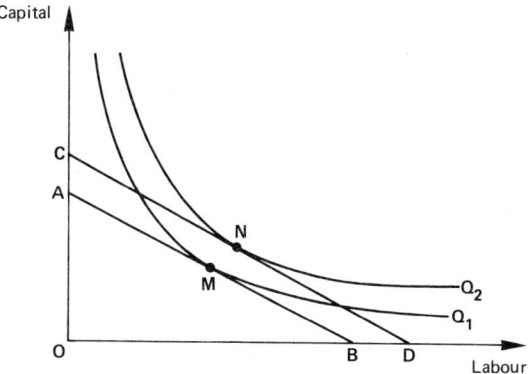

1.7 Reaching a higher isoquant by increased spending

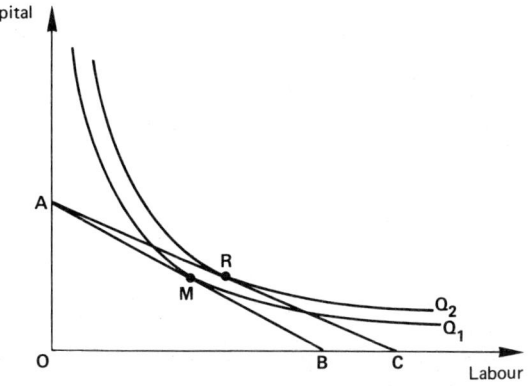

1.8 The effects of a fall in the price of labour

2 Types of firm and methods of financing them

Types of firms

As we have seen in the previous chapter, firms can exist in many different sizes. They can also exist in any one of five major forms.

1 *Sole proprietor*

The sole proprietor or one-man business exists when there is only one entrepreneur or owner. This entrepreneur will have to perform all the managerial functions and may also form all or a large part of the firm's labour force. The biggest advantage of this form of business is that all the profits go to the one person – but, of course, this one person takes all the risk and has sole responsibility for losses, if they occur. The sole proprietor has to raise all the necessary money and is responsible for the debt. Indeed, even private possessions must be sold to meet the firm's debts, if necessary. A sole proprietor is taking a big risk, but the rewards may be high and he or she may be able to expand the firm into a 'safer' form later.

2 *Partnership*

A partnership is slightly safer. Here a group of people enter into an agreement to be partners in ownership of a firm. The advanages and disadvantages are similar to that of a sole proprietor, except that the risks are spread and finance can come from slightly more sources (though the profits also have to be shared). Sometimes a 'sleeping' partner may be brought in – someone who contributes money, but is prepared to let the other partners do the actual management. Managerial economies of scale are likely to exceed those of a one-man business.

One extra disadvantage is that if a partner leaves or dies, he or she (or his or her beneficiaries) must be paid their share of the firm and the remaining partners must sign a new partnership agreement.

Sole proprietors and partnerships occur largely in the professions (eg doctors, lawyers, accountants) and in small-scale retailing and service trades, but they are by no means unknown in manufacturing, when one or two people set up a small workshop, for example.

3 Joint-stock companies

This is the most common type of firm in manufacturing industries and can be found in many other fields as well. A joint-stock company can obtain finance by issuing stocks and shares. Thus, the firm is owned jointly by all those who possess shares. Shareholders appoint directors, who aim to run the company so that the shareholders receive profits. A shareholder becomes an owner by buying shares and gives up his or her title to ownership merely by selling those shares.

In small firms the directors often own most or all of the shares and the division between entrepreneur and manager scarcely exists. The minimum legal number of shareholders is two, so a managing director may own virtually all the shares and his wife (or her husband) or accountant or other close associate the remaining few. The main advantage of corporate status is that *limited liability* is gained. Unlike the sole proprietor or partner, a shareholder in a company has legal protection; if the firm goes bankrupt he or she loses the money invested in the company, but his or her private possessions cannot be touched – liability is limited to the stake in the company. Any money he or she has taken out of the company in previous years, for example in distributed profits, cannot be touched.

There are also, in some instances, tax advantages in forming a company. For example, a professional footballer may be paid wages as an employee of a club, but may also earn other income from advertising, sponsorship, personal appearances at social events and so on. If the latter type of earning is paid into a company he can avoid his entire earnings going directly into his private income and thus raising his tax liability. Yet his company can pay him, as the major shareholder, a dividend.

For large companies the main advantage of becoming a company is that shares can be offered to the public on the Stock Exchange. Yet fewer than 5,000 companies enjoy this status as 'public companies' (note that the word 'public' in this instance does *not* refer to the public sector). There are about 600,000 'private companies' whose shares are not traded or 'quoted' on the Stock Exchange, but are held and traded privately. Many shares in private companies only change hands when they are inherited or when the firm is sold. A private company is often a 'family firm'; the number of shareholders cannot, by law, exceed 50.

Some quite large firms (eg Mars, the confectionery manufacturers) remain private, but often a large firm decides to take the big step of 'going public' in order to tap the massive resources of the Stock Exchange. To achieve this, a firm's share must be accepted by a firm of brokers or underwriters. These brokers operate as *issuing houses*. They buy (or 'underwrite') the firm's shares and then sell them on the Stock Exchange. (Only brokers may operate there – companies cannot sell the shares directly themselves.) The issuing house requires a company prospectus, describing its history, asset structure and future prospects. Only if the broker regard the firm as a 'good risk' do they agree to buy the shares and issue them. Once a company has 'gone public' it is easier for it to issue new shares in the future, by offering existing shareholders the new shares at an attractive price. This is called a *'rights issue'*.

In a public company the directors are unlikely to be the major shareholders. ICI, for example, has millions of shareholders, none of whom owns even 1% of the shares. Yet few shareholders exercise their rights by attending the annual meeting and voting. A dissatisfied shareholder is more likely to sell shares than to try to overthrow the management. Many shareholders are more concerned with speculating in shares rather than collecting the annual dividends. This can, of course, make a public company vulnerable to a take-over bid. Another company can obtain a controlling interest merely by offering an attractive price for the shares on the open market.

Nevertheless, it is clear that corporate status brings many advantages and economies, notably financial and managerial, and probably diversification as well, particularly in public companies.

4 *Public corporation*

A public corporation is owned by the State and run by the government, which appoints the managers. There are no shares, though the government may raise money by issuing stocks, which is a form of borrowing, or by subsidising the corporations itself. There are many types of public corporation (eg BBC, Totalisator Betting Levy Board, London Passenger Transport Board) but the most well-known example is the nationalised industry. Control over these industries is exercised in theory by Parliament, the people's representatives, but in practice the Government decides on policy and there is little real public control.

The distinction between private and public status is now getting rather blurred. BL still has shares – but the government owns over 96% of them. Though BL is not officially a nationalised industry, British Aerospace is – yet that body issued shares to the public in 1981 and the government has promised to follow suit with other nationalised industries. Nationalised industries will be dealt with in more detail in Chapter 13.

5 *Co-operative societies*

This type of organisation is rare in the UK. Several were set up in the 19th century in retailing, but form only a minor part of that sector. The idea is for the customers to own shares and elect the managers.

A newer type is the Workers' Co-operative. Here, the workers own the company, helping to make the decisions and sharing the profits. Several have been set up, notably the Norton Villiers Triumph Meriden Co-operative; Scottish News Enterprises; Kirby Manufacturing and Engineering, but have had little success. It must be said, however, that they have all been set up as a last resort when the company had gone bankrupt, which can hardly be said to be ideal circumstances.

Stocks and shares

The Stock Market bears its name because it originated in the eighteenth century when investors dealt only in stocks, which are loans. The growth of industry since then has meant that the market now deals mainly with shares, which are now often called 'equities'. Stocks and shares are collectively known as 'securities'.

1 *Stocks*

A stock is a fixed-interest security. A purchaser of a stock is entitled to a certain rate of interest or sum of money each year. The stock is also usually dated, bearing a date in the future on which the issuer of the stock will redeem it – ie buy it back at face value. Stocks are issued by the government and local government authorities. Government stock is still known as *'gilt-edged'* because until 1931 any paper issued by a government promising to pay a sum of money (including bank notes) had to be backed by the country's gold reserves. Companies also issue stocks, and these are known as *'debentures'*.

2 *Shares*

Whereas a stockholder is a *creditor* of a firm (he or she has lent it money), a shareholder is an *owner*. A shareholder owns that fraction of a firm equivalent to the fraction of the total shares issued which he or she possesses. There are several types of share.

a) *Preference share*
   This, like a debenture, carries a fixed interest return and is dated. The difference is that a firm must pay its debenture holders, but a preference shareholder is only paid if the firm makes a profit.
b) *Cumulative preference share*
   If a firm cannot afford to pay in any year, the holder of a cumulative preference share must be paid his or her arrears as soon as possible in subsequent years.
c) *Ordinary share*
   This is the most common type of share. Its main feature is that there is no fixed rate of interest. The shareholder takes the risk that there may be no reward in the hope that there may be a large one. In return for taking this risk he or she has the right to attend shareholders meetings and vote. Usually, only ordinary shareholders have these full entrepreneurial rights.
   Companies prefer to issue ordinary shares, but relatively

unknown firms or firms trying to raise money in difficult economic times may be forced to issue fixed-interest securities in order to persuade the public to part with their money. The proportion of fixed-interest securities to ordinary shares is called '*gearing*'. A 'highly-geared' firm is more vulnerable than a 'low-geared' firm because it is committed to paying-out fixed interest rates each year.

An imaginary example may show how the system operates. Suppose a firm has issued £3m of securities, £1m in the form of 5% debentures: £1m in 5% cumulative preference shares and £1m in ordinary shares; the original purchase price of each security was £1. The profits available for distribution rise gradually from years 1 to 4 of the firm's operations, as shown in Table 2.1.

Table 2.1

	Distributed profits			
	Year 1 £60,000	Year 2 £140,000	Year 3 £200,000	Year 4 £400,000
1 million £1 5% debenture shares	£50,000	£ 50,000	£ 50,000	£ 50,000
1 million £1 5% cumulative preference shares	£10,000	£ 90,000	£ 50,000	£ 50,000
1 million £1 ordinary shares	–	–	£100,000	£300,000

In Year 1, only the debenture holders are fully paid – as they would have been even if the company had made no profits. The preference shareholders get a little, but have to wait until Year 2 to get all their entitlement. Ordinary shareholders get nothing and the market price of these shares might well slump. In Years 3 and 4, ordinary shares are paying 10% and 30% on their purchase price. This is very attractive, so the price of these shares would rise and fixed-interest securities would simultaneously become less attractive, as they cannot participate in this increasing prosperity. Some firms have schemes to convert fixed-interest securities to ordinary shares after a few years, which is attractive to investors.

How firms finance themselves

There are many ways in which firms finance themselves. Stocks and shares can only be issued by companies; other firms must use other methods – indeed, companies also tap many other sources.

The main sources of finance are:

1 *Retained profits*

The main source of finance is revenue from trade – the money which customers pay to the firm. The excess of revenue over costs is excess profits, and firms wish to plough much of this back into their activities. Companies retained 53% of their income in the UK in 1978.

2 *Self-finance*

For small firms in particular, the entrepreneurs have to dig into their own pockets, especially to set up their business and carry it through its early stages.

3 *Loans from banks and other UK institutions*

This is the major form of finance for firms which are not companies. With the economy in slump at the end of the 1970's and early 1980's, even companies have had to make tracks to the banks as almost their only source of finance. Other institutions also lend money to firms. For example Finance for Industry (FFI), a company incorporating the Finance Corporation for Industry (FCI) and the Industrial and Commercial Finance Corporation (ICFC) is backed by the Bank of England and the commercial banks. FCI was originally set up to lend to large firms and ICFC to small firms, in 1945. Equity Capital for Industry (1976) is a body sponsored by insurance companies and pension funds. The 'Committee to Review the Functioning of Financial Institutions', set up in 1976 under the Chairmanship of Sir Harold Wilson, recommended in 1978 that new loan corporations be set up, to be sponsored by both government and the private sector, but this suggestion has not so far been implemented.

4 *Stocks and shares*

Companies issue these, as explained earlier in the chapter. In times of prosperity, shares are quite popular. In times of low profits, shares are difficult to issue. This is especially true when other interest rates are high and investors are offered more attractive temptations by other institutions.

Nearly half of public companies' ordinary shares are owned by institutions like insurance companies, pension funds and investment trusts; only about 40% are owned by individuals resident in the UK. (The rest are owned by overseas investors, the public sector or charities.) Many new shares are '*rights*' issues; this means that they are offered by a company directly to existing shareholders. No less than 88% of new shares issued in 1978 and 92% in 1979 were rights issues. The way in which new issues vary according to the economic climate can be seen in Table 2.2.

Table 2.2 New capital issues (£m)

	Companies	Public sector	Total
1967	421.1	250.4	671.4
1968	656.4	207.9	864.3
1969	571.3	161.7	733.0
1970	353.4	185.4	538.8
1971	663.6	264.9	928.5
1972	956.4	139.5	1096.9
1973	210.5	72.2	282.7
1974	162.5	421.8	584.9
1975	1578.4	415.0	1993.4
1976	1160.9	302.9	1463.8
1977	947.3	553.5	1500.8
1978	662.5	339.7	1002.2
1979	885.1	82.1	967.2

Source: Midland Bank Review, Spring 1980, p 16.

5 *Government*

The government does not confine its financial assistance to nationalised industries. There are many schemes in existence for the assistance of firms in areas of high unemployment, and governments have also give special aid to various firms (especially in the car industry) and projects.

In 1975 the Labour Government set up the *National Enterprise Board*, which aimed to assist industrial development by providing state aid for any scheme which would improve efficiency, international competitiveness or productive employment. This would include encouraging and helping new firms and amalgamations. Also, the NEB was supposed to increase the State's holding of company shares. The change of government in 1979 caused this last aim to be dropped, and the role of the NEB to be diminished. The decision to take responsibility for BL out of NEB's hands caused the resignations of the entire Board. Although the NEB has put money into dozens of small firms and has helped to set up the UK's first microprocessor enterprise, INMOS, most of its fund had been sunk into propping-up the ailing BL and Rolls-Royce companies at least until 1979.

6 *Loans from overseas*

With several hundred foreign banks operating in London and with many overseas sources available, borrowing from overseas sources, often at easier interest rates, has become increasingly common.

7 Factoring

Factoring occurs when a firm is pressed for cash and has trouble collecting the debts which are owed to it by others. These debts can be sold (albeit at less than face value) to a firm of factors or debt-collectors, who take the responsibility of collecting them.

8 Leasing

It is an increasing trend for firms to lease machinery and property instead of owning it. Firms have even sold equipment and agreed to lease it back from the new owners. These arrangements save money in the form of maintenance and replacement costs. Also, the firm does not have to try to dispose of obsolescent and depreciating assets. The share of leased equipment in gross new investment rose from 3% in 1971 to 10% in 1978; machinery, cars, computers, even ships and aircraft, are major categories of things leased, largely from the Equipment Leasing Association.

9 Credit: hire-purchase

Firms also obtain equipment through hire-purchase agreements, and obtain trade credit, both of which assist their cash flow problems.

Recent trends

As the economic situation became more bleak in the early 1980s and many firms have gone bankrupt, all types of firm have run into financial difficulties. Companies' retained profits slumped from £12,121 million in 1978 to £7,904 million in 1980, few new shares were issued and all sorts of firms resorted to borrowing. Companies alone borrowed £6,460 million from banks in 1980 as opposed to £2,398 million in 1976. Even the booming leasing industry, which had grown over 50 per cent per annum in the previous five years, fell 7 per cent in real terms in 1981. Until business prospects improve, firms will continue to have financial problems. Companies cannot offer good prospects to investors, retained profits are low, and only the financial institutions and government are keeping large sectors of industry going through lending.

Summary

1 Firms can exist in the form of sole proprietor, partnership, joint-stock company, co-operative society or public corporation.

2 Companies have the advantages of limited liability and issuing stocks and shares.

3 Only public companies can issue securities to the public via the Stock Exchange.

4 Ordinary shares are the commonest type of security, but fixed-interest securities are often necessary for a firm to obtain finance.

5 Firms raise money in many ways, principally by retained profits, borrowing and (for companies) issuing securities. Their methods will vary as economic circumstances dictate.

3 The labour supply

Division of labour

One of the most fundamental principles of economic theory is *division of labour*. According to this principle, economic wealth is increased if each worker specialises in just one task. Modern industrial economies are based on this specialisation. Workers earn their living by performing one specific job – as driver, mechanic, clerk, doctor, farmer or any one of thousands of different occupations. With the incomes they receive from performing their individual tasks, each worker then purchases the goods and services produced by others.

This principle may not seem particularly profound, but division of labour is, in fact, comparatively new. Before the rapid economic growth engendered by the Industrial Revolution in the last two centuries, most people did *not* specialise. They had to be self-sufficient in most respects, especially food production, and also probably in providing their own shelter, clothing, fuel, basic tools and utensils. There were some specialists, of course, such as doctors, priests and lawyers, but the mass of peasantry had to be largely self-sufficient.

Division of labour was stimulated by industrialisation, particularly by the creation of the factory system. For the first time, workers performing similar tasks were gathered together in one place, a factory, to work. One of the earliest and most famous of modern economists, Adam Smith, first drew attention to the principle of division of labour when he visited a pin-making factory in the 1770's. Smith found that the workers each had a specific task, such as drawing the wire, or shaping the head, or sharpening or cutting, and this created much greater output than if each employee tried to perform all the functions. This principle of division of labour has subsequently developed into linked processes through assembly lines and thus to many of the Economies of Scale firms now enjoy.

Advantages of division of labour

1 *Utilisation and development of skill*

Clearly, it is best for the economy, the firm and the worker if a person uses his or her skills and abilities in their job. This may not always be possible, and there may not be an opportunity to use a particular skill (eg a first-class blacksmith may find it difficult to earn a living in the 1980's) or a person may go through life not knowing about potential skills he or she may possess. People also can make bad judgements about their skills and abilities. Some people have many skills and others comparatively few. A person may be the best available manager for a firm, but may also be the best available salesperson, production engineer or caretaker. From the point of view of the firm, it would be best to employ such a person in the most vital of these posts (and the different salaries offered for the various jobs will reflect this), as manager, and fill the other posts from candidates who can perform these tasks better than they could fill the post of manager.

Even if someone's skills are not best employed, everyone can improve with practice. A student with little aptitude for French may never obtain a certificate in French, but will learn a little French and know more than if he or she had never taken the course. 'Diminishing returns' will appear eventually because everyone's talents are limited, but an optimum level of skill does exist and can be reached.

2 Time and effort

An expert does a job more quickly than a novice. Programming a computer, stacking shelves or even working a pocket calculator can be done more quickly with practice. This increases the amount of work done in the time available.

Fatigue is also lessened with experience and practice. A learner driver emerges from his first attempt to propel a vehicle on a busy road in a state of exhaustion and tension; a person who drives for a living can cope with heavy traffic without experiencing so much strain. The same can be applied to most jobs, especially those associated with appearing in front of an audience, such as broadcasting or teaching.

3 The factory system and the use of machinery

Division of labour reinforces the factory system which helped to stimulate it. With many people working at the same task, machines are developed which increase economies of scale. These machines can replace the most unpleasant and repetitive manual tasks and create more skilled and less physically demanding jobs in design, supervision and maintenance of the machinery. Machines are less susceptible to fatigue, produce standardised products and make fewer mistakes than human labour.

Disadvantages of division of labour

1 Boredom and alienation

All jobs are to a greater or lesser extent repetitive, even apparently 'glamorous' occupations like acting or playing sport. Some jobs are *extremely* boring, especially relatively unskilled jobs and those associated with operating machines or performing clerical tasks. The 'optimum' efficiency is soon reached – indeed, it may be dictated by the machine, and boredom then sets in. Boredom leads to carelessness, loss of interest in the job, and even to accidents or a desire to stay away from work or go on strike, just for a change of scene. In extreme forms, even mental illness can be experienced, as a person has no outlet for their energies or initiative. Perhaps this is why so many people seem to devote much energy to hobbies, for which they do not get paid or at which they are not all that good, (eg playing golf, gardening) but at which they have some freedom for self-expression and are 'their own boss'.

2 Factory discipline

The modern system of employment means that most people have to work a structured day, working set hours at a particular place in a disciplined framework. The pre-industrial peasant had a hard life, but could decide how and when to perform his or her tasks. The modern office or industrial worker works in a system imposed by someone else. Even if the system is not harsh, it can be an irritant – shift work, fixed holiday times, rush-hour travel, deadlines to be met. All this reduces 'job satisfaction'. Because few workers have much opportunity for self-fulfilment or self-expression, only high wages can compensate or act as a motivating force.

Self-employed people, with a stake in their own destiny and the power to influence their working life take more risks and have more worries than their employees, but this very element of control over their actions which they possess may make their jobs and existence more satisfying. It is no coincidence that the majority of serious industrial relations and strike problems occur in large firms where the individual worker may feel that he or she is little different from the machine he or she works with and has no status or importance.[1]

3 Unemployment

The continued introduction of new and better machinery is doing away with jobs, particularly in the manual and clerical fields. This process has been going on for at least two centuries, indeed one of the most famous examples of it come in the early 19th century when the handloom weavers lost their jobs to the new stocking frames causing the Luddite Riots of machine-smashing in 1811-1812. There has never yet been an example of automation causing permanent unemployment, because newer, usually more skilled, jobs are created by these technological developments. But new jobs require new skills, and an over-specialised worker may not be able to adapt.

Since 1945 there has been a decline in many industries in the UK – shipbuilding, textiles, coal-mining, steel making, now even car and aircraft assembly and clerical occupations. Many people have become unemployed and have had either to re-train or take a less skilled job. Division of labour can make workers less adaptable, particularly if they have been working in one job for all or most of their working life. Despite the boredom of many modern occupations, workers often fear losing these jobs because of the greater problem by unemployment and inability to learn new skills. One noticeable trend during the recent rise in unemployment has been redundant skilled men and women taking business courses so that they can try to continue to practise their skills, but as self-employed people.

4 Interdependence

Because we all now specialise, we rely on others to provide the vast majority of goods and services which we do not produce for ourselves. If something happens to reduce or cut off the supplies of these things we are in trouble. Thus, a threat to imported oil or food supplies, a transport or electricity strike, a bad harvest, can have wide repercussions. Even our jobs can be at risk – for example a strike in a component manufacturer soon causes car assembly workers to be laid-off; a rail strike stops materials getting to factories.

Nevertheless, despite these economic, social and psychological problems which division of labour brings, it is the basis of our modern industrial society and our current standard of living would be quite unattainable without it.

The labour force

The labour force is composed of those people who are either self-employed or who offer themselves for paid employment. Thus, it excludes housewives, people doing voluntary work, students and pensioners. Many of these people work, but are not officially paid; housekeeping allowances, student grants and pensions are not designated officially as 'pay'. Many of the workforce are unemployed. The main figures available in the UK for unemployment are those officially registered as seeking work – ie 'signed-on' at the Job Centres and receiving unemployment benefit. There may be many other potential workers, for example married women who are not registered but who would take a job if one came their way. Some estimates suggest these unregistered potential workers might double the official unemployment figures.

In the UK, the workforce (including those registered as unemployed) is about 26 million – less than half the population. The fraction of the population of a country which is in the labour force depends on many factors. These include:

1 Size of population

This is an obvious limitation to the potential size of the workforce. It can be affected by migration, however. The UK has been a net exporter of population since early colonial days, except for the 1950's and early 1960's, when labour was imported because of shortages. West Germany has introduced many overseas workers to fill gaps in the 1960's and 1970's. The USA's labour force was boosted by millions of immigrants in the 19th century and early 20th century. Yet except for examples like that of USA, most migrations are fairly small and account for a small fraction of both population and workforce.

2 Age-structure of population

An economy with a large population of older people or a large number of children has many people who are unlikely to take part in the workforce – though the children will eventually do so.

3 Sex structure

In all countries, men are more likely to be part of the employed workforce than women. The tendency is for more male births, but for a surplus of females in the population, because women live longer. These normal patterns can be emphasised or changed by events. For example, the millions of casualties of young men in the First World War not only altered the age and sex structure of several European countries by reducing the post-war workforce, but also by reducing the post-war birth rate and increasing the number of women in the workforce, who could not find marriage partners.

4 Laws and customs concerning the employment of women

In Moslem countries religious principles prevent women entering the workforce. In the Western world young women are expected to get jobs when they leave school. This was not always so. In Victorian England, women of humble origin began to find work in mills and factories, but the middle-class woman did not work unless she was unmarried, when she might get a job as a governess or, after Florence Nightingale, perhaps as a nurse. Now about 43% of the women of the UK are in the labour force, as opposed to 35% in Germany, 41% in

France and 25% in the Netherlands. In underdeveloped (developing) countries, of course, women and children work on the family's plot of land, as they did in pre-industrial Europe, but this is rarely counted as 'paid employment'. In the USSR women are a large proportion of the workforce and are in all jobs – for example two-thirds of doctors are women.

5   Laws concerning education and retirement ages

In the UK education is compulsory to 16 and the retirement age is usually 65 for men and 60 for women. Any raising of the school leaving age or reduction of the retirement age reduces the workforce (though some people work beyond official retirement age, just as others retire early). The introduction of compulsory education to the age of 12 in 1881 reduced the workforce in Britain, child labour being common before then, and successive rises in the leaving age have continued the trend. Yet many children exist on the fringe of the workforce via newspaper delivery rounds and Saturday and evening jobs in retailing.

Although education is compulsory in most countries, leaving ages differ as does the rigorousness with which the law is applied. By no means all countries have pensions and retirement ages.

6   Further education

In the industrial world in particular, education beyond the compulsory age has increased. In the UK, universities, colleges and school Sixth forms contain over three-quarter million students, all of working age. The availability of this education, the financial sacrifices involved by those receiving it, who could be in paid employment, and the ultimate benefits, particularly in terms of job prospects, all have effects on the size and structure of the labour force. This higher education and further education is expensive to the state and, in lost earnings, to the individual and underdeveloped countries cannot afford it to the extent richer countries can.

These students are not entirely lost to the labour force, as many of them enter it with regard to summer vacation jobs, often in leisure and service industries which need temporary workers at that time of the year.

7   The economic climate

In poor countries almost everyone works, usually in agriculture on the family plot of land. In Victorian Britain, women and children of poor families worked, but only the men in the middle-class families – hence the term the 'breadwinner'. As the 20th century has developed, more women have entered the workforce. This has partly been because of 'female emancipation' but also because of the economic climate. In order to preserve the standard of living they desire, to pay high rents or mortgages, run a car, take holidays, families decide that both partners shall work. Wives work after marriage and often return to the workforce after rearing children. The economic climate can also influence decisions about retirement (people whose pensions are based on their earnings dare not retire when inflation is prevalent) or about whether children shall leave school as soon as possible.

8   *Working hours*

If the labour supply is measured on the basis of hours worked rather than just numbers employed, then laws about working hours, holidays, overtime are important. Hours of work have not declined much in recent years – official hours have been reduced, but overtime has risen.

Recent trends in UK working patterns

1   *Increasing role of women in the workforce*

The most significant post-war trend in this field has been the increasing role of women in the workforce. Women now constitute over one-third of the labour force. Not only young women are in paid employment; 53% of the 45–59 age group (as opposed to 22% in 1951) are employed. The reasons for this trend include:

a)   The rise of part-time jobs
     One if five of the workforce in the UK is a part-time worker (as compared with one in ten in Germany and one in twenty in Italy). Part-time work is especially attractive to married women, particularly if their hours correspond with but do not exceed school hours. It is reckoned that 2¾ million part-time jobs have been created since the War, the vast majority of which are filled by women.
b)   Economic climate
     It is now thought necessary by many families for wives to contribute to the household budget in order to preserve the family's standard of living.
c)   Tax advantages
     Married women can now be taxed independently from their husbands instead of both incomes being combined which increased the risk of being pushed into a higher tax bracket.
d)   Fall in family sizes
     Despite early marriages, many couples are having their families at later ages and also family sizes have fallen to an average of only a fraction over 2 children.

e) Increase in divorces and separations
The increase in the number of broken marriages has raised the number of women who need to work when they revert to 'single' status, especially when they have responsibility for the children of their marriage.

f) Women are cheaper to employ
Despite the Equal Pay Act of 1970 (which did not fully come into effect until December 1975), women's earnings are still lower than those of men (see Table 3.1).

Table 3.1 Female/Male earnings ratio, 1970–1978
Average gross weekly earnings (excluding overtime)

Year	Manual males (£)	Manual females (£)	% Female/Male	Non-manual males (£)	Non-manual females (£)	% Female/Male
1970	26.8	13.4	50	35.8	17.8	50
1973	31.9	18.9	59	46.7	24.4	52
1974	36.6	22.7	62	52.7	28.3	54
1975	47.8	31.2	65	66.3	39.2	59
1976	61.7	42.4	69	87.3	53.5	61
1978	69.1	47.7	69	96.3	58.5	61

Source: New Earnings Surveys, HMSO

The reasons for this are the predominance of women in part-time jobs and the fact that women tend not to be promoted to higher grades, either because their career is interrupted by marriage or because they do not seek this extra responsibility. Women also tend to work less overtime and 'unsocial hours' for which pay exceeds the basic rates.

g) Female emancipation
Undoubtedly women now desire to be much more independent from their husbands both financially and even socially, especially when not 'tied' to the house by young children, and work gives an outlet for both these aspirations.

h) Shortage of labour
Although this is not longer true, in the 1950's and 1960's when unemployment never exceeded 2½% and was often below 1½%, women filled vacancies which existed and established the trend which was to follow.

2 *The decline in manufacturing; the rise in service trades*

Employment in manufacturing, mining, transport and other 'basic' industries has declined. This is not only because some of these industries have declined; also, they have become more automated and mechanised. Consequently, now more than half the workforce finds employment in service trades, which have expanded.

3 *Decrease in geographical mobility*

As well as occupational mobility, the workforce has become more mobile geographically. This has been true since the Industrial Revolution started – before this, generations of families never left their native village. Yet the trend has increased due to the growth of new industries, the decline of old ones, and the developments in transport and communications, which make movement easier.

4 *Rise in trade union membership*

The membership of trade unions has risen steadily until roughly 60% of male employees and 40% of females belong to a union. The increased and proven strength of unions has attracted members, particularly to the large and powerful unions like TGWU, which has nearly 2 million members out of a total union membership of 11 million. Laws protecting 'closed shops', where only union members can work in certain jobs, have also increased membership. The first decline in membership since the War was experienced in 1980 as unemployment rose.

5 *Growth of the public sector*

The state now employs about 30% of the workforce. The growth of nationalised industries, the rescue by the state of 'lame ducks' like BL and Rolls-Royce, the increase in civil servants, local government officers and other administrators, the extension of education – all these have increased the role of the state as employer. Yet 63% of the workforce still work in the private sector – and another 7% are self-employed.

6 *Rise in unemployment*

This will be dealt with in greater detail in the next chapter and in Section nine. Nevertheless, a dramatic change has taken place in the economies of most countries in the industrialised world since 1970 – the return of large-scale unemployment for the first time since the 1930's. In 1970, the UK unemployment was 2½%; in 1982 it exceeded 12% – over 3 million people. Some trends (increasing union membership; women's part-time jobs) were beginning to become reversed, but the major trends are increased unemployment among school-leavers (especially those with few qualifications) and older workers, many of whom have been encouraged to retire early. From 1975, even women's employment, previously rising quickly, began to decline.

The next chapter will have more light to shed on this problem.

The population base

Despite the existence of trade, demand for goods and services in an economy is closely related to the size of the population and its purchasing power. This purchasing power is largely determined by what the population earns. People's roles as producers and consumers are closely linked. Thus, it is important to look briefly at the structure of the population of the UK.

Every 10 years since 1801 (except in 1941) a census has been taken of the UK's population. The results take several years to analyse and the most up-to-date information on the April 1981 census will appear in the mid-1980's. Nevertheless, some trends and developments can be identified.

Recent trends in the UK population structure

1 Birth-rate changes

The *Birth-rate* is defined as the number of births per 1000 of the population taking place in a given year. So, if a country had a population of 50 million and the birth-rate were 10, the actual births would be:

$$\frac{50m}{1000} \times 10 = 500,000$$

The UK birth-rate has shown noticeable trends since 1947. It fell from 1947–55: rose from 1955–64: fell until 1979 and began to rise thereafter.

The rate was high after the War because many marriages and families had been postponed and couples had been separated. It fell to more 'normal' levels by the mid-1950's, then picked up again as comparative prosperity returned. Then, squeezes on incomes, inflation and unemployment drove it down again. Birth-rate changes depend on factors such as:

a) Economic climate and cost of living
   The opportunity-cost of a child is high. Children cost a great deal of money for at least 16 years before they can earn. It is usually the mother who has to give up her job, so the family has increased expenses and reduced income, perhaps for years. This rather callous view of parenthood is one which prospective parents have had to take in what they regard as difficult economic circumstances since the mid-1960's. The attitude is different in poor countries. Here children can work at an early age and are an insurance against their parents' proverty in old-age.
b) Contraception
   Families can now be planned. The widespread introduction of the contraceptive 'pill' in the last 20 years has increased this control and has clearly reduced family size. A similar and even more spec-

tacular trend accompanied the introduction of earlier forms of birth control in the early part of the 20th century. Needless to say, religion and custom plays a part; the Roman Catholic Church disapproves of contraception and it is, for example, banned in the Irish Republic.

c) Emancipation of women
   This clearly combines with the first two factors.
d) Medical provisions
   The infant death-rate is still high, compared with death-rates of those aged 5 to middle-age. Medicine can make few improvements in this field. In other countries this is not so, and improvements in child and maternity care can dramatically improve the live birth-rate.

2 Death-rate changes

The death-rate is defined as the number of deaths per 1000 of the population in a given period. The death-rate in the UK since 1945 has been remarkably stable. Medical developments have reached a plateau and the life expectancy of people has not been raised for some time. This is not true in many countries and has not been so here in the past. The death-rate fell dramatically in Britain from 35 in 1880 to 15 in 1939.

3 Migration

The UK has been a net exporter of population since its early colonial days, with the exception of the 1950's and early 1960's. Both emigration and immigration have slowed dramatically in the last few years because of the world-wide rise in unemployment. Most countries have Immigration Acts, including the UK, which introduced such legislation in 1962.

To obtain entry into the UK, Commonwealth citizens have to have certain skills or have jobs to come to. Only 6,000 vouchers are issued per year (since 1976), but immigrants can bring in dependents and most immigrants now are dependents. Thus, the age, sex and occupational structure of migrants are important – they are a microcosm of the whole population.

Emigrants tend to follow the same pattern as other countries also only want certain skills. UK emigrants go mainly to USA or the 'white' Commonwealth countries. The exodus has sometimes been called the 'brain drain' because of the skills of the people involved.

Two other types of immigration affect the UK. One is that of UK passport-holders. When Commonwealth countries become independent, citizens were offered British passports. Many Asians living in West Africa accepted this offer and they entered the UK in the 1960's and 1970's to avoid persecution in Africa. There are still 200,000 UK passport-holders in Africa.

Table 3.2 Birth and death rates in the UK 1947–1980

Year	Birth rate	Death rate
1947	20.7	12.5
1948	18.1	11.1
1949	17.0	11.9
1950	16.2	11.7
1951	15.8	12.6
1952	15.7	11.5
1953	15.9	11.5
1954	15.6	11.5
1955	15.4	11.7
1956	16.0	11.7
1957	16.5	11.5
1958	16.8	11.8
1959	16.9	11.7
1960	17.5	11.5
1961	17.8	12.0
1962	18.3	11.9
1963	18.5	11.9
1964	18.8	11.3
1965	18.4	11.5
1966	18.0	11.8
1967	17.6	11.2
1968	17.2	11.9
1969	16.7	11.9
1970	16.3	11.8
1971	16.2	11.7
1972	14.9	12.1
1973	13.9	12.0
1974	13.2	11.9
1975	12.5	11.8
1976	12.1	12.2
1977	11.8	11.7
1978	12.3	11.9
1979	13.1	12.1
1980	13.5	n.a.

Source: Annual Abstract of Statistics 1982.

The other category is aliens – people from outside the Commonwealth. Aliens must have work permits and must be registered for the period of the permit.

According to EEC legislation, any Common Market citizen can move and obtain work without discrimination. Surprisingly, there has been little movement within the EEC. West Germany which employs much foreign labour, tends to recruit from the cheaper sources of Yugoslavia, Greece, Turkey and Spain.

Although migration has declined recently, there are still problems. Skilled emigrants have been hard to replace. Many social problems have been created by immigration and 'second-generation' migrants have particular difficulties, often because they aspire quite naturally to better jobs than their parents took in the 1950's.

Table 3.3 UK migration 1969–1980

	Immigrants (thousands)	Emigrants (thousands)	Net migration (thousands)
1969	205.6	292.7	− 87.1
1970	225.6	290.7	− 65.1
1971	199.7	240.0	− 40.4
1972	221.9	233.2	− 11.4
1973	195.7	245.8	− 50.1
1974	183.8	269.0	− 85.3
1975	197.2	238.3	− 41.2
1976	191.3	210.4	− 19.1
1977	162.6	208.7	− 46.1
1978	187.0	192.4	− 5.5
1979	194.8	188.6	+ 6.2
1980	174.0	229.0	− 55.0

Sources: Annual Abstract of Statistics 1982 and N Tree: 'The Year in Review 1981–82', Anforme Ltd., 1982, p 19.

Table 3.4 Geographical distribution of population of Great Britain 1971–81

Area	Population (thousands)		% change
	1971	1981	
North	3,142	3,097	− 1.4
Yorkshire and Humberside	4,856	4,854	− 0.1
East Midlands	3,633	3,807	− 4.8
East Anglia	1,669	1,865	+11.7
South East	16,993	16,733	− 1.5
(of which, Greater London)	7,452	6,696	− 10.1
South West	4,081	4,326	+ 6.0
West Midlands	5,110	5,136	+ 0.5
North West	6,597	6,404	− 2.9
Wales	2,731	2,790	+ 2.2
Scotland	5,229	5,117	− 2.1

Source: N Tree, op cit, p 18.

4 Geographical distribution

The geographical distribution of the UK's population has tended to follow the occupational distribution. Internal and international migration have similar causes – career and standard of living prospects (though religious or political persecution can also be a cause of international migration). The changes in geographical distribution reflect the areas and industries of growth and those of decline, as the next chapter will illustrate more fully.

The consequences of a static population

With the birth-rate not much above the death-rate and migration comparatively low, the UK's population, unlike that of the underdeveloped or developing world, is virtually static. The consequences are that the pattern of demand and employment has changed. Education and youth-oriented products are no longer growth industries; provision for old people needs expansion and a relatively smaller workforce must provide the funds for this. Yet this slowing of the growth of the population has not helped unemployment, indeed it may have worsened it. It is a fallacy to think that exporting 2 million people would erase the 2 million unemployed, because *demand* would fall by 2 million – so fewer workers would be required as production fell. Only increased exports or increased demand at home can raise employment. If the population is static, demand can only rise if the wealth of the existing population increases – and that needs income, stimulated by output which is stimulated by demand – a vicious circle.

Unless demand rises, the stimulus to invest, innovate and raise production is blunted. The gloomy *Rev. Thomas Malthus* (he who called Economics 'The Dismal Science') was wrong when he wrote in 1799 that world collapse was imminent because the population was too high. In fact, there is even today enough food in the world – the problem is that it is unequally distributed. Rising population in the 19th and 20th century stimulated increased production and new techniques, not only in agriculture. Malthus's thesis may be true one day and the fact that the world's population may double to 8 billion in the next 50 years is daunting, but the situation the UK faces, of a static population, may also cause problems.

Summary

1 The modern economy is based on division of labour, despite its disadvantages.
2 The labour force in the UK exists of less than 50% of the population.
3 The entry of women into the labour force on a large-scale is a noticeable post-war phenomenon in the UK.
4 The pattern of working is changing in the UK as manufacturing jobs decline and service industries expand.
5 Unemployment is now a serious and general problem, for the first time in over 40 years.
6 The UK's population is static due mainly to a fall in the birth-rate

in the late 1960's and throughout the 1970's, and to a fall in immigration.
7 A relatively declining population can create problems, just as a expanding one does.

Footnote

1 See Introduction, p. 6 on the Hawthorne Experiments.

4 Structural and regional unemployment

Entrepreneurs have to decide not only what to produce and how to produce, but also where to produce and for whom. This chapter considers the question of location of industry and goes on to discuss the problems which arise when industries in certain areas decline and unemployment occurs.

Location of industry

The factors attracting firms to set up in particular areas may be divided into two groups, natural and acquired.

1 *Natural*

a) Climate
   This clearly has a great effect on the type of agriculture found in an area – grain in sunny areas, rice in monsoon climates and so on. To some extent, climate can be created artificially today, as the market-gardening industry illustrates, but this is expensive and can only be done on a relatively small scale.
   Other industries are also influenced by climate, such as tourism (winter sports as well as summer resorts). The cotton industry of Lancashire was created there partly because of a damp climate and soft water supplies.
b) Terrain and site
   Soil clearly links with climate as an important determining feature in agriculture. Mountainous areas support little except grazing and perhaps tourism; marshy areas are unsuitable for building. Terrain can influence the siting of almost any enterprise involving buildings and communications.
c) Raw materials
   This has always been important, especially where an industry uses a product which is mined locally (though there are exceptions, such as Cornish china clay, which is transported to the potteries for its industrial use). Other examples are the woollen industry in sheep-rearing areas, brewing near hop-fields, furniture-making in the beech woods of the Chilterns and paper-manufacture near pulp mills in Essex.

d) Fuel and power

This factor probably had more influence than any on the siting of industries in the Industrial Revolution. The introduction of coal as the main fuel, especially in iron and steel making helped to determine not only the location of the iron and steel industry (three tons of coal were needed to smelt one ton of iron in the early processes) but also the many industries using iron and steel products.

The most important modern fuel, oil, does not have such a determining factor, except for oil refining which takes place near the oilfields or near ports through which oil is imported. Oil is relatively easily transported. Gas and electricity are available on national networks or grids, though hydro-electric power can influence industrial location.

e) Market

This is the most important factor influencing location in the modern world. Industry wishes to go where there is a market, in order to reduce transport costs. Retailing (shops, garages, supermarkets) and services (banking, medicine, schools) exist in all populated areas with the biggest units (eg supermarkets) in the largest centres of population.

Most products today are meant for mass, not local markets, so they tend to go where the largest sector of the market is. One third of the population of England and Wales lives in the South-East of England, so this attracts a major part of industry. These industries attract labour, so the market expands and the process continues. Thus, the market is both natural and an acquired factor in attracting new firms and industries.

f) Communications

Settlements grew in ancient times near a water supply. Water was also a major form of transport. Villages grew at river crossing-points, in valleys, on major routes. Market towns grew at central points on which routes could easily converge. Nowadays, communications have become an acquired factor, with first canals, then railways, now roads, motorways and airports being important influences on an entrepreneur's decision where to produce. One of the clearest examples of settlement and therefore industry being determined by modern communications was in 19th century USA where towns opening up along the trans-continental trails and railroad tracks.

2 *Acquired*

a) Labour supply

Market and labour supply tend to go together as factors attracting new firms. If there is no local market in the area, then labour supply could be the decisive motive, particularly if certain local skills exist. Mass labour for the unskilled and semi-skilled jobs is still important, but much labour will need expensive training, so often a firm will be more influenced by the existence of some desirable skills in an area rather than by a mass of unskilled labour. Towns like Coventry and Luton, based on vehicle manufacture, attract many other forms of engineering, particularly connected with vehicles. There is expertise in the area, even if it has to be attracted from existing firms.

Tradition and skills can keep an industry in an area long after the natural factors have gone. There is no reason why biscuit-making should continue to exist in Reading or furniture-making in High Wycombe or blanket manufacture in Witney. The local materials are no longer needed, but the skills, reputation and tradition remain, particularly experienced and trained labour, so the industry survives and new firms may even be established there rather than somewhere else.

b) Subsidiary and supply industries

Often when industries are linked together, like cotton-weaving and cotton-spinning, or where one industry supplies another or uses another's waste products, these industries will become established near to each other. Component firms will be set up near car assembly plants, marine engineering near shipbuilding ports.

c) Specialist sources

The existence of the Stock Market, bullion market, foreign exchange market, Lloyds Shipping Insurance and other such institutions in London clearly attracts all sorts of monetary institutions to London – for example, over 200 foreign banks. Specialist insurance or warehousing facilities, marketing outlets or training facilities may also attract firms in related fields.

d) Financial incentives

Factors affecting land and labour have been mentioned; capital is also important. Financial aid, either locally or centrally provided may be available in certain areas as an extra incentive. Firms can benefit from loans, grants, tax allowances or cheap rents in areas wishing to attract investment.

Structural unemployment

There are *four types of unemployment.*

1 *Voluntary* unemployment exists among those of working age who choose not to enter paid employment. This could include students, those who retire early, housewives with young children and the often popularly exaggerated small number of people who do not need to work or who can exist on social security as successfully as in a low-paid job. By its very nature, voluntary unemployment does not create a problem which governments need to cure.

2 *Frictional* unemployment is temporary unemployment, particularly seasonal such as affects people in the construction industry or tourism, as well as professional sportsmen and women or actors.

3 *General* unemployment occurs when unemployment spreads throughout the whole economy, due usually to lack of demand. This will be dealt with fully in Section nine of this book.

4 This chapter is concerned with *structural* unemployment, caused by a change in the structure of the economy, as some sectors expand and others decline. Thus, structural unemployment is concerned with declining industries. In the UK these industries are mainly those dating back to the Industrial Revolution – coal, steel, textiles, shipbuilding. These have a strong regional basis, so that structural unemployment in the UK often tends to be *regional* unemployment. This is not always the case. Industries like railways and education are in decline because of falling demand for their services and these are not based only in certain areas. Nevertheless, many of the UK's declining industries are regionally-based and the impact of unemployment on these areas has been most marked.

The regional problem

The UK has had a growing problem of regional unemployment since the First World War. The world-wide slump of the 1920's and 1930's hit certain industries and regions worse than others. These same regions suffered above-average unemployment after 1945. Indeed, until the mid-1970's regional unemployment was probably the UK's only unemployment problem. Even though general unemployment increased tremendously in the early 1980, these traditional areas still display above-average figures, as Table 4.1 shows.

Table 4.1

	% workforce registered as unemployed					
Area	1950	1960	1970	1975	1980	1982 (February)
UK	1.6	1.7	2.6	4.2	7.4	12.6
South East	1.1	1.0	1.6	2.8	4.8	8.7
East Anglia[1]			2.1	3.5	5.7	9.7
South West	1.5	1.7	2.8	4.7	6.7	10.3
West Midlands	0.5	1.0	2.0	4.1	7.8	14.3
East Midlands	0.8	1.1	2.2	3.6	6.4	10.4
Yorkshire and Humberside[2]			2.9	4.0	7.8	12.2
North West	1.6	1.9	2.7	5.3	7.8	14.1
North	2.8	2.9	4.7	5.9	10.9	14.8
Wales	3.7	2.7	3.9	5.6	10.3	15.0
Scotland	3.1	3.6	4.2	5.2	10.0	13.7
N Ireland	5.8	6.7	6.8	7.9	13.7	18.1

1 East Anglia is included in South East figures before 1970.
2 Yorkshire and Humberside included in East Midlands figures before 1970.

Sources: Economic Journal 1978 and N Tree: 'The Year in Review 1981-82': Anforme Ltd., 1982, p 12.

The main reason for the high figures in Scotland, Wales, Northern Ireland and the Northern regions is that the main industries in these areas have declined. The rising figures in the Midlands are partly due to the decline in the vehicle and engineering industries. There could be several reasons for the decline of an industry.

1 The industry's product is outdated and has been overtaken by newer products from other areas. Thus, the woollens industry was overtaken by cotton in the 18th and 19th century; coal has been largely superseded by oil; transistors by silicon chips.

2 The industry has lost ground to competitors from other areas or countries. Thus, Lancashire cotton has failed to compete with Japanese and other Asian countries' products; car manufacturers have lost ground to foreign competitors; the UK motorcycle industry has virtually gone out of existence, again mainly because of the Japanese.

3 The industry faces a general decline in demand perhaps because of world-wide over-capacity (eg shipbuilding) or a world recession (eg steel).

4 The industry employs few people and the area cannot provide alternative jobs, so population moves away, hastening the decline in both area and industry. This applies to crofting and sheep-farming areas in Scotland and Wales, or to the Hebridean Islands where fishing has declined and tweed-making can only provide a few jobs.

5 The industry is in an area away from the main markets and transport costs harm its competitive position. As population and industrial activity concentrate ever increasingly in the South-East of England, this problem has applied to Scotland, Wales, Northern Ireland and the North. This has fostered a feeling of resentment in these regions against the dominance of London and the South-East and has shown political repercussions in a resurgence of Scottish and Welsh nationalism. The Scots have been particularly anxious that the oil revenues from the North Sea fields, all nearer to Scotland than England, should be of benefit to the Scottish economy.

The accession of the UK to the EEC in 1973 has tended to increase the problems of these areas. The UK is itself on the periphery of the Common Market so the northern and western regions are on the edge of the periphery, far from the central markets of France, Belgium, Germany and Northern Italy. Southern Italy's problems have shown a similar continuing trend, though it must be noted that the economy of the Republic of Ireland has grown rapidly since it joined the EEC. With the market such a dominant factor in determining industrial location today, however, areas on distant frontiers, such as Scotland and Wales, do have increased problems.

6 The adoption of automation in an industry has replaced labour with capital; the industry is not in decline, but the number of unskilled and semi-skilled jobs has dropped. This applies to most forms of manufacture (eg ships, vehicles, steel) and even to clerical occupations.

7 Mining and extractive industries may suffer from exhaustion or increasing inaccessibility of resources in certain old-established areas. Coal mining and Cornish tin mining are examples of this; the same will be true one day of North Sea Oil.

Regional policy

It is clearly not good sense either economically, socially or politically to allow large areas to have unemployed resources. Labour is the factor of production to which most publicity is given, but it is equally wasteful to squander resources of land and capital, leaving derelict factories, rusting machinery and under-used utilities such as gas, water, public transport and other amenities. In 1972 the EEC Commission listed three criteria for identifying a declining area. Two are obvious – a low level of income and output per head, and a relatively high level of unemployment. The third criterion was a high net outward rate of migration. Thus, the problem corrects itself to some extent, as people leave for more prosperous areas, or even for other countries. Yet this exodus wastes land and capital resources, denudes an area of its younger, more qualified workers and leaves an ageing, unskilled workforce and a general air of decline.

The prosperous areas have their problems – congestion, a high cost of living (especially housing), a need for more schools and other amenities. The great discrepancy between house prices in expanding and declining areas makes movement impossible for many people, especially the large sector of people who live in council accommodation (as much as 50% of the semi-skilled and unskilled workers). Social and family ties are also a problem.

Thus *'taking workers to work'* is a policy which can only be of limited value. *'Taking work to the workers'* is much more necessary. Jobs must be provided in the areas of decline to use the factors of production there; removing the factors to other areas can only be done to a smaller extent.

The *aims* of regional policy could be summarised as:
1 Making use of the resources available in less prosperous areas.
2 Avoiding the costly and socially undesirable mass exodus of workers and their families from an area.
3 Helping *some* movement of workers to other areas, if it is in their interest and will also benefit the economy without doing irreparable harm to the area they leave.
4 Encouraging a more broadly-based industrial structure in areas hitherto too reliant on one industry, or even one firm.
5 Maintaining provincial cultures and identities.
6 Maintaining a general planning strategy which will assist *all* areas of the country to obtain steady rate of economic growth.

Regional policy in practice

There has been an active regional policy in the UK since the *Special Areas Act of 1934* identified the so-called depressed areas and outlined government policy to assist them. Post-war policy was based on the *Distribution of Industry Act of 1945*, which listed the 'development areas' as they were more optimistically named, and the aid available. The *Local Employment Act of 1960* replaced the 1945 Act and several more measures followed in the next twenty years. There is little point in ploughing through all this legislation; instead, the principal measures and trends of regional policy will be identified and the current position discussed.

Regional policy has had more than its share of critics. For example, a House of Commons sub-committee reported in 1973 that 'Regional policy has been empiricism gone mad – a game of hit and miss played with more enthusiasm than success'.[1] Professor Nevin described post-war policy as 'a confetti-type approach . . . at no stage adding-up to a coherent and really substantial development in any region' and added, perhaps cynically, that 'Regional policy has been predominantly governed by political considerations rather than by long-run economic considerations. Thinking has been conditioned by the need to defend marginal constituencies'.[2]

It is impossible to say just how many jobs have been either created or saved by regional policy, though surveys of firms at different times have found that regional incentives have played some part in aiding their decisions about where to place factories or increase their investment. As always it cannot be known what would have happened had there been no regional policy, but it is safe to surmise that thousands, perhaps tens of thousands of jobs have been saved or established by regional aid.

Major features of regional policy

1 Apart from Northern Ireland, which is dealt with under separate legislation, there are now four grades of assisted area – Special Development Areas (SDA's) set up in 1975; Development Areas (DA's) started in 1945; Intermediate Areas (IA's) created in 1970 and Inner Urban Areas (IUA's) established in 1978. IUA's are now ranked second in priority to SDA's.

IUA's were created when the decay of inner city areas led to social unrest, expressed in riots and demonstrations. Derelict areas, like London's Dockland, Central Liverpool and Manchester, Clydeside and the North East of England could offer few jobs; housing was old or in the form of grim multi-story flats, often vandalised; amenities were poor and crime figures high; those who could move away did so. After the War, new towns were encouraged by the New Towns Act (1964) and Town Development Act (1952) partly because of inner city slums and wartime bomb damage. Hatfield, Basildon, Bracknell, Harlow, Crawley and Stevenage in the South-East; Aycliffe and Petrelee in the North; Cwmbran in Wales; Glenrothes and East Kilbride in Scotland, were examples of over twenty such towns. Although Milton Keynes in North Buckinghamshire is still expanding towards its 250,000 target, the New Towns policy has clearly been replaced by a movement towards the social rescue and economic revival of inner cities and urban areas.

2   All these areas quality for financial aid, which goes directly to firms in the areas. Grants of up to 15% (22% in SDA's) are available for capital expenditure of over £5,000 in DA's for the manufacturing, mining or construction industries. Grants of up to 15% are also available in SDA's and DA's for expenditure of more than £500 on plant and equipment. Firms can also claim tax and depreciation allowances on their plant, buildings and machinery in the assisted areas.

Specific subsidies are also available, such as that to British Shipbuilders (most of whose yards are in assisted areas) to help to obtain a large order from Poland in the late 1970's. The inner urban areas tend to receive more piecemeal and specific aid, though firms going to these areas can all receive 100% capital allowances and exemption from development land tax and some rates liabilities. Seven 'Enterprise Zones' were listed for special aid in IUA's in 1980 – the Isle of Dogs, Belfast, Clydebank, Lower Swansea Valley, Speke, Newcastle/Gateshead and Salford/Trafford Park. More were added in 1982.

3   Until 1976 a Regional Employment Premium existed whereby firms in assisted areas were paid a subsidy per head for the number of workers they employed. This ended because it contravened EEC law. In 1975 the EEC had itself set up a Regional Fund, but this takes only 3.2% of the EEC Budget (1981) and the UK received only a quarter of the Fund's total budget of £335m. this aid goes not to firms or local authorities, but to central government which decides how to distribute it. The sum available for re-training from the EEC's Social Fund is even more meagre. For most of the EEC, the regional problem consists of declining rural areas, not decaying industrial cities and towns, so most of the aid comes from the Agricultural Fund. The Common Agricultural Policy benefits the UK's regions very little, except for some aid to hill farmers.

Local authorities in assisted areas can, with central government's permission, float loans on the open market, and can also use their own finances to attract and assist industry.

4   Building controls (Industrial Development Certificates) have existed in one form or another since 1945. Firms wishing to build or expand may need a certificate, which may be refused in areas of low unemployment. It has been estimated that: 'In terms of employment creation in development areas, IDC's would seem to have been the most effective instrument of all in the past, achieving over the 1960's an annual average of jobs created which was 40% greater than the

next most effective instrument'.[3] With general unemployment rising in the later 1970's and into the 1980's, however, IDC's are now rarely refused even in the more prosperous areas.

The government has also gone in for advance factory building – building factories to demand or even in advance of demand in assisted areas and then offering them to prospective entrepreneurs at concessionary rates or rents.

5   Several schemes of movement grants have existed at times, to assist people to move to other areas or even to move so-called 'Key Workers' in from more prosperous areas to help train the unemployed for work in a new industry coming into the area. The most recent scheme is the Skilled Workers Mobility Experiment of 1978, offering £500 to skilled workers who wish to move to find jobs in certain industries. In none of the schemes has the sum offered been remotely useful for buying a house in a more expensive area.

6   Re-training is one of the most vital parts of regional aid. In the UK it has long been regarded that it is the task of industry or further education establishments to train labour. Recently, this view has changed and governments have done more training themselves. Skill Centres (formerly known as Government Training Centres) have expanded, where people can go for six months to learn a new skill. The grants they receive while being trained are small and trade unions sometimes block the trainees chances of employment by quoting closed shop and apprenticeship rules, so that places are often left vacant in skill centres. Nevertheless, up to 100,000 places a year are available, and many people have been re-trained, though more of the trainees have left jobs to attend the Centres than have come from the dole ueues. Re-training of the unskilled is also a big problem.

Aid to attend more orthodox courses is also available. The Training Opportunities Programme (TOP's) gives grants to young people to go on certain courses at Further Education Colleges in order to learn a new trade.

Industry carries out its own training schemes but the government assists Industrial Training Boards (ITB's). The ITB's levy a charge of 1 per cent of the wage bill on all firms except those who are regarded as having adequate training schemes of their own. In 1981 the government reduced the number of ITB's from 24 to 7. They remain only in clothing, construction, engineering, hotel and catering, road transport, rubber and plastics, and petroleum industries. There is a separate training board for agriculture.

7   The government has assisted the spreading of information about job prospects. The Job Centres display local vacancies and often also publicise jobs available in other areas.

8   The biggest unemployment problem today is among the young, most especially those with no qualifications who reside in the assisted areas. In 1981 one in six of the unemployed was in the 16–18 age group and unemployment in this age group exceeded 50 per cent in some

areas. The Youth Opportunities Programme (YOP) has grown in piecemeal fashion since 1976. Many schemes exist to subsidise employers to take on young workers, including the encouragement of early retirements to create vacancies. The main plank of the YOP scheme is the work experience scheme. Here, youngsters are paid a small sum (£23.50 per week in 1981) to be employed for six to twelve months. Over 100,000 employers provide the vacancies and the scheme catered for 360,000 teenagers in the year ending in March 1981. The aim is to offer a place to every unemployed school-leaver, plus those under 19 who have been unemployed for over a year. Only three out of ten YOP trainees found jobs at the end of their work experience in 1981, however. The YOP improves 'employability' but scarcely creates a permanent new demand for labour. Trade unions estimate that every three youths on the programme may cost one adult a job, because some employers use the YOP as a source of cheap, subsidised labour. Thus, some trade unions have become restive about the scheme which was originally meant for the unqualified but has to cater for youths with several GCE 'O' levels.

Although the YOP applies nationwide, it is most heavily involved on the worst areas; in 1981, only 3 per cent of its money was spent in London, whereas 19 per cent went to the north-west, for example.[4]

60 per cent of the UK's workforce has no vocational qualifications (compared with 33 per cent in West Germany) and the decline in unskilled vacancies has focused attention on the need for much more vocational training, reform of the apprenticeship system. Yet the youths in the UK are paid relatively more than those in other countries – about $\frac{2}{3}$ of the average national wage in 1981. The government started a scheme in January 1982 to try to increase youth employment, yet reduce young people's earnings. Employers taking on youngsters at less than £40 per week (the average youth earnings were double that figure) would receive £15 per week subsidy from the government. Wages between £40 and £45 would be subsidised by £7.50; wages above £45 would receive no help.

Many of these policies have been operated since 1973 by the *Manpower Services Commission* (MSC), a body of government, business and union representatives, which is concerned with both training and finding jobs through its two agencies the Training Services Agency and Manpower Services Agency. The operations of the MSC are summarised in Diagram 4.1.

9 The government has also assisted areas of high unemployment by moving its own departments or setting-up new ones in the provinces. The Post Office Headquarters moved from London to Edinburgh in the 1960's, for example, and the Driving and Vehicle Licensing Centre was created in Swansea in the 1970's. A government may also place an order with a firm in an assisted area in order to provide work, such as ordering a ship from a British Shipbuilders yard or an aircraft from British Aerospace, or even ordering such mundane articles as office

equipment or ministry cars from British sources.

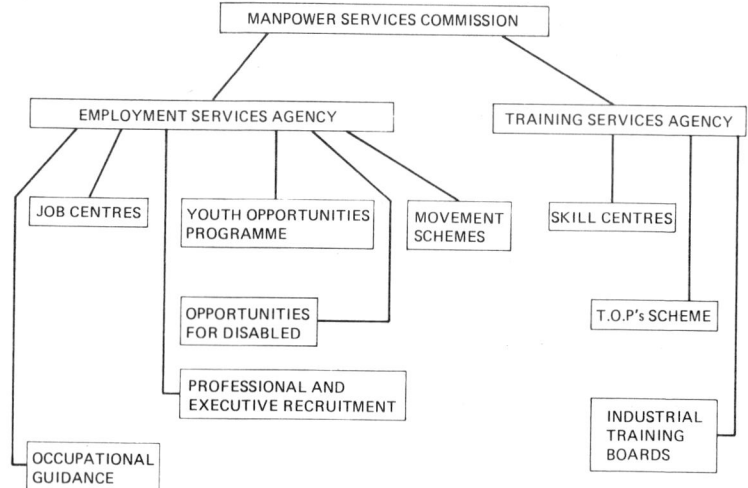

equipment or ministry cars from British sources.

Regional policy in the 1980's

In its desire to reduce government spending the Conservative Government elected in 1979 immediately cut regional aid by one third. Several hundred SDA's, DA's and IA's were downgraded in status and their aid reduced. Only 25% of the workforce now lives in areas covered by regional aid, whereas before 1979 40% were in assisted areas. Regional Planning Councils, set up in 1965, and the Location of Offices Bureau were disbanded. It was also decided that a firm would only get assistance if it could persuade the government that their project could not go ahead without it.

Thus, regional policy is now in decline. The growing problems of general unemployment, especially among the young, has given prominence to the YOP, TOP and other such schemes.

Regional policy has often encourage investment, but not necessarily jobs; machines have perhaps benefited more than labour. Only the Regional Employment Premium and the latest YOP and other piecemeal schemes, like the Short-term Working Compensation Scheme, have directly subsidised the wage bill. Aid has now become more selective and specific with the newest problem being the inner cities. Indeed, it has been said that this realisation of inner city problems has been 'the most dramatic and important reconsideration of spatial economic problems since the inception of an offical regional policy in the early 1930's ... the emphasis has switched from regional problems to urban policy and industrial strategy'.[5]

Although regional policy can claim some successes, the problem remains. Indeed 'After forty years of experience, the UK governments still seem to be uncertain as to the role of regional policy and the most efficient methods by which this role can be fulfilled'.[6]

Summary

1 Industry settles in areas because of natural and acquired factors possessed by an area; of these, the most important ones are now the market and communications.
2 Areas dependant on one industry can suffer great problems if the dominant industry declines.
3 This structural unemployment in the UK caused by declining industries has often been regionally-based and given the UK regional unemployment problems not experienced until recently by other EEC countries.
4 Regional policy has mainly concentrated on providing new jobs in the declining regions, through financial incentives, building controls and re-training aid.
5 There has been a change of emphasis in the 1970's with regional aid becoming subservient to more general measures, especially to aid youth unemployment.
6 Despite this, the regional problem remains serious and to it has been added the special problem of inner urban areas.

Footnotes

1 Trade and Industry Subcommittee of House of Commons Expenditure Committee – 'Regional Development Incentives – Report', House of Commons Paper 85, London, HMSO, p 72.
2 Quoted in British Economy Survey, Summer 1979. Regional Issues – G Wardell, p. 34.
3 Brownrigg and Greig: 'Regional Policy in the IDC's', Economics Spring 1980, p. 4.
4 In September 1983 the YOP is to be replaced by the Youth Training Scheme (YTS), guaranteeing training and work experience for a year to all unemployed school leavers.
5 KJ Button: 'Spatial Economic Policy' in The British Economy in the 1970's, ed PJ Maunder, Heinemann Education Books, London, 1980, p 190.
6 Brownrigg and Greig: op. cit., p. 6.

5 Cost and supply schedules

Costs

In a competitive economy, entrepreneurs must pay considerable attention to their costs of production. So far, we have examined the problems of the search for efficiency in terms of concepts like diminishing returns and economies of scale. These principles must now be converted into financial concepts and expressed in terms of costs.

Costs can be categorised into two main groups – fixed and variable. *Fixed costs* are those which do not vary when output changes. Examples are rent and rates, managers' salaries and the original purchase price of a machine. These fixed costs, or overheads, as they are sometimes called, remain the same whether the firm is producing no units or working to full capacity. As production increases, however, average fixed costs steadily decline; if fixed costs are £1000 and output is 10, AFC = £$\frac{1000}{10}$ = £100 per unit; if output is 1000, AFC = £$\frac{1000}{1000}$ = £1 per unit.

Variable costs do vary with output. They include the cost of labour, raw materials and transport. Average variable costs fall at first, then rise. This is because of the law of diminishing returns – efficiency rises at first, then falls as diminishing returns set in.

This division of costs is only valid in the short-run. In the long-run, *all* costs are variable. New factories can be built, machinery installed and managers employed. The firm will expand in the best optimum scale of all its factors of production.

Even in the short-run it is difficult to categorise all costs. A telephone is paid for partly by a fixed rental (fixed costs) and partly according to the calls made (variable costs); gas and electricity are paid for in similar ways. Depreciation of plant, machinery and vehicles is usually regarded as a fixed cost, but the article may depreciate more quickly if used constantly – or if hardly used at all. The same principle could be applied to maintenance costs, usually regarded as fixed.

These fixed and variable costs appear on a firm's Profit and Loss Account. Economists recognise two other types of cost which do not appear in a firm's accounts. One is *social cost*, defined as cost suffered by a community because of a firm's activities. For example, houses near an airport may need double-glazing and also lose part of their value, because of noise pollution. This pollution may also create more intangible costs to the community, such as problems of declining mental health created by tension and disturbances due to the noise. The other non-accountable cost is *imputed cost*. A farmer or shopkeeper may be assisted by his wife or family, who may not be paid a wage equivalent to that which would have to be paid to an assistant in the open market. If an outside employee were brought in to replace the entrepreneur's relative, costs would appear to go up, though the amount of work would remain unchanged. Thus a factor of production which is being paid less than its market value should have an extra 'imputed' cost added on to make up the difference between true cost and actual cost.

In accounting terms, however, *total cost* is simply fixed cost plus variable cost. The most efficient level of production for a firm is where *average cost* is at its minimum. Average cost (often called *average total cost* to distinguish it from average variable cost or average fixed cost) is, of course, total cost divided by output. If a firm produces 10,000 pencils for a total cost of £1000, the average cost per pencil is 10p.

The entrepreneur is also interested in the concept of *marginal costs*. These are defined as the extra cost of raising output by one unit. For example, if it costs £25m to produce 5 aircraft and £32m to produce 6, the marginal cost of the 6th aircraft is £7m.

A typical example of the types of costs might be as illustrated in Table 5.1.

Table 5.1

Output	Fixed costs	Variable costs	Total costs	Average costs	Average variable costs	Marginal costs
0	128	0	128	–	–	
1	128	32	160	160	32	32
2	128	42	170	85	21	10
3	128	50	178	59	16	8
4	128	56	184	46	14	6
5	128	62	190	38	13	6
6	128	72	200	33	12	8
7	128	87	215	31	$12\tfrac{1}{2}$	15
8	128	112	240	30	14	25
9	128	148	176	31	$16\tfrac{1}{2}$	36
10	128	200	328	33	20	52
11	128	279	407	37	$25\tfrac{1}{2}$	79
12	128	376	504	42	31	97

Note that marginal costs are plotted on a graph half-way between the relevant outputs – eg the marginal cost of the 5th unit of production is plotted against an output of 4½.

If Table 5.1 were to be reproduced on graph paper, the result would be similar to that of Diagram 5.1. The optimum (most efficient) short-term level of output (OX) is, in this case, 8. This is the level where average costs are as low as they can be. Maginal costs crosses average cost at *the optimum*. As long as marginal cost is below average cost, then average cost is falling; if marginal cost is above average cost, average cost is rising. An analogy with cricket may help some readers. If a batsman's marginal innings (ie his most recent one) produces a score of more runs than his current average for the season, his average will rise; a score below his average will reduce his average.

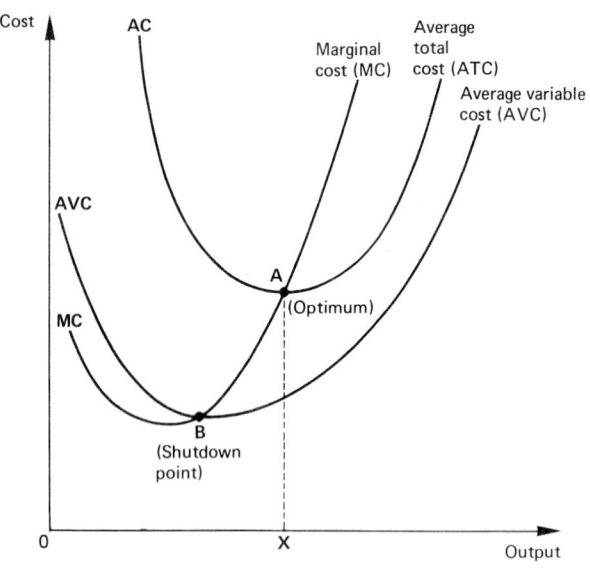

5.1 The optimum and shut-down points

In order to break even (ie to make normal profits) an entrepreneur must receive a price equal to his or her average costs. The price must, in our example, never fall below £30, which the entrepreneur must receive for an output of 8. For any other output price must exceed 8 – eg to sell only one unit, the price must be £160 because average cost is £160 for one unit.

In order to make excess profits, price must exceed average costs. *'Marginal cost pricing'* (ie charging a price equal to marginal costs) will achieve this for any output beyond 8. The marginal cost of the 10th unit is £52: if this is plotted against an output of 9½ units, the marginal cost curve crosses output 10 at 65. If 10 units are sold at 65 each, total revenue is 650. Total cost of producing 10 units is £328, so excess profits are +322. Marginal cost pricing brings in excess profits.

Any price below £30 will produce a loss, as average costs can never be below £30 per unit in this example. For outputs below 8 an entrepreneur would like to charge on an average cost pricing basis. But raising the price for a reduced output (eg charging £31 for 7, £33 for 6 etc) is not likely to be acceptable for consumers. Average cost pricing may not be possible. Marginal cost pricing is not a disaster – in fact, it minimises losses. As long as price exceeds average variable costs, losses are minimised. For an output of 7 for example, marginal cost pricing brings a price of £20. Total revenue is therefore £140. As total costs are £215, losses are £75 – less than producing O at a cost (and loss) of £128. As long as variable costs are more than covered, some of fixed costs can be covered, and losses are less than fixed costs. When price (ie marginal cost) equals average variable costs (in our example at output of 6), losses are £128, and the entrepreneur is indifferent between carrying on and shutting down. This is the shut-down point – point B on Diagram 5.1, at an output of 6.

Thus, a firm's supply schedule is its marginal cost curve from point B onwards (when MC exceed AVC); this minimises its losses and maximises its profits in the short-run. In the long-run, of course, *all* costs must be covered, so the profit-maximizing supply schedule is the marginal cost curve from point A onwards. (When MC exceeds ATC).

The industry's supply curve

The supply schedule for the industry is derived from the supply curves of all the firms in the industry. It is obtained merely by adding up the relevant parts of the marginal cost curves of the firms. Suppose there are 5 firms in an industry and their marginal costs for various levels of output are as illustrated in Table 5.2.

Table 5.2

Output	Marginal costs (£)				
	Firm A	Firm B	Firm C	Firm D	Firm E
1	1	2	1	1	2
2	2	4	2	3	3
3	3	6	5	7	4
4	4	8	7	10	5
5	5	10	9	13	6

If the market price were £1, firms A, C and D could produce one unit each; firms B and E could not produce anything. Thus, the industry's supply would be 3.

If the market price rose to £2, firms A and C could afford to produce two units each; firms B, D and E could only produce one; the industry's supply would thus be 7.

If the price rose to £3, firm A could produce 3; firms, C, D and E would produce 2; firm B could still only produce 1; supply would total 10.

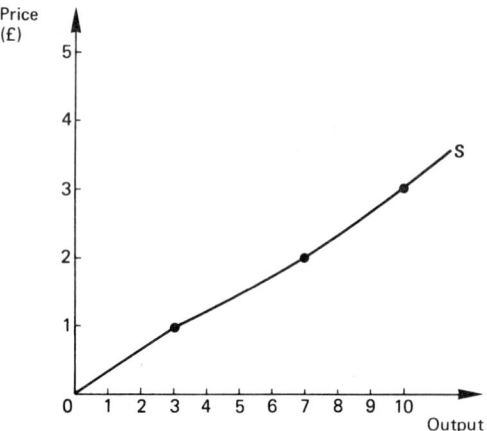

5.2 The industry's supply curve

This schedule of supply is illustrated by Diagram 5.2. The curve shows what the industry *would be prepared to supply* at each price. It also reflects the responsiveness of supply to changes in price. This responsiveness is called the *elasticity of supply* and is defined as:

$$\frac{\text{Proportionate change in quantity supplied}}{\text{Proportionate change in price}}$$

Thus, the calculation is:

$$\frac{\text{Change in quantity supplied}}{\text{Original quantity}} \text{ divided by } \frac{\text{Change in price}}{\text{Original Price}}$$

This can be rearranged as:

$$\frac{\text{Change in quantity}}{\text{Change in price}} \times \frac{\text{Original price}}{\text{Original quantity}}$$

Mathematically, the Greek delta Δ is used to denote 'change in', so the formula is:

$$\frac{\Delta Q}{\Delta P} \times \frac{P}{Q}$$

In our example, when price rises from £1 to £2, supply rises from 3 to 7.

Thus, by the above formula,

$$\frac{(7-3)}{(2-1)} \times \frac{1}{3}$$

simplifies as $\frac{4}{1} \times \frac{1}{3}$

and gives elasticity of 1.33.

As elasticity is greater than one, supply is said to be *elastic*. If elasticity is less than one, supply is said to be *inelastic*.

An anomaly occurs here, however. Suppose we take the same example, but in reverse. Price falls from £2 to £1, causing supply to fall from 7 to 3.

The elasticity formula gives us:

$$\frac{3-7}{1-2} \times \frac{2}{7}$$

or $\frac{-4}{-1} \times \frac{2}{7}$

or 1.12.

Clearly, it is strange for the same line or curve to have two different elasticities depending on whether one moves up or down. In order to eliminate this, mid-points between the two output and price figures are used. The formula becomes:

$$\frac{\Delta Q}{\Delta P} \times \frac{P_0 + P_1}{Q_0 + P_1}$$

where P_0 and Q_0 are the original price and quantity and P_1 and Q_1 are the new ones.

Thus, when prices rises from £1 to £2 and supply rises from 3 to 7, the formula gives us:

$$\frac{4}{1} \times \frac{(1+2)}{(3+7)}$$

or $\frac{4}{1} \times \frac{3}{10}$

or 1.2.

And when the reverse occurs, with £2 and 7 the original price and quantity levels:

$$\frac{\text{minus } 4}{\text{minus } 1} \times \frac{(2+1)}{(7 \times 3)}$$

or $4 \times \frac{3}{10}$

or 1.2

The theoretical extremes occur when elasticity is infinite ('perfectly elastic') or is zero ('perfectly inelastic') as illustrated in Diagram 5.3. Perfect elasticity is theoretical; it means that the industry can supply an infinite amount at the market price. This would assume that the industry's average and marginal costs remain constant. Perfect inelasticity is possible; it means that the industry will not raise or lower supply whatever the price. This could be true of a unique article, such as an art treasure. Whatever the price offered, supply remains unchanged – the article is unique.

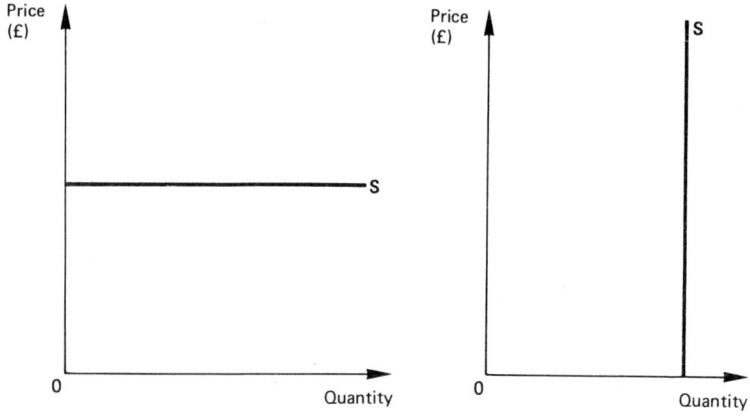

5.3a Perfectly elastic supply   5.3b Perfectly inelastic supply

Any straight line supply schedule originating from the origin of the graph has an elasticity of supply of one. Diagram 5.4 illustrates this.

S_1 is an obvious case – price and quantity rise by equal amounts; the axes are on the same scale and the supply curve is at 45°. In S_2, quantity rises half as much as price each time – again a constant elasticity of unity. S_3 also shows a constant and unitary relationship between price and quantity.

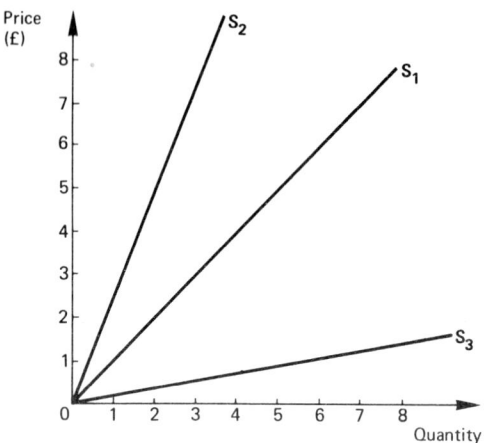

5.4 Unitary elasticity of supply

The long-run

In the long-run a firm has to cover *all* its costs in order to break even. Prices must at least equal average costs. Also, in the long-run, *all* factors of production can be increased. This leads to economies of scale and possibly eventually to diseconomies.

As the factors of production are increased in supply, the average and marginal cost curves shift to the right and also move downwards because of economies of scale. Diagram 5.5 illustrates this. At point A, the firm is beyond the optimum (point q) and average costs are rising. Yet if it then installs new capital, buys more land and employs more labour (ie increases the supply of all its factors of production) it can move down AC_2 towards a new optimum at point w. If output eventually reaches B, a similar situation arises – it would benefit the firm to leave AC_2 and set off down AC_3 towards optimum x. If diseconomies eventually set in, AC_4 and AC_5 lead to gradually increasing inefficiency. Thus, the firm's long-run expansion path would follow the jagged path illustrated. This jagged path is usually smoothed out to form the long-run supply curve (sometimes called the 'envelope' curve) as shown in Diagram 5.6.

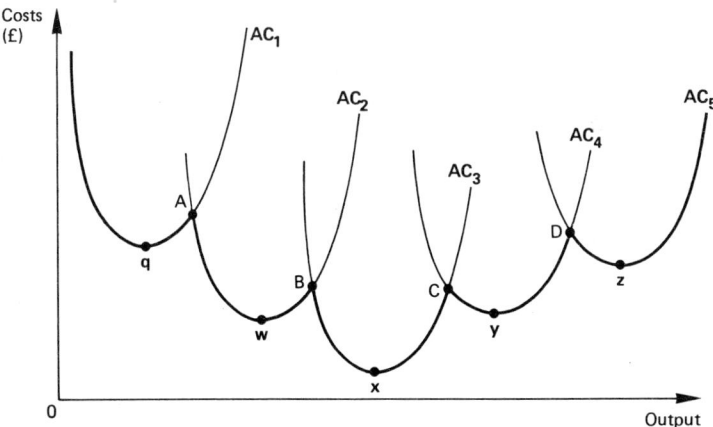

5.5 A firm's long-run expansion path

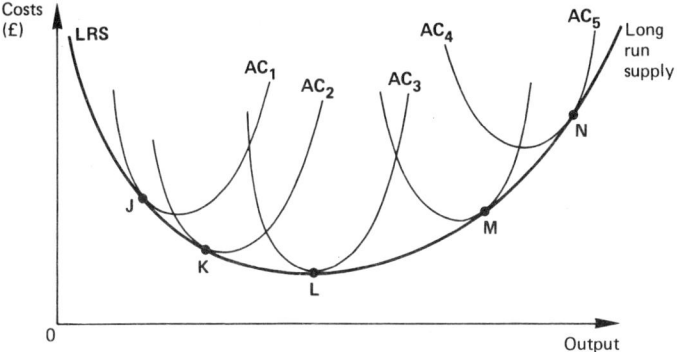

5.6 The long-run supply or 'envelope' curve

The industry's supply curve shifts as the firms in the industry can produce more efficiently. The process is quite simple – the supply curve merely moves to the right as more can be supplied at each possible price (Diagram 5.7).

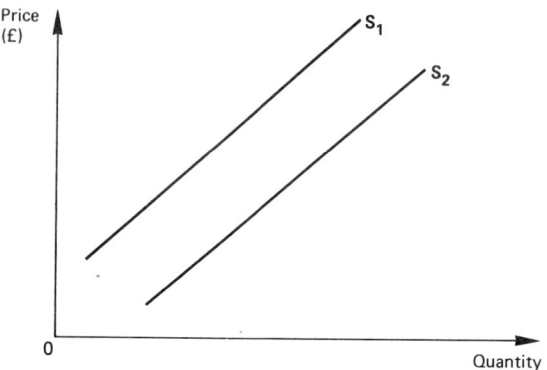

5.7 An increase in supply

Joint supply

Some products are in joint supply. For example, the production of coal gas necessarily increases the output of coke, whether or not more coke is desired or needed. Thus, there may be a fall in the price of coke, because of surplus supply. The marginal cost of the coke is usually said to be the total cost of the extra units of both products minus the extra revenue gained from sales of coal gas.

There can be an opposite relationship between products. Sheep can be bred for meat or wool. If there is a boom in the demand for wool, producers may produce more wool at the expense of mutton. This can lead to a shortage of mutton.

Conclusion to Section one

This section has dealt with the main problems of an entrepreneur – what to produce, where, how and for whom. The ultimate problem for an entrepreneur is fixing the price, involving the problems of costs and supply. Yet entrepreneurs do not exist in a vacuum. They cannot set their prices in isolation. There is another side to market – demand. The next section deals with this subject of demand. When both production and consumption have been understood, the third economic problems – exchange – can be explained.

Summary

1 Firms incur fixed and variable costs; variable costs change when output changes.

2 Average cost = $\dfrac{\text{total cost}}{\text{output}}$: marginal cost is the extra cost of producing one more unit.

3 Firms will maximise profits or minimise losses in the short-run by a policy of marginal-cost pricing.

4 In the long-run, price must at least equal average cost for profits to be made.

5 Elasticity of supply = $\dfrac{\text{proportionate change in quantity supplied}}{\text{proportionate change in price}}$

6 A supply curve shows what the industry is prepared to produce and sell at different prices.

Section two Demand

6 Individual demand

Utility

The assumption made by economists about the behaviour of consumers is that a consumer seeks to obtain the maximum benefit from the money he or she spends. This principle of 'getting one's money's worth' is called 'maximizing utility'.

Utility can be defined as the pleasure, satisfaction or benefit which a consumer obtains from consuming the products that he or she chooses to buy. Each decision to buy involves the principle of 'opportunity cost'. A consumer has a limited amount of money to spend and if he or she spends it all on Good A, then he or she has foregone the opportunities of spending the same amount on Goods, B, C, D etc. The consumer has decided that Good A is the one which will bring maximum utility. Alternatively, the consumer could purchase different amounts of several goods to achieve his or her wishes.

Factors which influence demand

When making a decision about what to purchase, a consumer is influenced by the following factors:

1 *The relative prices of the goods available*

If a consumer wishes to travel from London to Glasgow, the choices of travel are by air, rail, road transport, driving in his or her own car or hiring a car. The relative prices of all these modes of transport would be important. If the initial idea was to travel by train, he or she would want to know the cost of the train journey, but this price would not be the only one of interest. It would also be sensible to find out the prices of possible *substitutes*, like the air fare or car hire.

As well as substitutes, there are goods known as *complementary goods* – ie a product which complements or goes together with others. The demand for torch batteries will be influenced by the demand for torches. When purchasing a car, a consumer would not only be influenced by its price and the price of possible substitutes, but also by the price of servicing, spare parts or other essential complements.

2 *Tastes*

This is a subjective factor and one which is difficult to measure or quantify. If someone does not like a particular product he or she will be unlikely to consider buying it. Our traveller, contemplating the journey from London to Glasgow may be scared of flying or may like driving, so this will influence the decision. He or she might decide to drive even though the train is cheaper, because he or she prefers to drive; individual tastes outweigh the price factor.

A consumer's views concerning the qualities of the products available are a strong influence on his or her buying decisions: the cheapest product or brand may not be the best! Indeed, the nineteenth century American economist, Torsten Veblen, noted a phenomenon called *conspicuous consumption*, whereby people preferred to buy expensive goods either in order to prove to their neighbours that they could afford them or else because they thought that an expensive product must, by definition, be of superior quality.

Clearly, consumers are influenced by advertising and tend to buy well-known brands. They can also take the advice of friends and relatives about what to buy. Thus, tastes can be changed by a variety of factors, even time of year (eg increased demand for ice-cream during warm weather) but each consumer's tastes will be personal and different from other people's.

3 *Disposable income*

Whatever we would all *like* to buy, our consumption pattern is limited by the financial resources at our disposal. Some of our demand decisions involve spending money on essential everyday products like heat, light and basic foodstuffs. Some people may not have much left after buying these essential products and thus may have only limited power to exercise choice based on tastes, though they can exercise *some* choice, even in purchasing their essential products of food, clothing and shelter.

For all demand decisions these factors come to bear. 'What does it cost?' (price effect): 'can I afford it?' (income effect) and finally 'is it worth that much to me?' (taste effect).

The law of diminishing marginal utility

Total utility is defined as the total benefit or satisfaction a consumer obtains from the purchases. *Marginal utility* is the extra utility he or she gains from consuming one more unit of a commodity. People usually act in a way which conforms with the *law of diminishing marginal utility*. This Law states that:

'The more units of a commodity which a consumer purchases, the less value he places on obtaining additional units of that commodity'. (ceteris paribus).

For example, if all my shoes are falling to pieces, I need new ones. I may place great importance on buying a new pair – the marginal utility (the extra benefit I receive from having one pair rather than none) is high for a new pair. Having bought them, however, I am not quite so desperate to obtain a second pair. The marginal utility conveyed by the second pair is less than that of the first.

Table 6.1 The law of diminishing marginal utility

Quantity	Total utility (£)	Marginal utility (£)
1	3.00	3.00
2	5.50	2.50
3	7.50	2.00
4	9.00	1.50
5	10.00	1.00
6	10.50	0.50

Suppose my demand for hats is illustrated in Table 6.1 (which supposes that marginal utility can be measured and expressed in money terms). The marginal utility table shows that I place £3 of value on obtaining one hat, but only £2.50 on a second one and £2 on a third. Thus, I will pay up to £3 for one hat, but only £2.50 for a second and so on, until the hat makers will have to reduce the price to 50p to persuade me to buy a sixth hat. If the price is above £3, I will buy no hats at all – my income and tastes will not allow me to buy hats.

Suppose I buy five hats at a price of £1 *each*. I am spending £5. Yet I would have been prepared to pay £3 for the first, £2.50 for the second, £2 for the third and £1.50 for the fourth, plus £1 for the fifth – a total of £10. I have made a sort of 'saving' of £5 on the first four hats. This is known as *'consumer's surplus'* – the surplus utility a consumer gains when he or she pays less for a product than he or she would have been prepared to pay.

Exceptions to the law

As so often in economics, there are exceptions to the Law. For some consumers, marginal utility may *increase* as they purchase more units of certain commodities.

1 *Completing a set*

If I collect stamps or antiques, for example, I may be willing to pay a great deal to get one item to complete a set. A set is more valuable than a few odd items, so I am more anxious to buy the last item in the set than I was to buy the first one, which had no special significance.

2 *Addiction*

Someone who has an addiction, for example to drugs or alcohol, must have more and more – so he or she becomes increasingly desperate and is prepared to pay more for successive units of the product to which he or she is addicted.

3 *Conspicuous consumption, or the Veblen effect*

Because of their desire to show off their wealth some people may deliberately buy highly priced goods or may purposely buy a second or third car in order to demonstrate their ability to pay.

4 *Speculation*

If the price of a share or other similar asset rises, speculators may rush to buy because they anticipate a further rise in its value. They wish to buy now and sell later when the value has risen more; if prices fall, they may sell for the converse reason.

5 *Giffen goods*

In the late nineteenth century Sir Robert Giffen discovered that very poor people, who could afford only the most basic foodstuffs, tended to buy more of these foodstuffs when their price rose, and compensated by stopping or reducing their consumption of slightly more luxurious goods.

Suppose a consumer needs 3,000 calories per day to survive and he has £1.80 to spend. If bread provided 1,000 calories and cost 10p per loaf, and meat provided 500 calories and cost 80p per pound, he or she could consume two loaves (2,000 calories: 20p) and 2lbs meat (1,000 calories: £1.60).

If the price of bread rose to 40p per loaf, the consumer could only obtain 3,000 calories by buying 2½ loaves and 1lb meat. This would provide 2,500 calories at a cost of 80p from the bread and 500 calories at a cost of 80p from the meat. The bread price has increased – but he or she has consumed more bread.

The law of equi-marginal returns

We are making the assumption all the time that rational consumers seek to maximise their utility. They will be seeking to maximise their 'consumer's surplus' by buying goods at a price equal to or below the prices they would have been prepared to pay. The principle that was explained in Table 6.1 (the example about hats) will apply to all their purchases. The law which describes this is the law of equi-marginal returns, which states that:

'A rational consumer will distribute his expenditure among a variety of goods in such a way the marginal utility of the last unit of each commodity purchased is in the same proportion to the price of the commodity'. (ceteris paribus).

This law is illustrated in Table 6.2, which illustrates a consumer's marginal utilities for different quantities of three products.

Suppose this consumer had £4.60 to spend and that meat cost £1 per lb, cheese 50p per lb. and potatoes 20p per lb. He or she would purchase, with £4.60:

2lbs meat   (£2) : Total utility 450p
4lbs cheese   (£2) : Total utility 750p
3lbs potatoes (60p) : Total utility 220p

At all these points, there is an *identical ratio of marginal utility to price (2:1)*.

Table 6.2 The law of equi-marginal returns

	Marginal utilities (pence)		
Quantity	Meat (£1 per 1b)	Cheese (50p per 1b)	Potatoes (20p per 1b)
1	250	290	110
2	200	210	70
3	160	150	40
4	130	100	20
5	110	70	10
6	90	50	5

Any other combination adding up to £4.60 would lead to a loss of utility. For example:

3lbs meat   (£3) : would gain 160p more utility
2lbs cheese   (£1) : would lose 250p of utility from not consuming the 3rd and 4th lbs.
3lbs potatoes (60p) : utility unchanged.

The net loss of utility would be 90p. A similar loss would occur for any other combination adding up to £4.60.

Indifference curve analysis

A more common way of illustrating the law explained in this chapter is by the use of indifference curves. Assume that a particular consumer has the choice of purchasing varying amounts of just two commodities, apples and pears. He or she has to work out what value of utility different amounts of the two commodities convey. If this consumer had 10 apples and no pears, how many apples would he or she be prepared to give up to obtain a pear? A schedule can be drawn up showing what each apple is worth in terms of pears (see Table 6.3). At all these points the consumer is 'indifferent' between consumption of the two products. On Diagram 6.1, for instance, 7 apples and 4 pears are as acceptable as 3 apples and 19 pears.

The indifference curve is convex to the origin because of the law of diminishing marginal unity. The consumer values the first apple more than each successive one, so he or she needs more pears to be persuaded to give up the first apple than subsequent ones. The same applies to the consumer's valuation of pears. Thus, the curve is steeper at its extremes than in the middle, where the two goods are exchangeable with less relative sacrifice. The slope of the curve represents the *diminishing marginal rate of substitution*; towards the extremes substitution takes place on increasingly stringent terms.

Table 6.3 An indifference schedule

Apples	Pears
10	0
9	1
8	2
7	4
6	7
5	10
4	14
3	19
2	26
1	35
0	50

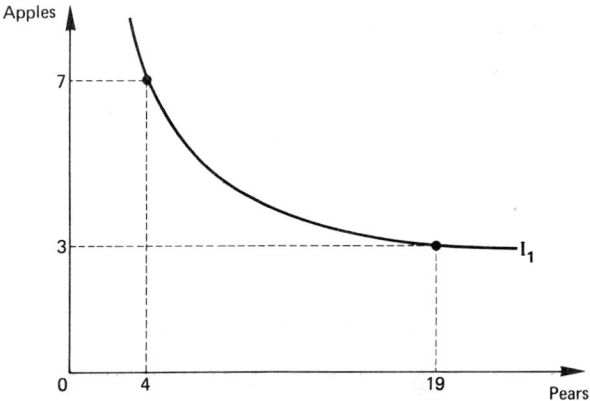

6.1 An indifference curve

A consumer possesses an infinite number of indifference curves. He or she has another schedule of pears starting at 11 apples; another commencing at 12 and so on indefinitely. A consumer wishing to maximise utility desires to reach the furthest possible indifference curve from the origin of the graph, but is limited in this ambition by a budgetary restraint – ie by disposable income.

At any particular moment, there is a ratio between the prices of goods. If, for example, apples cost 10p each and pears cost 5p, the

73

price ratio is 2:1; two pears can be bought for the same outlay as one apple. A series of lines can be drawn on the graph showing this ratio. Yet, as just stated, the consumer's disposable income is fixed in the short-run. Thus, the line that will be drawn representing the relative prices of the two commodities is determined by his or her income. In Diagram 6.2, this so-called *'budget line'* is XY: the consumer's budget will allow him of her to purchase any combination of apples and pears along XY. The consumer will find out which of the infinite number of indifference curves will touch XY. Where a tangency occurs (at point H in the diagram), the ratios of the prices of the goods will equal the marginal rate of substitution of apples and pears (ie their relative marginal utilities). Thus, the law of equi-marginal returns is satisfied. Oa apples and Ob pears will be consumed.

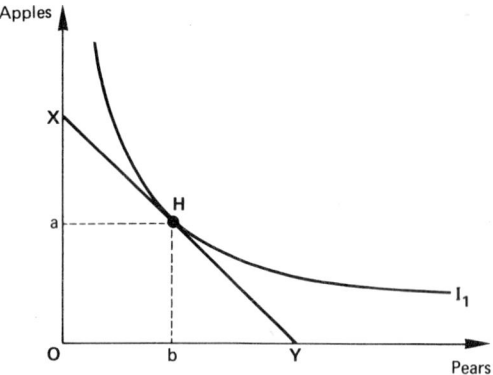

6.2 The interaction of the budget line and an indifference curve

Income effects

If the consumer's disposable income increases, the budget line can be moved further from the axis because he or she can afford more goods – from XY to WZ in Diagram 6.3. (WZ will be parallel to XY because we are assuming that the relative prices of the goods are unchanged.) Thus, a new indifference curve can be reached – at point K. Oc apples and Od pears will be assumed.

There is an exception to this process, involving goods called *inferior goods*. These are, as their name suggests, basic low quality goods. For example, a poor person may only be able to afford margarine or minced meat. If their spending power increases, they may decide to buy butter or joints of beef instead, so consumption of the poorer quality goods will *fall*. We measure margarine in Diagram 6.4 against 'all other goods' because it is inferior with regard to all other goods in the consumer's mind. When income rises, consumption of margarine falls from Oa to Ob units. Point K is to the left of Point H.

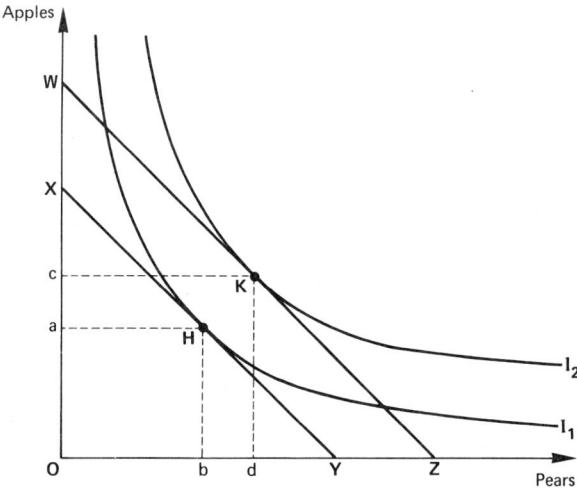

6.3 Income effect

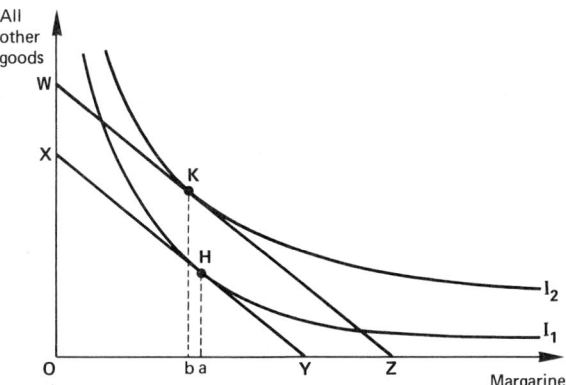

6.4 An inferior good

Price or substitution effects

There is another way in which a consumer can increase consumption and reach a new indifference curve. This occurs if the price of one of the commodities falls. In Diagram 6.5, pears have become cheaper, so the budget line moves from XY to XZ. The ratio between the prices has changed. For example, if the price of pears falls to 2p each, *five* pears can be bought for the equivalent of one apple. The consumer's income can purchase more goods. In this example, Oc pears can be purchased instead of Ob.

75

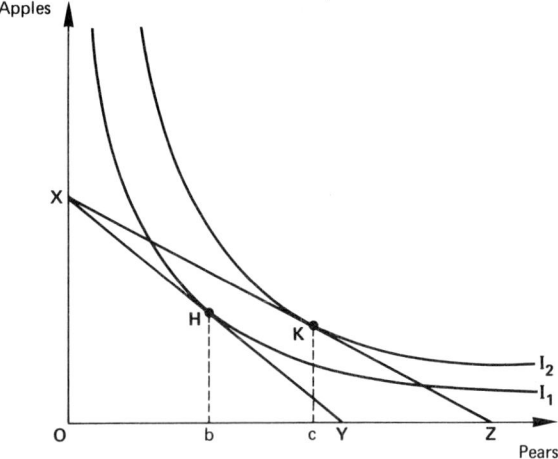

6.5 Price effect

Had pears become expensive (and apples remained unchanged in price) the budget line would have had to move closer to the origin and less could be purchased. To illustrate this, imagine that in Diagram 6.5, XZ and Oc had been the starting position, and XY and Ob the position after the pear price had risen.

If *both* goods became simultaneously cheaper, the budget line would have moved further from the origin in a similar way to the income effect (though it would not move parallel to the old budget line unless the two goods became cheaper in the same proportion to each other); the budget line would move to the left if both goods became more expensive.

Yet again, there is an exceptional case – the *Giffen good*, illustrated in Diagram 6.6. For a Giffen good, consumption *rises* when price rises. If potatoes are regarded as inferior to all other goods, the budget line moves from XY to XW and there is a movement from indifference curve I_1 to I_0. But this time, *more* potatoes (Ob) are consumed than before (Oa). Point K is to the right of Point H.

How to distinguish between the price and income effects

When the price of a good falls (assuming it is not a Giffen good) more of it will be purchased, as was illustrated in Diagram 6.5. Yet there is both a price and an income effect mixed together here. The price (or substitution) effect occurs because the good is now relatively cheaper than other goods; the income effect occurs because the fact that the good is cheaper means that the consumer is relatively better off; his or her disposable income will command more purchasing power.

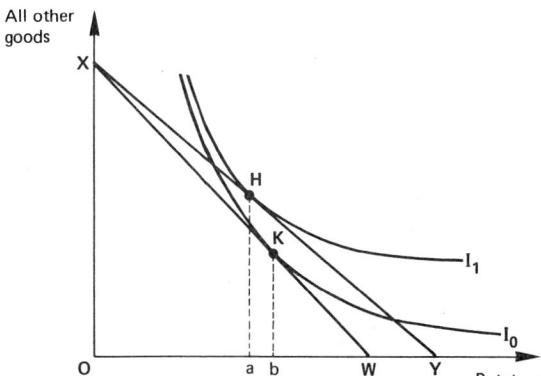

6.6 A Giffen good

In order to separate these two effects the procedure shown in Diagram 6.7 must be followed. When books become relatively cheaper the budget line moves from XY to XZ and Ob books are now bought instead of Oa. If a new budget line (MN) is drawn parallel to XZ, touching the original indifference curve, the two effects can be separated.

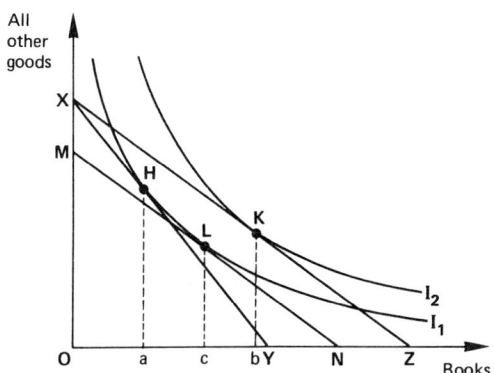

6.7 Income and substitution effects

MN represents the change in relative prices without moving to a new budget line so is the *price effect*; cb is the *income effect* – it shows how much of the extra consumption is due to a move to a new budget line (ie extra disposable income) and indifference curve.

For a Giffen good, the price effect is still positive, but the income effect is negative and this outweighs the price effect. Thus, the overall effect is negative, and Ob is *less* than Oa – the price fall has *reduced* demand (Diagram 6.8).

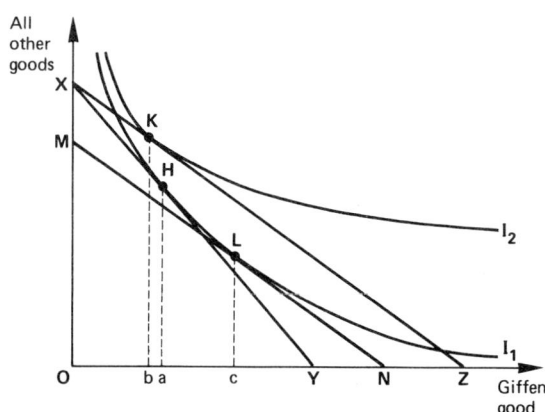

6.8 A Giffen good

Summary

1 The benefits conveyed to a consumer from purchases are called 'utility'. A rational consumer seeks to maximise utility.
2 A consumer's demand is influenced by prices, incomes and tastes.
3 For most goods the law of diminishing marginal utility applies – a consumer values the first unit of the good more than the second unit, the second more than the third and so on.
4 Utility is maximised when the marginal utilities of the last unit of each commodity consumed are in the same ratios to the prices of the goods. This is the law of equi-marginal returns.
5 An indifference curve shows the points where a consumer is indifferent between various quantities of two goods. The budget or relative price line shows the ratio of the prices of the goods. Where these schedules meet dictates the actual quantities of the goods consumed.
6 Should a good become relatively cheaper or a consumer's income rise, the consumer can reach a higher indifference curve and increase his utility.
7 The main exceptions are Giffen goods, whose consumption rises when price rises and falls when the price falls, and inferior goods, for which demand falls when the consumer's disposable income rises.

7 Market demand

The demand curve

Market demand is the total demand for a particular product. It is obtained simply by adding up all the individual demands of each consumer for that product. The individual demands are, of course, based on marginal utility and are influenced by all the relevant factors referred to in the previous chapter, such as price of the product, price of other products, tastes and disposable incomes. The principles which determine total demand for a product are therefore the same ones which influence an individual consumer's demand. As a result of this a commodity will be demanded in greater quantities when its price is low than when its price is high (unless it is a Giffen good).

The amount which all consumers in the market are prepared to buy at different prices is shown by a demand curve (Diagram 7.1). A demand curve is a *schedule* which shows what consumers *would be prepared to buy* at different prices. For example, at price OA, quantity OX would be demanded; at price OB, demand would be OY.

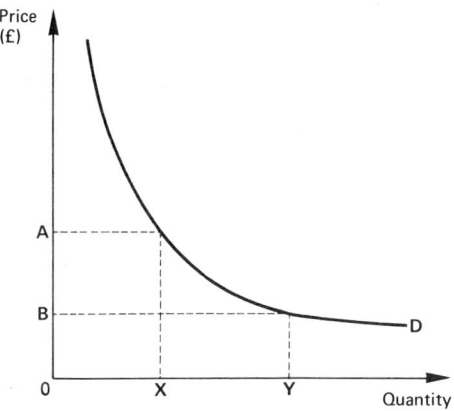

7.1 A demand curve

Price elasticity of demand

As illustrated in Diagram 7.1, a change in the price of a commodity will cause a change in demand for it; the extent of this change can be found by moving along the demand schedule from the old price to the new one and identifying the new level of demand. The extent to which demand responds to a price change is called the *price elasticity of demand* and is defined as:

Proportionate change in quantity demanded

Proportionate change in price

Using the Greek delta to denote 'change in', the formula is expressed in similar terms to that of elasticity of supply (see pp 62), ie:

$$\frac{\Delta Q}{\Delta P} \times \frac{P}{Q}$$

As a price rise will lead to a fall in demand (except for Giffen goods) and a price fall will lead to a rise in demand, then mathematically elasticity of demand will produce a negative result. If elasticity is between -1 and 0, demand is said to be inelastic; beyond -1 demand is said to be elastic.

In order to eliminate the anomaly of achieving a different result when moving up the demand curve to that achieved when moving down it, again, as with elasticity of supply, mid-points are chosen and the formula is amended to read:

$$\frac{\Delta Q}{\Delta P} \times \frac{P_0 + P_1}{Q_0 + Q_1}$$

Suppose Table 7.1 illustrates the demand for economics textbooks. If the price were £5, 20 would be demanded; if price fell to £4, demand would rise to 30.

Table 7.1

Price (£)	Quantity demanded	Total revenue $(P \times Q)$ (£)
6	8	48
5	20	100
4	30	120
3	40	120
2	55	110
1	80	80

The elasticity formula would be:

$$\frac{10}{-1} \times \frac{(5 + 4)}{(20 + 30)}$$

or $\quad \dfrac{10}{-1} \times \dfrac{9}{50}$

or $\quad -1.8$.

For the reverse process, with price rising from £4 to £5 and demand falling from 30 to 20, elasticity would be:

$$\frac{-10}{1} \times \frac{(5+4)}{(20+30)}$$

or $\frac{-10}{1} \times \frac{9}{50}$

or -1.8.

Between prices of £4 and £3 in Table 7.1, elasticity is unity. When price falls from £4 to £3, for example, quantity demanded rises from 30 to 40

Thus:

$$\frac{10}{-1} \times \frac{(4+3)}{(30+40)}$$

or $\frac{10}{-1} \times \frac{7}{70}$

produces $\frac{10}{-1} \times \frac{1}{10}$

or elasticity of -1.

The same result is achieved for a price rise from £3 to £4. When elasticity is unity, the total revenue (the amount sold multiplied by the price at which it is sold) will be unchanged. The change in demand exactly counteracts the price change.

Diagram 7.2 illustrates the only demand curve which has an elasticity of unity (ie of minus one) throughout its length. It is a rectangular hyperbola; total revenue (ie all the areas of the P × Q rectangles) is always the same.

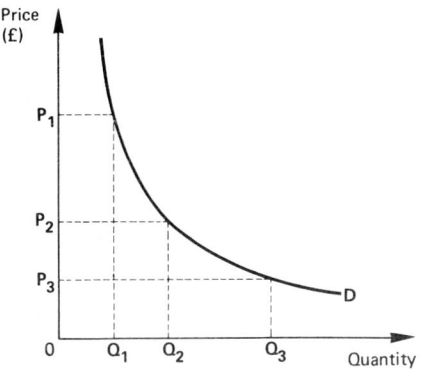

7.2 A demand curve with unitary elasticity

There is a simple way of finding out whether demand is elastic or inelastic in a particular instance. If, when price *falls*, total revenue *rises*, demand is elastic. If, when price *falls*, total revenue also *falls*, demand is inelastic. The area of the rectangle OP₂XY in Diagram 7.3 is *greater* than the area OP₁AB, so demand in the segment of the curve AX is elastic. In Diagram 7.4, total revenue OP₂XY is *smaller* than OP₁AB, so demand is inelastic.

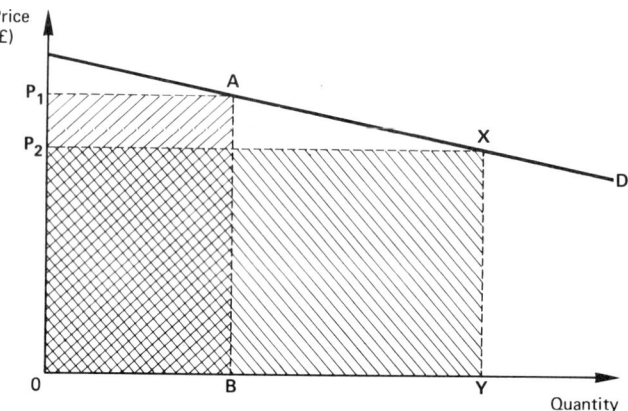

7.3 Elastic demand

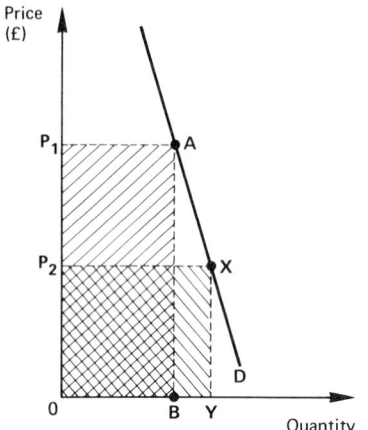

7.4 Inelastic demand

As with elasticity of supply there are theoretical extremes of elasticity of demand. Diagram 7.5 shows a perfectly inelastic schedule (elasticity = 0): there is no response of demand to any price change. A perfectly elastic schedule is also shown. Here, demand is infinite at the market price (elasticity = infinity).

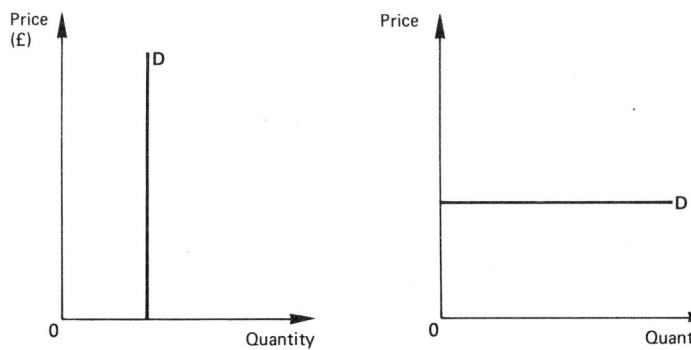

7.5a Perfectly inelastic demand   7.5b Perfectly elastic demand

Other elasticities of demand

When price changes, demand responds and moves *along* the demand curve. Yet there are factors which cause demand to move to a *new* curve. In this case the *conditions* of demand have changed, causing the original demand curve to be obsolete. The factors which can cause demand to shift to a new curve are changes in consumers' income or tastes, or changes in the prices of other goods. For example, demand for a particular commodity may increase because tastes have changed in its favour, or disposable incomes have risen, or rival commodities have become more expensive. Diagram 7.6 shows this. More is demanded at each possible price (eg OZ is sought at price OA, instead of OX). An opposite movement in disposable incomes, tastes, or prices of rival goods would shift the demand schedule to the left and less would be demanded at each price (eg OW at price OA).

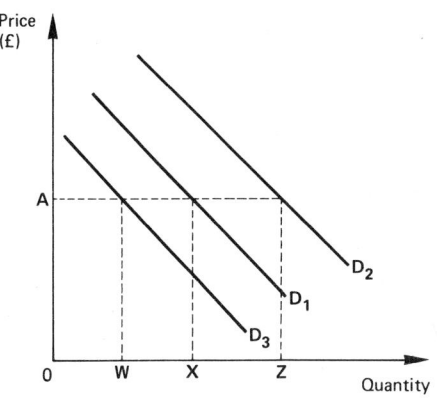

7.6 Changes in demand

1 *Income elasticity of demand*
If consumers receive a rise in their disposable income, their demand for certain commodities may increase. The responsiveness of demand for a particular item to a change in disposable income is known as *income elasticity of demand* and is defined as:

$$\frac{\text{Proportionate change in quantity demanded}}{\text{Proportionate change in disposable income}}$$

So, a 10% rise in disposable income which resulted in a 20% rise in the demand for petrol would mean that income elasticity of demand for petrol was $\frac{20}{10}$ or 2.

Income elasticity of demand will almost invariably be positive, because a rise in income will usually cause consumers to buy more of the goods at their disposal. Should income elasticity be greater than one, the good can be regarded as a luxury; if income elasticity is between 0 and 1, the good is a necessity. If income elasticity should be negative, then this is the exceptional case – an inferior good (see Chapter 6, pp 74–5).

2 *Cross-elasticity of demand*
Cross-elasticity of demand measures the responsiveness of demand for one good to a change in the price of another one, ie:

$$\frac{\text{Proportionate change in quantity demanded of product 'X'}}{\text{Proportionate change of price of product 'Y'}}$$

Goods and services may be related to each other in two ways. They may be substitutes (eg gas, electricity, oil and coal as methods of domestic heating) or they may be complementary goods, which are products which go together or 'complement' each other, such as pencils and pencil sharpeners, football boots and laces.

Let us suppose that tea and coffee are substitutes for each other. Clearly not everyone will regard them as substitutes, because of differing individual tastes, but we are talking about *total* demand, so we will assume that a sufficiently large proportion of the population do regard them as substitutes to make the assumption valid.

Diagram 7.7 shows the cross-elasticity relationship. When the price of tea falls from OPT_1 to OPT_2, demand increases from OQT_1 to OQT_2. Although the price of coffee has not changed coffee is now less attractive in comparison with tea; some consumers will stay loyal to coffee because of tastes, but others (whose disposable income is limited, of course) will switch to the cheaper item, so as demand for tea increases, demand for coffee falls (from OQC_1 to OQC_2).

Cross-elasticity will be positive – a fall in the tea price has led to a fall in the demand for coffee. A rise in the price of tea would have led to a rise in demand for coffee, tea being less competitive than before.

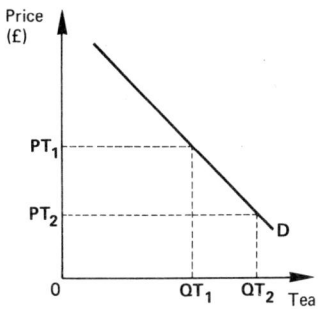
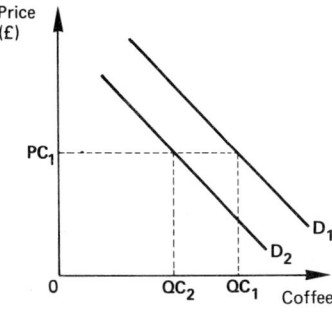

7.7a Demand for tea   7.7b Demand for coffee
Cross-elasticity of demand – substitutes

For complementary goods, the cross-elasticity relationship produces a negative number as its result. As Diagram 7.8 shows, when the price of torches falls, there is a rise in demand not only for torches but also for a complementary good, torch batteries.

Should the price of torches have risen, the demand for batteries would have fallen in line with a fall in the demand for torches.

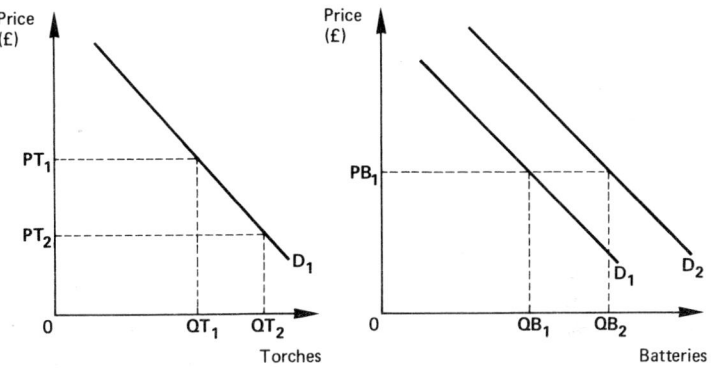

7.8a Demand for torches   7.8b Demand for batteries
Cross-elasticity of demand – complementary goods

3 *Taste elasticity of demand*
Because tastes cannot really be quantified, there is no measurable formula or definition of taste elasticity of demand, but the concept follows the same principle as income elasticity. Changes in tastes will shift the demand curve, as was shown in Diagram 7.6.

Perverse demand curves

It is possible to visualise a demand curve in which demand *rises* when price rises. A Giffen good should follow this pattern, as should a good exhibiting the Veblen 'conspicuous consumption' effect. A share or foreign currency which is increasing in value should also produce rising demand. Yet economists dispute whether, in fact a rising demand curve (see Diagram 7.9a) is valid. For example, if a share price rises or a fur coat becomes an article of prestige, have not tastes changed, or has not the good in question become a different article – its nature has changed in the eyes of consumers? If this is accepted, then it is the *conditions* of demand which have changed, so the demand curve should have shifted to the right, as shown in Diagram 7.9b.

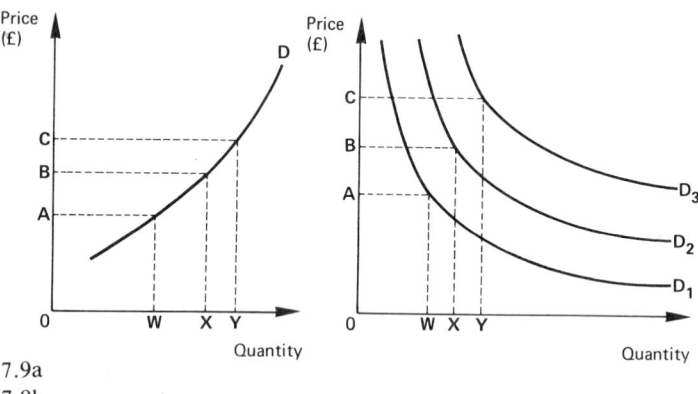

7.9a
7.9b

'Perverse' demand – two possible explanations

Generally, economists prefer the second explanation and are reluctant to acknowledge a 'perverse' or rising demand curve.

Elasticity of demand in the real world

It is most important in the real world for entrepreneurs and for governments to have some idea of the various elasticities of demand for different products. If the price of a commodity rises, how much will demand fall? Will total revenue fall? The price elasticity of demand for petrol in the UK is about −0.23 ie demand is inelastic; if the price rises most consumers will grumble but still consume almost as much as before, so total revenue will, in fact, rise. Petrol is now a necessity. Foreign holidays are a luxury and demand is relatively elastic; price rises will cut demand significantly (though research has shown that the rising unemployment has *not* reduced holidays as much as was expected – people seem determined to 'get away from it all' once a year).

Clearly, demand for necessities (eg food, clothing) is inelastic compared with demand for luxuries. Lack of availability of substitutes (eg in the case of petrol) makes demand relatively inelastic.

Durability makes demand for a good more elastic – if the price of a car or refrigerator goes up, people make do with their old one for a bit longer. For similar reasons, demand for a product is always more elastic in the long-run than in the short-run. Relatively cheap items, like newspapers, tend to have inelastic demand – a rise in price only affects a small proportion of the average consumer's expenditure and therefore is not important enough to warrant cutting consumption.

Cross-elasticity is probably easier to measure, especially with regard to substitutes. In the 1970's gas became much cheaper for central heating than electricity and oil, and there was a significant swing in demand which the government had to counteract in order to prevent excess demand for gas and also to protect the electricity industry in particular.

Governments are also concerned about income elasticity of demand. If consumers receive a pay rise or a tax cut, what will they spend the extra money on? Income elasticity of demand for food is low. The 19th century statistician Ernst Engel, produced *Engel's Law* proving that, as people became richer, they spent a smaller proportion of their income on food. Income elasticity for consumer durables and vehicles and holidays is much higher and a 'consumer-led boom' will greatly affect such industries. In the UK there is an exceptionally high demand for imports (a 'propensity to import'), so that income rises will result in higher imports of cars, consumer durables and electronic gadgets as well as more demand for holidays abroad.

This relationship between supply and demand is clearly vital to both producers and consumers. This (plus the government's role in the market) is the subject of the next section.

Summary

1 Total demand for a product is shown by a demand curve or schedule showing the quantities demanded at different prices.
2 The responsiveness of demand to changes in price is called the price elasticity of demand. There is usually an inverse relationship between price and demand changes.
3 If total revenue falls when price rises or rises when price falls, demand is relatively elastic. If the opposite occurs, demand is relatively inelastic.
4 The responsiveness of demand for a product to changes in disposable income is called income elasticity of demand. It is positive, except for inferior goods.
5 The responsiveness of demand for one product to changes in the price of another is called cross-elasticity of demand. The relationship is positive for substitutes but negative for complementary goods.
6 Entrepreneurs need to know the various elasticities of demand which consumers have for their products in order to anticipate what

will happen if prices change. Government's policies should also take note of demand patterns.

Section three The price system

8 The free market in operation

The function of price

A free market is one where there is no intervention from the government. In a free market, the price of a good is determined by the interaction of supply and demand. Price equates supply with demand and thus provides a solution to the economic problem – it allocates resources. The previous three chapters have been concerned with either demand or supply; now, we can put them together. Only where they cross do the wishes of consumers exactly match those of producers. Thus, in Diagram 8.1, the quantity traded will be OQ_1 and the price charged will be OP_1; only at this point are both sides prepared to do business. The market for this product is in equilibrium here.

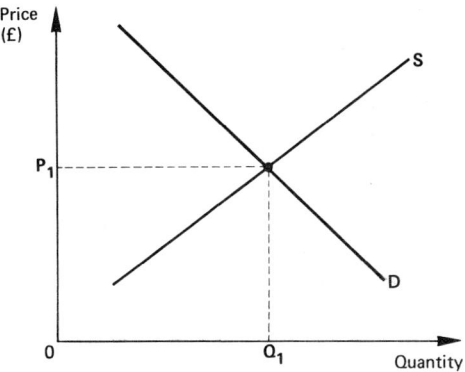

8.1 The determination of price

Changes in demand and supply

If the conditions of either demand or supply change, the equilibrium point will change because one of the curves will have moved. Suppose demand rises because of a favourable change in consumers' incomes or tastes, or because a rival product has become more expensive. In Diagram 8.2 demand has risen to D_2 and thus a new equilibrium is found at price OP_2 and quantity OQ_2. Consumers are really asking for quantity OX at the market price, but the industry cannot meet this demand because supply is not perfectly elastic. In the short-run not all factors of production can be increased in supply (machines and land are probably fixed); the law of diminishing returns operates. Thus, supply can only be increased at greater marginal cost, so the price producers ask for will rise. Consumers *will* get more of the product, but they will get OQ_2 not OX and they will have to pay OP_2 for it.

To see what happens when demand falls, imagine, in Diagram 8.2 that D_2 was the original schedule and demand then fell to D_1. Supply will fall and a new equilibrium will occur at OP_1 and OQ_1.

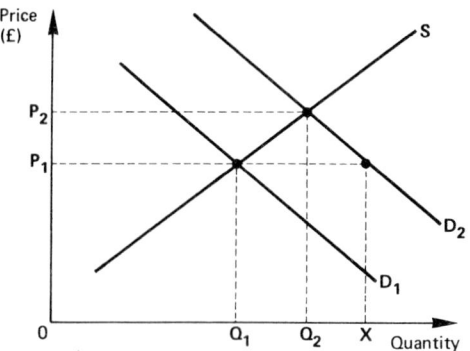

8.2 A change in demand

Suppose supply were to rise (eg firms might become more efficient and be able to supply more at the market price). In this case, the industry is willing to supply OX at the market price of OP_1, but consumers will not agree. They will only buy more if price falls – so they get more (OQ_2) but the industry has to reduce its price to OP_2. Again, to see the effects of a fall in supply, reverse the process in Diagram 8.3 and regard S_2 as the original supply and S_1 as the fall in supply.

The extent of the change in price and quantity will depend on the relative elasticities of demand and supply. These will also determine whether total revenue rises or falls as a result of the changes in price and quantity. When demand rises, total revenue will always rise, and vice versa. When supply changes, total revenue may rise or fall depending on the elasticity of demand.

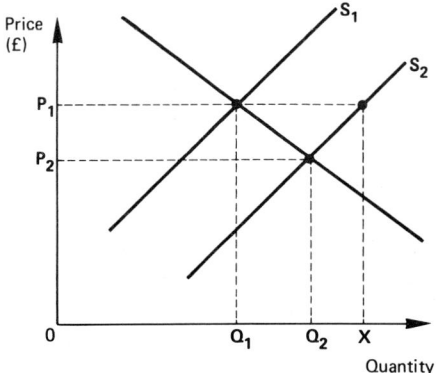

8.3 A change in supply

For agricultural products, the same process happens but in slow motion. This process is explained by a phenomenon known as the *Cobweb theorem*, illustrated in Diagram 8.4.

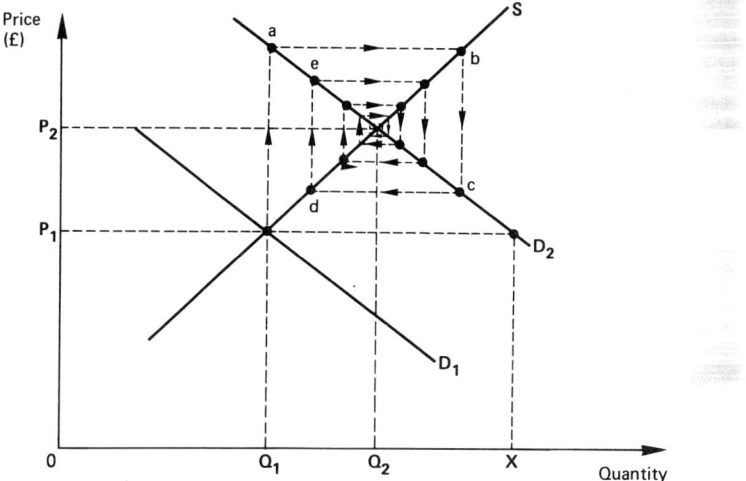

8.4 The cobweb

What is really happening when demand rises is that consumers are asking for quantity OX at the market price. They cannot have this because supply is not perfectly elastic, so there is, in fact, excess demand. Indeed, for agricultural producers, the very short-run supply curve may be completely inelastic – no more can be supplied until next harvest. Thus, the immediate reaction of the industry may be to 'ration' this excess demand by raising the price (point a). As soon as

91

possible though, the industry will produce more in order to meet the new demand (in the real world there will probably be some stocks available) and will move up their supply schedule to point 'b' at the new market price. Consumers will not agree to this, however. They will only buy this quantity at a price determined by point 'c'. Now there is excess supply, so firms, seeing the price drop, will reduce output to 'd'. Now there is excess demand, so price shoots up to 'e'. The process continues until equilibrium is reached at OQ_2 and OP_2. Remember, producers do not know exactly how much demand has risen. All they know is that it *has* risen, and they are trying to reach a new equilibrium.

Farmers, when deciding what crops to plant or animals to rear, do not know what demand will be in the coming year. They can only estimate what to produce by identifying the current year's demand. If demand has changed, their output level is wrong. They can 'chase' demand by moving up and down the supply curve as shown by the Cobweb theorem. Hopefully, they will eventually 'catch up' demand and reach equilibrium, but some Cobwebs have been known to 'explode' (Diagram 8.5). Here, as time goes on, the movement is *away* from equilibrium.

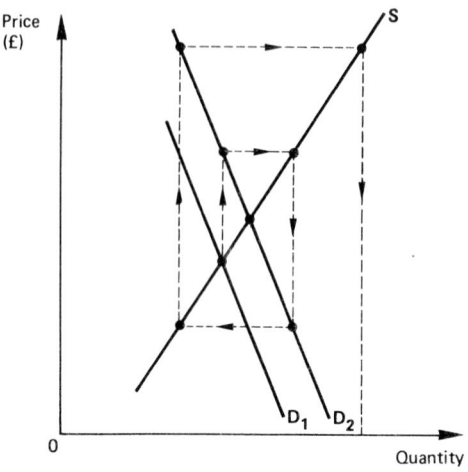

8.5 An exploding cobweb

Eventually, the industry will enjoy some technological change and its productivity will increase. Then supply will rise, as shown in Diagram 8.6, and price will come down towards or perhaps even below the original level.

If demand had fallen instead of risen in the original instance, a similar Cobweb system would evolve, producing either a new equilibrium at a lower price and output, or an exploding situation.

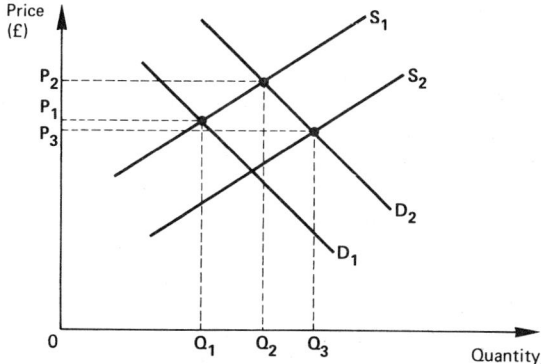

8.6 Changes in demand and supply

Special cases

1 *Perfectly inelastic and elastic curves*

It is possible that a rise in demand may not always lead to a rise in quantity supplied. Supply may be perfectly inelastic – for example a unique article like an art treasure; whatever the demand, supply cannot increase, so price will rise dramatically. Should supply be perfectly elastic, any increase in demand can be met in full. Similar special cases apply if demand is completely inelastic or elastic (Diagram 8.7).

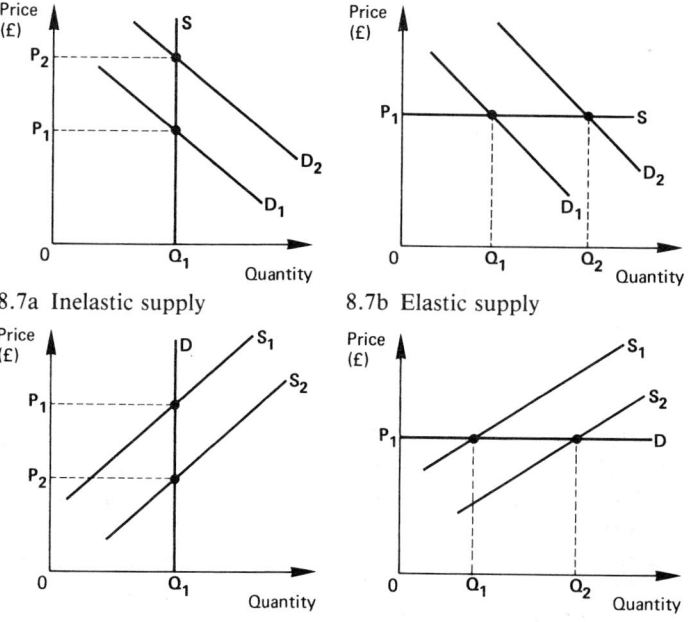

8.7a Inelastic supply   8.7b Elastic supply

8.7c Inelastic demand   8.7d Elastic demand
Perfectly elastic and inelastic cases

2 *Backward-bending supply curve of labour*
When demand for labour rises, the supply may not rise after a time – indeed it may even fall; the supply curve may bend backwards (Diagram 8.8). There are two reasons for this. First, no-one can work 24 hours a day, 7 days a week. Workers must take some rest even if offered higher wages to work more. At some point (eg at wage level W_1) a 'trade-off' occurs between extra work and leisure; workers prefer more leisure instead of work, even if extra earnings are sacrificed. For example, a school teacher may prefer leisure to taking night classes or private pupils in the evening. Also, the taxation system which taxes the rich relatively heavily may deter people from working longer only to lose a large part of their extra earnings. This backward-bending curve is obviously more likely to apply to richer people in more sophisticated economies, not to poor workers or countries.

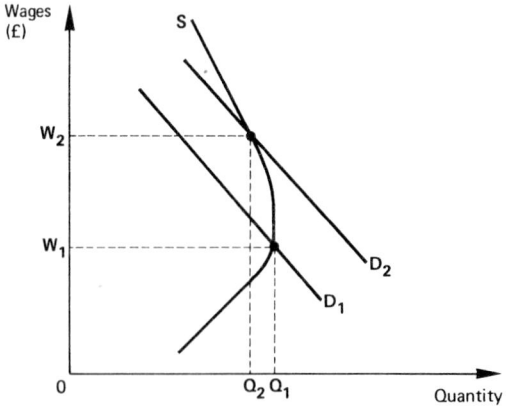

8.8 Backward-bending supply curve

3 *Joint supply*
Suppose two products are produced together and it is not possible to increase the supply of one on its own. Thus a rise in demand for coke would produce more coke but also more coal gas, so the price of coal gas would fall. As Diagram 8.9 shows, the increase in coke production from OQ_1 to OQ_2 means that coal gas output must also rise. This causes its price to fall.

4 *Joint demand*
This takes us back to cross-elasticity of demand (see Chapter 7, pp 84–5). Goods can be jointly demanded if they are complementary goods or substitutes. Diagram 8.10 shows what happens if the supply of cigarettes rises. More are consumed at a lower price. For a complementary good, like matches or cigarette lighters, demand will rise, as will the price. For a substitute, like cigars (or even

sweets or chewing-gum, perhaps), demand will fall, causing the price to come down as well.

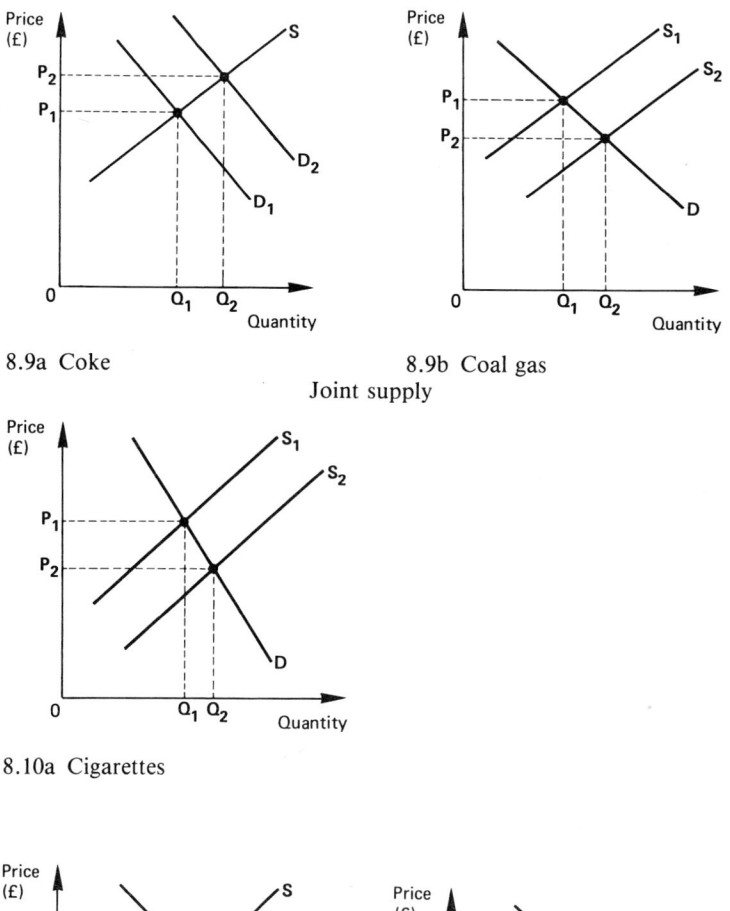

8.9a Coke   8.9b Coal gas
Joint supply

8.10a Cigarettes

8.10b Cigarette lighters (complement)   8.10c Cigars (substitute)
Joint demand

5 *Derived demand*
A producer's demand for a factor of production is derived from the public's demand for that product. An increase in the demand for cars will cause a rise in demand for car workers, assembly lines and components, for example.

6 *Composite demand*
Suppose an article has several uses. For example, sheep could be bred for wool or meat. If the demand for mutton rises, sheep will be reared for meat, not wool. This could cause a shortage of wool and a subsequent rise in the price of wool.

Summary

1 Price is determined, in a free market, by the interaction of supply and demand.
2 Price allocates resources.
3 If demand or supply changes, a new equilibrium is reached via the Cobweb theorem.
4 There are several 'special cases' but the basic theory remains valid.

9 Government intervention in the price system

Why and how governments intervene in free markets

Although the free market interaction of demand and supply allocates resources efficiently, this allocation may not be acceptable on social, moral or political grounds. In a time of famine, for example, should food supplies be sold only to the richest consumers? Thus, governments often intervene in the market and they push supply or demand schedules into another position, which naturally moves the position of equilibrium to another place, altering both price and quantity traded. The main reasons why governments do this are as follows:

1 *One side of the market may be being exploited by the other side*

It is unlikely that the elasticities of demand and supply will be identical in the market for a particular commodity. The side of the market with the *relatively inelastic* curve will get the worst of the deal and may be exploited. There is an inelastic demand for food, so if food prices rise consumers will still need to buy it; a monopolist supplier could withhold supplies, force prices up and exploit the desperate consumer. A group of producers could get together and form a cartel to restrict supplies with similar results. Alternatively, supply could be inelastic relative to demand, so that consumers could force a low price on the sellers – for example in a period of high unemployment employers could obtain labour (which is in inelastic supply) for a low wage. Such forms of disadvantage or exploitation may not be acceptable to a community, so the government intervenes to alter the price.

2 *Taxes on goods and services raise revenue*

Taxes placed on goods and services are called 'indirect taxes' because they are placed on the supplier who passes them on to the consumer by raising the price. (A 'direct tax' is paid by the person on whom it is levied, like income tax). The revenues accrue to the government. All governments use both forms of tax. In the UK, indirect taxes include Value-Added Tax (VAT), excise duties on petrol, alcohol and tobacco, and tariffs on imports.

3   *Taxes can deter consumption and re-allocate resources*

Taxes on goods can be used to alter consumers' spending patterns. 'Undesirable' products, like cigarettes, can be taxed in order to deter consumption of them. Similarly taxes can be used to discriminate between products, in the way that tariffs raise import prices and encourage consumers to buy home-produced goods, thus re-allocating resources to domestic industries.

4   *Subsidies can also re-allocate resources*

In the same way that taxes are used, government subsidies to particular firms or industries can also be used to re-direct consumers' spending. Governments in the UK have often subsidised firms like BL, or have helped firms to compete against foreign rivals. A large subsidy to British shipbuilders in the 1970s helped them to obtain a large order from Poland in the face of foreign competition.

The use of indirect taxes and subsidies to re-allocate resources or, in the case of taxes, to raise revenue, is illustrated in Diagrams 9.1 to 9.5.

Indirect taxes are levied on producers, who pass them on to consumers. Thus, the supply schedule will move to the left. In each of the cases illustrated in Diagrams 9.1 to 9.4, price rises from OP_1 to OP_2 and the quantity bought falls from OQ_1 to OQ_2. The 'true' cost of producing OQ_2 is OA (or Q_2B). Therefore, AP_2 (or BC) is that part of the price which is due to the tax. The tax revenue, therefore, is P_2CBA.

As can be seen from the diagrams, the best taxes for raising revenue are those levied on commodities for which demand and supply are inelastic (Diagram 9.4). The best taxes for reducing consumption are those with elastic demand (Diagrams 9.1 and 9.2). Thus, in the real world, attempts to reduce the consumption of goods like petrol and cigarettes, for which demand is inelastic, is difficult; these commodities (plus alcohol) do raise considerable revenue, however. Each diagram also shows how the tax burden is shared. The consumer pays the amount *above* the free market price (P_2CXP_1); the producer bears the amount below (P_1XBA). Whoever has the relatively inelastic schedule pays the larger share – ie the producer in Diagram 9.2, the consumer in diagram 9.3.

A subsidy has, of course, the opposite effect on the market to that of a tax. The supply schedule moves to the right and the consumers obtain a greater quantity at a lower price, as shown in Diagram 9.5.

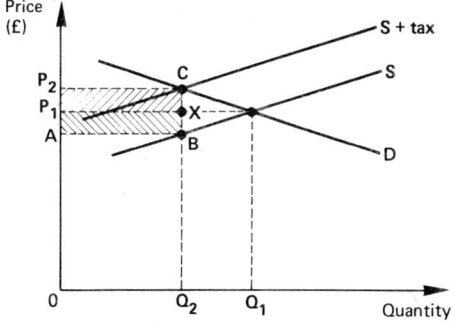

9.1 Effects of tax on a good with elastic demand and elastic supply

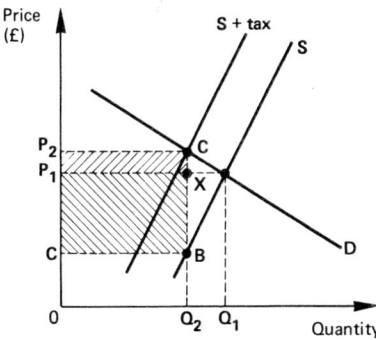

9.2 Effects of tax on a good with elastic demand and inelastic supply

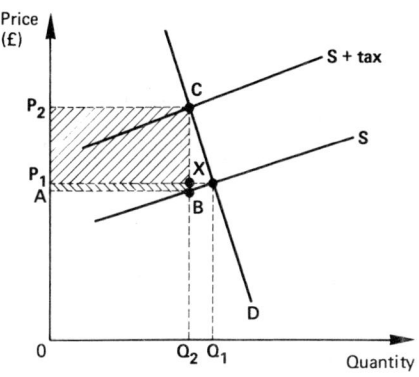

9.3 Effects of tax on a good with inelastic demand and elastic supply

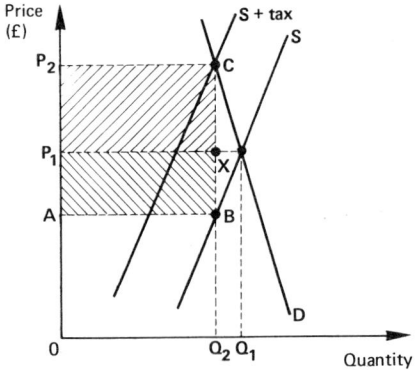

9.4 Effects of tax on a good with inelastic demand and inelastic supply

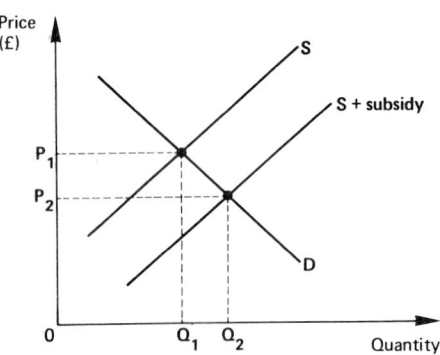

9.5 Effects of a subsidy

5 Social costs and benefits can be considered

A government can intervene to make allowances for social costs and benefits, which the price system may not include. Governments have overruled proposed motorway routes and even the proposed siting for a third London Airport, because of social cost factors. Beneficial projects, however, like clearing derelict canals or buildings, can be subsidised. The tobacco tax referred to on page 98 is another example of an attempt to deter a socially undesirable product.

6 Wild fluctuations in price can be avoided

Primary products, like food, minerals, cotton or rubber, can fluctuate in price very much if demand changes, or if there are production difficulties. Failures of harvests can cause great rises in food prices just as a glut can cause a steep fall. Thus, the EEC's Agricultural Fund buys up surplus products in years of high production and can release them in years of shortage, keeping prices fairly stable. World bodies exist to do the same for several commodities like rubber, cotton and coffee. A similar arrangement sometimes occurs to stop wild fluctuations in currency prices (ie exchange rates). Central banks co-operate to buy or sell a currency if its price seems likely to fall or rise dramatically and cause insecurity to traders.

7 *Emergency measures may be needed*

Emergency conditions, most obviously a war, may cause a government to take emergency measures, like *price-fixing* or *rationing* of vital goods, especially food. Even in less extreme circumstances governments may resort to 'prices and incomes policies' to try to control the rises in prices and incomes, stopping firms from setting their prices or trade unions from negotiating wage rises above a certain level. These are both interferences in a free market, but may be thought necessary in order to reduce inflation, improve the balance of payments or preserve jobs.

Price control takes the form of fixing maximum or minimum price limits for certain commodities.

a) *Maximum prices*

A maximum or 'ceiling' price may be fixed in order to help consumers. Examples of prices held down below the free market price include council house rents and some nationalised industries and public transport prices.

Diagram 9.6 illustrates a maximum price. The government has decreed that the price must not exceed OP_M although the free market price would be OP_F. This results in OQ_D being demanded buy only OQ_S supplied, so there is excess demand of $OQ_D - OQ_S$ (ie AB).

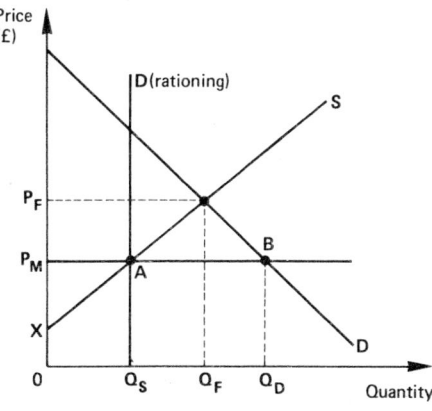

9.6 A maximum price

This excess demand could be dealt with in two ways. The government could subsidise the producers so that their supply curve becomes kinked at point A, in fact becomes XAB. Alternatively, the government could ration the good, so that only OQ_S will be sold. *Rationing* makes demand completely inelastic, as shown by the schedule D (Rat) in Diagram 9.6. Rationing will almost certainly lead to a *'black market'* in which illegal supplies will be sold 'off the ration' at a price above OP_M. Rationing does not remove excess demand, it pushes it underground on to the black market. Even without rationing, a black market will probably arise, because excess demand exists. Without rationing, excess demand will be dealt with by *queueing* and 'first come, first served'. This is commonly seen in Communist countries, where the state fixes prices and demand exceeds supply.

Queueing, rationing and the free market are all perfectly valid ways of allocating resources. The free market is the most efficient. None is necessarily the 'fairest' – but the concept of fairness is, of course, a normative judgement!

b) *Minimum prices*

A minimum or 'floor' price may be fixed to help producers. Examples of prices fixed above the free market price include the EEC's agricultural prices or a trade union negotiated minimum wage for a particular job.

Diagram 9.7 shows that a minimum price can lead to excess supply of $OQ_S - OQ_D$ (or AB). This excess supply can be dealt with by artificially making demand reach point B. The demand curve becomes YAB kinked at point A. This is precisely how the EEC agricultural system works. The Agricultural Fund buys the surplus AB at the guaranteed price of OP_M. Alternatively, suppliers can be given a quota to produce, so that production does not exceed OQ_D (illustrated by S. quota in Diagram 9.7).

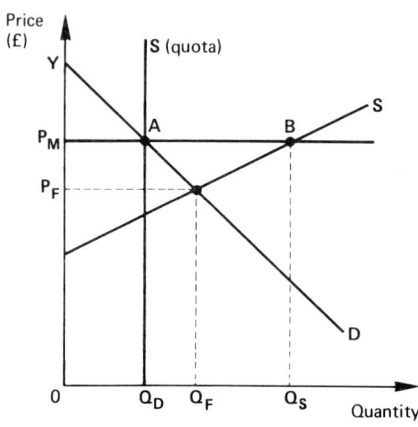

9.7 A minimum price

Quotas, like rationing, equate supply and demand at a level of sales below that of the free market. This can produce unemployment and dissatisfied consumers. Indeed, any interference with the free market distorts the allocative function of the price system and forces equilibrium to an unnatural position. Distortions prevent the free market from acting as an indicator of trends via the functioning of price. Either producers or consumers are protected – but on political or social grounds this protection may at times be thought to be essential.

8 Governments have to provide 'public goods'

There are some products which do not enter the price system at all. These include vital services like defence, police and fire services, courts and prisons, roads and street lighting. These are provided 'free' to consumers and are paid for by central or local government out of their tax or other revenue. All people derive derive some benefit from these 'public goods', even though they may not use them all very much. It would be difficult to allocate a price to the consumer. How much do I benefit from defence or the police service, for example? How could I 'buy' my portion of defence?

Some public goods *could* be provided in a free market. Education and health services are provided virtually free in the UK, but there are also private sectors in these fields. One can pay fees to go to a private school or pay for private treatment. By no means all countries include the same items in their category of public goods. In France ambulances are privately-owned; in the USA medical services are mostly privately provided. In the UK the government sector is growing and government intervention in the price system has become increasingly prevalent.

Summary

1 Governments intervene in free markets to protect consumers or producers from exploitation and to re-direct resources.
2 Certain goods are public goods and are provided free. Other methods of intervention are taxation, subsidies, rationing, quotas and price control.
3 Indirect taxes can raise revenue (best done when demand and supply are inelastic) or deter consumption (most effective when demand is elastic).
4 Price control leads to excess demand or supply. Government subsidies to producers or consumers, or rationing and quotas may be needed to settle this.
5 Black markets and queueing may result when excess demand exists.

Section four   Monopoly and competition

10   The firm in equilibrium

The nature of equilibrium

It is generally assumed in economic theory that the aim of an entrepreneur is to maximise profits. In reality, this might not always be the case. Some entrepreneurs may like just to make enough profits to satisfy their personal needs, this being especially true in small firms. Some producers may seek to maximise sales, or alternatively to produce at minimum average cost. (Chapter 1 was based on this assumption.) Nationalised industries may well have other targets to achieve, like providing a cheap and efficient public service. Nevertheless, for the purposes of this Section, we will make the simple assumption that firms seek to maximise profits.

When firms succeed in maximising profits, they are said to be in *equilibrium*. There is no incentive to move from this level of output. Equilibrium output is reached where *marginal cost = marginal revenue*.

Marginal cost is the extra cost of increasing output by one more unit (see Chapter 5, pp 59–61); marginal revenue is the extra revenue gained by producing and selling one more unit. Revenue is what the firm receives from selling its product, so *total revenue* is clearly quantity sold multiplied by the selling price. Thus, *average revenue* equals total revenue divided by quantity sold and *marginal revenue* equals total revenue of selling 'n' units minus total revenue accruing from selling 'n − 1' units.

If it is assumed that a firm sells identical products at the same price, then average revenue equals price - eg if 10 pencils are sold for 5p each, average revenue equals 50p divided by 10 - ie 5p. In the real world this assumption may not necessarily be true; firms may sell identical goods at different prices to different people. The charge for telephone calls and rail fares varies according to the time of day; domestic users pay for electricity at a different rate than industrial users; bulk buyers may get discounts from some suppliers; exports may be subsidised and be cheaper than the same good in the home market. Nevertheless, to keep the theory relatively simple at first, we will assume that average revenue equals price.

We shall also assume for the moment that firms generally face orthodox falling demand curves for their products; in order to increase sales and persuade consumers to spend more of a limited income on a particular good, its price must be reduced. Table 10.1 illustrates this, and Diagram 10.1 shows the table in graphical form. From this we see that price = average revenue and that more is sold as price is reduced. The average revenue curve, in fact, is the *demand curve* facing the firm. Notice that marginal revenue falls faster than average revenue. This is because we are assuming that price equals average revenue. One unit can be sold at 10p, but to sell two items, the price must be 9p each; the firm sells both at 9p *not* the first at 10p and the other at 9p. Thus, marginal revenue is the difference between selling two at 9p each and one at 10p – ie 8p. Marginal revenue can eventually become negative because total revenue eventually falls; maximising sales is not necessarily going to maximise revenue or, as we shall see, profits.

Table 10.1

Number sold	Price (£) (= Average Revenue)	Total revenue (£)	Marginal revenue (£)
1	10	10	10
2	9	18	8
3	8	24	6
4	7	28	4
5	6	30	2
6	5	30	0
7	4	28	−2

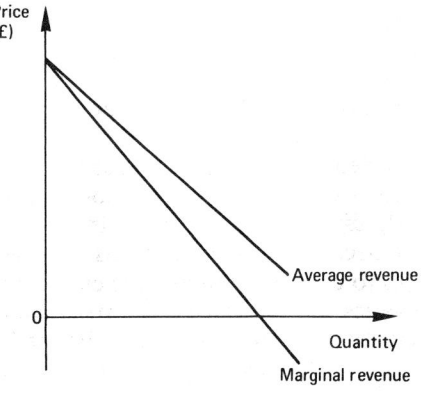

10.1 Average and marginal revenue

Diagram 10.2 shows why profits are maximised when marginal cost equals marginal revenue. Suppose a firm decided to produce OL units: the extra revenue of the last unit is LA but the extra cost is only LB, so that unit brings in an excess of revenue over cost of AB. If another unit is produced (LM), that units costs MD but brings in additional revenue of MC. Thus, CD 'profit' is earned by that unit. This surplus is, of course, *in addition* to surplus AB earned by unit L. Thus, the firm will continue to expand production until all the surpluses between the marginal revenue and marginal cost curves have accrued – ie at output OX. Here, profits are maximised. Should the firm continue to produce units beyond OX, the marginal cost of each additional unit exceeds the marginal revenue brought in by it, so a loss ensues on these units.

Thus, *all* firms aiming to maximise profits will aim to produce at a level where marginal revenue equals marginal cost. This is true, whatever type of market the firm operates in.

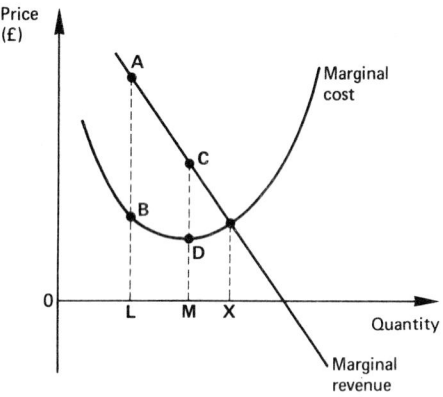

10.2 Equilibrium for a firm

Types of market

1 *Monopoly*

A firm is a monopoly if it is the only one producing a particular commodity. There are very few examples of a firm producing 100 per cent of the output of a commodity, but a firm can be regarded as a monopolist if it is by far the largest one in an industry and is not harmed or influenced by the actions of such small firms as may exist. Thus, British Rail is not influenced by the actions of the handful of privately-run railway companies; the Post Office takes little notice of private carrier services.

Most nationalised industries are monopolies (though some, such as British Airways, who face competition from foreign and privately-owned British airlines, are not) but in the private sector monopolies tend to be mainly local. In a small village or a remote area the only or doctor or garage has a monopoly inasmuch as consumers have to make expensive journeys in order to find other sources of supply. Monopoly is less likely to exist in the long-run, because potential rivals can grow and encroach into the market. The British Oxygen Company produced over 90 per cent of industrial gases in 1956: by 1980, it produced about 35 per cent; competition had grown as the market grew and foreign supplies came in as consumers looked for alternative suppliers. Consumers will always seek greater choice and in the long-run will often obtain it.

In reality, few goods or services have no substitutes. The British Gas Corporation has a monopoly over gas supplies but if I wish to install central heating I may turn to electricity or oil-fired central heating. British Rail monopolises railway transport, but has to compete against road transport and internal air services. Nevertheless, particularly in the short-run, firms can be dominant enough to be regarded as monopolies in their particular industry.

2 *Duopoly*

If two firms dominate an industry, duopoly is said to exist. For example, Unilever and Proctor and Gamble each have about 45 per cent of the detergent market. Broadcasting in the UK is split between the BBC and the IBA.

3 *Oligopoly*

Oligopoly is common in the modern world. An oligopolistic market is one where there are a few large firms, each of which has a sizeable market share. The actions of one firm will affect and cause a reaction by the other firms. No single firm dominates, but all have considerable power and are in strong competition (unless they agree with each other not to compete and instead share out the market and profits). Oligopoly is clearly seen in the UK banking system, the oil industry and vehicle manufacture.

4 *Imperfect competition*

In an imperfectly competitive market there are more firms than in oligopoly, but competition can still be fierce. Firms influence each other, but there are more competitors than in oligopoly. Demand for the products of each firm will be just that bit more elastic than for the product of an oligopolist because consumers have greater choice. Many branches of the engineering industry or types of retailing are examples of an imperfectly competitive market.

In oligopoly, there are usually entry barriers against new firms, because of the need for huge financial resources, or because the firms act together to keep out new competitors. For example, oil companies buy up garage franchises and squeeze out smaller competitors, perhaps by initiating a price-cutting war. In imperfect competition these entry barriers do not exist.

5 Perfect competition

Perfect competition is largely a theoretical concept. In a perfectly competitive market, there is a huge number of small firms. No single firm can dominate the market or influence other firms. A detailed explanation of perfect competition will be given in Chapter 12.

6 No market

Public goods, like defence and state education, are provided by the government without the consumer having to pay a price for them. Thus, there is no market for these products, in the true sense, because there is no price mechanism.

The next two chapters will deal with monopoly, oligopoly, imperfect and perfect competition. In each case the entrepreneur's aim will be assumed to be to maximise profits by producing at equilibrium.

Summary

1 An entrepreneur seeking to maximise profits will aim to produce at equilibrium, where marginal revenue equals marginal costs.

2 There are several types of market from monopoly to perfect competition, though both these two extremes are difficult to identify in pure form in the real world.

11 Monopoly, oligopoly and restrictive practices

1 Monopoly

Sources of monopoly power

A firm can rise to a position of dominance by several methods:
1. *Nationalised industry*
   A nationalised industry is usually formed by the state take-over of the private firms in an industry. Occasionally, as with the Atomic Energy Authority or the British National Oil Corporation, the state sets up a brand new organisation, but usually the industry was already in existence in the private sector. Not all nationalised industries are monopolies. British Airways has to face competition from the private sector (firms like British Caledonian and Dan Air) and from foreign airlines. Indeed, foreign competition can occur in many industries, preventing a firm from gaining a complete monopoly. In 1981, the UK government set up INMOS for making micro-processors – Britain's first such firm. INMOS will still have to compete with foreign micro-processors, however. Nationalised industries are dealt with in detail in Chapter 13.
2. *Patents*
   A patent is a document giving a firm the right to manufacture a new product or process. This gives a monopoly to the producer for the duration of the patent, which is sixteen years.
3. *Government protection*
   Protection against competition, especially from imports, may maintain or create artificial monopoly powers.
4. *Franchises*
   Local monopolies may be established by the issue of licences or franchises. For example, garages are usually tied to oil companies and public houses to breweries, so that only that company's products may be sold there.
5. *Take-overs and amalgamations*
   Firms may grow through sheer success. This may drive rivals out of business, or may cause them to be taken-over by the successful firm. Alternatively, firms may amalgamate with each other on a more equal basis to form a strong unit.
   There are several ways in which take-overs and amalgamations

may take place. Four types of *'integration'* are possible:

a) *Horizontal integration*

This is probably the commonest method and it occurs when firms come together which produce virtually the same article. Examples of this include the merger of National Provincial and Westminster Banks in 1968 or the *Times* and *Sunday Times* Newspapers in 1966.

b) *Vertical integration*

This occurs when a firm takes over a firm which supplies it with components or raw materials (backward vertical integration) or with a retail outlet or some firm involved in a process 'further down the line' of production (forward integration). Examples include the merger of British Motor Corporation and the component firm Pressed Steel (which made steel for car bodies) in 1966.

c) *Lateral integration*

This occurs when firms amalgamate which make similar products, but not ones which normally rival each other. An example is the merger of BMC and Leyland – car makers joining with commercial vehicle manufacturers. Sometimes, firms merge which produce very different products, such as Cadbury's and Schweppes (1969) or British Match Corporation and Wilkinson Sword (1973). These mergers, called *conglomerates*, bring marketing, financial, diversification and (perhaps) managerial economies, even if not technical ones.

d) *Geographical integration*

This obviously happens when a firm concentrates its activities in a certain area. This type of integration can have horizontal, vertical or lateral elements.

6 *Financial and technical barriers*

Some industries are very capital-intensive and it is just too expensive for potential rivals to start up and pose a threat. Alternatively, there are technical barriers. Even if the law permitted it (which it does not), it would be technically wasteful, indeed impossible, for a private gas company to lay a new and rival set of gas pipes under a town in order to rival the Gas Corporation's existing facilities.

Monopoly equilibrium

Like any entrepreneur, a monopolist is in equilibrium where marginal revenue equals marginal costs. The full picture is seen in Diagram 11.1. Equilibrium occurs at point Z, so profit-maximising output is OM. The price at which OM is sold is OP (because average revenue, which equals price, at output OM is MX). The average cost of an output of OM is YM (which equals OW). Therefore, excess profits are PXYW. It must be remembered that normal profits are part of the average cost curve. If price (ie average revenue) equals average cost, only normal profits are earned. If price *exceeds* average cost, then excess profits accrue to the firm. This happens in monopoly conditions. Because there is no competition, these excess profits cannot be competed away by other firms and they remain in both the short and long-run.

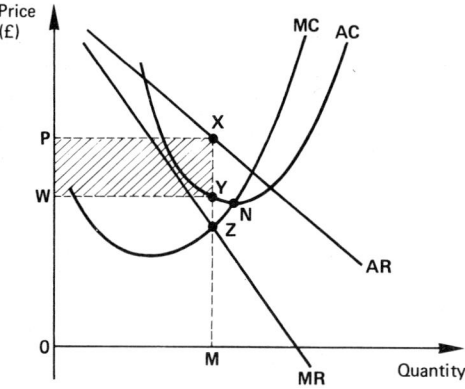

11.1 Monopoly equilibrium

It will also be noticed that the profit-maximising level of output is *not* the same as the optimum or most efficient level (point N in the diagram).

Table 11.1 shows a tabular representation of an equilibrium diagram. Marginal revenue equals marginal cost at an output and sales of 4, and at this point profits are maximised.

Table 11.1 Profit maximisation in monopoly

Quantity	Total costs (£)	Average costs (£)	Marginal costs (£)	Price (£) (= average revenue)	Total revenue (£)	Marginal revenue (£)	Profit (£)
0	100						
			150			200	
1	250	250		200	200		−50
			75			140	
2	325	162.5		170	340		+25
			50			80	
3	375	125		140	420		+45
			20			60	
4	395	96		120	480		+85
			60			20	
5	455	91		100	500		+45
			35			10	
6	480	90		85	510		+30
			10			−20	
7	490	70		70	490		0

Discriminating monopoly

At this stage we can drop for the moment the assumption that firms always charge the same price for identical goods. Monopolies often discriminate between various customers, charging different prices to different consumers for the same service. For example, rail passengers pay more to travel in the rush hour than at off-peak times; regular travellers may obtain season tickets which provides each journey at a cheaper rate. Telephone calls cost different amounts at different times of the day or week (cheaper per minute after 6.00pm or at weekends). *Discriminatory pricing* is not the same as *differential pricing*, incidentally. The Post Office provides an example of differential pricing by providing first and second class mail – different prices, but also different services.

Diagram 11.2 illustrates a discriminating monopoly. The entrepreneur's aim is to maximise profits. A transport operator is faced with different conditions of demand for peak hour and off-peak travel. The peak hour demand is, of course, the more inelastic. He or she could provide the service at one price, as Diagram 11.2c shows: produce OQ_3 at a price of OP_3 and make excess profits of P_3XYZ. Discriminatory pricing can increase profits, however. The operator's cost schedules are the same in both markets, so he or she uses a single market diagram (11.2c) to locate the equilibrium position where MR = MC. The appropriate outputs (OQ_1 in the peak hour market and OQ_2 in the off-peak market) are produced where the respective MR schedules meet the MC schedule. A price of OP_1 will be charged in the peak hour market (Diagram 11.2a) and OP_2 in the off-peak market (Diagram 11.2b). Excess profits of P_1ABC and P_2DEF will be made in the respective markets. Consumers whose demand is inelastic will pay the higher price and those with elastic demand the lower one. The lower price in the off-peak market will raise the quantity sold and revenue gained; the higher price in the peak hour market will not deter sales very much and will also increase revenue.

A firm does not have to be a monopolist to charge discriminatory prices. For example, football clubs or theatres or concert halls may offer season tickets to regular attenders. Season ticket holders obtain entry to the events at a cheaper rate than a casual attender who pays for each fixture or event. It is difficult for non-monopolists to discriminate, however, because competitors may undercut them in the market where they are charging the higher price.

Criticisms of monopoly

There are some obvious criticisms which can be levelled at monopolists. The fact that there is no direct competition puts them in a position to exploit the consumers, especially if demand is inelastic. Monopolists do not aim to raise prices indiscriminately, of course; they aim to maximise profits by producing at the equilibrium output. Yet even at equilibrium there is an element of exploitation because price exceeds both average and marginal costs, so excess profits are made. The equilibrium level of output is not the optimum level, so production is not at its most efficient level, either.

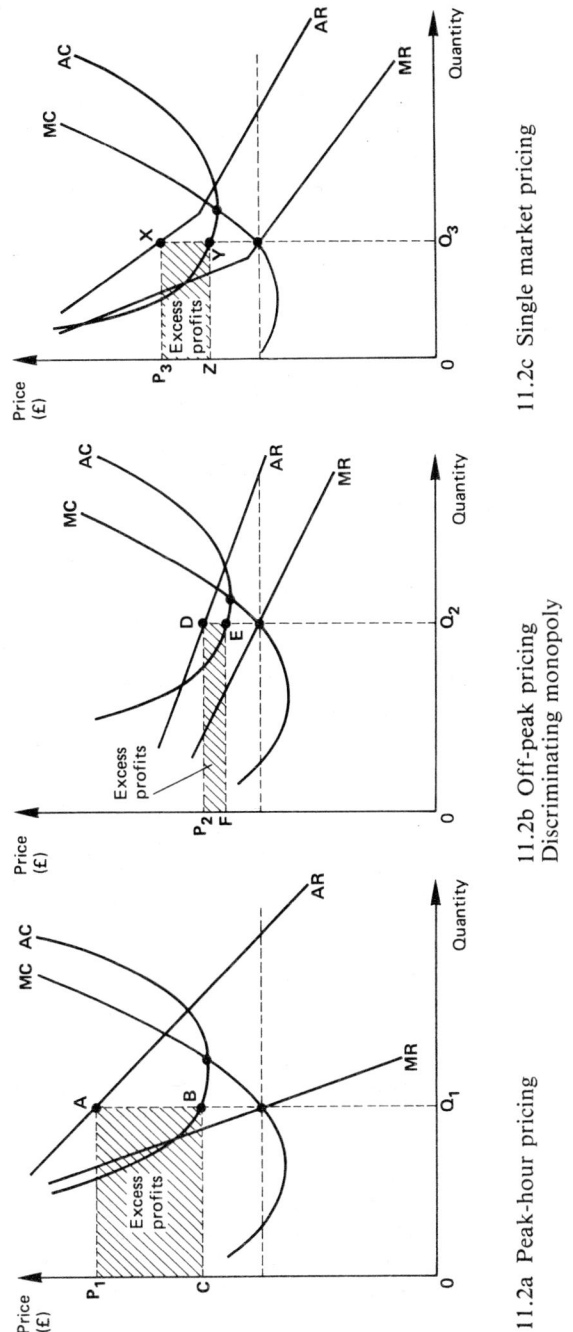

11.2a Peak-hour pricing

11.2b Off-peak pricing
Discriminating monopoly

11.2c Single market pricing

In theory, a monopolist should enjoy economies of scale, as the firm is almost certain to be a large one. Yet without competition, there is no great incentive to implement these economies. The monopolist is rather cushioned from competition and may become inefficient because of this.

Monopolists may not necessarily set out to maximise profits. If they make really large excess profits they may fear government intervention, for example, via the Monopolies Commission. They may also fear the long-run growth of competition because the high profits may attract ambitious entrepreneurs who (as in the British Oxygen case) will eventually bring the monopoly position to an end.

Nevertheless, it is clear that monopolists *could* exploit the consumers and they *might* become inefficient without the stimulus of competition. Thus, legislation exist to control monopolies in the UK.

Monopolies legislation in the UK

The *Monopolies Commission* was set up in 1948. It is an advisory body which can investigate monopolies at the government's request. It has no enforcement powers. In 1965 it became the *Monopolies and Mergers Commission*, because it was considered that existing monopolies were known about and the more important problem was the potential monopolies which might come about through mergers. As Table 11.2 shows, the 1960's and early 1970's was a period of considerable merger activity. Then 20 per cent of the net assets of UK manufacturing firms was involved in mergers. Indeed, half the manufacturing output of the UK is now in the hands of little more than 100 companies (whereas this proportion was shared by 2,000 companies in 1913); this so-called '*Concentration Ratio*' is very high by comparison with other countries.

The Monopolies and Mergers Commission has to weigh the advantages of economies of scale against the dangers of lack of competition. Although only a tiny fraction of monopolies and mergers have been referred to the Commission (eg only 3 out of 558 mergers in 1979) there are still many cases, and it is necessary to refer to the specialist literature on the subject to gain a full picture.[1] Yet several monopolies have not been found to be against the public interest. The Commission reported largely favourably in the cases of Rank Xerox (1976), which had control of over 65 per cent of the sales and leasing of photocopiers in Western Europe and held 2250 patents, and in the case of Petrol Wholesaling (1979) whereby 96 per cent of garages are tied to exclusive dealing by franchise to certain oil companies. Some firms have been criticised, however, such as Courtaulds (1968), who held 98 per cent of the market for cellulose fibre, Kelloggs (1973), who had 60 per cent of the breakfast cereal market and the particularly contentious case of Hoffman La Roche (1973) who were accused of charging exploitation prices for the drugs Librium and Valium, for which they controlled 99 per cent of the market. The Swiss firm refused to obey a UK government order to reduce prices and refund the NHS because it said that EEC law overruled British law, and the case went to the EEC court.

Table 11.2 Mergers and acquisitions of industrial and financial companies

Year	No of mergers
1963	888
1964	940
1965	1,000
1966	807
1967	763
1968	946
1969	967
1970	793
1971	884
1972	1,210
1973	1,313
1974	570
1975	388
1976	402
1977	521
1978	596
1979	558
1980	469*

* Industrial Companies only
Source: Annual Abstract of Statistics, 1982.

Several famous mergers were approved by the Commission, including BMC and Pressed Steel (1966), *Times* and *Sunday Times* (1966), Cadbury and Schweppes (1969) and the National Provincial and Westminster Banks (1968). Yet the proposed merger between Barclays and Lloyds Banks was disapproved of, as the Commission would not accept a reduction to just three banks, which would also 'squeeze' Midland Bank.

The government is under no obligation to act on the Commission's findings and several times its reports have been overruled (eg it disapproved of the proposed merger between Babcock and Wilcox and Herbert Morris in 1977, but the merger went through.)

A somewhat stronger line against mergers appeared in 1981–82 when, for the first time, the Commission recommended against proposed mergers in three successive cases, those of Lonhro and House of Fraser, European Ferries and Sealink, and separate bids for the Royal Bank of Scotland by the Standard Chartered Bank and the Hongkong and Shanghai Bank. The Commission's Report on the banking case caused the *Economist* to state that 'On the basis of this and the House of Fraser reports, nobody advising companies on British takeovers can have much idea of the criteria that might lead a client's bid to be referred to the Commission, or of the rhyme or reason likely to cause the Commission's judgements'.[2] It is still entirely a matter for the Minister as to which cases to seek the Commission's opinion on, and entirely up to the Commission to decide each case on its merits, regardless of precedent or any pre-determined guidelines.

The scope of the Commission was increased by the 1980 *Competition Act*, which empowered it to investigate nationalised industries and 'uncompetitive practices' by firms which controlled less than 25 per cent of the market. The test case on uncompetitive practices was heard in 1981 resulting in TI Raleigh being condemned for refusing to supply cut-price retailers.

It must be mentioned that governments sometimes *encourage* mergers. The Industrial Reorganisation Corporation in the 1960's and the National Enterprise Board in the 1970's were set up with government money partly to assist mergers which were in the public interest. Mergers may bring financial, marketing and diversification economies of scale (evidence of technical economies is disappointingly small) but management diseconomies are possible. Official enthusiasm for mergers and economies of scale began to wane in the mid-1970's, however, as recent cases show.

2 Oligopoly

Oligopoly is common in the modern world. Large firms compete, as in oil or banking, yet patents, financial barriers and technical economies of scale keep out potential rivals. In oligopoly, producers' actions affect each other; cut-price competition, advertising, product differentiation through brands and 'special offers' ie 'non-price competitiveness' are features of this type of market. The main feature in theory is the 'kinked' demand curve, illustrated in Diagram 11.3. At the market price the demand curve is kinked. This is because, if the firm *raises* its prices, other firms will not respond; instead, they will take away some of the firm's customers, so demand for its product becomes more elastic. But if the firm *reduces* its price, rivals will have to react in order to avoid losing customers, so by keeping their share of the market they will not allow the first price-reducer to increase sales dramatically.

Yet, does this happen in the real world? Often we see one oil producer raise its petrol prices only for others to follow days later. Instead of rubbing their hands and taking customers away from the price raiser, rivals follow, thus apparently refuting the kinked demand curve thesis.

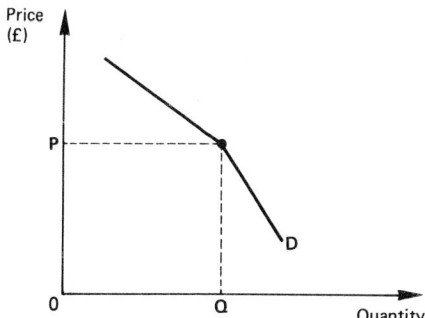

11.3 Oligopoly – 'kinked' demand curve

There are perhaps four reasons for this anomaly. One is that all the firms have similar cost schedules; materials and labour cost roughly the same to all entrepreneurs in the same industry. If one firm incurs higher costs and thus raises its price, the rivals may well soon be in the same position. Secondly, particularly in the case of oil, demand is inelastic. Raising the price will raise total revenue, because sales will not fall much, so all firms may be inclined to raise their prices whenever possible.

Thirdly, companies may be competing in many other ways than price. Advertising, trading stamps or other special offers and inducements, after-sales service or a host of other devices may be used to entice customers, who do not make their buying decisions on grounds of price alone.

Fourthly, the firms may be operating a *cartel*. A cartel is an agreement between firms to fix prices or mutually to divide the market. Thus, consumers can be forced to pay higher prices, because the element of choice has been removed now that competition has been eliminated. All the disadvantages of monopoly occur, with none of the advantages (eg economies of scale) to compensate for this.

Cartels are likely to arise whenever there are a few firms in the industry and their powers are roughly equal. It also helps if the product is homogeneous and consumers have comparatively little brand preference. Cartels can also be formed to keep out rivals or to drive out another firm. There are some famous international cartels, like the Organisation of Petroleum Exporting Countries (OPEC) and IATA, which fixes air fares. There has been evidence of IATA members trying to defeat price-cutting non-members, like Laker Airways, which was forced out of business in the transatlantic air fares war in February 1982. Laker Airways had, perhaps unwisely, started the fare-cutting war, but their relatively slender resources caused them to be the first casualty. Both OPEC and IATA have many members, so there is always a danger that someone will break ranks and cut prices to attract more customers. Cartels prosper best with relatively few members.

Cartels are illegal in the UK, but their existence is difficult to prove. After all, companies producing the same product will have roughly the same costs to cover. Rivals cannot be allowed too many advantages. If one bank alters its interest rates other will have to follow or may lose customers in an industry where there is comparatively little consumer brand loyalty. Despite difficulties of detection, there is a structure of anti-cartel legislation in the UK.

Restrictive practices legislation

Again, it is necessary to refer to specialist literature to gain a full picture of hundreds of cases[3], but here is a brief outline. The *Restrictive Practices Court* was set up in 1956 to investigate any agreement between three or more suppliers affecting the price or conditions of sale of their product. As a Court, it has the power the enforce its decisions and has the power or precedent (ie all similar cases are automatically condemned if a particular case is held to be illegal). By 1976, 3150 restrictive practices had been registered; only a few had come to court, but these few had caused 2800 to be abandoned.

Firms have to argue their case by attempting to pass through any of 8 'gateways' listed in Acts of 1956 and 1968. They can argue:
1   The agreement is necessary to protect consumers from physical injury.
2   The removal of the agreement would deny the consumers 'other specific and substantial benefits and advantages'.
3   The agreements is necessary to counteract measures taken by others in the industry to restrict competition.
4   The agreement is necessary to enable to signatories to negotiate fair terms with a monopolist or monopsonist buyer.
5   The removal of the agreement would cause persistent and serious unemployment in certain areas.
6   The removal of the agreement would adversely affect export earnings.
7   The agreement is necessary in order to maintain another agreement which is not against the public interest.
8   The agreement does not restrict competition in any relevant trade or industry and is not likely to do so.

The Court takes an overall view; cases are not decided on a number of gateways passed or refused. Few cases have been allowed to stand, but price-fixing was allowed on books (1959) because otherwise the number published would fall – best-sellers have to subsidise specialist books. Cement makers (1961) proved their agreement had kept prices down and Metal Window Frames (1962) proved competition against a monopolist.

Although most cases have been condemned, proof of an 'unofficial' cartel (ie not a written agreement) is almost impossible to produce. One reason for re-nationalising steel in 1967 was given as suspicion that it was a cartel.

In 1964 the Court took on responsibility for cases under the Resale Prices Act, which condemned *Resale Price Maintenance* (RPM) whereby producers laid down a minimum price for their products in the shops and forbade pricecutting. Supermarkets, with their desire to offer cut-price offers, were just beginning to blossom at this time. The Court condemned the 'test case' of Chocolate and Sugar Confectionery in 1967 and few other cases were heard. The only RPM allowed is with regard to books, for similar reasons to the cartel case, and drugs, on public health and safety grounds.

Despite several efforts to strengthen laws to protect the consumer, including the Fair Trading Act of 1973, which attacked misleading contracts and high-pressure selling, monopolies can still be a potential danger and restrictive practices still continue. The next chapter investigates the advantages of *competitive* markets, as opposed to those where competition is stifled.

Summary

1   Monopolies may occur through take-overs and sheer success in the market, or may be created by the government.
2   A monopolist makes excess profits in equilibrium and may be in a position to exploit the consumer.
3   The Monopolies and Mergers Commission can investigate monopolies and mergers which may be against the public interest, but most mergers are not investigated and some are actively encouraged by governments on the grounds of efficiency.
4   Oligopoly dominates in several industries, but fierce competition may be replaced by a cartel.
5   Cartels and Restrictive Practices have been attacked by governments mainly through the Restrictive Practices Court, but they are impossible to eliminate completely.

Footnote

1   See Bibliography.
2   *The Economist*, 23 January 1982.
3   See Bibliography.

12 Imperfect and perfect competition

The argument for competition

Consumers have limited incomes at their disposal and firms have to compete in order to gain as much of these limited resources for themselves as they can. In order to do this, they must satisfy consumers' desires. In theory, therefore, competition is in consumers' interests; they dominate the market. Although consumers are influenced by advertising, they can rarely be persuaded for long to buy something they do not want. Despite consumer research and advertising campaigns, many new lines do not succeed in breaking through permanently.

The most important feature of competition is *price* competition. Consumers will usually be influenced by comparative prices. Yet quality, design, after sales service, delivery dates and other non-monetary features are all used by firms in order to attract custom away from their rivals.

1 Imperfect competition

As its name implies, imperfect competition is not an ideal market; there are elements of monopoly present. Sometimes it is called 'monopolistic' competition because of this.

In imperfect competition, firms' actions do influence each other; one firm's price change can influence other firms and thus alter the market price. Yet there is always some brand preference in consumers' minds in imperfect competition; some will stay loyal to a brand regardless of what the firm in question or its rivals do. Other customers will switch from brand to brand, though. On the supply side the main difference between imperfect competition and oligopoly is that there are no entry barriers in imperfect competition. New firms can enter the industry. This is a vital factor in affecting the long-run equilibrium position.

Equilibrium in imperfect competition

In the short-run the position of equilibrium is exactly the same as in monopoly, as was illustrated in Diagram 11.1: price is greater than average costs, so excess profits are earned. Yet because there are no entry barriers new firms can enter the industry and existing firms can change their levels of output. This will cause supply to rise and, assuming demand is unchanged, price will fall. The excess profits will be competed away and long-run equilibrium will occur in the position shown in Diagram 12.1. At output OQ, price will be OP. Average revenue will equal average costs and there will be no excess profits. Price will equal average costs, normal profits will be earned, so there will be no incentive for firms to enter or leave the industry.

Although the firm is in equilibrium, resources are wasted. Average revenue and average cost can only be at a tangent when average revenue is falling. Thus, output is below the optimum level (shown at point Y) so firms have surplus capacity. In addition, price is above marginal cost. The 'true cost' of providing a good is its marginal cost which is the exact cost of producing that unit. The consumer is paying more than this 'true' cost, so is not maximising his or her welfare or benefit. Yet imperfect competition has some good points. Consumers do have choice, and entrepreneurs are not making excess profits in long-run equilibrium.

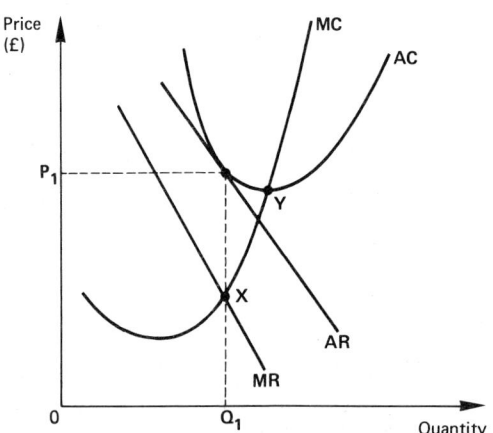

12.1 Long-run equilibrium in imperfect competition

2 Perfect competition

Perfect competition, as its name suggests, is an ideal situation. That is why it does not exist in the real world. The conditions necessary for perfect competition to exist are:

a) A large number of small firms, each of which has a tiny fraction of the total market and none of which is important enough to influence the market price or each other.

b) Firms can sell as much as they are capable of producing at the existing market price.

Thus, perfectly competitive firms are *price-takers*, not price setters, and demand for their products is *perfectly elastic* (Diagram 12.2). Thus average revenue equals marginal revenue, as all goods are sold at the same price.

c) There is no dominant consumer.
d) Consumers have no brand preference.
e) There is perfect knowledge in the market; producers know of each other's actions and consumers know the prices the producers are charging.
f) Additional factors of production can be employed at the existing levels of wages, rent and interest.
g) There are no obstructions to entry for new firms.

These conditions can never all be met in the real world, particularly perfect knowledge. The foreign currency market has some of the features (many buyers and sellers; little brand preference) as has small farming in underdeveloped countries.

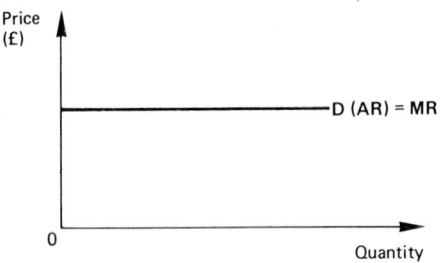

12.2 Perfectly elastic demand for perfect competitor's product

Perfect competition equilibrium

Equilibrium in perfect competition is found by an identical process to that used in other markets. The profit-maximising perfect competitor will produce an output where marginal revenue equals marginal costs. Diagram 12.3a shows that, in the short-run, excess profits can be earned (P_1XYZ).

Because of unobstructed entry and the existence of competition, these excess profits will be competed away in the long-run. Greater supply will reduce the market price, as shown in Diagram 12.3b. It must be noted that, for the *industry*, the demand curve is downward-sloping. This is because the industry is not in perfect competition with other industries in the economy. Suppose egg production took place in conditions of perfect competition. Consumers would not care which farm produced their eggs (each egg-producer would face a perfectly elastic demand curve) but if the egg industry as a whole altered its price, consumers would react and change their level of consumption. Thus, in Diagram 12.3b, the market price falls.

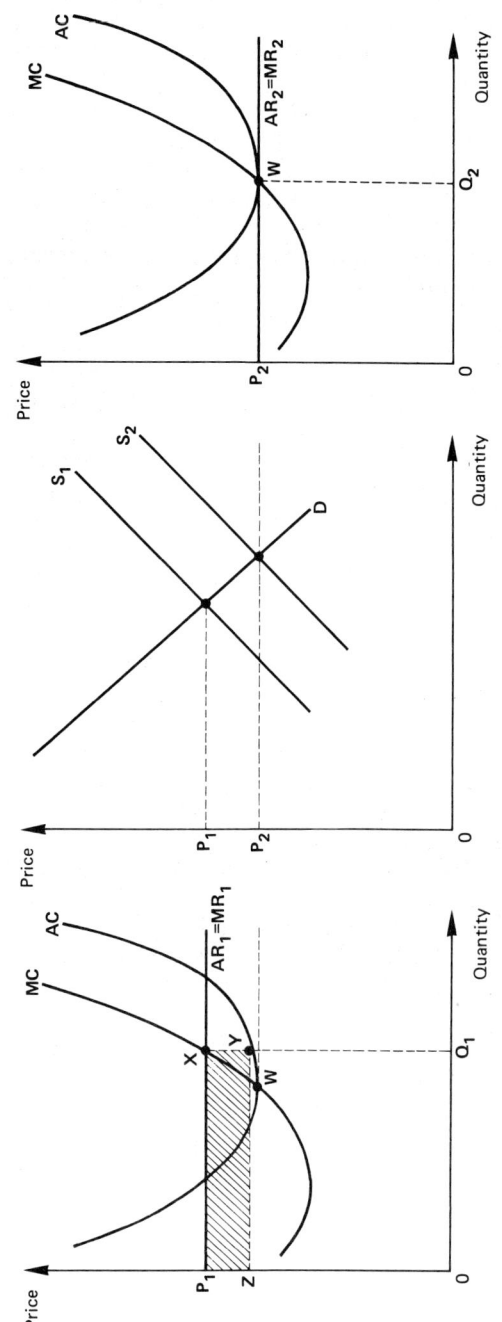

12.3a Firm in short-run equilibrium

12.3b Industry equilibrium
Perfect competition equilibrium

12.3c Firm in long-run equilibrium

Each firm is a price-taker, so its price falls. Thus, the long-run equilibrium position is shown in Diagram 12.3c. Only normal profits are earned; there is no tendency for firms to enter or leave. Firms and industry are in equilibrium.

The most important point about a perfect competitor's long-run equilibrium is that the *equilibrium and optimum points coincide*. Production is at the minimun point of average cost; *price equals both average and marginal cost*. The price is as low as it possibly can be (without firms making losses and leaving the industry). Production is at its most efficient level and the consumer's welfare is maximised. The consumer gets the best possible deal.

3 Monopoly and competition

A glance at all the long-run equilibrium diagrams will show that perfect competition is best for the consumer, whose welfare is maximised when price equals marginal cost. Also, resources are used most efficiently, because production is at the optimum level. Monopoly, conversely, is worst for the consumer, who has to contribute to excess profits. Monopolists and imperfect competitors also waste resources by not producing at the optimum. Yet a fallacy must be recognised. Perfect competitors are small; even at optimum efficiency and lowest possible price their output level is small. A monopolist or imperfect competitor will almost certainly enjoy greater economies of scale than a perfect competitor. Thus, a less-than-fully efficient monopolist, even when earning excess profits, may be more efficient than a fully-efficient perfect competitor. The output scales on the monopoly and competition diagrams are not identical. A monopolist will almost certainly produce more than even the most efficient perfect competitor, and the price may well be lower. It is a mistake to assume that perfect competitors will have lower prices and greater outputs than imperfect competitors or monopolists merely because perfect competitors product at their optimum level.

It is also true that, in the real world, no firm in any type of market is likely to be in equilibrium, anyway. In the real world demand is constantly changing and cannot exactly be forecasted. Costs are also changing, as indeed is technology. Perfect knowledge does not exist. Thus, the position of equilibrium moves. In short, the real world is a dynamic place whereas equilibrium analysis is static. Nevertheless, equilibrium theory shows what firms are trying to achieve and shows general trends of movement and behaviour. It is a useful tool of analysis in showing how firms and markets work.

Summary

1 Competition is considered to be in the interests of consumers and is mainly seen through price changes, though there are many non-price features of competition.

2 In imperfect competition, equilibrium is not at the optimum, but there are no excess profits in the long-run.

3 Perfect competition is best for the consumer and for resource allocation, because price equals marginal cost, with equilibrium coinciding with optimum price and output. There are no excess profits.

4 Though a perfect competitor in equilibrium is as efficient as he or she can be, economies of scale can make a monopolist or imperfect competitor more efficient.

13 Nationalised industries

The state sector

Monopoly is encountered to the greatest extent in the UK in the public sector. The state (ie local and central government) employs about one-third of the workforce and uses an even greater production of the country's capital equipment. The provision of public goods, like defence, emergency services and education, has been long established, but two new state ventures were established almost immediately after the Second World War – the National Health Service and the Nationalised Industries. The big era of nationalisation came in 1945–50, when for the first time ever a Labour Government with a large majority came to power. Coal, Steel[1], Gas, Electricity and Railways were nationalized then. Some other industries have been nationalised since, mostly in the 1966–70 period (the second time Labour had a workable majority) and now nationalised industries employ about 8 per cent of the workforce and account for as much as 15 per cent of the country's fixed capital investment.

A nationalised industry is a public corporation which is funded by the government and whose board of directors are appointed by the government (although they are not civil servants). Their overall aims and policies are laid-down by the government and the board is responsible to the appropriate minister for running the industry along the prescribed lines. There are many examples of chairmen and board members resigning because of differences of opinion with their minister, particularly when elections produce a change of government and thus of policy. Nationalised industries belong to the nation; the government is accountable to the people's representatives in parliament for its handling of the industries.

There may be some debate about what exactly can be defined as a nationalised industry, especially since the *National Enterprise Board* was set up in 1975. The NEB is a public corporation with state funds which it can use to benefit particular firms or industries, either to help their international competitiveness or to maintain employment. The NEB was also empowered to extend public ownership, if necessary. NEB funds have gone to over 50 firms, yet most of its money went to two important concerns, Rolls Royce and British Leyland. The Conservatives had had to take over Rolls Royce Aero Engines in 1971 to prevent its collapse; successive governments had been involved in rescuing BL. The NEB ended up owning all the voting shares of Rolls Royce and 98.9 per cent of those of BL: it also owned 79.7 per cent of the shares of Cambridge Instruments, 50 per cent of Ferranti and 100 per cent of Alfred Herbert. The government removed the NEB's responsibility for Rolls Royce in 1979 and legislation to reduce its role led to the resignation of the entire board.

Yet none of these firms is officially a nationalised industry, because they still have shareholders, though the government's majority shareholding means that they are as much under government control as a fully-fledged nationalised industry. In addition, the position of some 'official' nationalised industries was changing in 1981. The government issued shares in British Aerospace in 1980 and sold Cable and Wireless and the National Freight Corporation in 1981. In addition, 51 per cent of the British National Oil Corporation's oil-producing (but not its oil marketing) activities were to be sold to private investors. So, were British Aerospace and BNOC still to be classed as nationalised industries and yet BL not to be so classified, when the state would own more of BL than of the other two? The boundaries between what was and was not a nationalised industry were becoming blurred. This chapter will regard any firm or industry whose assets are entirely or mainly state-owned as being a nationalized concern.

Motives for nationalisation

The following arguments have been advanced at various times:

1 Political and ideological
   It is no coincidence that virtually all the nationalised industries were created by the Labour Party. Clause four of the Party's Constitution calls for nationalisation of the important sectors of the economy. This is because of socialist ideas that profits should accrue to the nation, not to shareholders, and that important industries should be run in the public interest. One reason given for re-nationalising steel in 1967 was that the firms were operating a cartel, which was against the public's interest.
2 Natural monopolies
   It would clearly be a waste of resources to have rival gas or electricity companies laying pipes and cables in the same streets to serve different houses; the industries are 'natural' monopolies. There is also need for national grids or systems of distribution to ensure supplies to all areas. Thus, industries like these have become monopolies.
3 Essential industries
   On the same lines, the natural monopolies should be placed under public ownership in order to guarantee essential supplies to the public. People who live in remote areas might not receive gas, electricity or transport if private firms were the only suppliers, or

would only receive them at astronomical prices, because of the impossibility of making such services pay. Industries can also be classed as essential on strategic grounds, such as the Atomic Energy Authority.

4 Decrepit industries which private enterprise can no longer support. Many nationalised industries have been created from industries which have been in great difficulties. Railways, coal and shipbuilding were in urgent need of huge new investment, which private enterprise could no longer provide; the industries were run-down and making losses, yet preservation was regarded as essential in the national interest. The problems of many nationalised industries have not been helped by the fact that they were in a poor financial state in the first place. Many are the old, original industries of the Industrial Revolution – virtually all of these except textiles have been nationalised. Ominously, newer industries have also come under state control more recently, because of their difficulties, eg aircraft manufacture, BL vehicles. Very few nationalised industries are originals, except the Atomic Energy Authority and BNOC. Most were created by taking-over existing struggling firms.

5 Safeguarding jobs

For social and political reasons, several industries have been nationalised or aided in order to prevent unemployment. BL and Rolls Royce are recent examples.

6 Assisting overall planning

Transport is the prime example of this. In the 1940's railways, canals and a large part of road haulage[2] were nationalised: the 1968 Transport Act set up the National Freight Corporation and the National Bus Company. Much of this was done in order to establish an overall transport policy. Similarly, the Bank of England was nationalised in 1946 because it was the vehicle through which governments implemented their monetary policies.

Needless to say, a government can exert a considerable measure of control over firms without nationalising them. Factory Acts, Companies Acts, Monopolies and Restrictive Practices Legislation are long-established controls. Prices and incomes policies, taxes and subsidies, or buying of shares (for example via the NEB) and the issuing of franchises or licences, for instance for North Sea Oil exploration or to the Independent Television Companies, are other measures which have been used over the years.

Finance of nationalised industries

1 *Pricing policy*

All price changes by nationalised industries have to be sanctioned by the government. Although nationalised industries do not have the aim of maximisation of profits, huge losses cannot be maintained for long, either. Usually, their terms of reference include instructions like 'breaking-even over a period of time'. If some of their services are loss-making, then cross-subsidization would seem to be necessary. There is a fixed charge for being connected to the telephone system, yet it may cost several thousand pounds to connect an isolated farm in the Scottish Highlands. Thus, should new subscribers in the London area pay more than the actual price of connecting them?

There are two methods of cross-subsidisation, *discriminatory pricing* and *differential pricing*. Discriminatory pricing involves charging different prices for the same product in different markets, as illustrated in Chapter 11 (Diagram 11.2). Examples of this include cheaper off-peak travel and telephone calls, season tickets and stand-by air fares. Differential pricing involves providing two types of service, for example first and second class postage, first and second class rail and air fares.

The 1967 White Paper stated that 'consumers should pay the true cost of providing the goods and services in every case where these can be sensibly identified'.[3] This was identified with a frequently-heard call for *'marginal cost pricing'*. It will be remembered from Chapter 12 that in perfect competition, price equals marginal cost in equilibrium. Perfect competition is the type of market in which consumer welfare is maximized. Nationalised industries are supposed to be run in the consumers' interest, so should equate price with marginal costs. That is the logic of the argument. Unfortunately, in practice things are not that simple. Measurement of marginal cost is not easy. For example, should the first person getting on to a train pay a huge sum and the last arrival pay nothing? After all, the cost of providing the service to the last passenger is virtually nil – the train is not going to use more fuel or labour to transport that person.

Diagram 13.1 illustrates marginal cost pricing and shows it is no panacea. In case (a) the price is still above average costs, so excess profits (P_1XYZ) are made. In case (b) the industry makes a loss (P_2XYZ); only in case (c) are normal profits made. Yet it would be a fluke if case (c) could be created to order in the real world. Marginal cost pricing is a feature of perfect competition and cannot easily be applied to monopoly. Average cost pricing would perhaps be easier to achieve; average costs are certainly easier to identify.

An additional problem for pricing policy is that 'breaking-even' actually means making a profit. This is because most of the industries have debts to the government to pay off. Some of these debts were incurred when the industry was set up; the government had to buy out the private shareholders when the industry was nationalised and the industry has to recompense the government for this. Several industries have been saddled with these charges for over 30 years. On the other hand, many loans have been written-off (as much as £5 billion grants and loan write-offs were conceded in 1980) which relieves some of the industries' burdens.

2 *Investment policy*

Most of the nationalised industries are capital-intensive, notably Telecommunications, Steel and Electricity. Their re-equipment and re-investment needs are large. Electrification of railways, purchases of new aircraft, oil exploration costs are just a few examples. Like private firms, nationalised industries are supposed to make enough profit in order to be able to plough back some resources into new equipment. From time to time nationalised industries have been given targets to reach, such as the 'Test Discount Rate' of 10 per cent in 1969, whereby investment projects had to bring in a 10 per cent return. In 1978 a 5 per cent 'required rate of return' was imposed. Social costs and benefits are sometimes included in these targets.

Since 1978, most of the industries have been given specific rates of return to achieve on investment. This has been tried in the past and often the targets have not been met any more than have various profit or turnover targets. Even though government permission is needed for investment programmes and targets are set, there are no real sanctions which can be applied. Unlike the private sector, nationalised industries cannot really go bankrupt, because the state backs them up. The industries can borrow from the National Loans Fund and often receive government grants as well.

Criticisms of nationalised industries

1 Political interference and lack of consistent policy

As the industries are the responsibility of the government they are frequently the victims of changes of government and hence changes of policy. There have been many such changes. Labour Governments have tended to favour the social and political aims of the industries; Conservative Governments have tried to make them profitable and have also been inclined to try to denationalise parts of them (eg Road Haulage, 1951; Steel, 1953; Cable and Wireless, 1981; National Freight Corporation, 1981). Various Commissions, White Papers and investigations have come up with different policy aims and recommendations without achieving consistent results. Prices have been kept down at times but allowed to rise quickly at other times.

In the early years, emphasis was placed on the social service aspect which was emphasised in the terms of reference of the industry. For example, the National Coal Board was charged with 'making supplies of coal available, of such qualities and sizes, in such quantities and at such prices, as may seem to them best calculated to further the public interest in all respects'.[4]

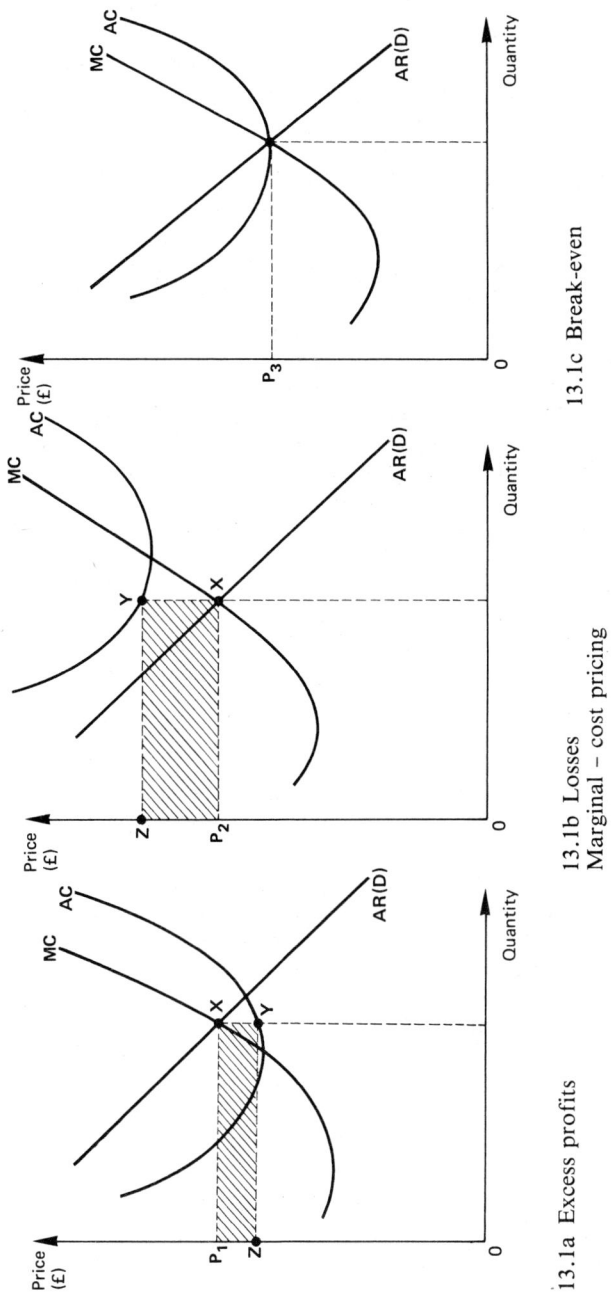

13.1a Excess profits

13.1b Losses
Marginal – cost pricing

13.1c Break-even

During the years of Conservative Government (1951-64) the policy clearly changed. The Herbert Committee of Investigation into the Electricity Industry made its views quite clear, when it said that 'the governing factor in the minds of those running the Boards should be that it is their duty to run them as economic concerns and to make them pay'.[5]

The 1961 White Paper seemed to sit on the fence. It stated that nationalised industries 'cannot be regarded only as very large commercial concerns which may be judged mainly on their commercial results: all have, although in varying degrees, wider obligations than commercial concerns in the private sector. The object of these proposals is to find for each Industry or Board a reasonable balance between these two concepts'.[6] In the 1960s, in fact, there was an effort to make the industries more commercially viable, with many railway and coal mine closures.

The 1967 White Paper proclaimed the 'arm's length' policy; the industries were not to be too closely interfered with, although they were encouraged to implement marginal cost pricing. Since 1967, government pressure and intervention has increased, however. Several more industries have been nationalised; detailed rates of return and pricing policies have been given to specific industries. Few of which have been achieved (see Appendix). Then, the Conservative Government which came to power in 1979 started to implement some denationalisation, or as it became known, 'privatisation' programmes. Lack of consistency in governmental policy towards the industries throughout nearly four decades have not helped the industries.

2 Some are heavy loss makers

Steel, shipbuilding and railways have been fairly consistent loss-makers. Electricity, gas and telecommunications have usually made profits, on the other hand. Losses have to be subsidised from the National Loans Fund or government grants. Unfortunately, the statistics produced are often misleading. There are different accounting procedures followed by various industries; trading figures often include loans or write-offs of debts, which make the results seem better than they really are. In 1977-1978 an apparent trading profit of £25.4m. for British Rail was really a £461m. loss after deducting a government subsidy; the Coal Board's £21.7m profit was really a £70.0m loss for similar reasons; the Post Office, however, showed a £367m profit which was in reality a £717m. profit. Trading profits are often turned into losses after debt interest, taxation and central charges have been paid.

Even profits are not always approved of - in 1977 the Post Office was reprimanded for making too much profit and was instructed to give a £7 rebate to all telephone subscribers. In reality, the clash between operating on commercial, profit-making lines and yet providing cheap and efficient services has never been resolved. Table 13.1 shows the pre-tax profit and loss figures for the industries for 1980-81. The result was a net loss of £150m, though the different accounting methods make this figure unreliable. The industries also contributed £800m of tax payments and dividends in 1980-81, but grants and write-offs of loans in that period totalled nearly £5 billion.

Table 13.1 Nationalised industries: profit and loss, 1980-81

Industry	Workforce	Pre-tax profit (£m)	Loss (£m)
British Gas	106,011	£710	
BNOC	1,926	£309	
British Telecommunications	246,725	£181	
Bank of England	3,600	£ 64	
British Airports Authority	7,459	£ 50	
Cable and Wireless	12,000	£ 44	
Post Office and Giro	185,195	£ 29	
Central Electricity Generating Board	59,729	£ 27	
NRDC	250	£ 12	
Docks Board	11,272	£ 11	
Crown Agents	1,964	£ 1	
British Waterways Board	3,263	£0.6	
National Freight Corporation	30,595		£ 8[1]
National Bus Company	58,399		£ 12
National Enterprise Board	65		£ 24[2]
British Shipbuilders	67,000		£ 37
National Water Council	13,919		£ 77
British Rail	178,059		£ 78
Atomic Energy Authority	13,919		£136
British Airways	53,399		£141
National Coal Board	224,841		£186
BL Ltd	120,720		£387
British Steel	120,900		£665

1 Figures for 9 months only.
2 Excluding BL and Rolls Royce.
Source: The Observer, 30 August 1981.

3 Lack of incentive to achieve targets
Many targets for profits or rates of return on investment have not been met, yet few sanctions can be applied. Private firms who make losses eventually go out of business; nationalised industries do not have this incentive or deterrent, because they are so often 'bailed-out' by the government. Yet many targets have been unrealistic and have reflected yet again the confusion of aims in this sector.

4 Overstaffing
It is clear that several industries were operating beyond their optimum level and diseconomies were setting-in. 'The consequence of government intervention through subsidy and control has been to fossilise the services of the nationalised industries at a level which is arguably no longer required by the public and to allow cost escalation on a scale which would not have been tolerated in a private industry'[7] wrote W.R. Redwood in 1976. Although some industries have shed a lot of labour over the years (the Coal Industry employed nearly three quarters of a million on the day of nationalisation in 1947), some closures have been averted and jobs preserved. Yet, in 1980 the government sector began to share in the rising unemployment. In 1980–81, the workforce in nationalised industries declined by just over 100,000, with steel closures particularly prominent. Subsequently, many other industries shed labour, including British Airways and BL Ltd. The problem of overstaffing was beginning to diminish – but redundancy payments became a financial burden.

5 Poor labour relations
In fact, the strike record in nationalised industries is not bad. Certain years and events stand out – miners' strike in 1974 and steel in 1980, but these are exceptions. In docks and shipbuilding the strike records were bad *before* nationalisation, and may have played some part in causing the industries to have to be rescued. Workers in nationalised industries (and elsewhere in the public sector) have to negotiate directly or indirectly with the government. Incomes policies are more easily enforced in the public sector, though job security there has usually been greater. For a long time wages in the public sector were relatively low, but they became relatively favourable in the late 1970's when loss-making private firms could not afford to pay their workers such big rises. Certain nationalised industry workers have found themselves in strong positions, especially gas, electricity and water workers; others are not so well-placed and redundancies have begun to occur when wages rise, just as in the private sector.

6 Lack of accountability
Public control over nationalised industries is not strong. Consumers' Councils exist, but cannot achieve much. Parliament only debates nationalised industries for 3 days a year, unless special debates are granted. Day-to-day problems (eg late trains, lost letters and parcels) are almost impossible to get to grips with, even by Members of Parliament. The NEDO investigation ('A Study of UK Nationalised Industries'), commonly called the McIntosh Report of 1976 recommended a change in the structure of the industries to reduce political interference, provide more continuity of policy and establish broader control, but these suggestions were not accepted and government control has subsequently increased, if anything.

Conclusions

Nationalised industries often make losses. Despite moves towards de-nationalisation in some areas, the bulk of the old, capital-intensive, declining, yet socially or strategically essential industries will remain in government hands. No private firm would want to buy steel, coal, or railways, for example. They are destined to remain in the public sector.

It would seem to be inappropriate to judge the success or failure of nationalised industries solely on commercial grounds; their aim is not to maximise profits. Yet, on what grounds should they be judged? Returns on investment have been suggested and tried with little success; productivity is difficult to measure in the service trades, but is used in determining coal miners' pay; external benefits and costs to the community are also difficult to measure (eg do steel furnaces pollute the environment; does an airport stimulate the economic development and prosperity of an area?). Perhaps the standard and reliability of the service provided would be an appropriate measure. Do trains arrive on time; are they clean; are power cuts common; is steel of reliable quality; does BL Ltd honour its delivery dates? Perhaps these are the sort of criteria on which judgement should be based.

There is no guarantee of consistent government policy in the future, however. Selling-off profitable parts of the industries will bring in revenue on a 'one-off' basis, but will not solve the problems of the older, declining, industries. The role of the nationalised industries seems destined to remain a bone of contention in the future.

Summary

1 Nationalised industries employ 8 per cent of the workforce and an even larger proportion of fixed investments. Many are capital-intensive industries.
2 The government's involvement in industry has increased, partly through the activities of the NEB.
3 Many industries became nationalised when they were in steep decline.
4 The government sets prices, profit and investment targets, but many targets are not reached.
5 The main problem faced by the industries is inconsistency of aim, caused by government policy changes and the overall impossibility of resolving conflicting objectives with which the industries are faced.

Footnotes

1 Steel was denationalised by the Conservatives in 1951, but renationalised by Labour in 1967.
2 Road haulage was first nationalised in 1947 but largely denationalised in 1951.
3 Nationalised Industries: A Review of Financial Objectives, Cmnd 3437, HMSO, November 1967.
4 Coal Industry Nationalisation Act, 1946, Section 1(c).
5 Report of Committee of Inquiry into the Electricity Supply Industry, Cmnd 9672, HMSO, 1956, para. 372.
6 A Review of the Financial and Economic Obligations of Nationalised Industries, Cmnd 1337, HMSO, April 1961, para. 2.
7 WR Redwood: Government and the Nationalised Industries, Lloyds Bank Review, April 1978.

Appendix Performance targets

Performance targets allocated to nationalised industries in 1979-80 included the following:

British Airways : 6 per cent return on mean net assets revalued at current cost before interest after depreciation, for 1979-80 and 1981-82.

British Gas : 6½ per cent profit on turnover after interest and depreciation, before tax, for 1979-80, and an average of 8 per cent profit (after current cost depreciation before interest and tax) on net assets valued at current cost, April 1980 to March 1983.

British Shipbuilders : Maximum trading loss (before interest, tax and extraordinary items) of £100m. in 1979-80 after crediting intervention fund assistance, and a maximum loss on identical terms of £90m. in 1980-81.

British Steel : Break-even after depreciation and historic cost interest in 1980-81.

Electricity Council : 10 per cent return on average net assets, before interest after historic cost depreciation plus 40 per cent for 1979-80, and an average of 1.8 per cent on net assets valued at current cost in 1980-81 to 1982-83.

N.B. few of these targets were achieved.

Source: Doing the Sums for Britain's Nationalised Industries: The Economist 'Business Brief', March 18th 1980.

Section five Money and banking

14 Money

Introduction

Money is a device invented by human beings to make the basic functions of production, consumption and exchange work more easily. Money itself has no intrinsic value; it cannot be eaten or worn, for example. Money only assumes value when it is used, most obviously when it is exchanged for a good or service.

Money can take any form which the community using it accepts. Two important forms of money in the modern world are notes and coins. These tokens have been used for centuries, especially coins. Notes are a more recent convenience which have been introduced because they are easier to carry than coins. In fact, *anything* a community accepts can be money. Primitive tribes have used sea shells, beads or even animals as money. In prisons and prisoner-of-war camps, cigarettes and soap have been used. The most important modern form of money, as will shortly be seen, is bank deposits – a non-tangible type of money.

The concept of value is subjective. Things only have value inasmuch as a community or person ascribes value to them. Apparently worthless articles can have 'sentimental value' to a particular person, for instance. Gold and silver have been used as forms of money for centuries, yet the main reason why they were chosen to perform this function was that they were useless for anything else. Unlike tin, iron or wood for instance, gold could not be used for any other purpose. Only because gold and silver became used as money did they assume value in the eyes of the community.

The other main reason for the use of gold and silver as money was their relative scarcity. Again, we see the concepts of scarcity and value at work in economics. Unless money is relatively scarce it has no value; tobacco is used as money in prisons because it has this quality of scarceness. In inflationary times money is relatively abundant, so its value falls. Money must be relatively scarce, yet there must be enough to serve the needs of the economy; it must not be so scarce as to be virtually unobtainable.

Perhaps now we can attempt a definition of money. A common definition is that money is: 'Anything a community accepts in payment for goods and services, or in settlement of a debt'. The form of money used should have certain properties. For example, it helps if it is portable, durable, recognisable and divisible into units representing different values. Coins are more durable than notes, but less portable; tobacco in prisons is scarce, but is not necessarily recognisable or identifiable as money at a particular moment – it might be performing another function as an article to be smoked.

Whatever the drawbacks of a particular form of money, some monetary system is essential in the modern world. The only alternative to money is *barter* – direct exchange of goods and services. Barter existed in primitive economies and may still take place today in certain transactions. For example, football clubs sometimes exchange players, small children swop toys, the Leyland firm in the 1960's once sold buses to Cuba in exchange for sugar. Yet barter usually takes place as a second-best alternative. The football club or the child do not have enough money; Cuba did not have the necessary foreign exchange. (Leyland, of course, sold the sugar and thereby obtained the more useful commodity – money.) The superiority of money over barter can be seen if the functions of money are explained.

The functions of money

1 *A medium of exchange*

This is the most obvious function. Money is used for purchasing things; in other words, it is exchanged for goods and services. This is, of course, a form of barter, but the difference is that the recipient of the money has confidence in it and is willing to accept it, whereas another good in exchange may not be acceptable. For barter to take place there must be a 'double coincidence of wants'; both sides must need what the other side is offering. Latin teachers would starve unless they can find a baker anxious to learn some irregular verbs in exchange for a loaf of bread! Most people will accept money, because they recognise it, trust it and know it will be useful to them when they want to exchange it for goods. Money, therefore, is the most *'liquid'* of assets. It can be most easily changed for other assets.

Money facilitates the functioning of modern economies. In a barter system there would be severe limits to the levels of specialisation and division of labour which could take place. With money, specialisation and mass production can take place and we can all rely on the knowledge that we can buy goods and services instead of needing to produce many of them ourselves.

2 *A measure of deferred payments*

This is the other feature in our definition of money – a measure of debt. With a barter system, if one person owes another two chickens or three pineapples, the age, condition and size of these articles is not specified and may cause disagreement. If someone owes me £5, though, we both know what £5 represents; the debt is specifically defined.

This function of money allows a sophisticated debt system to exist – banks, stock market, building societies all deal in debts. This debt market is an essential element in industrial economies, particularly in facilitating investment, savings and consumption.

3 A measure of value

Another important function of money is that it facilitates a price system. Instead of all goods and services being valued in terms of each other, they can be measured against a neutral standard, money. This function is again vital to a modern economy. Prices of goods and of factors of production (eg wages) can be established.

4 A store of wealth

Assets can be kept in several forms, like goods or property for example. Money is another form in which assets can be stored. Thus 'savings' in all its forms (shares, deposits in banks or building societies, cash) is possible. Money can be accumulated for future use.

Bank debt

So far, notes and coins have been mentioned as important monetary forms. In fact, these are *not* the major forms of money. The most important form of money today is bank deposits. In most large monetary transactions today tangible money (notes and coins) does not change hands. Instead, alterations are made in bankers' books; bank debt is transferred from one person to another.

How bank deposits are created

Banks are not philanthropic institutions – they are firms which aim to make profits. Thus, cash deposited with a bank will not just be kept in the vaults. The bank will use this money to make profits for itself by lending or investing some of it. If I deposit money in a bank, then by definition I do not want to spend this money at the moment. If the banks know that, at any particular time, say 10 per cent of deposits will be reclaimed by customers in cash form, then the other 90 per cent of deposits can be used by the bank to make profits for itself. The 'cash ratio' of cash to total liabilities need only be 10 per cent.

Assuming this to be the case and assuming that banks can either keep cash or lend, suppose I deposit £100 in a bank. The bank's assets and its liabilities rise by £1,000. But the bank may decide to lend £900 of this money, knowing that I will probably not want to draw on more than 10 per cent of it at any one time. Thus, the additions to the banking sector's assets and liabilities looks like this:

Liabilities   *Assets*
+ £1,000   Cash + £100
                Loans and investments + £900

The customers who receive this £900 will use the money for whatever purpose they borrowed it – they will invest it or spend it, for example. It will circulate for a time but will probably eventually find its way to someone who will bank it. In fact, if the money is borrowed and transferred by cheque, it never really leaves the banking system. Thus, bank assets and liabilities will rise by another £900. Yet the bank knows it can lend 90 per cent of this £900, so that the new addition to the banking sector's liabilities and assets will look like this:

Liabilities   *Assets*
+ £900   Cash + £90
                Loans and investments + £810

The £810 will be lent, may circulate and probably get back into a bank eventually. 90 per cent of it will be re-lent and so the system continues. The total amount of bank liabilities created is £1,000 + £900 + £810. . . .etc. The process only stops when (in this example) £10,000 has been created. In other words:

$$\text{Liabilities created} = \text{Original deposit} \times \frac{1}{\text{cash ratio}}$$

In our example,

$$\text{Liabilities created} = £1,000 \times \frac{1}{10\%}$$
$$= £10,000.$$

If the cash ratio had been 20 per cent, the liabilities created would have been £1,000 $\times \frac{1}{20\%}$ or £5,000. If no cash had been kept, the liabilities created would have been infinite; if all had been kept, no money would have been created. The '*money supply multiplier*' depends on the cash ratio.

There has been no official cash ratio since 1971. Banks decide their own rates and these will vary. At times of heavy spending like summer holidays or Christmas shopping banks will make slightly more cash available. Needless to say, banks can only lend money if people are willing to borrow it. The state of the economy, particularly business prospects and banks' interest rate charges, will influence people's willingness to borrow. If prospects are bad, banks may be left with 'idle balances', which create neither extra money for the economy nor income for the banks. Thus, the money supply multiplier, which was 5.8 in 1973 fell to the region between 4.8 to 5.1 between 1975 and 1980 as business prospects worsened.

Needless to say, if all customers wanted their money in cash from the banks, they could not have it; the cash simply does not exist. As long as people are willing to do most of their deals by transferring bank deposits to each other (by cheques or credit cards) instead of by cash, the system works. Any system of money works as long as the community using it has confidence in it – indeed, *confidence* is the keynote. If communities lose it, the system collapses. Thus, on 10th December 1980 the main four banks in the UK had sterling liabilities of £42,042 million and cash assets of only £1,433 million. Yet as long as confidence remains, the system works. Indeed, a money system without any notes and coin at all is possible. In the USA so many deals are done by credit card and cheque transactions that the actual amount of notes and coin in circulation is no larger than in the UK which has a much smaller population and money supply. There is, after all, no reason why money should include cash as a major component if a more convenient system is accepted.

Summary

1 Money is anything that a community accepts which performs the functions of being a medium of exchange, measure of debts, measure of value and source of wealth.
2 The taking of deposits and re-lending of them creates money according to the money supply multiplier.

15 The Bank of England and the commercial banks

Bank of England

The hub of the UK's banking sector is the Bank of England, which is the UK's 'Central Bank'. The Bank of England was set up as an ordinary bank in 1694 but because it was the only bank to be a joint-stock company (until 1826) and was also involved at times in raising money for the government, it became the strongest and most reliable bank and consequently its functions changed.

Until 1844 any bank could issue banknotes. A banknote was merely a token representing a certain amount of gold, issued for reasons of greater convenience and portability. Thus, a £5 note 'promises to pay the bearer on demand the sum of £5' – it should be presented to the Bank of England in return for £5 of 'real money', ie gold. Today, although the old words are kept on banknotes, the notes themselves are regarded as 'real money'; they cannot be changed for gold. When all banks issued notes which were only tokens the system was unreliable. A bank might collapse, or a person might refuse to accept a note of a bank he or she did not know. Most banknotes were only accepted in the locality of the bank; only the Bank of England's notes were generally acceptable as being "as good as gold". Thus, the Bank Charter Act of 1844 decreed that no new bank could issue notes. Existing note-issuing banks gradually faded away or were taken-over, until by 1921 only the Bank of England's notes survived.

Throughout its history the Bank of England has assumed specialist roles and has given up its ordinary banking business. Its role was formally recognised when it was nationalised in 1946. The Governor of the Bank is appointed by the government and is responsible to the Treasury and the Chancellor of the Exchequer.

Functions of the Bank of England

1 *Domestic*

a) *Issues notes*
  The *Issue Department* of the Bank is responsible for the issuing of banknotes in accordance with the instructions of the government. All banks must have assets to match their liabilities and until 1931

(except during the Napoleonic and First World Wars) the notes had to be backed by the country's gold reserves. Now, notes are backed only by the government's word: currency issue is *fiduciary*, or backed by faith in the government. Thus, the Issue Department holds mainly government securities as backing for its issued notes (see Table 15.1). The securities are a tangible expression of this faith.

Table 15.1 Balance sheet of Bank of England Issue Department, 10 December 1980

Liabilities	£m	Assets	£m
Notes in circulation	10,611	Government securities	8,430
Notes in banking department	14	Other securities	2,195
	10,625		10,625

Source: Annual Abstract of Statistics 1982.

b) *Acts as banker for government and the commercial banks*

The *Banking Department* of the Bank performs similar functions to those of an ordinary or 'commercial' bank – it takes deposits and invests them. The only customers of the Bank, however, are the commercial banks and the public sector of the economy. The government banks at the Bank of England. The commercial banks keep some of their cash there. Occasionally though not on the day chosen in Table 15.2, the government orders the Bank to take extra or 'special' cash deposits from the banks in order to reduce their credit-creating powers (see Chapter 17, pp 158–9). Table 15.2 shows a simplified balance sheet of the Banking Department (some small items are omitted, so the accounts do not quite balance). The deposits are mainly invested in government securities, though some money is loaned to other financial institutions.

Table 15.2 Balance sheet of Bank of England Banking Department, 10 December 1980

Liabilities	£m	Assets	£m
Public sector deposits	33	Government securities	446
Commercial banks' deposits	487	Advances and other accounts	175
Reserves and other accounts	627	Value of premises, equipment, plus other securities	526
Special deposits	0	Notes and coin	15
	1,147		1,162

Source: Ibid

c) *Manages the national debt*
   The Bank is responsible for issuing government bills and bonds. It also redeems those that have a redemption date, pays the interest and, as Tables 15.1 and 15.2 show, holds some itself. The Bank also manages the securities of nationalised industries, local authorities and some Commonwealth governments. This trading in government debt is known as *Open Market Operations* and is performed by the Issue Department.
d) *Lending of the last resort*
   Some monetary institutions in the City of London can, under certain circumstances, borrow from the Bank on the security of such government debt as they hold. They only do this as a last resort because the rate of interest they pay compares unfavourably with other sources of borrowing. Chapter 16 explains this in more detail.
e) *Carries out the government's monetary policy*
   The Bank of England is the institution through which the government carries out its monetary policy. As bank liabilities are an important component of the money supply and interest rates are a major influence on the level of liabilities created, the Bank of England's control over the system is vital to any government's monetary policy. A detailed explanation of monetary policy mechanisms appears in Chapter 17.
f) *Regulates the banking system*
   The Bank is responsible for issuing certificates of authorisation to banks and similar institutions and ensuring that they operate responsibly.

2 *International*

a) *Manages the country's gold and foreign currency reserves*
   The Bank is the custodian of the country's gold and foreign currency reserves. Since October 1979, when exchange controls were abolished, there have been no controls on the conversion of sterling, currency imports and exports, or the holding of gold by UK citizens. Thus, enforcing exchange controls is no longer a Bank function, but it still deals with currency conversions. With exchange rates floating since the early 1970's the Bank often intervenes in the international currency markets if it sees the exchange rate going higher or lower than the government wishes. A high exchange rate, which raises the price of British exports, can be counteracted by the bank's selling of sterling; a low exchange rate can cause the Bank to buy sterling in exchange for foreign currencies. These activities of the bank's '*exchange equalisation account*' had to take place when exchange rates were fixed, because sterling had to keep within certain limits. Even though there are now no fixed limits, the government and the Bank do not wish sterling's exchange rate to fluctuate too greatly and thus

create uncertainty in the minds of traders and producers, so intervention still takes place.
b) *Takes part in international currency agreements*
All countries have central banks (eg Federal Reserve Bank of the USA, Banque de France; Deutsche Bundesbank) with broadly similar functions to the Bank of England. These banks, acting usually at the command of their governments, often co-operate to prevent speculative movements against certain currencies. Support operations for troubled currencies (including sterling) have taken place several times. The Bank of England co-operates; indeed, when sterling is involved, it has to initiate these operations.

Commercial banks

Hundreds of banks have been set up over the centuries. Many have gone bankrupt through bad management or robbery; others have amalgamated or been taken over by stronger banks. Since 1968 there have been just four leading banks in the UK – Barclay's, Lloyd's, Midland and National Westminster. These 'big four' banks are often called the *clearing banks*, because they belong to the London Clearing House, which is the organisation through which inter-bank debts are settled or 'cleared' each day. For example, if a Barclay's customer writes a cheque in favour of a Lloyd's customer, Barclay's must transfer some debt to Lloyd's.

Although there were, in 1979, 352 listed banks in the UK the 'big four' dominate the domestic banking scene – a contrast to the USA, for example, where there are 14,700 independent banks.

Functions of commercial banks

1 *Take deposits*
The most basic function of a bank is to take and look after deposits. Customers can place money into sight deposits or time deposits. A sight deposit, or current account, can be drawn upon at any time, but usually does not earn interest. A time deposit, as its name suggests, involves placing the money for a period of time. It cannot be withdrawn at will, but it earns interest for the depositor. Money can be withdrawn from a bank in cash or by transferring customer's credit via a cheque or credit card. The cheque and credit card themselves are *not* money; they are merely means of transferring it.

2 *Customers' services*
The provision of cheque books, credit cards, cash cards and confidential deposit boxes are but a few of the services banks offer their customers. Advice on investments and tax matters, foreign currency conversions, payment from customer's accounts of

regular bills by standing orders or direct debiting are also available. Banks offer dozens of convenient services to their customers.

3 *Loans*

Banks make their profits by re-lending the greater part of their customers' deposits. This lending can take many forms. It can be for as little as 24 hours or for years. Borrowers can be the government, other banks and financial institutions, firms or private individuals. Loans can be for a fixed period or can be for a fixed sum; alternatively, customers may be granted overdraft facilities by which they can overdraw from their accounts up to an agreed limit.

4 *Investments*

Banks do not buy shares, but they hold government stocks (gilt-edged securities) and also sometimes take part in consortia with firms to provide money for specific projects.

Asset structure of banks

In the previous chapter it was assumed that banks either kept their deposits in cash, or else lent them. In fact, they keep a wide variety of assets. Table 15.3 shows how the commercial banks spread their assets to balance their liabilities. It is noticeable that most of their business is done in sterling. Many of the categories need explanation.

Certificates of Deposit, introduced in 1968, are certificates issued by a bank which certify that a deposit has been made with them for a certain period, on which interest is being paid. Yet these certificates are negotiable – they can be traded. The person making the deposit can sell the certificate and the person holding it collects the sum on the maturity date. Banks not only issue these certificates, they also buy them, so they appear as both liabilities and assets.

Treasury bills and other bills (items 4 and 5 in the Assets section) are *bills of exchange*. These originated from medieval and early modern times when banks as such did not exist. A producer made goods and then sold them to a merchant, who sold them to the public. But should the producer have to wait until after the final sale to the public before being paid, or should the merchant have to pay before receiving his revenue from selling the goods? The dilemma was resolved by the invention of the *promissory note*, whereby the merchant gave the producer a note promising to pay a certain sum on a fixed date in the future. This note was negotiable, though, so if the producer was in need of immediate cash he could sell it. A goldsmith or moneylender might buy it at slightly less than face value (ie at a 'discount') and then recover the full amount on the maturity date. The moneylender thus took over the risk, but made a profit if he had assessed the risk correctly. The producer was willing to take a small loss in order to get the money quickly. The merchant retained the breathing-space he needed before he had to pay.

Table 15.3 Balance sheet of the London clearing banks, 10 December 1980

Liabilities	Sterling (£m)	Other Currencies (£m equivalent)	Total (£m)
Sight and time deposits:			
UK residents	38,026	2,878	40,904
Overseas residents	2,603	8,060	10,663
Certificates of deposit	1,412	616	2,028
Capital and other liabilities			9,855
	42,042*	11,514	63,452*
(of which, sight deposits 16,816)			
Assets			
1 Notes and coin on premises	962		962
2 Notes and coin at bank of England	471		471
3 Money at call	2,161		2,161
4 Treasury bills	494		494
5 Other bills	1,073		1,073
6 GB Government stocks with less than a year to maturity	352		352
7 Special deposits	0		0
8 Loans and advances to:			
Financial institutions	6,032	4,366	10,398
UK public sector	533	387	920
UK private sector	25,310	716	26,026
Overseas	3,027	5,988	9,025
9 Certificates of deposit	692	44	736
10 Investments in:			
GB Government stocks with more than a year to maturity	1,787		1,787
Other stocks	1,686	500	2,186
11 Other bills	90	23	113
12 Other assets (eg property and equipment)			6,755
	44,670	12,024	63,459

*some totals are rounded up.
Source: Ibid

Treasury bills are bills of exchange issued by the government. The banks hold some of them. Trading companies still issue bills just as in former centuries (commercial or trade bills) and local authorities also issue bills. They are short-term liabilities, for example a treasury bill is issued by the government for 91 days.

Treasury bills are bought directly from the government by institutions called discount houses, whose functions are fully explained in the next chapter. Banks provide funds to the discount houses in the form of loans called 'money at call' (item 3 in the assets table in Table 15.3)

Examples of a certificate of deposit, commercial bill and treasury bill are seen in Figures 15.1, 15.2 and 15.3.

The table shows what a tiny proportion of assets are kept in cash form. Yet more is kept in the form of liquid assets which can easily be turned into cash (items 3 to 6 in the asset table). The most profitable business for banks is long-term loans and advances, however (item 8). About 70 per cent of assets are held in this category, mostly in the form of loans or overdraft facilities to the UK private sector. Thus, the traditional pattern of banking business (taking deposits and making loans) remains the commercial banks' primary function.

Summary

1 The Bank of England is the UK's Central Bank. It is responsible for note issue, keeping the public sector's reserves and regulating the banking system.
2 The Bank of England also performs international functions.
3 Commercial banks take deposits and create money by lending and investing.

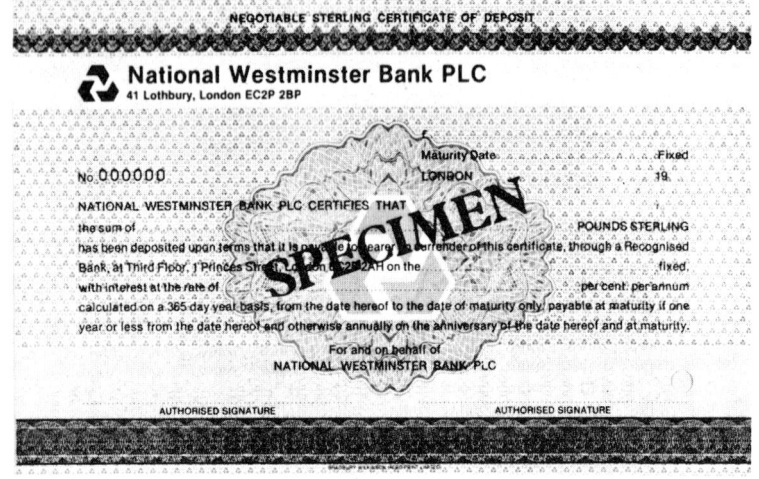

15.1 A sterling certificate of deposit

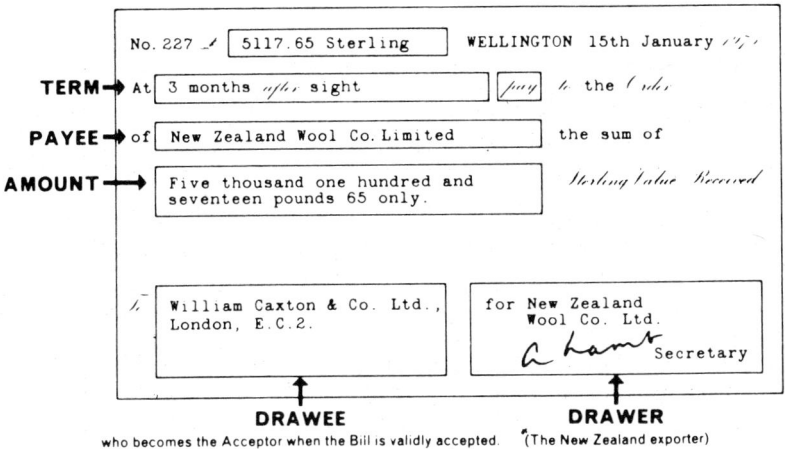

15.2 A commercial bill

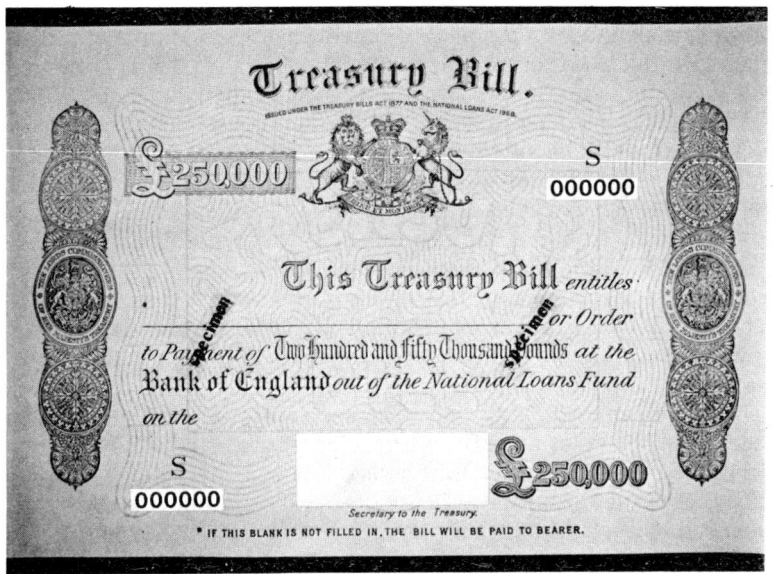

15.3 A treasury bill

16 The discount and secondary money markets

Discount houses

Discount houses are unique to Britain. There were 11 in existence in 1980. Their primary function is to discount bills – ie to buy them at less than face value. Discount houses tender (ie bid) for the treasury's weekly issue of treasury bills. The houses guarantee to cover the weekly issue of bills, however many are offered for sale. The difference between the purchase price and the face value of a bill is called the discount rate. For example, a £5,000 treasury bill bought for £4,900 represents a discount rate of 2 per cent; as these bills are 91 day bills, a 2 per cent rate is expressed as an annual rate of 8 per cent.

Discount houses also buy commercial and local government bills, short-term gilt-edged securities (including longer-term bonds with less than a year to maturity), and certificates of deposit. The funds they use are obtained by borrowing, mainly from the banking sector (money at call) at lower interest rates than the discount rate. The danger, as always with a policy of borrowing on a shorter-term than lending, is that the houses' borrowings may be called back before the bills' maturity date. In that case, they may have to sell or 'rediscount' the bills. If no customers appear, the discount houses may have to sell the bills to the Bank of England before maturity date. If the Bank rediscounts bills, it does so at its own rate called *Minimum Lending Rate* (MLR). (It is called a 'lending' rate because, technically, the houses borrow from the Bank on the security of the bills they deposit there). MLR is *above* the discount rate, so that the houses have to rediscount at a loss – eg if MLR is 10 per cent and the discount rate 8 per cent, a £5,000 bill is bought for £4,900 and rediscounted for £4,875. Thus it should be impossible to make a profit out of the Bank, though with all interest rates being rather volatile since the early 1970's, sometimes the rates have become misaligned and assets have been rediscounted at a profit, albeit temporarily.

The balance sheet of discount houses is shown in Table 16.1. They have their critics (after all, other countries do without them) but are defended on the grounds that they ensure that the government's need for short-term loans is always met and that they help trade through their purchase of commercial bills. They provide a cushion between banks and the Bank; it is the houses rather than the banks which are 'forced into the Bank' in times of financial squeeze.

Table 16.1 Balance sheet of Discount Houses, 10 December 1980

Borrowed funds	£m	Assets	£m
Sterling:		Sterling:	
UK banking sector	4,804	Treasury bills	556
Other sources	296	Other bills	2,485
		GB Government securities	956
Other currencies:		Certificates of deposit	613
UK banking sector	16	Local authority securities	377
Other sources	24	Other assets	234
		Other currencies:	
		Bills	22
		Certificates of deposit	50
		Other assets	12
	5,140		5,305

Source: Annual Abstract of Statistics 1982.

Secondary money markets

London has been one of the world's major banking and financial centres for decades. There were 244 foreign banks with branches in the UK in 1980, plus 352 other 'listed banks'. Included in the latter category are the 17 *Merchant Banks*, sometimes known as *Accepting Houses*. Their function is to 'accept' or underwrite trade and foreign bills and new issues of shares on the Stock Exchange. Underwriting means taking-over the risk. An exporter holding a bill of exchange from abroad can sell it at a discount to a merchant bank before maturity date. This is almost identical to the process experienced in medieval days from which the system originated.

Both foreign and merchant banks are, of course, largely involved in foreign currency business. With interest rates volatile in the 1970's and currencies also floating, there has been a tremendous movement of money round the world's money markets, as investors seek the best and quickest profits. The abolition of exchange control in 1979 only served to increase this trend. With interest rates generally on the high side in the UK in the 1970's, money has poured into the country at times, especially from the wealthy oil-producing countries. Huge USA deficits caused by the Vietnam War also released large quantities of dollars into the world economy. Since the 1950's, in fact, the so-called '*Eurocurrency*' markets have mushroomed. A Eurocurrency is defined as a deposit made with a bank and denominated in a currency other than the currency of the country in which the bank is situated. Thus, the money is beyond the control of the government of its country of origin. These deposits came from central banks, multinational companies, governments (especially the oil-producers) and individuals. Deposits can be from 24 hours up to 15 years and account for over 20 per cent of world currency reserves. Eurodollars are the largest single component.

The Eurocurrency market is very difficult to control. It is probable that the huge influx of foreign currencies in the early 1970's added fuel to the flames which were growing because of the British Government's policy of reducing controls on the banks in 1971. A huge amount of money was suddenly available in the City of London. Several 'secondary banks' were set up to cash in on this. They offered high interest rates, attracted custom away from the more conservatively-minded 'big four' banks, and invested heavily in the booming property market. The property market crashed, the secondary banks had too low a cash ratio, and some could not meet their liabilities.

Since the secondary banking crash of the mid-1970's the Treasury has increased its control over this sector. The 1979 *Banking Act* separated the traditional commercial banks, dominated by the big four, from other institutions, to be called 'licensed deposit-takers', which could not use the title of 'bank'. All institutions taking deposits need Bank authorisation and must join a deposit protection scheme to insure depositors against losses if members collapse.

The liabilities of the secondary banking sector totalled over £200 billion in 1979 – but only £34 billion was in sterling. Similarly, their loans were mainly overseas (£114 billion in 1979). Thus, they not only dwarf the traditional banks' foreign currency deposits but also begin to challenge their sterling liabilities position. Most of their deposits are time deposits.

Several other markets arose in the 1970's. The local authorities have increasingly issued bills and securities in order to help to finance their activities. Also, the inter-bank market has grown. The many different interest rates and the mass of money available has encouraged banks to lend to each other and buy each others' certificates of deposit.

Other markets

There are, of course, many other institutions which take deposits and re-lend them. *Building societies* take deposits and lend them to people wishing to buy property. These advances are called mortgages. Insurance companies, finance houses (which provide hire-purchase facilities), savings banks, pension funds and both investment and unit trusts all receive immense deposits. Some of these funds are lent to borrowers, others are directly invested in stocks and shares. Table 16.2 shows the liabilities of these institutions. Far more money (in sterling) is deposited with non-bank institutions than with banks. Nevertheless, as the next chapter describes, the government has more control over the banking sector than these other institutions.

Table 16.2 Liabilities of financial institutions at the end of 1978

	£m
Major deposit-taking banks	36,113
Discount houses	4,111
Accepting houses	6,796
Other banks – UK residents in £	20,116
– non-residents (in other currencies)	103,513
National savings bank	3,002
Trustee savings bank	5,340
Finance houses	2,617
Building societies	39,723
Investment and unit trusts	11,374
Insurance companies	46,829
Pension funds	28,939

Source: Rethinking Monetary Policy: M Lewis. Lloyds Bank Review July 1980 p 42.

Summary

1 Discount houses exist to provide short-term finance by discounting bills.
2 The City of London's institutions are involved in acceptance business and Eurocurrency dealing as well as normal banking business.
3 Huge sums of money are deposited with institutions other than banks.

17 The mechanisms of monetary policy

The money supply

The main aim of monetary policy is to control the money supply. In addition, a government may wish to control interest rate changes, although this has become more a means of affecting the rate of growth of money rather than an end itself. Governments are concerned with the total supply of money, the forms it takes and the directions in which it is flowing.

Controlling the aggregate supply and the various components of it is a very complex task. The first problem encountered is in defining just what constitutes money. The simple assertion that money consists of notes, coin and bank liabilities is now no longer accepted as a definition. There are three official measurements used in the U.K. today. They are:

M_1: Notes and coin in circulation plus the private sector's sight deposits in sterling with banks.

Sterling M_3: M_1 plus the private sector's time deposits in sterling plus the public sector's deposits.

M_3: Sterling M_3 plus the UK residents's non-sterling deposits.

The most commonly used definition is Sterling M_3: that is the one quoted by the authorities when measuring the money supply. Government targets for monetary growth are expressed in terms of Sterling M_3. Table 17.1 shows how great the difference is between the three definitions. Sterling M_3 is approximately twice the size of M_1. Thus, governments have often been able to control M_1 more easily than Sterling M_3, which has additional components, but sometimes have had more success with Sterling M_3 than with M_1. There are arguments that even Sterling M_3 or M_3 are not adequate explanations of what constitutes money. In 1981 the government declared that an additional definition of money would be used, called 'PSL$_2$', which stands for private sector liquidity 2 (and please do not ask what happened to PSL$_1$!).

PSL$_2$ consists of:
The private sector components of Sterling M_3
plus some other money market instruments, including commercial bills and deposits with local authorities

plus savings deposits and securities, including those with building societies.

The inclusion of the vast building society deposits makes PSL_2 nearly twice as big as Sterling M_3. There is logic in including these deposits because they can be drawn upon by depositors almost as easily as can bank deposits.

Every country has a different definition of the money supply. Unless money can be accurately defined, there would seem to be problems involved in trying to control it.

Table 17.1 The money supply, 1980 (£m)

Notes and coin in circulation	10,425
UK private sector sterling sight deposits	20,805
M_1	31,230
UK private sector sterling time deposits	36,766
UK public sector sterling deposits	1,595
Sterling M_3	69,591
UK residents' deposits in other currencies	6,383
M_3	75,974

Source: Annual Abstract of Statistics 1982.

Aims of monetary policy

Monetary policy can be used to increase, restrict or re-direct the growth rate of the money supply. Usually, in recent years, restrictionary monetary policies have prevailed. The aims of monetary policy include the following:

1 *Controlling the general level of prices*

If prices in general are rising the government may wish to restrict the rate of growth of the money supply. Rising prices *could* be caused by 'too much money chasing too few goods' (ie supply cannot keep pace with demand) especially if there is full employment when output cannot easily be increased in the short-run. According to the views of '*monetarists*', inflation is caused by too high a money supply. The theory is based on the equations:

$$MV = PT \text{ or } MV = PQ$$

where M = the money supply
V = the velocity of money's circulation
P = the general level of prices
T = the number of transactions
Q = the quantity of goods and services produced
(All the above apply to a given period of time.)

Thus, if the money supply rises, spending power increases and the velocity of circulation will go up as more goods are bought. The number of transactions will rise, though if there is full employment, output cannot rise. Thus, prices will rise; there is a relationship between 'M' and 'P'.

Past evidence supports the validity of the theory. Gold and silver discoveries in the sixteenth and nineteenth centuries increased the minting of coins and the money supply – and prices rose. Similarly, spectacular currency collapses, like that of Germany in 1923, when banknotes with face values of billions of Deutsch marks were printed and prices rose to stupendous levels, lent credence to the theory. Not all economists agree (eg the huge printing of money in Germany may have been a *reaction* to rising prices, not a *cause*). In addition, there are many other theories about inflation. It may be caused by rising production costs (eg wages), for example. A full discussion both about inflation and its possible causes and about the value of monetary policy will appear in Chapter 29. Whatever the rights and wrongs of the case, monetary policy will continue to be used as a way of controlling spending power. Governments will attempt to control the supply of notes and coin and of bank lending.

2 *Assisting the balance of payments*

If producers cannot meet demand there is a probability that consumers will turn to imports instead. Indeed, if consumers think that foreign goods are better anyway, imports can rise regardless of the level of domestic output. Governments may wish to prevent this balance of payments problem, so restricting general spending power may be used as a way of restricting spending on imports. This policy may also release more goods for export. There are, of course, other ways of dealing with the problem (see Chapter 20) but monetary policy may be used.

3 *Alleviating unemployment*

If unemployment is high, governments may wish to *create* spending power in order, by the principle of derived demand (see Chapter 8, p 96) to increase the demand for labour. Thus, an expansionary monetary policy may be used.

4 *Directing funds into certain forms*

Governments may decide to encourage certain forms of deposits and lending at the expense of others. For example, it may want exporters to borrow, but not importers; or it may desire people to deposit money in building societies instead of banks.

5 Controlling the cost of managing the national debt

Sometimes the government is more concerned with controlling the level of interest rates rather than the money supply itself. This may be because borrowing for investment or exporting is being handicapped by high rates or because the government itself is having to pay a great deal to service the national debt.

Each year governments (indeed, the whole public sector) spend more than they collect from tax revenue and other sources. Thus, there is a *Public Sector Borrowing Requirement* (PSBR). This borrowing is mainly financed by the selling of gilt-edged securities by the Bank. In 1980/81, for instance, when the PSBR was £13,192 million, the gilt issue was £13,083 million, over two-thirds of which went to the non-bank private sector. If interest rates rise, the interest paid by the government to holders of gilts must rise. So must payments to holders of National Savings Certificates. As inflation caused interest rates to rise during the 1970's three new types of gilt-edged stock were invented in order to help the government compete for funds. These were Convertible Stocks (bought for short periods with the option of converting to a longer investment later) in 1973 and Partly-Paid Stocks (where buyers could buy over a period) in 1977. Most significantly, in 1977, stock with floating rates was issued. If inflation accelerated, the interest paid would rise. Similar guarantees were written into some new National Savings issues. Thus, governments could be involved in expensive interest payments if rates rise.

Mechanisms of monetary policy

In this section, we will assume that the main aim of monetary policy is to reduce the rate of growth of money and possibly also to re-direct it. An expansionary policy would broadly be followed by reversing the policies explained below. Whether M_1 or Sterling M_3 is involved, the main category of money is advances to the private sector in the forms of loans and overdrafts. The main aim of a restrictionary policy is to control these advances. Sometimes, however, rather roundabout methods have to be used.

1 *Moral suasion*

The Bank of England's position in the monetary system as the government's agent in the application of monetary policy means that its requests to banks have the force of commands. The Bank can actually issue *directives*, but has not so far had to do so. Requests, or moral suasion, have usually taken the form of telling banks about to whom to lend. Twelve such requests were made in the 1970's, starting in 1972 with an instruction to "make credit less readily available to property companies and for transactions not associated with the maintenance and expansion of industry".[1] In 1973 banks were instructed not to pay depositors a rate above 9½ per cent on deposits of £10,000 or less. This was an attempt to direct depositors to building societies, who were threatening to raise the mortgage rate because of shortage of funds.

2 *Raising interest rates, usually by raising MLR*

If MLR is raised, discount houses will raise the discount rate to minimise losses incurred if they are forced to rediscount at the Bank. The commercial banks will raise their rates on money at call. Many markets rates used to be automatically linked to MLR by formulae. Although this no longer applies, a change in MLR is known by the banks and other institutions to be a signal for them to act similarly with regard to the rates they both pay and charge. Thus, depositors will be encouraged and borrowers discouraged.

3 *Open market operations*

Open market operations are the Bank's selling of gilts to the non-bank private sector. The buyers pay for the gilts by drawing money from their bank accounts. Thus, the cash reserves of the banks fall, so the money supply falls. Also, as banks' liquid assets have fallen, they cannot lend so much money. Indeed, they may have to reduce their lending in order to replenish their liquid assets. The money supply multiplier will work in reverse when cash is withdrawn from rather than deposited in a bank.

If gilts are bought by the banks, then the money supply does *not* fall – one asset (cash) has been replaced by another one (gilts) in the banks' list of assets. Thus, if a government wishes to use open market operations to reduce the money supply, it will try to find customers for gilts *outside* the banking sector. Yet to succeed in this, high interest rates may have to be paid, thus increasing the government's own debt burden.

4 *Funding*

Funding can be used to help enforce open-market operations. When banks' cash reserves are squeezed, they can obtain cash by selling treasury bills. To stop this the Bank goes in for funding, which is replacing maturing bills by issuing gilts, thus lengthening the period in which the holders' cash is tied up in the Bank.

5 *Special deposits*

This device was introduced in 1960. Whenever bank lending is thought to be too high, the banks may be asked to deposit *extra* amounts of cash with the Bank. These 'special' deposits, although they earn interest, are 'frozen' – the banks cannot use them, so cash is effectively taken out of the system. Varying amounts of special deposits were called-in during the 1960's and 1970's.

All these weapons have traditionally been used against the commercial banks. The aim is to attack their cash reserves by taking some of them away (special deposits) or pushing them into other forms like gilts or money at call. If banks' cash reserves are squeezed they cannot lend so much and indeed they may have to cut back on lending in order to replace depleted cash. By these roundabout routes, the authorities hope to restrict bank lending.

The Bank can wield some weapons against other institutions, however, including these:

6 Selective credit controls

Instructions like those mentioned above about directing cash towards building societies have been used. The Treasury can also single-out Finance Houses for attention. Customers purchasing items via hire-purchase may be required to make larger down-payments and pay off the residue of their debt over a shorter period at higher interest rates.

7 Foreign exchange regulations

Controls over the convertibility of sterling and the export of currencies can particularly affect the foreign banks and can affect the size of Sterling M_3. Altering sterling's exchange rate also affects the flow and composition of funds into and out of the country. The abolition of exchange controls in 1979 has reduced the government's powers in these fields, however, and made the sector even more volatile.

The problems of monetary policy in the 1970's

All the weapons of monetary policy produce problems, and these became particularly acute in the 1970's, when governments tried to control the money supply more precisely than before. The first announced target was in 1967, when the Chancellor had to agree to an agreed limit of monetary growth as part of the terms of a loan from the International Monetary Fund. The government also agreed in 1969 to limit *Domestic Credit Expansion* (DCE) to £400 million in the next year. DCE is most simply described as:

      The PSBR
minus   the net acquisition of public sector debt by the UK non-bank sector
plus   the increase in bank lending in sterling to the UK private sector and overseas.

This really means the government spending in excess of its revenue *minus* the money collected in by selling gilts *plus* the increase in bank lending.

Although DCE is still a concept in use, the measure used more commonly is Sterling M_3. Governments have published targets for Sterling M_3 annually since 1976.

Policy in the 1970's was based on *competition and credit control* (CCC), introduced in 1971. The aims of CCC were, as its name suggests, to increase competition and to control credit creation more efficiently. Banks were accused of acting rather like a cartel and the government wished to see more competition, including competition from other institutions. Yet it also desired to control institutions outside the commercial banks more closely.

The main feature of CCC was that banks had to keep 12½ per cent of their *eligible liabilities* (deposits which were for less than two years) in the form of *eligible assets*. These eligible assets included cash at the Bank of England (not special deposits), bills, money at call and government stocks within a year of their maturity date. Banks were free to decide how much cash to keep apart from their deposits at the Bank of England. CCC also established an eligible assets ratio of 10 per cent for finance houses and instructed discount houses to keep a certain proportion of their funds in specified public sector assets.

The government hoped to reduce its interest rate activities and MLR was allowed to 'float' according to market pressures between October 1972 and May 1978. An important weapon was special deposits and these were strengthened between 1973 and June 1980 by *supplementary deposits* (the 'corset') whereby banks had to make extra Special Deposits if their eligible assets rose too quickly.

CCC was far from an unqualified success and many of its features had been supplanted by 1981. The problems encountered during the life of CCC included the following:

1 *Banks evaded the controls*

Although banks could not defy the Bank, they found ways of dragging their feet or circumventing the controls. For instance, when special deposits were called in or their reserve assets were hit, they replenished these categories by selling treasury bills, buying commercial bills (the issue of which rose by 43 per cent between July and December 1979, for instance) or dealing in the growing inter-bank market for certificates of deposit.

2 *Borrowers could by-pass the banks*

CCC did not succeed in controlling adequately all the institutions. Even if the commercial banks were squeezed, borrowers found other sources of funds, including overseas sources. This so-called *disintermediation* (avoiding the banks, the normal intermediaries) led to the money supply continuing to rise.

3 *There was a banking crisis in the early 1970's*

The idea of letting MLR float led to some anomalies (at times it became out of line with other rates and institutions found that they could rediscount bills to the Bank at a profit, for instance) and governments had to step in and alter it in the old fashion. Also, money tended to circulate around the City's institutions for speculative reasons as interest rates fluctuated, instead of financing industry. Even as late as February 1981 only 26 per cent of bank lending went to manufacturing firms (see Table 17.2) and much of this was 'distress borrowing' by declining firms who were borrowing to pay wages or redundancies or repay past loans instead of borrowing to invest. The so-called *'round tripping'* of money within the financial sector also helped institutions evade controls as they swapped one form of asset for another to avoid technical restrictions on certain categories.

Table 17.2 Clearing bank advances to UK residents, February 1981

Services	30%
Manufacturing	26%
Personal	19%
Agriculture, mining, construction	12%
Financial institutions	12%

Source: *Annual Monetary Survey* 1980, *Midland Bank Review*, Summer 1981, p 15.

The worst problem came with the *secondary banking crash*, which reached a climax in 1973-75. Encouraged by the new impetus for competition, new 'secondary' banks offered high rates for deposits, hoping to cash in on the property boom by lending to and investing in that sector. The property price collapse found certain institutions with inadequate cash reserves and sometimes inadequate assets to meet their liabilities. Several banks crashed and the Bank had to mount rescue operations. Perhaps the most extreme example was Cedar Holdings, 96 per cent of whose deposits were for less than one year, yet whose assets were tied-up for long periods. Thus, the 1979 *Banking Act* tightened the regulations for bank and deposit-taking institutions to observe. The widening of institutional activities has continued to increase, however. For example, banks increasingly lend for house purchase, thus competing with building societies.

4 *Money supply targets were not achieved*

CCC released funds for lending. Before 1971 banks had had to keep 28 per cent of their funds in short-term assets: now they had only to keep 12½ per cent plus cash reserves. The Conservative Government envisaged a consumer-led boom. The credit card revolution also hit the UK (though the traditionally-minded British still do 94 per cent of their deals in cash). Sterling M_3 rose 27.2 per cent in 1973 alone. The secondary banking crash resulted and inflation soared. Even opponents of Monetarism saw a relationship between the astonishing rises in money supply and the rate of inflation. Attempts to control the situation from 1976 onwards met with mixed success, as Table 17.3 shows. Indeed, the introduction of the 'rolling' (ie regularly revised) targets from 1978 onwards shows the problems of control. The high growth figure for February 1980 to April 1981 is partly explained by 'Re-intermediation' when several controls were relaxed, including the abolition of the 'corset' in June 1980. This, in itself, shows how large Disintermediation had been and thus how controls had been evaded.

Table 17.3 Monetary growth targets

	Target limits for M_3 growth (%)	Actual growth (%)
1976/77	9–13	7.7
1977/78	9–13	16.0
1978/79	8–12	10.9
October 1978–October 1979	8–12	13.3
June 1979–April 1980	7–11	10.0
February 1980–April 1981	7–11	18.5

Source: *Monetary Control in Britain, 1971–1981*, Bank Information Service, 1981, p 2.

5 High interest rates attracted 'hot money'

High interest rates aimed to restrict the growth rate of money. Yet they attracted 'hot' money from foreign speculators. Although not part of Sterling M_3 these funds might still be a base for monetary creation. Also, they could flow out (hence the word 'hot') as soon as rates elsewhere became more attractive. Twice, OPEC's huge funds entered and left the UK in the late 1970's – a very unstable situation.

6 High interest rates restrict investment and growth

High interest rates may succeed in restricting borrowing for consumption, but they will also discourage borrowing for investment. Thus, long-run growth and technological improvements do not occur and the country's competitiveness falls.

Thus, monetary policy encounters a fundamental dilemma. If it does not work, the evils it is trying to prevent may continue. If it does work, it also deters consumption and investment, thus creating unemployment and stagnation. It may also clash with other government policies. For example, an influx or outflow of hot money will affect sterling's exchange rate; distress borrowing may come as a result of a high tax burden on companies, and it, like any form of borrowing, raises Sterling M_3. To be fair, of course, other policies aiming to solve the country's problems, may also create as many problems as they solve (see chapter 29). Despite the fact that "successive Chancellors may have publicly extolled the diagnostic value of this or that monetary variable . . . The different monetary variables which came into favour from time to time did not imply the use of different instruments of policy,"[2] Yet another rethinking about monetary policy took place in 1979–80 and resulted in new measures being introduced in August 1981.

Because Sterling M_3 was proving more difficult to control than M_1 and because it is a rather disputed definition of money, there has been a search for something to replace it. *Monetary Base Control* (MBC) has been discussed. Advocates of MBC suggest that the government can only really control cash; all creation of money is based on original cash deposits; if these can be controlled, the base on which money is created is controlled, so lending can be restricted. Particular attention would be focussed on the cash the banks are required to deposit with the Bank. Whereas interest rates aim to affect the *demand* for funds, MBC hopes to act directly on the *supply*. The first tentative steps towards MBC were taken in 1981.

The August 1981 measures

1   The 12½ per cent 'reserve assets ratio' and its categories no longer apply. (The ratio had been reduced to 10 per cent in January 1981 as a first step).

2   All recognised banks and deposit-taking institutions which have eligible liabilities (maturity date less than 2 years) of £10 million must hold 0.5 per cent of these liabilities in non-interest-bearing cash deposits at the Bank.

3   Certain minimum levels of money at call must be held.

4   The Bank will discount bills accepted by a wide variety of banks (96 in November 1981).

5   Special deposits will be required from *all* these institutions, when necessary. The 'corset' was abolished in June 1980, however.

6   MLR will be allowed to fluctuate according to market pressures, but the Bank has a secret indictor formula for judge MLR's 'correct' level and may intervene if necessary.

These measures are similar to the aims of CCC – a desire to allow market forces to operate, yet also to control a wide range of institutions. As CCC did not work too well, the 1981 system may well encounter similar problems. Nevertheless, monetary policy will continue. Money supply growth rate targets will continue to be set. For the year 1981–82, the targets for M_1, Sterling M_3 and PSL_2 were all to be in the range of 8–12 per cent. The differences between the definitions make it likely that the actual growth rates will differ. For example, in the year ending in January 1982, PSL_2 rose by 12½ per cent, M_1 rose by 10 per cent and Sterling M_3 rose by 15¾ per cent, partly because the rise in banks' participation in the mortgage business took customers away from building societies, thus swelling Sterling M_3 more than PSL_2. Nevertheless, governments will continue to try to exercise some control over both interest rates and that most elusive concept, the money supply.

Summary

1 Monetary policy aims to control the aggregate money supply, its components, and the direction of its flow.
2 Increases in the money supply are widely, though not inversally, regarded as being a cause of inflation.
3 The mechanisms of monetary policy aim primarily to reduce banks' cash reserves in order to restrict the base of their lending.
4 Competition and credit control in the 1970's encountered many problems and monetary control was frequently evaded. The system was revised and changed in 1981 with a possible move towards monetary base control.
5 The money supply is very difficult to define. The official definition in the UK is £M_3, which consists mainly of sight and time deposits of the private and public sectors.
6 There are several reasons why a government tries to control the money supply, including the desire to control price levels, the balance of payments, unemployment, and the size of the national debt.
7 Monetary policy mechanisms include moral suasion, interest rate manipulation, open market operations, funding, special deposits and selective credit controls.
8 In the 1970's, monetary policy encountered many problems and the policy of competition and credit control was tacitly abandoned in 1980. The government found that effective control of the money supply was very difficult to achieve and an accurate definition of the money supply was also a question of dispute.

Footnotes

1 Bank of England Quarterly Bulletin: 'Bank lending,' September 1972, p 329.
2 'The Implementation of Monetary Policy in Post-War Britain', *Midland Bank Review*, Spring 1981, p 7.

Section six Index numbers

18 Index numbers

Measuring trends in economics

Planners and policy-makers need to be able to detect and measure trends in the economy. Thus, statistics need to be collected concerning what has happened and is happening in the economic sphere. Yet, to take the UK as an example, there are 56 million consumers, about 26 million workers, hundreds of thousands of firms and millions of transactions. Clearly it is rarely possible to collect *all* the information needed in the real world. Not every person can be quizzed as to spending patterns or earnings, for example. Indeed, the population is only fully counted and surveyed once in every ten years through the census. Yet a stream of information is required by governments and planners concerning output, prices, trade, population and so on. Thus *sampling* needs to be used. A sample of the population needs to be questioned and the results used as a basis for analysing the whole population's position. The most famous example of sampling probably comes in the sphere of politics, namely public opinion polls, whereby a sample of the population is asked abouts its voting preferences. Yet sampling is also used in the economic sphere. Firms are asked to provide information about production and trade, and consumers are requested to report on their spending patterns. Firms also engage in various forms of market research to see what new products consumers will buy and at what prices. A sample of consumers can be asked to try products and report on them, or products can be released in certain areas at various prices and the results tabulated. Sampling has, of course, some obvious problems:

1. The people questioned must be 'average' people, who represent accurately the group of people whose opinions are needed. It is no use questioning a millionaire if information is required about the spending of a person on the national average wage; it is of little value interrogating the proprietor of a small business which neither imports nor exports if information is being sought about trade trends.
2. Those supplying information may, through incompetence or unwillingness to co-operate, not supply accurate or complete information. It is well-known that political canvassers find many

people in a street agreeing to vote for their party because those people do not wish to stop and argue.
3 Circumstances may change during or after the sampling or an unusual event may take place during it. For example, if I am keeping my accounts for a week and it happens to be the one week in four years when I buy a new car, this must not be taken to mean that I (or people like me) buy a new car each week.
4 The question asked in the sample survey must not be biased, or be 'leading' questions, such as "Do you agree that......?". Psychologists tell us that people are more inclined to vote 'yes' than 'no' to most questions and so half the art of surveying opinion is to structure the question to ensure the result you want!

Information is often needed in the economic sphere in order to discover and measure *trends* over a period of time or to make *comparisons*. Often, it is difficult to measure trends in production, for example, because measurement of different products is made in different units (eg kilos, gallons, tons, tonnes). Similarly, price changes in or comparisons between different countries are handicapped by the use of different currencies. Many of these problems are overcome by using a device called *index numbers*.

Index numbers

Index numbers are really, at their simplest, a system of percentages. Table 18.1 shows how they can be used for measuring changes in output of commodities which are measured in different units. Suppose a country produces five different commodities and its output of them in Years 1 and 2 is as shown in the Table. It is not really possible to make a meaningful conclusion about production trends unless a common measuring-stick can be found. Index numbers provide this. The outputs of each item in Year 1 are all numbered '100' and Year 2's outputs ar calculated as percentages of Year 1's. Then it can be seen that output of the economy as a whole has risen by 13 per cent or an average of 2.6 per cent per industry.

Table 18.1 A production index

			Output (millions)	
Industry	Year 1	Year 2	Index year 1	Index year 2
1 Kilos of wheat	3	4	100	133
2 Barrels of oil	10	12	100	120
3 Vehicles	5	4	100	80
4 Tonnes of steel	20	21	100	105
5 Suits of clothes	16	12	100	75
		Total	500	513
		Average	100	102.6

Yet all the industries may not be equally important to the economy. A decline in clothing manufacture may not be so important to the country as an increase in oil production. Thus a method needs to be found which will give due emphasis to the important industries, either on the basis of the factors they employ, the revenue they bring in, or some other vital basis. In any index number system '*Weights*' are calculated to provide the proper emphasis which will reflect the relative importance of the various things being measured. In the UK, the *Index of Industrial Production* uses weights adding up to 1000. The index is multiplied by the weight to get the 'weighted index' of output. Table 18.2 lists the weights used in this index (they are, of course, subdivided into other categories; for example in the mining weight of 41, coal counts for 34; in the food, drink and tobacco weight of 77, food accounts for 54).

Table 18.2 Weights used in index of industrial production

Mining and quarrying	41
Construction	182
Gas, electricity and water	80
Manufacturing of which:	697
Food, drink and tobacco	77
Coal and petroleum products	9
Chemicals and allied industries	57
Metal manufacture	47
Engineering and allied industries	298
Textiles	40
Leather, clothing and footwear	27
Bricks, pottery, glass, cement	28
Timber and furniture	25
Paper, printing and publishing	58
Other manufacturing	31
Total	1,000

Source: Annual Abstract of Statistics 1982.

Weighting can make a considerable difference to an index system. Let us take a simple example, but this time in the sphere of *prices* rather than production. Suppose an economy produced just five goods, as illustrated in Table 18.3. An unweighted index system shows (Columns 3 and 4) that prices rose from an average of 100 to 104 between Years 1 and 2 – a rise of 4 per cent, of course. But suppose weights are added in order to emphasise the most important goods. If Commodity B was more important than Commodity A, for example, then the fall in the price of B is more significant than A's price rise. If weights are allocated to provide this emphasis (Column 5), then a different result is obtained (Columns 6 and 7) than was shown in the unweighted index. The weighted index shows that prices have really *fallen* by 2 per cent in Year 2.

Table 18.3 A weighted price index

Commodity	Price (£)		Index		Weight	Weighted Index (index × weight)	
	Column 1 Year 1	Column 2 Year 2	Column 3 Year 1	Column 4 Year 2	Column 5	Column 6 Year 1	Column 7 Year 2
A	0.20	0.25	100	125	10	1,000	1,250
B	1.00	0.80	100	80	30	3,000	2,400
C	0.10	0.12	100	120	15	1,500	1,800
D	0.50	0.45	100	90	25	2,500	2,250
E	2.00	2.10	100	105	20	2,000	2,100
Total			500	520	100	10,000	9,800
Average			100	104		100	98

Weighted indices are collected and published in the UK for many sectors of the economy – wholesale prices, retail prices, wages, earnings, trade, exchange rate of the pound, output. There is even an 'Index of Longer Leading Indicators' which attempts to forecast ups and downs in the business cycle a year or more in advance by using five other indices – short-term interest rates, company cash flow, new housing starts, Financial Times 500 share index and the CBI's quarterly survey of business confidence! Of all these indices, perhaps the most well-known is the Retail Price Index.

The retail price index

The Retail Price Index (RPI) measures changes in the prices of goods in the shops and retail outlets. These prices are obtained by collecting 150,000 prices of a basket of 350 goods each month from shops in 200 areas. Adjustments have to be made for quality changes – for example if a bar of chocolate remains the same price but is altered in size, a device often used by manufacturers to avoid raising prices. Thus, sampling is used.

The weights are also obtained by sampling. 3,000 households each year are asked to keep accounts of their spending for a two week period. The sample is drawn from nine-tenths of the population, leaving out the very rich and poor (thus, pensioners have a separate index). Allowances have to be made for exceptional purchases, like new cars or holidays, which would not occur each week. Despite all the allowances made, all sampling has an error margin (eg public opinion polls allow for 2 per cent either way of their results). The weights are altered each year in order to reflect changes in spending patterns. Table 18.4 shows the weights for selected years. In 1980, therefore, the average family was reckoned to have spent 21.4 per cent of its disposable income on food, 8.2 per cent on alcohol, 4.0 per cent on tobacco and so on. Trends since 1966 are clear – the smaller proportion spent on food, the decline in smoking but rise in the proportion spent on drinking, transport and vehicles.

Table 18.4 Retail prices index weights (selected years)

Product	1966	1976	1980
Food	298	228	214
Alcohol	67	81	82
Tobacco	77	46	40
Housing	113	112	124
Fuel and light	64	56	59
Durable household goods	57	75	69
Clothing and footwear	91	84	84
Transport and vehicles	116	140	151
Miscellaneous Goods	61	74	74
Services	56	57	62
*Meals consumed outside the home	–	47	41
Totals	1,000	1,000	1,000

*only became a separate category in 1968.

Source: Annual Abstract of Statistics 1982.

The weights for 1914 included food 600; housing, fuel and light 240; clothing 120 – ie 96 per cent spent on three basic essentials of life. These would now be quite out of date. As people have become better off, they buy a wider range of goods and services (thus 'meals out' have become a separate category). Engel's Law suggests that people spend a smaller proportion on food as they become richer; things that were luxuries become much less exclusive, so basic commodities take a lesser share of spending.

The weighted index can then reflect the 'true' price rises in different categories, as shown in Table 18.5. Prices rose 163.7 per cent in six years, 1974 – 80, and the variations between the different categories are also clear.

Table 18.5 The retail prices Index, 1980

Base Year: 15 January 1974 = 100	1980
Food	255.9
Alcohol	261.8
Tobacco	290.1
Housing	269.5
Fuel and light	313.2
Durable household goods	226.3
Clothing and footwear	265.4
Transport and vehicles	288.7
Miscellaneous goods	276.9
Services	262.7
Meals out	290.0
Average	263.7

Source: Ibid

The RPI includes indirect taxes, of course, as they are part of a good's price. Direct taxes and national insurance contributions are not included, however. Nor are mortgage payments (a very important item to many people), though rents are included. Betting, medical fees, subscriptions and donations are also excluded. Thus, the RPI is *not* a faultless Cost of Living Index, though trade unions have often based wage claims on it.

In 1979 the Government decided to start a new Index, which would be a more accurate cost of living indicator, the *Tax and Price Index* (TPI), which gave a 25 per cent weight to income tax and national insurance changes. This started when the government raised indirect taxes but reduced income tax. For a time the TPI showed prices rising at a slower rate than the RPI did, but by 1981 the TPI was climbing above the RPI. Thus, the TPI was quietly dropped (although some trade unions tried to base pay claims on it) and when the government decided to 'index' some tax allowances in the 1982 Budget (ie to raise the allowances when prices rose), the RPI, not the TPI was chosen as the price rise indicator.

Problems involving index numbers

1 Any sampling involved is open to the problems and errors of sampling referred to above.
2 The results are 'averages'; for example, the RPI fits the 'average family'. Yet no family distributes its spending in *exactly* the pattern reflected by the RPI's weights. Therefore, the RPI does not fit anyone exactly, but it 'most nearly fits' many people.
3 Weights are essential – but they need regular and accurate revision in order to take account of changes in the relative importance of the items being measured. For instance, as spending patterns change, the RPI's weights must change; as industries decline their weight in the Production Index must be reduced. The 1975 Index of Industrial Production gives oil and natural gas extraction a weight of 0.3 (out of 1000) – hardly an accurate reflection of the position in the 1980s. When weights are changed an *exact* comparison with previous years is not possible, but revisions are required to take account of changes in the economy.
4 The 'base' year (the one given the index of 100) must be a typical year. If it is a 'rogue' year, then the subsequent 'normal' years appear to be distorted. Often, an average of several years is taken as the base in order to eliminate irregularities. Like weights, bases also need to be changed from time to time. The exchange rate of the pound used to be valued against its 1972 level, the last time it had a fixed value before it was allowed to float. The pound has never reached this level again, so its index fell below 100, indeed to the 60–70 range in 1975–76. Eventually, it was decided that sterling would not approach its base year level again, so the base year was changed to 1976 because the

1971 base was thought to be obsolete.

Uses of index numbers

Despite these problems, index numbers are widely used, especially in official statistics. They enable comparisons to be made and trends to be identified. Thus, governments, producers, workers and consumers can see what policies they need to pursue in order to achieve their aims in the light of current events. The effects of recent and current policies can also be seen and lessons learned. If the indices are used jointly (eg earnings compared with prices and employment) more general conclusions can be drawn concerning how the economy and its component groups are faring.

All methods of measuring economic facts and trends have their drawbacks, including index numbers, but the necessity for attempting the exercise is clear, and index numbers have much to contribute.

Summary

1 Measurements of trends and the search for information include using sampling and index numbers.
2 Samplers need to choose their samples accurately and collect reliable information.
3 Index numbers enable trends to be identified and comparisons made through using percentage-based calculations.
4 Accurate weights need to be calculated in order to make the results more meaningful.
5 Index number systems are only 'average' results, which may fit no-one absolutely, but they 'must nearly' fit a large number of people.
6 Indices of most sectors of the economy are regularly collected, published and used to assist policy making.

Section seven International economics

19 International trade

The law of comparative advantage

There is no theoretical difference between international trade and trade between institutions within a country. There are some complications, such as the increased transport and insurance costs and the fact that countries use different currencies, so that an exchange rate system has to exist, but these factors do not invalidate the theory. Nor does the fact that countries may tend to restrict imports in order to favour their own industries.

The law on which international trade is based is the *Law of Comparative Advantage* (or *Law of Comparative Costs*), which states that, other things being equal, a country should specialise in the output of those products in which it has the greatest comparative advantage over other countries (other things being equal). Thus, countries with tropical climates product tropical foodstuffs, island nations tend to have fishing industries, temperate climates produce grain, mountainous countries favour tourism and so on. Climate, mineral deposits, labour supplies, technology are all influences on what a country produces. Whatever their resources, countries have to produce something; even those with few apparent advantages may specialise in services, as land-locked Switzerland does in tourism and banking or Liberia does in the registration of merchant shipping.

In order to illustrate the law, we will take a simplified example involving just two countries, A and B, and two products, food and machines. We will also suppose that the countries employ their factors of production in combined units of land, labour, capital and enterprise, and that these units are homogeneous, that is to say they are each capable of producing the same amount as each other. Thus, *constant costs* operate. The final assumption is that both countries have a total of ten production units.

In country A, each production unit can produce either 10 units of food or 4 machines. Therefore, the boundaries of production are 100 units of food and 0 machines, or 0 food and 40 machines. Table 19.1a shows some of the possible combinations of production. In the absence of trade the country will wish to produce some of both products, so let us assume country A employs 3 production units on food, thus producing 30 food units, and 7 units on machines, thus producing 28 units of that product.

Table 19.1 Production possibilities in countries A and B

Country A		Country B	
Food	Machines	Food	Machines
100	0	100	0
90	4	90	6
80	8	80	12
70	12	70	18
60	16	60	24
50	20	50	30
40	24	40	36
30	28	30	42
20	32	20	48
10	36	10	54
0	40	0	60

Country B's production units can each produce either 10 food or 6 machines. Table 19.1b shows some of country B's production-possibilities. Let us suppose that the country decides to devote 5½ units to food, thus producing 55 units, and 4½ units to machines, giving an output of 27.

Thus, country A is producing 30 food and 28 machines and country B's output is 55 food and 27 machines. If they decide to specialise, country B should concentrate on machines, in which its maximum output is 60, as opposed to country A's 40.

Tables 19.1a and 19.1b are reproduced diagrammatically in Diagram 19.1. What we have, of course, are two *Production Possibility Frontiers*, like those encountered in Chapter 1 (pp 11–12). These frontiers are straight lines because of the assumption that constant costs operate.

Before the countries specialise, Country A will produce at point W and Country B at point X. After complete specialisation, Country A will produce 100 food and 0 machines and B will produce 0 food and 60 machines. The aim of the countries is to exchange the two products so that they end up with more than they could have obtained by producing both articles themselves. That is to say that the countries both wish to reach a point *beyond* their respective production-possibility frontiers.

In order to trade, the two countries have to find a mutually-acceptable ratio of exchange between the two goods. Before specialisation in Country A, 10 units of food were 'worth' 4 machines, whereas in Country B, every 10 units of food produced involved giving up 6 machines. Thus, after specialisation, A will want at least 4 machines for every 10 units of food it exports, but B will not want to give more than 6 machines in exchange for 10 food units. If the exchange ratio took place outside this range of 10:6 to 10:4, then one of the countries would not benefit from trade – it would be better-off continuing to produce both goods itself. The exact ratio of exchange will depend upon which of the countries can drive the harder bargain. If B is more desperate for food than A is for machines, the ratio may be at or near B's 'limit' of 10:6. Whichever country had the less elastic demand for the other's product would get the worst of the deal – though it would not allow itself to be forced beyond its least-acceptable limit (10:4 for A, or 10:6 for B).

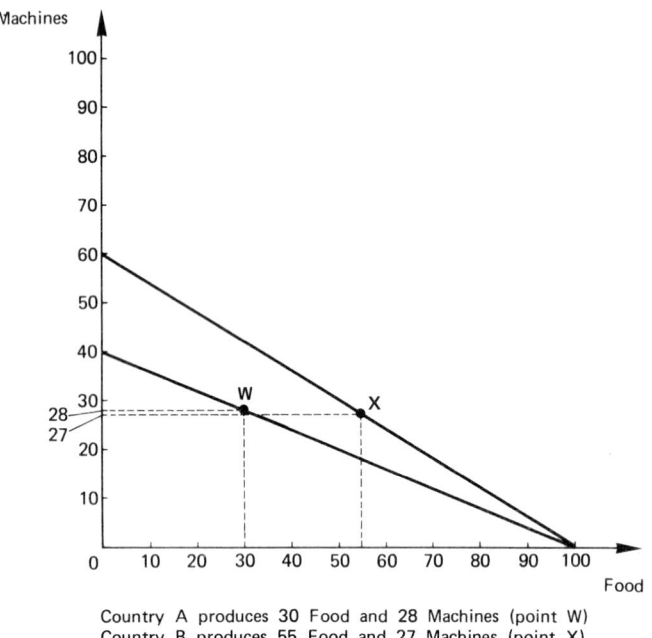

Country A produces 30 Food and 28 Machines (point W)
Country B produces 55 Food and 27 Machines (point X)

19.1 Production-possibility frontiers of countries A and B

For simplicity however, let us assume that the agreed ratio is 10 food for 5 machines. In Country A consumers can now go beyond the frontier of 100 food to 40 machines. A new frontier joining 100 food to 50 machines is now possible (Frontier 2A in Diagram 19.2). Country A could, for example, export 60 food in exchange for 30 machines and could consume at point Y – 40 food and 30 machines.

Country B's new frontier (2B) now joins 60 machines to 120 food, now that each of its 60 machines is 'worth' 2 food units. If B exports 30 machines, it imports 60 food. Thus, B consumes at point Z – 60 food and 30 machines. Both countries are consuming at a point *beyond* their frontiers of domestic production. Specialisation and trade (ie application of the law of comparative advantage) have benefited them.

This example is oversimplified, of course. In the real world, *increasing costs* exist, not constant costs. Factors of production are *not* homogeneous; some are suited to food, others to machines. In A, most factors are better suited to food, but *some* will better suit machines; in B, the opposite will apply. Because efficiency decreases as less suitable factors are employed, the production possibility frontiers are curved concave to the origin, as were those illustrated in Chapter 1, Diagrams 1.1 and 1.2 (pp 11-12).

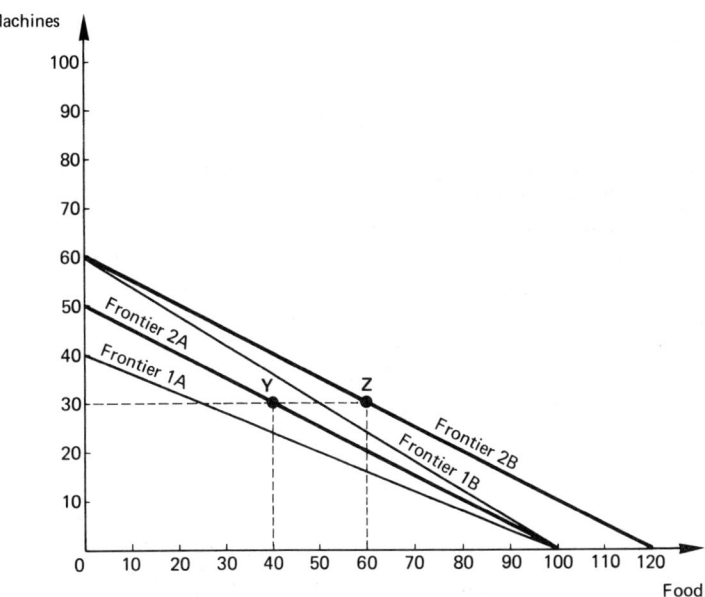

19.2 Countries A and B after trade

Diagram 19.3 shows such a frontier. AB is a segment of the domestic price ratio showing that a country would produce at point X. After trade, the price ratio or terms of trade shifts to CD. Production moves to point Y. More food is produced (OS instead of OR), in accordance with the specialisation principle, but specialisation is not total. *Some* machines (On) are still produced because *some* resources in the country are better suited to machines rather than to food. This accords with real world events. No country would specialise *completely* in one product and rely on other countries for their other needs. In our original example, A and B would have curved frontiers and though A would specialise in food and B in machines, they would not specialise absolutely.

175

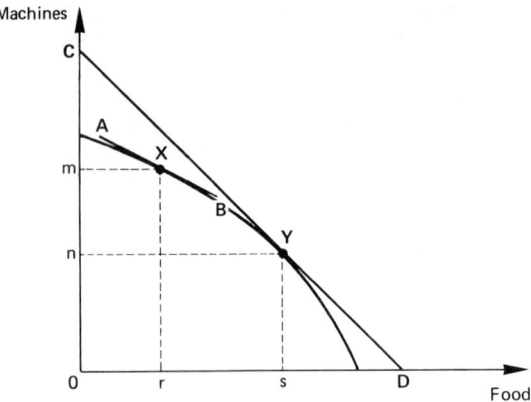

19.3 International trade with increasing costs

The real world also contains more than two countries and two products, so the Law of Comparative Advantage is even more difficult to illustrate. Yet the specialisation principle appears broadly to be borne out by the facts. Britain's trade pattern in the nineteenth and first half of the twentieth century seems to accord with the Law. Britain imported raw materials of which its domestic supplies were limited, or non-existent, like timber and cotton. It exported manufactured goods, based on its own reserves of coal and iron. The early development of coal-based steam power gave Britain an advantage in manufacturing, so it developed this sector.

Since about 1950, however, the UK's trade pattern has changed. The UK now imports steel, machines, vehicles, domestic appliances, textiles, even coal – all products in which it used to have a comparative advantage. Yet it still produces these goods as well. So the country both exports and imports similar products. This does *not* fit the Law of Comparative Advantage and seems difficult to explain.

Perhaps what is happening is that the UK is in a transitional stage. The advantages it used to have are being lost as technology and perhaps also management sciences advance more rapidly elsewhere. Much of the industrial sector is in decline, but because of the curved production possibility frontier reflecting increasing marginal costs, the sector will not vanish completely. Yet industrial structures will always be changing. Timber producers lost their advantage when coal power was developed; coal produces have now lost ground to oil producers. Production possibility frontiers move over time as technology in particular changes. UK is moving away from manufacturing towards service trades and oil production.

Another reason why the UK exports and imports similar products is that the products are not homogeneous. Japanese cars are not exactly the same as British cars; Saudi Arabian oil is not of the same quality as British oil; Italian refrigerators are not identical to those made in the

UK. In the eyes of consumers, the products are not the same; differences (real or supposed) in terms of quality, design or after-sales service are important. Some people will prefer the German camera or the Swedish furniture; other consumers will buy the British products. Complete specialisation is unlikely, at least in the short-run.

Free trade versus protection

The Law of Comparative Advantage benefits consumers, as the example showed. They can consume more and they get more choice, probably at lower prices. Yet for the benefits of specialisation to accrue in full, *free trade* has to exist. Free trade means trade with no artificial restrictions or barriers, a free market system, in fact. In the real world, however, free trade does not always exist. Instead, countries may *protect* their own industries and discriminate against those of other countries. Thus, the comparative advantage possessed by another country in a certain product may be obstructed.

Forms of protection

1 *Tariffs*

A tariff is a tax placed on an import. The result, of course, is that the price of the import rises. The tariff will probably be designed to raise the import price above that of the home-produced good. This aids output and employment in the home country, but reduces consumers' welfare by raising prices and reducing supply and choice. Tariffs can be of two sorts – a *specific* tariff levied per unit (eg per tonne) of the imported good or an *ad valorem* tariff, levied per money unit (eg per £) of the import. Tariffs may discriminate between different countries. By the old 'Commonwealth Preference' system the UK gave Commonwealth food and raw materials preferential treatment compared with similar products from other countries. The EEC regulations allow free trade between the members, but levy a common tariff on imports from outside the area. The existence of this common tariff (eg a Japanese car is subject to the same tariff whichever EEC country it tries to find a market in) makes the EEC a *customs union* as well as a *free trade area*.

Formation of a customs union or free trade area does not necessarily create conditions for the Law of Comparative Advantage to operate freely, because the area discriminates against products from outside. Trade may be created, but it may also be diverted away from the cheapest cost sources. Table 19.2 shows a hypothetical example.

Suppose country A places a 50% tariff on all its imports. This means that it does not import butter, though without the tariff country B can produce butter more cheaply. Countries B and C can produce vehicles more cheaply than country A and even after the tariff country C supplies country A.

Countries A and B now form a customs union, so A's 50 per cent tariff on B's goods disappears, but it remains on C's goods. B can now use its natural advantage with regard to butter. B will export butter to A; trade has been *created*. As far as vehicles are concerned, B will now also export them to A. Yet country C has the greatest natural advantage, which it cannot use because the tariff gives B an artificially-created advantage. In this case trade has been *diverted* from the cheapest source to a more expensive one.

Table 19.2 Trade creation and trade diversion

Butter	Country A	Country B	Country C
1 Production cost per million tonnes (£m)	10	6	16
2 Cost + 50% tariff (£m)	10	12	24
3 Cost after A and B form customs union (£m)	10	6	24
Vehicles:			
1 Production cost per million (£m)	10	7	6
2 Cost + 50% tariff (£m)	10	14	9
3 Cost after A and B form customs union (£m)	10	7	9

Trade diversion may well have occurred after the UK joined the EEC. Instead of importing dairy produce from New Zealand, the cheaper source, the common tariff diverts the UK to sources in Denmark and the Netherlands. Similarly, sugar cane imports from the Commonwealth have been largely replaced by EEC beet sources. In both cases, the UK had no tariff on New Zealand dairy produce or West Indian and Mauritian sugar to start with, so the case of trade diversion is even clearer than in our imaginary example.

2 *Quantitive restrictions*

Protection may take the form of quantitive restrictions like quotas or licences. The EEC has tried to negotiate quotas with Japan concerning the latter's car exports to Europe, for example. Some countries may only import certain goods, like armaments, under licence. In earlier centuries the famous trading companies like the East India, Levant and Hudson's Bay Companies were granted royal charters, creating monopolies or sole trading rights. The effects of all quantitive restrictions are to reduce supply, indeed to make the supply curve of the imported product completely inelastic. This is likely to raise prices.

3 *Exchange control regulations*

When international trade takes place, payment has to be made by mutual arrangement in an agreed currency. The supplier will wish to paid in a 'strong' currency and not one which is likely to depreciate in value. Therefore, countries will wish to conserve their supplies of popular currencies and importers will need government permission to buy these currencies. The scarce and vital currencies will only be released for approved imports. Similarly, limits may be placed on holidaymakers, emigrants and other travellers abroad with regard to the amount of foreign currencies they can take. After 1945, when gold had lost its pre-eminent position, much trade was done in dollars. Thus, there was a dollar shortage and countries hoarded their supplies.

The UK ended its exchange control regulations in 1979. On the other hand, like other countries, the UK may try to affect the exchange rate of its currency. When fixed exchange rates existed, a country might devalue its currency in order to make exports cheaper and imports more expensive. With floating rates, a country may find more difficulty in controlling its exchange rate, but may still seek to do so.

4 *Export subsidies*

Direct subsidies to exports are illegal by the terms of the *General Agreement on Tariffs and Trade* (GATT). Nevertheless, governments find many ways of aiding exporters. In the UK, the *Export Credit Guarantee Department* (ECGD) insures exporters against default or refusal to accept the goods on the part of other countries. Exporters may also receive credit or tax concessions from their governments. Nationalised industries are especially well-placed to receive government aid. British Shipbuilders received aid in order to gain an important Polish contract in the late 1970's; British Rail's subsidies indirectly help their ferry and hovercraft services; all countries' national airlines receive government aid. Subsidies may not directly help exports, but they may help firms to compete in their own markets and thus resist imports. This sort of aid is not illegal. Subsidies specifically designed to help an industry's international trading position are difficult to identify or counteract.

No form of trade restriction will guarantee success. Despite its common tariff, quota agreements and other protective measures, the EEC has failed to prevent the import of Japanese vehicles, for example.

Reasons for protection

Despite the advantages to the consumer of free trade, protection is common and the following reasons have been advanced.

1 *Strategically important industries must be preserved*

No country would wish to rely entirely on foreigners for imports of food, fuel or other vital products. Wars, political upheavals, natural disasters or other emergencies may result in supplies being drastically reduced or even cut off. In 1917 Britain's food supplies were down to 6 weeks' reserves; in the early years of the Second World War a similar German blockade was also effective. Threats and crises concerning

Middle East oil in the 1960s and 1970s demonstrated the vulnerability of many countries which had no oil of their own. Countries will try to preserve vital industries, even if they have no great natural advantages in that direction.

2 *Infant industries need protection*

New industries may need protection against more established and efficient competition. The industrialisation of Germany after its unification in 1871 was carried out behind high tariff walls. Germans had to buy German goods, which stimulated output in the new industries. Similar arguments are applied to the attempts to industrialise underdeveloped countries today. The danger of protecting infant industries is that the absence of competition may breed inefficiency. Competition is not there to stimulate the industries. Governments must ensure that new industries survive, but must make them fit for eventual competition.

3 *Dumping must be resisted*

Dumping is the selling of goods in foreign markets at a very low price, probably below the average or marginal cost of production, in order to drive other countries' industries out of existence. Unless specific government subsidies can be identified, dumping is hard to prove. The UK has taken action against the dumping of Eastern European clothing and tyres and is investigating several other products from these countries, including electric motors, alarm clocks and hardboard. Japanese electronic goods and motor cycles have virtually eliminated the UK's industries, but dumping has not been proved. The Japanese have not been selling at a price below production costs.

4 *Goods from low-wage countries must be kept out*

Some Asian countries have often been accused of producing cheap goods because their workers are exploited by being paid low wages. This argument is usually countered by statements that buying from these countries will make them richer, raise their wages and thus reduce their competitive edge. This process can take years, however, even decades and the importing countries may find their industries ruined in the process. The real counter argument is that it is *average* or *marginal* costs that are important. Thus, a high wage country like the USA or Germany can be competitive because productivity matches costs. If low wages automatically gave advantages, then the USA would not be able to export anything, while UK products should swamp the markets of Western Europe and North America, a situation which does not seem to exist in the real world!

5 *Declining industries must be protected*

Imports can create unemployment by ruining domestic industries. Thus, protection is needed to preserve jobs. The UK has aided its declining industries since 1945, including coal, steel, textiles, shipbuilding and vehicles. The economic arguments for this are rather shaky. Comparative advantage has turned against these industries and it is wasteful to preserve them, especially as it almost inevitably seems to involve fighting a losing battle. On political and social grounds, however, governments have to preserve employment, especially if there is a regional problem. Unemployment is costly in terms of redundancy payments, social benefits and waste of resources, and it may be that preservation is cheaper than closure, at least in the short run. Protection of declining industries is probably justifiable either if the industry is vital or serious unemployment would result, but the protection should usually be short term while attempts are made to start new industries and retrain labour. Also, protection should not aim at fossilising an industry at its existing level. In 1980 the UK government closed large areas of British Steel, thus concentrating on saving the most viable and promising parts of the industry.

6 *Membership of various organisations involves implementation of schemes which restrict trade*

When the UK joined the EEC in 1973 it had to apply the common tariff to all competing goods from outside the area, even though some of these were detrimental to the UK and other countries. In 1936 members of the League of Nations agreed to operate sanctions against Italy, as punishment for the invasion of Abyssinia, and for much of the 1960s and the 1970's United Nations countries operated sanctions against Rhodesia.

7 *Foreign currency reserves must be maintained*

A country with a huge import bill is in danger of running out of the means to pay as its foreign currency reserves become depleted. Thus, the country must restrict its imports and save its reserves for vital purchases. The obvious answer is to raise exports and thus obtain the funds to purchase imports. This is more easily said than done if the country concerned is poor and underdeveloped with few resources and probably reliant on exports of a cash crop or other primary product which is at the mercy of the weather or fluctuating world prices.

8 *Tariffs raise revenue*

Tariffs, unlike most domestic purchase taxes, usually aim to deter consumption rather than to raise revenue. There are usually more efficient ways of raising revenue, at least in industrialised countries. Only a tiny fraction of the UK government's revenue comes from tariffs, although the EEC raises 35 per cent of its revenue from the common tariff.

These reasons for protection have different degrees of validity, though all have some degree of justification. Many non-economic factors are involved, as is so often true in the real world, particularly when employment is involved.

Protection almost invariably leads to retaliation. Economic history books are full of accounts of trade wars, competitive devaluations and bilateral deals which exclude other countries. Eventually, in the 1930s, countries tried to get out of the slump by restricting imports and thus making their people buy home-produced goods. World trade collapsed and after the War priority was given to preventing a recurrence of such events and stimulating multilateral trade. In 1947 the United Nations attempted to set up an *International Trade Organisation*, but insufficient countries ratified the agreement and it never came into operation. GATT did come into effect in 1948 and this organisation has attempted to outlaw export subsidies, quotas and bilateral agreements. GATT members have also carried out seven 'rounds' of tariff-cutting, such as the Kennedy Round of 1964–67. Many trade restrictions remain, however, and the EEC is just one example of a preferential trade agreement which discriminates against non-members. No wonder the Law of Comparative Advantage has become rather blurred.

The terms of trade

When we were working out our example of the law of comparative advantage reference was made to the terms of trade, the ratio of exchange between the goods. In the example it was a 2 food units for 1 machine. In the modern world barter like this rarely occurs. In any case, most buyers and sellers are firms, not countries; they are not *exchanging* goods, one is buying and the other is selling. Thus, payment is made in an agreed currency and, in this era of floating exchange rates, probably at a pre-arranged rate of exchange.

The phrase 'Terms of Trade' is still used, however. A country's terms of trade are defined as:

$$\frac{\text{Index of the value of exports}}{\text{Index of the value of imports}} \times 100$$

ie a comparison of the relative prices of exports and imports.

'Good' terms of trade occur when export prices are higher than import prices. Good terms of trade do not necessarily mean a good trading performance. Oil producers like Kuwait or Saudi Arabia, whose customers have an inelastic demand, benefit from good terms of trade. A country like the UK, whose customers abroad have an elastic demand for its products, often prefer 'bad' terms of trade – cheap and competitive exports. Table 19.3 shows some trends in the UK's terms of trade. The relationship between these terms of trade and the balance of payments will be clearer when the next chapter examines the balance of payments in greater detail.

Table 19.3 UK's terms of trade index (1970 = 100)

Year	Index of average export price	Index of average import price	Terms of trade
1900	13	17	76
1920	49	55	89
1938	21	20	105
1946	41	42	98
1960	76	76	100
1974	171	215	80
1980	377	415	91

Source: British Economy in Figures, 1981. Lloyds Bank Ltd, 1981.

Summary

1 International trade is based on the Law of Comparative Advantage (or Law of Comparative Costs), which states that a country should specialise in the output of those products in which it has the greatest comparative advantage over other countries (other things being equal).
2 Specialisation on the basis of the law will raise world output. Countries should then work out mutually advantageous terms of trade so that each will end up with more of the various goods in question than it could obtain by trying to produce the whole range of goods itself.
3 Countries are unlikely to specialise completely in the production of one commodity or even a narrow range of commodities, because not all factors of production are suitable to this; even in an agriculturally-based country, *some* land, labour, capital and enterprise will be better-suited to manufacturing, and vice versa.
4 Free trade favours the consumer, through greater choice and lower prices, but protection, in the forms of tariffs, quotas, exchange control or indirect subsidies to exports, may exist.
5 Protection may exist in order to protect domestic producers, maintain employment, resist dumping, or avoid a balance of payments crisis. Political reasons (eg membership of an organisation like the EEC or United Nations) may also cause countries to erect trade barriers.
6 Terms of trade are defined as:

$$\frac{\text{Index of the value of exports}}{\text{Index of the value of imports}} \times 100$$

'Good' terms of trade may or may not be good for a country's trade performance. The elasticity of demand for imports and foreigners' elasticity of demand for the country in question's exports will be vital factors.

20 The balance of payments

The structure of the balance of payments

The balance of payments is a statement of a country's financial dealings with the rest of the world in a given period: it shows the inflows and outflows of currency during the period. Trade in goods, of course, is a vital element in the balance of payments, but it is by no means the only component. Yet the final figure in the balance of payments, showing whether there has been a net inflow or outflow of currency, is not necessarily the most important feature of the statement. A net inflow might occur because the country has borrowed a huge amount; a net outflow could possibly exist because the country has invested a large sum abroad. Thus, the final net figure in the balance of payments, although important, is not as important as the figures in the various components of the statement. Table 20.1 gives an outline of the UK's Balance of Payments for 1980, which will now be explained.

1 The first section in the statement is the *current account* which shows the balance of visible and invisible trade. Exports and imports of goods constitute visible trade. They are both valued '*free on board*' (fob), in other words excluding transport costs. If the cost of the goods at the UK port of entry is required, then imports need to valued '*cost, insurance, freight*' (cif), but the more common method today is to value imports as well as exports fob. The visible balance is referred to as '*the balance of trade.*'

The UK has had only a handful of visible trade surpluses since the Napoleonic Wars. Since the Second World War there have been surpluses only in 1956, 1958 and 1971 until the UK's oil boom produced a surplus in 1980 and set a new, though possibly short-lived trend for the 1980s. Table 20.2 shows some astonishingly large record deficits in the mid-1970s which were largely caused by the huge rises in the prices of oil and other vitally important imported materials. In the first half of the 1970s, the exchange rate of sterling fell sharply. For example, the pound was equal to $2.60 in 1971 and $1.57 in November 1976, and similar falls occurred in relation to other currencies. Imports thus became more expensive: £1 would only purchase $1.57 worth of American goods instead of $2.60 worth, for instance, but if the $2.60 worth of foreign goods were essential to the UK, much more than £1 (in fact, about £1.40) would have had to be spent. Oil, tin, rubber and other materials were vital to the UK, so they still had to be imported at the higher prices. (Exchange rates will be dealt with in detail in the next chapter.)

Table 20.1 UK balance of payments, 1980

	£m
1 Current account:	
Exports free on board	47,389
Imports free on board	46,211
Visible balance	1,178
Invisible balance	2,028
Current balance (visible plus invisible)	3,206
2 Investment and other capital transactions (net)	− 1,475
3 Balancing item	− 539
4 Allocation of special drawing rights by IMF	+ 180
5 Balance for official financing	+ 1,372
(current balance plus items 2, 3, and 4)	
6 Official financing:	
Net transactions with IMF	− 140
Foreign currency borrowing	− 941
Drawings on (+) or additions to (−) reserves	− 291
Total	− 1,372

Source: Annual Abstract of Statistics 1982.

Table 20.2 UK visible trade balance, 1969–1980

	1969	1970	1971	1972	1973	1974	£m 1975	1976	1977	1978	1979	1980
Exports fob	7,269	8,151	9,043	9,423	11,937	16,395	19,330	25,193	31,734	35,071	40,689	47,389
Imports fob	7,478	8,183	8,853	10,184	14,523	21,745	22,663	29,120	34,013	36,617	44,093	46,211
Visible balance	−209	−32	+190	−761	−2,586	−5,350	−3,333	−3,927	−2,279	−1,546	−3,404	+1,178

Source: Ibid

The UK's visible deficits have often been offset (though not throughout much of the 1960s and 1970s) by invisible surpluses. *Invisible trade* consists of trade in services rather than goods, and of certain transfers of currency between countries. An invisible export consists of some invisible trade involving an inflow of currency into the UK. An invisible import consists of an outflow. So, if I go on holiday to Spain, an invisible *import* has occurred from the UK's point of view. I have purchased services abroad, purchased some pesetas and spent them in Spain. Currency has flowed out of the UK.

The UK *always* has an invisible trade surplus, and Table 20.3 gives a breakdown of this sector for a recent year. The categories are:

a) General government

This includes expenditure by the UK government on maintaining embassies and consulates abroad, offset against similar expenditure here by foreign countries, and expenditure on keeping British armed forces overseas, especially in NATO countries. This defence expenditure is not offset by similar spending by foreign governments here, so is always a negative item.

b) Sea transport

The 'carrying trade' of the UK's merchant fleet used to be a huge earner. Before the War, it balanced as much as 10 per cent of the UK's import bill. Over-capacity in world market shipping since 1945 together with growing competition both from Japan and also from countries like Panama and Liberia which specialise in registering ships under 'flags of convenience', has reduced the UK's shipping surplus. Indeed, in many post-war years this category has shown a loss.

c) Civil aviation

British Airways and the privately-run UK airlines usually earn a small surplus here, because foreigners spend more on their services than the UK citizens do on foreign airlines. Increased competition in the later 1970s and early 1980s in the airline business (especially on the transatlantic route) has sometimes produced losses, however, and the Concorde services have been loss-makers as well. British Airways went into large deficit in 1981.

d) Travel

Throughout the 1950s and 1960s the UK made a loss in this category, but the decline in the exchange rate of sterling in the 1970s made the UK an attractive place for a cheap holiday, so tourism went into a surplus, reaching a peak of nearly £1 billion in 1978. The recovery of the pound in 1979/80 reduced this surplus, because UK was no longer so cheap to visit.

e) Financial services

The City of London's institutions earn a large surplus. The 1980 net surplus was composed of profits on insurance (£800m), banking (£310), brokerage (£370m), commodity trading, merchanting and legal earnings. London's pre-eminence as a banking, commodity trading and insurance centre guarantees a surplus here. Lloyd's of London, for instance, is the largest insurer of ships, aircraft and cargoes in the world.

f) Other services

This category has a vast number of components, including royalties, sales of films and TV programmes, consultancy, construction work overseas and advertising. The net earnings in this category have risen steadily.

Table 20.3 UK invisible trade, 1980

Category	Credit (£m)	Debit (£m)	Balance (£m)
General government	397	1,188	− 791
Sea transport	3,816	3,681	135
Civil aviation	2,210	1,815	395
Travel	2,965	2,757	208
Financial services	1,595	0	1,595
Other services	4,826	2,180	2,646
Interest, profit and dividends:			
(a) Government	943	1,598	− 655
(b) Private sector and public corporation	7,261	6,644	617
Government transfers	958	2,790	− 1,832
Private transfers	793	1,083	− 290
Totals	25,764	23,736	2,028

Source: Ibid

g) Interest, profits and dividends
Both the UK government and the private sector have large investments abroad, many of which originate from colonial days in tea plantations, gold mines, railways, rubber plantations and a host of other industries. Interest, profits and dividends from these sources guarantee a steady net inflow of invisible earnings. In recent years this surplus has declined, however. There is now much foreign investment in the UK, especially in North Sea Oil. Many foreign firms operate here so profits, interests and dividends accrue to the overseas shareholders. High interest rates in the UK have also encouraged foreigners to buy British government stocks so that interest payments on these stocks go abroad thus producing a deficit in the government sector.

h) Government transfers
Since the UK joined the EEC, subscriptions have had to be paid to the EEC institutions (£1,625m. in 1979). Subscriptions to other bodies, like the United Nations, some foreign aid, payments of pensions and benefits to persons overseas (eg to former employees of British embassies abroad) are also included. The UK receives some money from EEC funds, but this item, Government Transfers, is now the largest net invisible deficit. The EEC will be dealt with in detail in chapter 22.

i) Private transfers
This is also a negative item. It consists of transfers of money and goods across international boundaries, sent by people as gifts. For example, immigrant or foreign workers may send part of their earnings to relatives still living in their country of origin.

The sum of visible and invisible trade produces the *current balance*. This is probably the most important section of the balance of payments because it shows the country's current trading position. Normally, the UK has offset a visible deficit by an invisible surplus, but the invisible balance (though always in surplus) has been as volatile as the visible side, as Table 20.4 illustrates. Record surpluses were earned in the mid-1970s, but the government transfers to the EEC and the interest, profits and dividends flowing abroad have caused this to decline. Oil revenues began to offset this, from 1980 (the two are connected of course; oil exports earn income, some of which goes abroad to foreign shareholders of the oil companies) but the improving visible balance is somewhat misleading. The oil sector *is* in surplus, but the rest of the UK's manufacturing sector shows a deficit. Oil may offset the deficit earned by the rest of industry, but it cannot replace the jobs being lost elsewhere. Oil is also an exhaustible resource and the UK's visible balance, and indeed its entire industrial structure, may be in a poor state when the oil boom is over.

Table 20.4 UK Invisible trade, selected years

Category	1970 Balance (£m)	1973 Balance (£m)	1976 Balance (£m)	1980 Balance (£m)
General government	− 309	− 409	− 667	− 791
Sea transport	− 80	− 105	+ 48	+ 135
Civil aviation	+ 46	+ 65	+ 218	+ 395
Travel	+ 50	+ 31	+ 700	+ 208
Financial services	+ 439	+ 601	+ 1,286	+ 1,595
Other services	+ 291	+ 514	+ 679	+ 2,646
Interest, profits and dividends:				
(a) Government	− 269	− 199	− 648	− 655
(b) Private sector and public corporation	+ 823	+ 1,467	+ 1,953	+ 617
Government transfers	− 177	− 357	− 786	− 1,832
Private transfers	− 1	− 78	+ 28	− 290
Invisible balance	+ 813	+ 1,530	+ 2,811	+ 2,028

Source: Ibid

2 The second section of the balance of payments is *investment and other capital transactions*. This includes 'one-off' payments not connected with trade. For example, when an investment is made, it is recorded in this section of the accounts. Subsequent interest, profits and dividends paid or received from this investment appear in the invisible balance in subsequent years. Also in this category appear flows of money concerned with the buying and selling of government stocks (again, the interest received or paid occurs in the invisible balance) and the overseas currency borrowing or lending by the U.K. banks and other monetary institutions.

3 The *balancing item* occurs in the accounts because the balance of payments never balances. It is impossible to identify and catalogue the millions of visible and invisible trade transactions, and investment and capital transactions which involve millions of people and institutions. Often these transactions are identified late and thus the balancing item is reduced for a certain year as items are identified and distributed. Therefore, the balance of payments figures for a particular year are subsequently and continuously revised so all books and sources seem to quote slightly different figures for the balance in a particular year. The balancing item for 1970 is only − £39 million, as virtually all the 'lost' items have been found and allocated. Yet, in 1981, the balancing item for 1977 was still +£3186 million, with much research still needing to be done in order to discover hitherto unidentified items.

4 The *Balance for Official Financing* shows the sum total of the net current account, capital transactions and balancing item.

5 With a new allocation of *Special Drawing Rights* in 1980 (see Chapter 21), an extra item appeared in that year, thus revising the total figure (item 6).

6 The accounts then show Official Financing − ie how the surplus or deficit was financed. If the total balance was negative, then the deficit needed financing; if a surplus occurred, financing needs were negative. Official financing shows what the country borrowed or paid back and how much the reserves went up or down. Note that, if the country's reserves rose, financing needs were negative, so a *minus* sign means an *addition* to the reserves. A *plus* sign means reserves *fell* − financing was needed to pay off a balance of payments deficit.

It is, of course, quite possible that a country's reserves may rise in a year of deficit because it has borrowed more than enough to finance the deficit. Thus, an overall increase in reserves is not necessarily healthy. What countries seek is *'balance of payments equilibrium'*. Technically, equilibrium occurs when the balance for official financing is zero − there has been no net inflow or outflow of currency. Yet what a country really seeks to do is akin to what a firm does − make trading profits (ie a surplus on current account) and then *use* these profits to guarantee future earnings by investing them at home or abroad. This was Britain's policy in its Imperial era, investing its current account surpluses in tea plantations, railways, mines and other colonial assets. If oil restores a current account surplus to the UK for some years in the future, this policy of investing abroad may recur. It is certainly the policy which the OPEC countries follow, widening their industrial activities at home and investing abroad so that their prosperity will continue when the oil industry goes into decline.

Thus, a current account surplus is certainly desirable. World trade is, of course, a zero sum game; not every country can have a surplus. If one country turns its deficit into a surplus, another must incur a deficit. Nevertheless, countries incurring deficits try to cure them and they adopt the following methods.

Methods of curing a current account deficit

1 *Borrowing*

If the deficit is small, a country may take no action and just let its reserves decline, but a large or perpetual deficit over several years will need dealing with, so the first step may be to borrow from abroad. Government stocks could be sold abroad or a direct loan could be negotiated from the IMF or some other international organisation. Loans have to be repaid, however, so borrowing is only useful if the borrowed funds are used to restore the country's competitiveness by being invested in industrial modernisation. Borrowing merely to pay off debts is as senseless as a firm borrowing to pay the wage-bill. The borrowed funds must be profitably used. The lending authority may well impose conditions on the borrower as the IMF did to the UK in 1967 and 1976, when the UK had to promise to announce and achieve money supply targets.

2 *Trade controls*

A country may resort to protectionist policies by imposing tariffs, quotas or exchange controls, or subsidising exports. Many of these moves, especially subsidising exports, are illegal according to international agreements. The UK would have great difficulty in imposing restrictions on EEC goods, but presumably could try to impose selective restrictions against particular goods or countries, like Japanese vehicles or textiles. Trade restrictions are not a panacea. They may provoke *retaliation* from abroad. Also, the home country will have to produce goods itself to replace imports, or else shortages and price rises will result. For instance, if the UK banned car imports, the U.K. car industry would quickly have to double its output to keep pace with demand. Nevertheless, increased import restrictions are advocated by some authorities in the U.K. to stimulate demand for home-produced goods, and thus reduce the high level of unemployment.

3 *Deflation*

A method commonly used in the UK has been to deflate the economy by raising taxes and interest rates. The aim is to reduce people's spending. Some part of spending goes on imports (as high as one-fifth of all consumption spending in the UK), so a general squeeze on spending should reduce imports. Also, if home demand can be restricted, goods may be exported instead. Results (especially raising exports) usually take some time to come into effect. Any deflationary policy is also politically unpopular, as it reduces consumers' welfare. People may also reduce their savings in order to replace the consumption which is being squeezed.

4 Devaluation

Devaluation of a currency makes its exports cheaper in terms of foreign currencies and its imports more expensive in terms of its own currency. If sterling is devalued from, say, 4 Swiss francs to the pound to 3 Swiss francs to the pound, then a Swiss trader needs only spend 3 francs in order to buy £1 worth of British goods instead of 4 francs. If the trader continues to spend 4 francs, he gets £1.33 worth of British exports, so the quantity of exports will rise. Conversely, a British importer gets only 3 francs worth of goods for his pound, so needs to spend more than a pound in order to continue to import Swiss goods to the value of 4 francs.

Hopefully, foreigners will be tempted to buy more of the goods of the devaluing country, whereas home consumers will restrict their purchases of the more expensive imports. For devaluation to be successful, the *elasticities of demand for exports and imports must add up to more than unity* (the so-called Marshall-Lerner criterion). Only if this occurs will the devaluing country's current balance improve. Ideally, an elastic demand for both imports and exports will produce best results; imports will be cut drastically when prices rise, while exports will rise a great deal. The UK's exports do seem to benefit from devaluation, but it has proved difficult to reduce the import bill quickly.

Time lags also occur, because new export deals take time to obtain whereas imports are already ordered. The so-called *'J' curve*, shown in Diagram 20.1 illustrates that devaluation makes things worse before they get better. Imports are more expensive but it takes time to reduce them; exports do not immediately rise. Indeed, the elasticity of supply of exports is important. After the 1949 devaluation, the UK's exports were cheaper, but industry was too dislocated after the War to be able to take advantage of the competitive opportunities which devaluation provided.

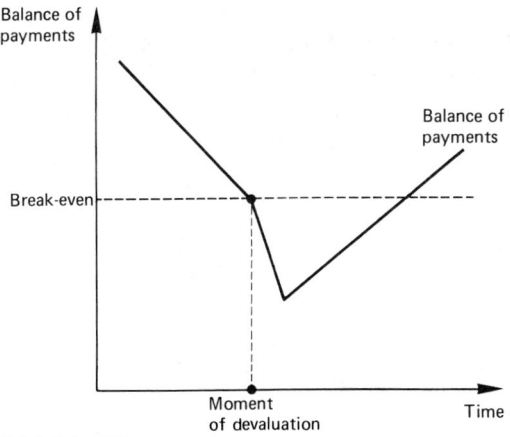

20.1 The 'J' curve

All these measures affect invisible earnings and capital flows as well as visibles. Devaluation aids the travel account; deflationary high interest rates attract investment; services like airlines and shipping should benefit.

Policies to assist the balance of payments contain two general principles – *expenditure-switching* and *expenditure-reducing*. Expenditure at home and abroad should be switched away from foreign goods, while expenditure at home should also be reduced, thus cutting imports and releasing goods for export. Usually a mixture of policies is required. For example, devaluation will raise the cost of living because imports are more expensive. Therefore, deflationary measures are required in order to prevent these inflationary pressure building quickly. Direct measures to boost exports will also be required to encourage firms to take advantage of better opportunities.

Exchange rate policy has become much more common now that a floating system exists. Previously, a country's exchange rate was almost regarded as a virility symbol, with devaluation being considered a signal of failure and disgrace. Devaluation or downward floating is not a guarantee of success, however. Treasury studies indicated that the advantages of the 1967 devaluation did not last indefinitely (though 80 per cent lasted for at least two years). In particular, the higher price of imported raw materials and fuel was soon passed on by manufacturers and began to erode the advantages of cheaper export prices while wage claims occurred as the cost of living rose. It is also noticeable that countries like West Germany and Japan, whose currencies have generally appreciated in value in the 1970's have produced better current balances than countries like the UK and Italy whose currencies have depreciated. International restrictions on trade controls and the difficulties created in using the rather crude tool of deflation have encouraged countries to fall back on depreciating or devaluing their exchange rate to an increasing extent, however.

The UK's balance of payments problems

The UK is a major trading nation, so its exchange rate and its balance of payments are vital factors in its economic performance. The balance of payments has been a major problem since the War and was by far the dominant factor in determining the economic policies of the Labour Government which held office between 1964 and 1970. Other problems, such as inflation and unemployment have subsequently become more urgent, but the balance of payments riddle is by no means solved.

Many of the problems stem from the Second World War itself. The UK lost ⅓ of its overseas investments, either by selling them to finance the War, or through enemy action, especially in the Far East. Markets were lost permanently. Debts of over £3 billion were incurred, which have never been paid-off. Indeed, these *sterling balances* have exchanged hands many times since, rather like undated securities which the UK has to pay interest on each year. One third of the merchant fleet tonnage was lost; damage to industry and manpower was serious (though not as severe as in Germany, which was aided to make a fresh start after the War, including being given a low exchange rate, while the UK tended to patch up its damaged machines instead of replacing or refitting them). There was a need to have a post-war export boom while keeping imports down, to restore invisible earnings and yet simultaneously to maintain the country's great responsibilities abroad (the colonial era did not end until the 1960s). Much of this daunting task was achieved, but the UK never really recovered its competitive position and serious problems were encountered in the 1960s. There is not space to go into a detailed history here, but the following events stand out:

1947:	Sterling fixed at $4.03 to the pound. Import controls continued. The UK tried to restore convertibility of sterling, but ran out of foreign exchange in five weeks. Strict exchange controls ensued. Rationing continued at home until 1954 in order to restrict demand.
1947–50:	Pay freeze.
1948–50:	Marshall Aid from the USA to former allies.
1949:	Sterling devalued from $4.03 to $2.80.
1950:	Korean War broke out. Fears of World War caused countries to stockpile raw materials: the UK had to buy them at expensive post-devaluation prices.
1951:	Record Current Account Deficit of £419m.
1957:	First UK borrowing from the IMF.
1958:	Import controls on foreign manufactures eased. From this date the pattern of UK trade began to change and imports of goods like vehicles, domestic appliances and machinery began to appear: sterling made convertible.
1961:	Pay restraint.
1962:	France vetoed the UK's application to join the EEC.
1964:	Current balance crisis – deficit nearly £500m: sterling crisis; new Labour Government resisted devaluation: borrowing and import restrictions instead.
1965–67:	Annual sterling crises: Incomes policy started in 1966.
1967:	Devaluation. £1 now worth $2.40: France vetoed EEC application: borrowing from IMF.
1970–71:	Large current account surplus (over £1bn in 1971). Squeeze relaxed – trade position deteriorated. Yet sterling revalued to $2.60 by Smithsonian Agreement.
1972:	Sterling floated.
1973:	UK joined EEC: World oil price quadrupled.
1974:	Record current deficit of £3,379m. From 1974 huge volatile hot money flows from OPEC have entered and left the U.K. several times as interest and exchange rates have fluctuated.

1976:   Sterling sunk to record low levels; borrowing from IMF.
1978:   Current account surplus.
1979:   Deficit of nearly £2bn: exchange rate of sterling had risen.
1980:   Current Account Surplus of over £3bn, mainly because of oil and decline of sterling's exchange rate.

So, the story is one of volatility. Squeezes of various sorts improve the situation then it deteriorates again rapidly as relaxation occurs. The basic problem of the declining competitiveness of the UK industry has not been solved. The size of the variations in the 1970s became astonishing, notably the turnaround of £5bn between 1979 and 1980. For the 1980s, the oil exports (and the saving of oil imports) should greatly aid the current account, but at the same time the rest of British industry is in apparent decline. Problems for sterling are particularly difficult. A rise in sterling's value would greatly aid oil earnings (demand for oil is inelastic) but would handicap other industries for whose products demand abroad is much more elastic. A fall in the pound might help other exporters – but what would happen to the import bill? Also, the decline in invisible earnings, partly connected both with oil and the unstable exchange rate, is worrying.

A debate occurred in the 1970s about what the UK should do with the expected oil surpluses. Should there be a spending spree, reduction of taxes, early payment of debts, research into other forms of energy or a recycling of money to other industries? In fact, events have overtaken these ideas. The surpluses earned by oil have largely gone to pay for the problems created by the high unemployment in the UK.

North Sea Oil has played a great part in causing the exchange rate of sterling to appreciate, with sterling being regarded as a 'petrocurrency'. The high interest rates prevailing and attracting foreign money also played a part in keeping sterling's exchange rate high. The relatively inelastic world demand for oil has benefited the UK's oil exports, but the rest of the UK's manufacturing exports, for which demand is more elastic, have suffered from the exchange rate's rise. As firms have failed, unemployment has risen. Demand (including demand for imports) has fallen relatively and firms have not stocked-up with so many imported raw materials. If Full Employment were restored, imports would boom and a deficit would occur. The so-called '*Cambridge School*' of economists calculated in 1981 that Full Employment would lead to a current account deficit of £8bn – including oil's surplus! Thus, they advocate trade controls in order not only to restore Full Employment by 'buying British' but also to prevent a horrific deficit recurring.

The UK's trade problems are deep-seated, however, and not all can be blamed on oil or exchange rates. Many problems originate in the UK manufacturing sector itself. It has not given high enough priority to exports or been competitive enough to compete with imports. Poor management, restrictive union practices, wages outstripping productivity, inadequate government aid, defaulting on delivery dates, poor quality, slipshod design and after sales service, inability of exporters to speak foreign languages, unwillingness to devise new products or keep abreast of technological changes – all these have been put forward as possible causes of poor performance. For some people, new hope came when the UK joined the EEC in 1973 – a new, rich market of over 200 million consumers was available. Yet not until 1980 was a trade surplus with the rest of the EEC achieved. Many problems have beset the UK in the trading field since markets were lost and debts incurred in the Second World War, but the conclusion seems inescapable that some of these problems have been of the UK's own making – and North Sea Oil does not provide a magic solution.

Summary

1 The balance of payments is a statement of a country's dealings with other countries. It is divided into the current account and investment and capital flows.
2 The current balance is usually regarded as the most important section of the balance of payments.
3 The UK usually has a visible trade deficit, but always has an invisible surplus.
4 Current account deficits are sometimes dealt with by expenditure-switching and expenditure-reducing policies, including trade controls, deflation and devaluation. None of these policies guarantee success and all can lead to retaliation.
5 The UK has tried all the expenditure-switching and expenditure-reducing policies with no permanent success. The overall loss of competitiveness of the UK industry has not ben counteracted by a continual decline in the value of sterling.
6 The growth of the UK's oil industry has improved the visible balance, despite the decline of other industries, but the invisible balance is declining and over-reliance on oil may be creating even bigger problems in the future.

21 Exchange rates

How exchange rates are determined

International trade is complicated by the fact that countries have their own currencies and therefore a system of exchanges rates is needed. There can be four elements in the price of an imported good – its production cost, transport cost, possibly a tariff or duty, and fourthly the exchange rate element. As was explained briefly in the previous chapter, if a country *devalues* its currency, its exports become cheaper in terms of foreign currencies and its imports become more expensive in terms of its own currency. If sterling is devalued from £1 = $3 to £1 = $2, a British good costing £100 can be obtained by $200 instead of $300 – it has become cheaper to the foreign consumer. On the other hand, an American good costing $300 to make and transport to the UK will cost £150 to buy here instead of £100. Prices have been artificially altered by changing the exchange rate. If a country *revalued* its currency, the opposite process would occur.

We must investigate how exchange rates are actually determined and must also examine how much control a country has over its exchange rate.

In an ideal situation, a country's currency could be determined by the *Purchasing Power Parity Theory*, which suggests that exchange rates should reflect the relative purchasing power of the currencies. If a basket of goods costs £10 in the UK and 100 francs in France, then £1 should be exchangeable for 10 francs. This theory is not really adequate, however. For a start, a common basket of goods cannot easily be found; patterns of demand tend to differ between countries, particularly if an industrialised country is being compared with an underdeveloped one, or a free market economy with a centralised one where prices are imposed by the state. More important, exchange rates are determined by many more factors than purchasing power. Currencies can be bought and sold in *foreign exchange markets* in many financial centres in the world in a similar fashion to the way in which shares can be traded on a Stock Exchange. The foreign exchange markets are in telex communication with each other, so pounds could be bought at, say, $1.90 each in London and sold at $1.91 in New York. This dealing is known as *arbitrage*. Indeed, currencies can be bought and sold in the same market, just as shares are, taking advantage of price (ie exchange rate) fluctuations. When huge sums are traded, profits can be made from tiny variations between different markets.

This arbitrage is really speculation, so movements of supply and demand will influence price. If speculators all wish to buy yen, the price of yen will rise; if they all wish to sell lire, the exchange rate of lire will fall. Thus, currency exchange rates are greatly affected by the actions of speculators. Like everyone involved in the sphere of economies, speculators' actions are governed by their expectations, which are largely influenced by their experience. If a country announces bad trading figures it is like a company publishing an unhealthy balance sheet – the price of its shares will fall. In the same way, the country's currency value will fall. A likely change of government, a feared or actual strike in a vital industry, unhealthy trends in inflation or unemployment, poor trade figures – all these can make speculators want to sell a country's currency. As always in asset markets, this very action (people selling an asset because they fear its value will fall) will cause the asset's value to fall. On the other hand, good trade figures, improved economic performance or, in the UK's case, the mere possession of that valuable asset, oil, can cause a rush to buy a currency, which will push sterling's exchange rate upwards.

Interest rates will also play a part in determining exchange rates. Between 1977 and 1980 sterling's exchange rate rose, partly because oil was beginning to produce heavy revenues for the UK, but also because interest rates in the UK were generally higher than in other countries. Much money (especially the large OPEC surpluses) came to the UK to take advantage of these interest rates. Thus, an inflow of money improved the balance of payments and sterling's exchange rate rose.

Most of the factors discussed so far relate to the demand side for a currency. The supply side is also important. Countries can alter their exchange rates by changing the supply of their currencies available on foreign exchange markets. If the UK, for example, thinks that sterling is valued too highly, it can buy foreign currencies. To do this, it sells sterling (the sterling is used to buy the foreign currencies) and by simple demand and supply principles, the price (ie exchange rate of sterling) falls. Diagram 21.1 illustrates this. Conversely, the UK could buy its own currency (thus selling its foreign currency reserves) in order to raise sterling's exchange rate.

Thus, a country's exchange rate is determined by many factors in the real world, including purchasing power parity, balance of payments performance, speculation, interest rates and consequent capital flows, and the policy of the government of the country.

Changes in exchange rates will, of course, primarily affect export and import prices and subsequently trade performance. The exact effect on trade will depend on the Marshall-Lerner criterion explained in the previous chapter. Capital flows will also be affected.

Much of this analysis assumes that exchange rates are able to vary in value – a so-called *fluctuating* or *floating* system of exchange rates exists. It is possible, of course, to have a *fixed* system of rates.

With a fixed rate system, traders know exactly what they are going to have to pay or are going to receive, so confidence and security exists. Yet there may be irresistable pressure on a currency and it may not be able to keep to its fixed rate; devaluation or revaluation may be forced upon it. A fixed rate system has no flexibility. Indeed, a country may wish to alter its exchange rate in order to improve its trading position or stave off speculation. The world had a mainly fixed rate system from 1947 to the early 1970s, but since then a floating rate system has been in existence.

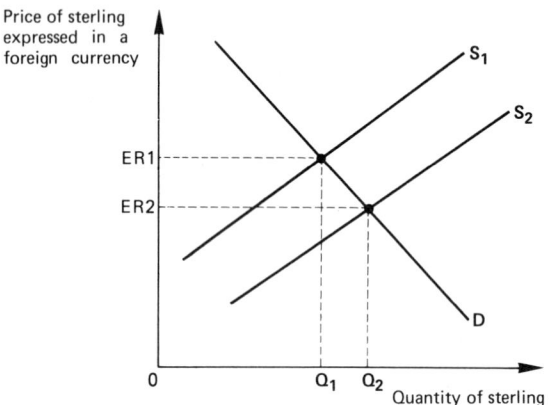

21.1 The determination of the exchange rate

Floating rates breed uncertainty. When a deal is struck, the traders either have to fix an exchange rate in advance or wait until the day of settlement, by which time the rate may have changed to the disadvantage of either buyer or seller and the advantage of his counterpart. Speculators are also able to operate freely. The system is more flexible, however, and should avoid dramatic devaluations or revaluations and replace them by more gradual day-to-day changes, though speculative pressure can exacerbate these changes as rumours spread.

The foreign exchange market has, incidentally, many of the features of a *perfect market*. There is a large number of buyers and sellers, little 'brand preference' on behalf of the buyers, near-perfect knowledge and the ability to take advantage of it, and prices are largely determined by supply and demand. The market is not absolutely perfect, of course. There is not completely free entry, the currencies are not all homogeneous (some are regarded as 'stronger' than others) and alterations to rates sometimes are imposed from outside the market by a government or international agreement.

Just as the foreign exchange market is not completely perfect, so also in the real world exchange rate systems are neither completely fixed or freely floating. There are several variations of the two systems of fixed and floating rates that can exist.

Possible types of exchange rate systems

1 *Completely fixed rates*

This is too rigid to be workable in the real world. Countries' economies do not stay in fixed relationships to each other as some countries prosper and others decline. As an economy's performance diverges from its exchange rate its trading position declines and there is pressure on it to change its exchange rate. Speculation and rumour mount and a country has to spend much of its reserves maintaining its rate or has to change it, thus creating the risk of retaliation.

2 *Adjustable peg*

This system was used in the world from 1947 to the early 1970s, the so-called *Bretton Woods System*, created at the conference at Bretton Woods in 1944. Exchange rates were fixed within narrow limits – 1 per cent fluctuation allowed either side of parity. Thus, speculation could exist but there was some leeway allowed. In 1971 the band of fluctuation was increased to 2¼ per cent either side of parity. Thus, a country did not have to devalue or revalue quite so readily. Also, by consultation with the International Monetary Fund, a devaluation or revaluation of more than 10 per cent could be negotiated. The scheme attempted to combine the advantages of both fixed and floating systems. Diagram 21.2 shows that an exchange rate could vary within the limits of the agreed ban; if it left those limits it must be brought back or officially altered in value. Between 1949 and 1967 the value of sterling was £1 = \$2.80; it could not fall below \$2.78 (eg to \$2.77 in the diagram). If it did so the UK government had to sell some of its foreign currencies to create an artifical demand within the permitted band. The *Exchange Equalisation Account* of the Bank of England (see Chapter 15, p 144) conducted this process.

Various sorts of adjustable peg systems could exist; wider bands could be used; a regular review of exchange rates could occur and adjustments be made, perhaps according to a formula (a '*crawling peg*' system); or adjustments could be made by mutual consent, as is supposed to happen in the *European Monetary System* of the EEC, whose members set up a fixed rate system (2 per cent fluctuation allowed for 'strong' currencies and 6 per cent for weaker ones) in 1979.

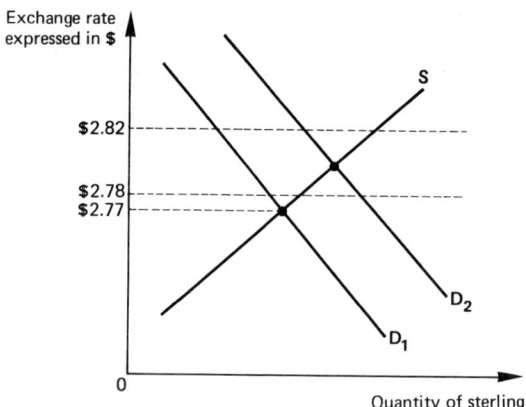

21.2 The adjustable peg system

3   Managed floating

After the collapse of the Bretton Woods system, the world entered a system of 'managed floating'. Currencies had no fixed exchange rates. Yet governments still had their own view of the limits beyond which they did not wish to see their currencies go, so they still stepped-in, in the manner shown in Diagram 20.1, to affect their exchange rates. For example, when sterling sunk from the official level of $2.60 it had just before it started to float in 1972, to $1.57 in October 1976, and the government stepped in. In 1978–79 sterling rose almost to $2.30, and the government was equally alarmed at the effect on export prices, so it took action to hold the exchange rate down.

4   Free floating

This, the 'purest' form of floating exchange rates, is generally impracticable, except for short periods, because of the instability likely to arise.

Post-war developments in the world monetary system

Bretton Woods

Until the 1930s the world operated under the *Gold Standard*. Countries could only issue currency equivalent to the amount of gold in their reserves (originally, of course, coins were actually made out of gold). International payments were often made in gold and currencies were priced in terms of gold at so many pounds, dollars, francs etc per ounce of gold. A small band of fluctuation was allowed.

As with all basically fixed systems, domestic policies were tied to exchange rate obligations. Fiduciary issues of money were not possible. When the world slump tightened its grip from 1929 onwards, countries found they could not issue enough money to relieve the unemployed. The desire to alleviate poverty and the wish to restrict imports and raise exports to create jobs caused the UK to devalue (ie leave the gold standard) in 1931. Other countries followed, competitive devaluations resulted and a floating system resulted.

The Bretton Woods Conference in 1944 wanted to prevent such unproductive competitive devaluations and trade restrictions, and thought that the best way to achieve this was to restore fixed exchange rates. There was not enough gold to finance world trade, though, and countries had begun to trade in currencies in the 1930s, usually the dollar, or (in the case of the British Empire, mainly) in sterling. Thus, the Bretton Woods Conference of the world's leading nations set up the *Gold Exchange Standard*. Currencies were to be measured against the dollar, but the dollar was fixed at $35 per ounce. The British plan (the 'Keynes Plan') of creating a new international currency to replace gold (Keynes called it 'bancor') was rejected as too revolutionary and the American 'White Plan' was accepted. The USA was particularly worried as to who would control a new currency like bancor.

Bretton Woods also set up the *International Monetary Fund* (IMF). Each member (there were 39 in 1947, 140 in 1980) paid a quota, according to its relative wealth, into the IMF pool, a quarter in gold and the rest in its own currency. Countries faced with the threat of having to devalue ('fundamental disequilibrium') could borrow from the pool up to 125 per cent of their quota under increasingly stringent terms. The first 25 per cent could be regarded as part of a country's reserves and could be drawn automatically; the rest had to be approved by the IMF; interest rates rose and conditions were usually imposed. Six more quotas were called for from members by 1980 and the quotas were changed as countries' relative wealth changed. Of course, some currencies lie dormant in the pool, others are more popular.

Devaluation of more than 10 per cent needed IMF approval, but this clause was never invoked mainly because discussions about devaluation would be likely to hasten it because of speculative rumour.

It took more than ten years from the start of the IMF's existence in 1947 before countries abandoned their restrictions on convertibility of currencies. Indeed, the UK did not fully abolish exchange control until 1979. Similarly, trade restrictions have continued. Marshall Aid from the USA was used to restore Europe's fortunes and the IMF was not really used for borrowing until the mid-1950s.

As world trade did eventually recover and trade and exchange restrictions were diminished, great pressure was put on the dollar, in which many transactions were done, and on sterling, also commonly used by Commonwealth countries. USA deficits were needed to finance the world's needs. There was, in fact, a shortage of international money.

One solution would have been to raise the gold price. As a scarce asset, gold was in demand, so in 1968 a *Two-Tier Gold System* was set up – gold would remain at $35 per ounce for official dealings, but float freely in the speculative market. Not surprisingly, gold illegally found its way from one market to the other.

The second solution was to invent a new currency, but this was still too radical an idea. A compromise was reached in 1970 with the creation of *Special Drawing Rights* (SDR's). Each IMF member was allocated extra borrowing rights above its quota. For instance, if the UK wanted to borrow dollars, the UK's SDR's would fall, but the USA's would rise until repayment (plus interest) was made. SDR's were allocated, equivalent to 5 per cent total world reserves, in 1970, 1971 and 1972, but disagreements concerning the allocation meant that no more were created until 1979, 1980 and 1981. By 1980, SDR's were no more than the equivalent of one fiftieth of foreign currency reserves and one thirtieth of gold reserves.

Despite these patchwork moves, the Bretton Woods system was cracking. 'Rescue operations' by central banks were increasingly being mounted to prevent devaluations by several countries. Nevertheless, devaluations and revaluations were taking place as countries found that they could no longer subject their domestic policies to the requirement of keeping a fixed exchange rate. The *Smithsonian Agreement* of December 1971 devalued the dollar to $38 per ounce and widened the band of allowed fluctuations around parity, but this rescue operation failed. In June 1972 sterling floated (and promptly sank); in 1973 the dollar was devalued to £42 per ounce of gold; the Two-Tier Gold System was abolished and in 1976 the official world gold price was abolished. Thus, the dollar was floating and there was no longer a fixed measure of value in the international monetary system. The dollar could no longer support the system.

The post-Bretton Woods system

Since the mid-1970s countries have no longer had to disrupt interest rates in particular and domestic policies in general in order to maintain a fixed exchange rate. The burden of adjustment has not necessarily fallen on those countries whose position has declined relative to others, which seemed to be the case under Bretton Woods. Yet speculators have had a field day and there have been wide fluctuations. Sterling has been below $1.60 and above $2.40 and its fluctuations against currencies other than the dollar have been even greater. The gold price reached a peak of $835 per ounce in January 1980, so that gold, hitherto of declining importance, suddenly became more important when gold holders found their assets increasing in value by hundreds of per cent.

The IMF has increased its pool via higher quotas; SDR's have revived; conferences have been held to try to restore a fixed rate system, but little has been achieved. Nothing has been invented to replace the dollar, though the role of gold could revive, now it is so valuable, and the world seems too volatile to allow a fixed rate system to be maintained, even if it could be created, except within very wide bands each side of parity. 'Managed floating' seems somewhat similar to a wide band system, anyway.

The sudden rise in wealth of the OPEC countries stemming from big rises in oil prices has caused a liquidity problem. The IMF has played its part in getting OPEC countries to recycle their money to the rest of the world, though the volatility of this money is still a destabilising feature, particularly causing interest rate competition between would-be recipients which may not be in the best interests of their domestic needs. Yet this liquidity problem is not as severe as the problem of having no measure of value in the international monetary system since the dollar was floated. One of the functions of money is to act as a measure of value: the international monetary system has no such measure.

For instance, sterling is still expressed in terms of the dollar, but the dollar itself is floating. There is no measuring-stick except the awkward system of comparing a country's currency to a 'weighted basket' of other currencies. Thus, to find out whether sterling is rising or falling it is necessary to compare its movement to that of the average movements of other major countries, each weighted according to its importance. Some countries have tried to express their currencies in terms of SDR's – but SDR's are measured against a weighted basket of five currencies.

The European monetary system

When the Smithsonian Agreement established wider bands of 2¼ per cent each side of parity in 1971 ('The Tunnel'), several European countries tried to keep their currencies fixed in relation to each other. They would float in a bloc ('The Snake') within these bands. This was called the '*Snake in the Tunnel*' system. It failed because countries could not keep in the snake, or even in the tunnel! The UK could only stay in the system for a month; France made three attempts to stay in, but failed.

The scheme was revived in 1977 and a new '*Supersnake*' was agreed in 1978 and came into operation in March 1979. All the members of the EEC joined, except the UK. Currencies are fixed within 2 per cent of parity (except 6 per cent for Italy). In addition, a fund was set up, financed by deposits from members who put in 20 per cent of their reserves. Loans can be obtained from this fund. A measure of value was created, called an 'ECU' (*European Currency Unit*). The ECU is measured against a weighted basket of the currencies of the EEC members (including sterling), weights to be changed when a country's value changes in real terms. The ECU will, it is hoped, eventually become the reserve asset of the EMS and inter-government dealing with take place in it.

The EMS shows a remarkable similarity to the IMF/Bretton Woods system – a fund, parity system, unit of account and measure of value. The UK was unwilling to join because it feared it would not keep within the 6 per cent band (ironically, sterling rose dramatically in 1979–80) and was worried about the system creating 'First and Second Division' currencies in the EEC. Critics in Europe see evidence of a continuing lukewarm attitude in the UK to the EEC and a looking outwards towards the dollar on the UK's part. The EMS, of course, excludes the dollar deliberately.

In its first two years, the EMS worked well, creating more stability than in any year since 1972. Some agreed small revaluations and devaluations have take place, but there have been no major crises.

The world outside the EMS has not sunk into disaster, either. Feeling still favours a return to a fixed system of exchange rates, but achievement of this seems unlikely. A fixed system would not, in any case, necessarily remove instability and speculative pressure or increase liquidity or stability if the agreed rates or measure of value could not be adhered to by everyone. There are many problems with the post-Bretton Woods system, but the floating rate system has demonstrated a remarkable capacity to absorb the shocks administered to it.

Summary

1 Exchange rates are an integral part in the cost of an import or export.
2 Exchange rates are determined by relative purchasing power capital flows, asset demand and speculative pressure. A country's economic performance and political changes can particularly affect this speculation. Governments may also act to alter their exchange rates.
3 Foreign exchange markets have some of the features of a perfect market.
4 Neither completely fixed nor floating exchange rates are feasible; the post-war system was basically fixed and has been replaced by a floating system.
5 The Bretton Woods system collapsed because of lack of liquidity and strains on the dollar as trade outstripped money supply.
6 The European Monetary System has restored a fixed system amongst some countries, but the world in general seems destined to continue a managed floating system.

7 The floating system has not solved liquidity problems and has the great problem of a lack of a stable measure of value, but it has not been as disastrous as was expected.

22 The United Kingdom and the European Community

Evolution of the European Economic Community

On January 1st 1973, three countries commenced their membership of the EEC, namely the United Kingdom, Denmark and Eire. These three, plus Norway, had completed successful negotiations in 1971, but a referendum in Norway had rejected membership. Referendums in Denmark and Eire expressed approval; one was not held in the UK because the Government claimed that the policy of joining was in its manifesto when elected and therefore had been approved already.

The EEC had been in existence since 1957, when six countries, France, West Germany, Italy, Belgium, the Netherlands and Luxembourg signed the *Treaty of Rome*. The UK had made unsuccessful applications to join in 1961 and 1967. Thus, the original members had been in the EEC for fifteen years before it was enlarged. The Community widened its boundaries again in 1981 when Greece was admitted (though a change of government in Greece threatened early withdrawal). The organization also decided to drop the word 'Economic' and call itself the 'European Community.'

The Community is often known as the 'Common Market' which is an amalgam of three organisations, the European Coal and Steel Community (ECSC) set up in 1952, and the Economic Community and Euratom (for co-operation in the peaceful uses of atomic energy) which were both created in 1957. Apart from some pious sentiments in the preamble to the Treaty of Rome, the Common Market is ostensibly an economic rather than a political organisation. Yet its origins are clearly political, springing from the aftermath of the Second World War, when it was resolved to end the divisions, especially between France and Germany which had helped to cause such bloodshed in the first half of the century. The fear of Russian expansionism after the setting-up of Communist regimes in Eastern Europe also accelerated the moves towards unity in Western Europe. Several organisations were set up, the most important being the military alliance, NATO, in 1949, others being mainly talking-shops, like the Council of Europe (1949).

The economic sphere was not neglected. Belgium, the Netherlands and Luxembourg formed the Benelux customs union in 1946. The Organisation for European Economic Control (OEEC) was created to assist post-war recovery and to help in the distribution of Marshall Aid from the USA. Europe relied greatly on the USA for assistance and both the American economy and the much-needed dollar dominated the post-war world. Some countries wanted to break away from American domination, at least in the economic sphere, and some even saw future possibilities of European Union or Federation – a powerful third force, politically and economically. Nagging fears of possible retreat into isolation by the USA as had happened after the First World War, also existed.

The results of this were first the formation of ECSC, dealing with the most vital products at that time of coal and steel, and secondly the Treaty of Rome itself. Although the EEC was almost exclusively concerned with economic matters, there is no doubt that some people saw it as the first step towards eventual political union amongst the peoples of Western Europe.

Main features of the Treaty of Rome

1 The member countries form a *free trade area*.
2 The members erect a common tariff against the outside world, thus forming a *customs union*.
3 There is a common agricultural policy specifically designed to protect the interests of the agricultural sector.
4 Labour, capital and enterprise should be able to move across frontiers and be employed without restriction or discrimination.
5 Treaties of Association should be signed with developing nations, especially former colonies of member states.
6 There should be a movement towards common policies in the social sphere, energy and transport.
7 Fair competition shall exist and members shall not subsidise their own industries to the detriment of other members.
8 Monetary Union shall eventually be achieved, possibly even including the use of a common currency.

The first three main features were achieved fully after a transitional period by 1958. By 1979, 57 countries had signed Treaties of Association via the Lomé Convention, and many others had signed specific trade treaties with the Community. Movement towards monetary union began with the foundation of the European Monetary System in 1979. Although progress was slow in some areas, notably in achieving common social policies, and the infamous Common Agricultural Policy was a bone of contention, the EEC made great strides in its first quarter century, at least towards achieving its economic objectives of achieving independence from the USA, stimulating trade between its members and increasing its wealth and technological development. Four new members had been admitted and several others, led by Spain, were wishing to join.

The Community has a permanent machinery of government.

Decisions are made by the member-governments. There is a Council of Ministers (one from each country) and also frequent and regular meetings between Heads of Governments, Finance Ministers, Agriculture Ministers, Industry Ministers and others who meet regularly to discuss specific matters. The right of veto still exists.

There is a parliament (410 members before the admission of Greece), directly-elected for the first time in 1979, but its powers are more limited than those of most national parliaments. It does question ministers and officials and discusses the Budget, but its powers of action are limited.

The Community has its own Civil Service – the Commission. Members appoint either one or two Commissioners, according to the country's size, who are given specific areas to cover, such as agriculture, regional aid, industry or foreign relations. Commissioners prepare policies for the Council and carry out the Council's instructions and, like top civil servants, wield considerable power and influence. For instance, it was Commission President Roy Jenkins who did much to revive the issue of monetary union in the late 1970s.

There is also a Court of Justice, to hear cases concerning possible violations of the Treaty of Rome, a Regional Fund, Social Fund, Investment Bank and other minor organs.

The UK's attitude to the Community

The UK declined to take part in the negotiations setting-up the ECSC and the EEC. The UK did not shed its colonial role until the 1960s. During the 1950s it still exercised a world role, politically, economically and even militarily. Sterling was still a reserve currency. The UK still claimed a 'special relationship' with the USA, stemming largely from the War; the American President from 1952–60 was Eisenhower, former Head of the Allied Armies in Europe during the War. The UK's trade was still largely with the Commonwealth; food, fuel and basic materials were imported and manufactures exported.

The position of the UK was changing, however. Tables 22, 1a and 1b show how the pattern of trade was changing between the mid-1950s and the mid-1960s, particularly with regard to imports. More manufactures were being imported; Western Europe was clearly now the UK's major trading partner. As early as 1961 the UK made an attempt to join the EEC. The economic troubles of the UK in the 1960s (eg the constant sterling crises and eventual devaluaton in 1967) and its lingering connections with the Commonwealth and the USA caused France to veto both these applications.

As the newly independent countries sought greater political and economic independence from the UK, and as the close relationship with the USA declined, the UK realised its destiny now lay more with Europe, and a final successful application was made in 1971. The UK saw a final chance for the UK's industrial sector to revive, faced with a sophisticated market of more than 200 million relatively rich consumers.

Table 22.1 The changing pattern of UK visible trade
a) *By area*

Area	% Imports (cif)			% Exports (fob)		
	1955	1965	1979	1955	1965	1979
Western Europe	25.7	35.8	59.8	28.9	41.8	58.2
of which,						
EEC[1]	12.6	23.6	43.1	15.0	26.3	41.8
North America	18.5	19.6	12.8	12.0	14.8	11.3
Other developed	14.2	11.9	6.1	20.5	14.8	5.8
Japan	0.6	1.4	3.1	0.6	1.1	1.4
Total developed	59.4	67.4	78.7	61.4	71.4	75.3
Centrally-planned	2.7	4.4	3.2	1.7	2.9	2.8
OPEC	9.2	9.8	7.0	5.1	5.6	8.9
Other developing	28.7	18.4	11.1	31.8	20.1	12.8
Total	100	100	100	100	100	100

[1] EEC refers to the original 6 members in 1955 (although the Community was not set up until 1958) and 1965, and included Denmark and Eire for 1979 figures.

Source: J S Metcalfe: Foreign Trade and the Balance of Payments, in *The UK Economy* ed. A R Prest and D J Coppock, 8 edition, Weidenfeld & Nicolson, 1980 p 129.

b) *By product*

	% 1955	1965	1977
Exports			
Engineering products	36.5	43.5	40.4
Semi-manufactured goods	29.7	26.8	23.7
Other manufactures	12.6	13.2	20.3
Food, beverages, tobacco	6.5	6.6	6.7
Basic materials	5.6	4.0	2.7
Fuels	4.6	2.7	3.4
Miscellaneous	4.5	3.0	2.8
Imports			
Industrial materials	47.9	43.1	36.5
Food, beverages, tobacco	36.2	29.7	16.1
Fuel	10.4	10.6	14.2
Finished manufactures	5.2	15.3	31.9
Miscellaneous	0.3	1.2	1.3

Source: Ibid pp 130 and 131

In 1960, seven countries including the UK, had signed the *Stockholm Convention*, creating the *European Free Trade Area*. The UK favoured free trade, but baulked at the EEC's common tariff and agricultural policy. Yet the small countries in EFTA (Denmark, Sweden, Norway, Switzerland, Austria, Portugal, plus later Finland and Iceland) offered limited market opportunities and the UK decided to take the plunge and agree to accept all aspects of the Treaty of Rome. No referendum was held until 1975 when a change of government in the UK led to Harold Wilson re-negotiating Edward Heath's original terms of entry. A referendum was then held as to whether the UK should *remain* a member, producing a two-to-one majority amongst the 65 per cent of the adult population who voted. Yet the UK has never seemed to be fully-integrated with the EEC, with constant expressions of dissatisfaction and a vehement lobby in favour of leaving. Much of the criticism has been directed at the Common Agricultural Policy (CAP).

Features of the common agricultural policy

When the EEC was founded, more than 25 per cent of its population was engaged in agriculture; even in 1980, over 10 per cent were in that sector (Eire and Italy still being well-above average with 24 per cent and 16 per cent respectively). In the UK, the figure is less than 3 per cent. Europe's agricultural industry contains a considerable backward sector and a high age-structure. Article 39 of the Treaty of Rome lists the CAP's aims as being:

a) to increase productivity by promoting technical progress;
b) to ensure a fair standard of living for the agricultural community;
c) to stabilise markets;
d) to ensure the availability of supplies;
e) to ensure reasonable prices.

In order to achieve these aims, over 70 per cent of the EEC Budget goes to support agriculture. The main features of the CAP are as follows:

1 The main vehicle is the European Agricultural Guarantee and Guidance Fund (*FEOGA* – Fond Europeéne d'Orientation et de Garantie Agricole).
2 FEOGA spends about 30 per cent of its funds on 'Guidance', including assisting retirements, amalgamations and modernisation, but the other 70 per cent goes on 'Guarantee'. Farmers are guaranteed that their produce will be bought at a certain price. For most products, a *Threshold Price* is set – the lowest import price plus levies. Transport costs are then added to find the *Target Price*. If the price of the product falls about 7 per cent below the Target Price, then FEOGA intervenes at the *Intervention Price*. Diagram 22.1 shows this. FEOGA intervenes and buys the surplus supply, ab in the diagram.

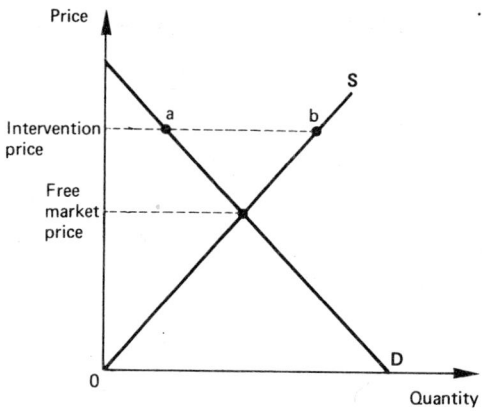

22.1 The CAP guaranteed price system

These surpluses can be huge; in 1979 there was a 20 per cent surplus of milk powder and a 25 per cent sugar surplus. Dairy produce surpluses occur every year; cereals, fruit, vegetables and beef 'mountains' have also occurred, plus 'lakes' of wine and olive oil. These surpluses are stored, if possible, or converted (eg to animal fodder); some are destroyed. All eventually need to be destroyed because of deterioration or sold on world markets (at world, not Community prices) unless there is a Community shortage in a subsequent year requiring stocks to be released. Community prices are also often well above world prices. For instance, in 1977 target prices were 204 per cent above world prices in wheat, 192 per cent above in beef, 176 per cent in sugar, 401 per cent in butter and 571 per cent in milk powder.

The CAP misallocates resources by encouraging surpluses. The more efficient and large-scale producers benefit more than the struggling farmers the policy was aimed to help. The UK, roughly 50 per cent self-sufficient in food in 1973, was 70 per cent so in 1981. The policy is also extremely expensive, both in the cost of subsidies and storage and the prices which consumers have to pay.

Before joining the Community, the UK mainly used a system of *Deficiency Payments* to support agriculture. Farmers were guaranteed a price, but the difference between the market price and the guaranteed price was paid by the government; the consumer paid the market price. Farmers were also issued with quotas; the deficiency payments would not apply to an unlimited level of production. The quota system also applied to Marketing Boards for products which farmers sold to a government marketing agency.

3 The Target Prices are fixed each February, before the actual output is known. Prices are fixed in terms of European Units of Account, then translated into domestic currencies at the prevailing

rates. These currencies are known as *Green Currencies*. Between February and harvest-time, of course, currencies float. Thus, there is a divergence between the Green Currencies and the exchange rates prevailing at the time the products are produced and sold. Thus, in 1973, *Monetary Compensation Amounts* (MCA's) were introduced to assist countries who suffered from a divergence between prevailing rates and Green rates. These MCA's subsidised countries near the bottom of the list when they sold to those higher up. Table 22.2 shows the MCA's for the years 1978–81 and demonstrates the dramatic recovery of sterling in this period.

Table 22.2 Monetary compensation amounts

	March 1978	*February 1979*	*February 1980*	*February 1981*
W Germany	+ 7.5	+ 10.8	+ 9.8	+ 8.8
Benelux	+ 1.4	+ 3.3	+ 1.9	+ 1.7
Denmark	0	0	0	0
Eire	− 5.7	− 3.0	0	0
France	− 21.5	− 10.6	− 3.7	0
Italy	− 26.1	− 17.7	− 2.3	− 1.0
UK	− 33.6	− 28.2	0	+ 18.2

Source: The Economist 9 February 1980 and 8 February 1981

The UK's problems concerning the Community

Despite a five-year transitional period, some special concessions and a re-negotiation of the terms in 1975, the UK has had a battle with its partners over several issues including these:

1. *Budget contributions*

   The UK's contributions to the Community Budget have risen, but the relative strength of the economy compared with the rest of the Community has declined. Thus, the UK has objected that its contributions are too high. The unfavourable movements of sterling have sometimes exacerbated the problem. In only one year has the UK made a net monetary gain from its membership of the Community as is shown in Table 22.3. By 1980 the UK was the third poorest member, but was paying the second largest contribution. Eventually, refunds of £762.5 million were negotiated for 1981 in return for an agreement on the raising of farm prices. Despite some valid problems, much of the UK's attitude seems to regard the Community as a fund from which one should expect to take out more than one puts in each year.

2. *The CAP*

   As Table 22.4 demonstrates, agriculture takes three quarters of the Budget. The UK sees little advantage in the CAP. Food prices have risen, expensive surpluses have to be bought and kept, cheaper imports have to pay the tariff – a classic case of *Trade Diversion* (see Chapter 19, p 178). The CAP is most unpopular, especially with consumers, but no worthwhile reforms have been achieved and its wastefulness continues.

Table 22.3 The UK's net budget contributions to the community

	£m
1973	111
1974	37
1975	− 45
1976	178
1977	481
1978	822
1979	829
1980	1,199*

*later reduced by negotiation

Source: The Economist, 17 November 1979, p 24

3 *Regional aid*

The EEC Regional Fund was set up in 1975 (see Chapter 4, p 53), but is small (see Table 22.4). The poorer areas in most Community countries are rural ones whereas the UK has decaying industrial areas. Thus, most of the Community's regional aid is channelled through the CAP. The UK's domestic regional policy has also been criticised by members under the Fair Competition rules. Problems encountered by some European industries recently (eg French and Belgian steel) may change attitudes towards the Regional Fund.

Table 22.4 Community Finance, 1980

		%
Revenue		
	VAT contributions	49.4
	Agricultural levies	15.2
	Customs duties	35.4
Expenditure		
	Agriculture	74.5
	Administration	6.0
	Refunds	5.3
	Social policy	3.9
	Overseas aid and development	3.5
	Regional policy	3.4
	Research, industry, energy	2.0
	Operation of EMS	1.4

Source: British Economy Survey, Summer 1981, pp 38-9

4 *Fishing limits*
 The UK has attempted to extend its territorial waters to prevent over-fishing by other countries, including Community partners. Since its exclusion from the extended Icelandic waters early in the 1970s the UK's deep-sea fishing industry has almost collapsed. Despite provisional agreements, no final settlement had been reached by the end of 1981 and the UK's in-shore fishing industry was following the rapid decline of its deep-sea fishing industry. The problem is not only a Common Market one – other trawlers, especially from the USSR, are fishing heavily in the North Sea areas which the UK wishes to preserve for itself. An agreement was reached in late 1982, but was unacceptable to Denmark.

5 *Energy policy*
 Despite the common energy policy aims of the Treaty of Rome, the UK has resisted Community attempts to share in the profits of North Sea Oil.

6 *Mounting trade deficit*
 The trend already existing of increasing trade between the UK and Western Europe illustrated in Table 22.1 has, of course, continued since 1973 as the Table demonstrates. Trade diversion, especially in food, has raised imports. The UK imported 31 per cent of its total food imports from the Community in 1972 and this percentage had risen to 49 per cent by as early as 1975. Transitional period concessions were made for New Zealand, who relied greatly on the British market, and for Commonwealth sugar producers, but these were short-lived. The UK's visible trade with the Community was in surplus in 1970. By the mid-1970s, annual deficits greater than £2 billion were experienced. 1980 saw the UK's first trading surplus with the rest of the Community since joining, but this was largely because of oil. In the rest of the manufacturing sector the picture is bleak. The competition has not stimulated British industry so much as it has destroyed parts of it, but it must also be realised that much of the fatal competition has come from non-members like Japan, despite the common tariff.

7 *Monetary union*
 There seemed little prospect of action in this sphere when the UK joined, but the relatively sudden developments in the later 1970s resulted in the formation of the EMS in 1979: the UK decided not to join (see Chapter 21, pp 203–4). Although sterling has shed most of its world role it is still an important currency, affected by speculative pressures and hot money flows. Gyrations in sterling's exchange rate have worsened many problems, including those of budgetary contributions and green currencies.

8 *Political objections*
 This account is primarily concerned with economic factors, but it must be noted that there are objections to the Community on grounds of loss of sovereignty and unwillingness to accept the

precedence of Community laws over domestic ones.

Should the UK leave the Community?

There is a vocal lobby urging the UK to leave the Community and the Community gets much of the blame for the country's problems. It is impossible to know, of course, what the UK's situation would be now had it joined the Community earlier or not joined at all. Similarly, it is difficult to estimate the effects of leaving.

1 Presumably, food prices would fall; contributions to the CAP would cease; deficiency payments might be restored. Whether cheap Commonwealth food would pour back in is problematical. These countries have found other markets; the pre-1973 situation could not be restored precisely.
2 There is no guarantee that the fishing limits problem would be more easily solved outside the Community.
3 Community goods would not enter the UK so freely, but non-Community countries would not be faced with the common tariff – whereas UK exports to the Community would.
4 The UK would probably have to pay some compensation for leaving and might be faced with subsequent retaliation against British goods.
5 The UK may be a relatively poor man in a rich man's club, and may find the membership fees a problem – but is such a country strong enough to survive outside the Community? Does it need to belong to an organisation and be inside at least some tariff walls? Would support for such problems as sterling crises, be so readily forthcoming?

Entry into the Community provided the UK industry with a new challenge. The evidence suggests that this challenge has not been successfully met. Large sectors of industry have declined and it is not clear what is going to replace them. Inflation was in double figures and unemployment over 3 million in 1982. It would be as foolish to blame the Community for these ills as it would be solely to blame trade unions, governments or any other favourite target. The CAP has been bad for the UK; many of the other problems seem to be of the country's own making. That membership of the Community has been disappointing is clear; that life outside would be significantly if at all better has yet to be proved. As stated in Chapter 20, the UK's basic problems lie in its industrial structures and practices and cosmetic changes in exchange rates and trading rules do not really attack this problem.

Summary

1 The EEC was set up in 1957 ostensibly in the economic sphere, but also with unstated political motives.
2 As well as being a Free Trade Area, the Community is also a customs union and has a Common Agricultural Policy. It has permanent organs of government and administration, but member governments still possess the power of veto.
3 The UK declined to be a founder-member, but subsequently made three applications to join, eventually entering in 1973.
4 The Common Agricultural Policy swallows 75 per cent of the Community's Budget, much money being wasted in buying surplus production at prices well above a free market level.
5 The UK objects to the CAP because of its cost and the high food prices it forces consumers to pay.
6 Other problems for the UK include budget contributions, fishing limits, the role of sterling and the apparent uncompetitiveness of much of the country's industry.
7 There is no guarantee that leaving the Community would improve the UK's economic position or solve its problems.

Section eight Income distribution

23 Wages – the marginal revenue product theory and its application to the real world

The demand for labour – the marginal revenue product theory

It will be remembered from the very first page of Chapter 1 that there are four factors of production, namely land, labour, capital and enterprise, which earn incomes of rent, wages, interest and profits respectively. Each of these factors is traded in a market, just like a finished product – there are *Factor Markets* as well as *Product Markets*. In every industry, indeed every firm, there exists a demand schedule for each of the various factors of production and there is also a particular supply of them available.

The entrepreneur's demand for a factor of production depends on the value of that factor to him, ie the value of the factor's output. This value is called *'Revenue Product'* because it is a combination of the factor's production and the revenue which that production brings to the entrepreneur. The work done by the factor is valuable not so much in its physical quantity, but in the value of that quantity as reflected in the price at which the product is sold. This value depends on the demand for the good or service which the factor makes. Thus, demand for a factor of production is *Derived Demand*, derived from the demand of consumers for the product the factor makes (see Chapter 8, p 96).

In this chapter we will examine the Marginal Revenue Product Theory and apply it to one factor of production, labour. It must be remembered, though, that the theory can apply to *any* factor of production, not just labour.

The theory states that:

'An entrepreneur will demand a factor of production up to the point at which the value of the extra output of the last unit of the factor employed is equal to the extra cost of employing that unit'.

Thus, as long as a unit of labour brings in at least as much revenue to the entrepreneur as it costs to employ the person, he or she will be employed.

The value of the output produced by factors of production is known as 'Revenue Product'. *Total Revenue Product* (TRP) is total physical product (ie the volume of goods produced) multiplied by total revenue. *Average Revenue Product* (ARP) is average physical product multiplied by average revenue. As Chapter 10 (p 104) showed, we can generally assume that average revenue equals price, so ARP equals average product multiplied by price.

Marginal Revenue Product (MRP) is marginal physical product multiplied by marginal revenue – ie the extra revenue brought in as a result of the extra output of each successive unit of labour. Thus, according to the definition of the theory stated above, the demand for labour is represented by the MRP of each successive unit of labour. Diagram 23.1 shows the ARP and MRP schedules; the demand curve for labour is the MRP curve. In fact, leaping ahead slightly, it is only the *downward-sloping* part of the MRP curve which is the Demand curve. Table 23.1 helps to show this.

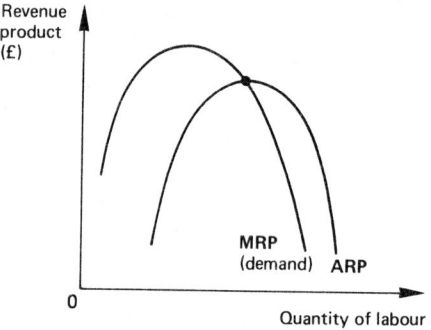

23.1 The average revenue product and marginal revenue product schedules

In Table 23.1, it is assumed that the firm sells its product in a *perfectly competitive market*, where demand is perfectly elastic and thus average revenue (price) equals marginal revenue. It is assumed that the price at which the good is sold is £20. The average and marginal product schedules rise and then fall because of the law of diminishing returns (Chapter 1, pp 13–14).

Table 23.1 Marginal revenue product theory as applied to a perfect product market
Price (AR) = MR = £20

No of men	Total physical product (TP)	Average physical product (AP)	Marginal physical product (MP)	Average revenue product (AP × Price)	Marginal revenue product (MP × MR)
				£	£
1	10	10	10	200	200
2	25	12.5	15	250	300
3	50	16.66	25	333	500
4	68	17	18	340	360
5	80	16	12	320	240
6	90	15	10	300	200
7	98	14	8	280	160
8	104	13	6	260	120
9	108	12	4	240	80
10	110	11	2	220	40

Suppose, in this example, 2 men were employed at a wage of £300 each, then the wage bill would be £600, but TRP would only be £500 (2 men multiplied by the ARP of £250). But if 4 men were employed at £300 each (the MRP of the 4th man is £300, if the MRP figures are plotted halfway between the number of men, the usual convention with all types of marginal analysis) then the wage bill is £1200 but TRP is £1360. Some of the men have to bring in more to the firm than they are paid in order that the firm can make a profit. This can only happen when the MRP schedule is falling.

The product market may be *imperfect*, however. In this case, average revenue (price) is *not* equal to marginal revenue (Chapter 12, pp 120-1). Thus, ARP and MRP diverge even more quickly, as Table 23.2. illustrates. The table assumes the same average and marginal product schedules as Table 23.1, but because the price falls when output rises, the ARP and MRP schedules will differ from Table 23.1. When TRP begins to fall (after the 7th man) then MRP actually becomes negative. If wages were £100, then approximately 5 men would be employed: a 6th man would only be employed if wages fell to approximately £50 in this example.

Table 23.2 Marginal revenue product theory as applied to an imperfect product market

No of men	Total product (TP)	Average product (AP)	Marginal product (MP)	Price £	Total revenue product (TRP)	Average revenue product (ARP) £	Marginal revenue product (MRP) £
1	10	10		20	200	200	
			10				200
2	25	12.5		19	475	237.5	
			15				275
3	50	16.66		18	900	300	
			25				425
4	68	17		17	1,156	289	
			18				256
5	80	16		16	1,280	256	
			12				124
6	90	15		15	1,350	225	
			10				70
7	98	14		14	1,372	196	
			8				22
8	104	13		13	1,352	169	
			6				-20
9	108	12		12	1,296	144	
			4				-56
10	110	11		11	1,210	132	
			2				-86

The supply of labour

The factors concerning the supply of labour for any particular job were explained in Chapter 3 (pp 34-7). Factors such as the age and sex distribution of the population, education and training, laws and customs (eg re child and female labour), taxation, mobility, motivation, pensions and unemployment benefit may all affect the number of people offering themselves for work and for particular forms of employment. Another vital factor, of course, is trade union power. Trade unions can force up wages or employment, restrict the labour supply by operating a 'closed shop', and affect retirement or redundancy terms. Governments can also affect the labour market through laws concerning redundancy or conditions of work or wage levels.

If the labour market were a *perfectly competitive* one, then all workers could be employed at the same wage level. Thus, the wage rate, being constant, would be the *average wage*. It would also be the *marginal wage* (ie the addition to the wage bill incurred by employing one more man). Diagram 23.2 shows this.

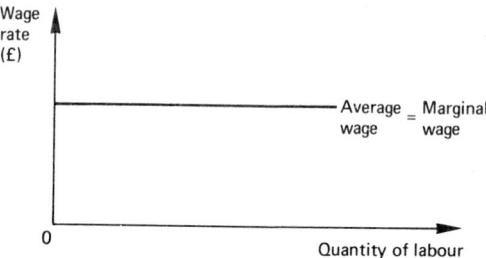

23.2 A perfect factor market

A more likely possibility is that the labour market would be *imperfect*; as more men and women are employed, the wage rate rises. There could be a shortage of labour, so that labour has to be won away from other firms by offering higher wages. If the last worker to be employed is paid more, then workers already in the firm would expect a wage rise to the same level, if they are doing the same job. Thus, the wage rate rises. The marginal wage rises faster. For example, if 5 women are each paid £200 per week, total wages are £1000. If a 6th woman is paid £210, and the first five have their wages raised to her level as a result of this, then the wage bill is £1260: marginal wage is £260 (£1260 − £1000) whereas average wage is £210. Diagram 23.3 shows this process.

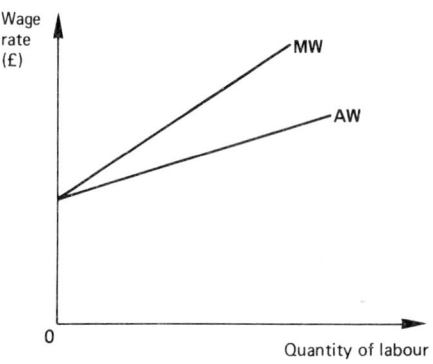

23.3 An imperfect factor market

Equilibrium in the labour market

Equilibrium in any market occurs where marginal revenue equals marginal cost, as explained in Chapter 10 (p 106). In the labour market, equilibrium is where *Marginal Revenue Product equals Marginal Wage*. Yet, as the factor market can be either perfect or imperfect, different situations can occur.

In Diagram 23.4, perfect competition exists in the factor market. Equilibrium is at point X, with OR wage rate paid and OM men employed.

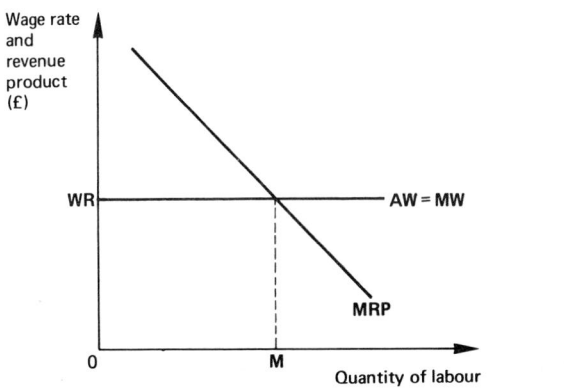

23.4 Equilibrium in a perfect factor market

In Diagram 23.5, there is an imperfect or *monopsonistic* influence in the labour market (ie there is not a perfectly elastic supply of labour). Equilibrium is at point X, with employment of OM. The wage rate must equal the average wage, assuming all workers receive the same wage rate. The employer than makes a surplus of WXYR when he employs OM men. Because of his degree of monospony power in hiring labour, he pays them less than their true MRP value to him. Yet the employees have some benefit from being employed by a monopsonist. The AW schedule shows what the wage rate would have been for all the various levels of employment. Between Z and Y, workers would have received *less* than OR wages, but because OM are employed, the wage rate has risen to OR. Thus, OM workers collectively receive a surplus of ZRY.

Factors affecting the wage determination in the real world

As is the case with virtually all laws in economics, wage determination in the real world does not work quite so simply or conveniently as the marginal revenue product theory suggests. There are clear differentials between what people earn in different jobs and indeed between people's earnings in the same job, and these differentials are not wholly explained by differencies in the value of what the workers produce.

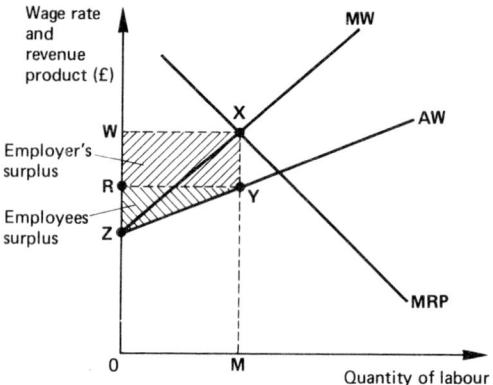

23.5 Equilibrium in an imperfect factor market

1 *Differentials between workers doing the same job*

Two workers doing the same job, like bus drivers working for the same company, teachers in the same school, bank clerks at adjoining tills, may not earn the same wage as each other. Possibly, one may have some extra responsibility (although this really means that he or she is not doing quite the same job as his or her companion) or one may actually be a more productive worker, for example a football club may pay its 'star' player more than other members of the team. Yet there are usually more mundane reason for these different wage levels, including the following:

a) age and experience

In several occupations, like banking, pay rises with age; in teaching, there are annual increments for several years, so that pay rises with experience. As division of labour suggested, experience and practice should improve performance and efficiency at least a certain amount.

b) special dangers or difficulty

Some people's jobs may take place in special conditions. People who work in London are often paid a 'London Allowance' because of the higher cost of living in the South-East and commuting to work; other employees of the same firm working elsewhere get paid less. Teachers who work in 'Educational Priority Areas' where attendance and discipline are poor or perhaps where many immigrants live, who have to be taught English before they can tackle the rest of the curriculum, are paid

extra allowances. These schools normally occur in inner urban areas. Paratroopers are paid slightly more than other soldiers because of extra danger in their job.
c) overtime or shift work
Some workers may do their job at 'unsocial hours'. Thus, night shift workers earn more than their companions who work during the day in the same factory. In many occupations, overtime can be earned, so those who work extra hours receive extra pay.

2 *Differentials between workers doing different jobs*

a) skills and abilities
Generally, skilled and qualified workers earn more than the unskilled, and non-manual earn more than manual workers, although this may not necessarily be true in every circumstance. This principle would seem to be in accordance with the marginal revenue product theory; the work of skilled workers is of more value of the entrepreneur than the work of the less skilled. Qualified and skilled people may also have had to give up earnings for extra years of study and need the incentive of eventual higher pay in order to make the sacrifice. Yet the skilled are not, as a matter of right, entitled to earn more. A skill has to be of use at a particular moment in time. If an industry is in decline, such as shipbuilding, even its skilled workers (eg riveters, welders) face redundancy. However high their skill, it commands little value because the price of the product is low so, through no fault of their own, the marginal revenue product of their labour is low. On the other hand, comparatively unskilled workers may earn a great deal if they work in a booming industry. Even mundane jobs in the oil terminals in the Shetland islands command wages far higher than in less profitable industries, though labour supply shortages are also a factor here.

One of the UK's problems in the 1960s and 1970s has been the erosion of differentials between skilled and unskilled workers. Apprenticeships have declined because the extra rewards expected in the future are not sufficient to justify foregoing present earnings. Similarly, it is being realised that a degree is not necessarily a 'meal ticket'. There is no reason why a degree should be a guarantee of higher earnings, of course, as it may not be connected with skill in performing a specific task in the world of production.

b) danger, unsocial hours
These elements apply, naturally. Coal miners, oil rig workers, steeplejacks and seamen may expect higher earnings than office workers because of the danger involved in their work. Car workers or train drivers on shift work, gas and electricity workers who must work at weekends, might also expect extra earnings. In

neither case (danger nor unsocial hours) are extra earnings necessarily guaranteed, however.

c) non-monetary factors

Some groups of workers may appear to earn relatively low incomes, but are compensated by non-monetary advantages. Teachers in universities, schools and colleges have longer holidays than other workers; some executives receive company cars, generous travel or entertainment allowances, school fees for their children to go to private schools, or other 'perks'. Other workers may receive subsidised lunches, company social and sports facilities or pay 'in kind' (workers in the confectionery industry may receive boxes of chocolates and sweets as a Christmas bonus). Workers who travel or reside abroad may receive generous leave periods; agricultural workers may live in 'tied' cottages at cheap rents, teachers in boarding schools live on the premises rent free; the list is endless. The great advantage of most of these arrangements is that, unlike direct monetary rewards, they are tax free. Generally, however, fringe benefits are higher for highly-paid workers than for the lower-paid.

d) Trade unions

Trade unions undoubtedly have a great effect on wage levels. *Collective bargaining* is clearly an advantage to workers. Instead of negotiating their own wage levels as individuals, they can bargain collectively through their union. Only about 50 per cent of employees belong to Unions in the UK, but those who do belong can usually expect to earn more than those in other jobs who do not belong to unions. Even without unions, workers can receive a 'surplus' above what they would have been prepared to work for, as Diagram 23.5 showed. Wages paid will depend mainly on the demand for labour, the MRP schedule. Yet unions can still affect both wage levels and employment levels, as Diagram 23.6 shows.

In Diagram 23.6, the free market equilibrium is at point X, producing OQ_1 labour and OW_1 wage rate. A union can force the employer to different points along this demand or MRP schedule. At point X itself, for example, a wage of OW_2 could be paid without reducing employment. Alternatively, wages could be pushed above OW_2, but employment will fall as employers move to the left of point X. Employers could be pushed to point Z, which will raise employment at the existing wage level. Both wages and employment could be increased by moving to point Y on the demand curve.

In the real world, the precise effect of unions on wages cannot be measured; it is impossible to know what wage levels might be in the absence of unions. Clearly, workers are stronger in bargaining collectively, however. Industrial action usually does force employers to concede more money. The extra wage cost is either passed on to the public in higher prices or perhaps the workforce is reduced in order to keep the total wage bill down. Thus, higher wages will reduce employment unless the extra wages are balanced by extra output or by a higher price of the output. This is in accordance with the shape of the MRP curve and thus with the marginal revenue product theory.

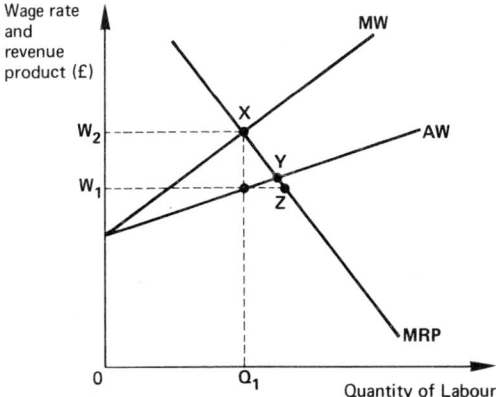

23.6 Influence of trade unions on the market

A fuller treatment of trade unions, whose duties and influence spread far beyond wage determination, will occur in the next chapter. The only other factor relevant at the moment is the operation of *closed shops* by unions, whereby only members of a specific union may work at a particular job. This reduces the labour supply available and, by simple demand and supply principles, keeps up wage rates. Employers, incidentally, do not necessarily oppose closed shops in all circumstances, because it is easier for them to negotiate with one union representing all the workers than with several unions or with a mixed union and non-union work force.

Trade unions tend, of course, to negotiate basic wage rates at a national level. Local plant bargaining usually results in local differences, however. Workers who are more productive (through their own efforts or the price their product commands) do receive more. Thus, Ford workers tend to earn more than those at BL, for example. The whole question of production and productivity is a problem in many industries, however, inasmuch that it is capital rather than labour which is really the productive factor. Workers may have low productivity through no fault of their own; their machinery may be poor or their working conditions bad (eg miners in some coal mines work in more difficult conditions than their compatriots in other mines).

e) Public or private sector
Traditionally, employees in the public sector tend to earn less than those in the private sector, particularly manual workers. This is partly because the government can impose its policies more closely on its own employees (eg the 1961–62 incomes policy was imposed on public sector but not private sector workers) and also because the public sector is mainly concerned with producing services, where output is difficult to measure. The trend changed in the later 1970s, however, as Table 23.3 shows. Non-manual workers in nationalised industries in particular were able to forge ahead of their equivalents in the private sector. This was due to the strength of workers in the power industries (gas, electricity, coal) and other vital sectors (transport, water and sewage). Actual or threatened industrial action by some of these workers greatly improved their earnings. Workers in other parts of the public sector are still notoriously badly-paid, however, particularly nurses, local government and hospital manual workers and some clerical grades – people with little industrial 'muscle'. The public sector is not so dependent on the profit motive, of course, and the dramatic decline in the profitability in the private sector of the later 1970s hit private sector earnings more than the more protected public sector.

Table 23.3 Comparison of earnings in public and private sector (selected years)
Public sector earnings as % of private sector earnings:

	1970	1974	1977	1980	1981
1 Central government:					
Manual	81	83	91	95	95
Non-manual	103	105	109	108	104
Total	102	106	112	111	108
2 Local government:					
Manual	78	81	84	91	91
Non-manual	102	103	107	98	106
Total	102	105	111	102	108
3 Public corporations:					
Manual	102	105	111	111	115
Non-manual	99	102	108	103	108
Total	98	101	107	105	109
4 Whole public sector:					
Manual	93.4	97.3	102.4	103.9	106.8
Non-manual	102.3	103.5	107.6	102.0	106.3
Total	100.0	102.7	107.2	105.3	108.4

Sources: Employment Gazette, December 1977 and New Earnings Survey each year 1978–81.

f) Regional differences and mobility

As mentioned in the London Allowance example, earnings can differ regionally, not only because of cost of living differences, but also because of unemployment differences. In high unemployment areas, workers may accept lower wages than those in areas where the opportunities to find other employment are greater. Mobility of labour tends to increase the differentials, increasing pressure on wages in expanding areas and leaving a hard core of the immobile unemployed elsewhere.

There is no official 'League Table' of earnings in the UK. The low paid try to climb up and those higher-up try to maintain their position. Thus, the competitive process raises wages all round, but rarely leads to one group permanently improving its position. Workers in one firm or job try to emulate others elsewhere who have gained a rise. No-one likes to see someone else, to whom they regard themselves as equal or superior, get ahead. Another common phenomenon in the UK is *wage drift*, whereby the growth of earnings is greater than the growth of wage rates, because of overtime and other 'extras'. Unions tend to negotiate on *wage rates* – but few people earn only the basic rate. Guaranteed overtime is by no means an unknown factor in wage negotiations.

The UK does not have a *National Minimum Wage Rate*, which some European countries do. Thus, some people are very low paid, especially part-time workers, notably women and youngsters. Children doing newspaper rounds and weekend or evening jobs are paid at lower rates than adults would accept. People not in unions are vulnerable, having little power. Workers in agriculture, textiles, catering and retail distribution are generally lower paid. Women and temporary workers abound in many of these trades. In 1978, 800,000 women and 100,000 men earned less than £40 a week for a full-time job.

A National Minimum Wage would seem to have more disadvantages than advantages, however. The poorly paid would not necessarily receive more money; instead they would lose their jobs if their MRP was not high enough to justify the higher wage. A National Minimum Wage would raise unemployment. It might also lead to more competition between workers. After all, no-one would want to earn the National Minimum – everyone would want to get off the bottom rung of the ladder.

The government and wages

The government plays a large part in wage settlements, not only in its role of employer. One third of the workforce are employed in the public sector but the government's influence also spreads to the rest of the employment sector. Government power is wielded through periodic impositions of Prices and Incomes Policies and through legislation concerning matters such as redundancies, dismissals and discrimination by employers on grounds of race or sex.

1 *Prices and incomes policies*

A prices and incomes policy aims to restrict the rises of prices and incomes to levels below those which would be attained in a free market. The usual method used is to pass a law restricting rises to a certain level or even forbidding them altogether. The policy may also include a formula for judging relativities between one sector and another, or for allowing rises under certain circumstances, for example giving automatic wage rises in accordance with rises in the Retail Price Index (so-called 'Indexation').

Prices and incomes policies may be used as part of a deflationary package to reduce inflation, especially if it is believed that high wages are a cause of inflation because producers pass on the higher wage bill to the public by raising their prices. Wage restrictions will also reduce consumers' spending power and prevent the pressure of increasing demand from raising prices. Prices and incomes policies may also be used to assist the balance of payments, as was the intention of the Labour Government's policy in the UK between 1966 and 1970. The ideas were to restrict consumption, thus reducing imports and releasing goods for export, and also to keep costs and thus prices down, increasing the competitiveness of the UK's products.

Prices and incomes policies can also be used to redistribute income, by helping the low paid while restricting the incomes of the more wealthy, or by encouraging productivity-based rises. Differentials can be narrowed by giving *flat-rate* incomes rises, or widened by granting *percentage* rises. For example, a man earning £5,000 pa relatively improves his position compared with a man earning £10,000 pa if they both receive a rise of £500 pa. On the other hand, a rise of 10 per cent per annum puts the richer man further ahead – his wage rises by £1,000 compared with the other man's £500.

Prices and incomes policies may also possibly preserve employment to the extent that an employer may not have to reduce his workforce as he might have done if he had had to concede a wage rise. On the other hand, restrictions on earnings may cause unemployment to the extent that spending power is restricted and firm's sales and profits are reduced. Cutting wages in the 1930s made the depression and unemployment worse, after all.

The prices and incomes policies of 1972–74 and 1976–79 were mainly used as attacks on inflation. These policies are not the only anti-inflationary policies available, however, as chapter 29 will show. Nor, indeed, are they the only possible policies available for assisting the balance of payments, redistributing wealth or preserving jobs. Nevertheless, these policies have been prominent in the 1960s and 1970s.

The main aim of prices and incomes policies is to control *wages*, which account for over 75 per cent of total costs. Yet unions will only accept wage controls if the government promises also to control not only non-wage incomes, such as rent, interest and profits, but also prices. Non-wage incomes can be controlled, but may work against government policy in other fields. Restricting interest rates and share dividends will deter investment and thus handicap efficiency and growth. Taxing profits will certainly not help industrial growth. A greater problem occurs with prices. National governments have little power to restrict import prices (except by constant juggling with exchange rates, which also has repercussions elsewhere). When OPEC raised oil prices by about 400 per cent in six weeks in 1973 the UK government was powerless to prevent the diastrous effects this had on its inflation rate – and on its prices and incomes policy. Yet governments have to try and control non-wage incomes and prices if they want wage control to succeed.

Wage control is difficult enough to achieve, anyway. Unions, through industrial action (actual or threatened) can resist it. Evasion is possible, for example by promotions, re-grading of workers, non-monetary awards and perks. Employers often co-operate with employees in evading the policy, especially if they are desperate to avoid a strike or if they can afford to pay. After all, these policies might prevent firms who can afford to pay or workers who have increased their marginal revenue product from respectively granting and receiving a rise. The allocative role of the free market (ie collective bargaining) is interfered with by an incomes policy. Earned rises are prevented, efficient firms are held back and factors of production are not encouraged to move from declining to growing sectors by the prospect of higher earnings. Any inteferences in free markets have this effect, of course, but the price paid may be thought to be worth if it other objectives, such as reducing inflation, are achieved.

One of the greater problems with prices and incomes policies is enforcement. What sanctions can be imposed if the restrictions are broken? Threats to fine unions or employers or take other action (the Labour Government of 1974–79 had a 'black list' of firms who broke the policy) are hard to enforce. The ultimate absurdity came in 1966 when the government punished one firm for paying too high a rise, but a union successfully prosecuted another firm for failing to pay a rise agreed before the policy started.

Another large problem of prices and incomes policies concerns what happens when they end. Some countries, notably Sweden, have had permanent policies to control wage rises; Labour Chancellor Dennis Healey envisaged this in the UK, but the unions would not accept this interference with their collective bargaining rights. Most policies have ended after about three years – and large wage claims have resulted. The classic example was in 1974, when in the year following the end of a three-year policy, wages rose at an average annual rate of 31.7 per cent. During that year, there was a voluntary policy (the 'Social

Contract') operating between government and unions. There have been several attempts at voluntary policies, as Table 23.4. illustrates. None has succeeded as well as the statutory, imposed policies. All governments seem to have prices and incomes policies, even if they are not statutory or openly admitted. In 1971-72, the Conservative Government tried to operate an unofficial 'n minus one' policy seeking to reduce public sector wage awards by 1 per cent compared with the previous settlement. In 1981-82 another Conservative Government tried to keep public sector awards to 4 per cent. Yet only a statutory policy succeeds – and mayhem seems to follow when the period of a statutory policy expires. There would seem to be an argument for a permanent policy, but politically this is not acceptable to the trade unions in the UK and could not be enforced, as the attempt to extend the 1975-79 policy demonstrated.

Because prices and incomes policies are somewhat arbitrary, exceptions are often allowed. Firms faced with cost rises they cannot absorb (for example, costs of imported raw materials or fuel) may be allowed to raise their prices. Wage rises above the limits laid down may be permitted under all sorts of circumstances. Indeed, the 1966-70 policy had so many exceptions allowed that virtually anyone could claim to be a 'special case'. Exceptions in past policies, as Table 23.4. shows, have included productivity, low-paid workers, labour retention problems, unsocial hours and the infamous comparability with other workers. Exceptions for comparability with similar workers are usually disastrous, leading to competitive league table climbing.

Productivity deals are often abused, mere promises of productivity improvements sometimes being accepted. Machines tend to be responsible for production to a greater extent than labour, anyway. Comparatively few workers are paid by results, or by 'piece rates', mainly because productivitiy is difficult to measure. Unions prefer 'time rates' or payment by the hour, week or year, regardless of work done. Many jobs, particularly service trades, are unsuitable for productivity deals. Miners have received extra pay for productivity in the later 1970s, but the deal was controversial because of differences in mining conditions in different coalfields. Although productivity is often not directly rewarded, promotions in administration, teaching or management for example, are indirectly related to it, if some sort of 'results' can be seen from a person's work. Nevertheless, productivity continues to be a controversial basis for pay awards.

Helping the low-paid or those with *special dangers* or *unsocial hours* is more acceptable for exceptional cases, though most people can find something especially nasty about their jobs if they think hard enough. Attempts to help the low-paid never bring permanent success. When differentials are reduced, the richer and stronger unions hit back to restore their advantages. The flat rate norms of 1975-77 were replaced by percentages in 1977 (as the table shows) because of union pressure.

Most policies have set up bodies to decide on exceptional cases – the *Prices and Incomes Board* of the 1960s, the *Pay Board* and *Prices Commission* (separate bodies) of the Health Government in the early 1970s and the *Comparabilities Commission* of 1979-80. The Comparabilities Commission had to compare public sector pay with the private sector, attempting to find equivalent jobs to ambulance drivers, hospital ancillary workers and school teachers among others. Pay and conditions had to be compared with a range of similar occupations. Any sort of comparability analysis is likely, of course, to lead to competitive leapfrogging.

The Heath Government attempted to reduce workers' fear by *indexing* earnings to the Retail Prices Index. After all, unions often base claims on rises in their members' cost of living. The Retail Price Index is not, of course, an accurate reflection of the cost of living, as explained in Chapter 18 (the miners embarrassed the Government in 1981 by basing a claim on the higher Tax and Price Index figures, which the Government had set up as a more accurate measure of the cost of living changes). Many workers negotiated indexation in 1973/4, receiving 40p per week for every 1 per cent rise in the Retail Price Index above 7 per cent. Although seemingly fair, the system of indexation is potentially inflationary as it causes wages to chase prices, thus pumping money into the economy. Indexation has been offered to several powerful groups, like gas and electricity workers, in return for a pledge not to strike, but the unions prefer the potentially higher gains of free collective bargaining. Weaker groups of workers might prefer indexation or a permanent wage mechanism which stops them from continuing to fall behind, however.

Incomes policies usually take the form of a period of *freeze* (often 6 or 12 months), than periods of a year with *'norms'*, which may contain criteria for exceptional cases. Needless to say, no worker will want less than the norm, which then tends to become a minimum rather than maximum level. The norms usually become more relaxed until the policy ends and the policy usually becomes less effective as the end approaches. In 1978 the Labour Government attempted for the first time both to have a formal Stage 4 *and* to reduce the norm for Stage 4. This was unacceptable to the Unions so both the policy and the next election in 1979 were lost.

Prices and Incomes Policies have many critics. Prices are difficult to control; incomes control tends to be somewhat arbitrary and inefficient. Yet free collective bargaining has hardly been ideal, either. In the short-run at least the policies certainly do affect wage determination, in the periods immediately before and after the policies as well as during them.

Table 23.4 Prices and incomes policies in UK 1945 to 1980

Policy	Period		Type of policy	Wage target	Exceptions
1 Wage freeze	February	1948-October 1950	Voluntary, but wage rises not allowed for cost pass through under margin controls	Zero norm	–
2 Wage and price plateau	March	1956-December 1956	Voluntary, undertakings on *price* stability from nationalised industries and certain private sector groups	–	–
3 Pay pause	July	1961-March 1962	Voluntary in private sector; imposed in public sector	Zero norm	Existing commitments honoured
4 Guiding light (a)	April	1962-March 1963	Voluntary	2-2.5%*	–
5 Guiding light (b)	April	1963-October 1964	Voluntary	3-3.5%*	–
6 Statement of Intent	April	1965-July 1966	Voluntary	3-3.5%	1 productivity bargaining 2 labour mobility 3 low pay 4 differentials out of line
7 Freeze	July	1966-December 1966	Statutory	Standstill plus rollback of previous agreements	–
8 Severe restraint	January	1967-June 1967	Statutory	Zero norm	1 productivity bargaining 2 low pay in exceptional circumstances 3 exceptional labour retention needs 4 gross anomaly correction
9 Relaxation	July	1967-March 1968	Statutory	Zero norm	as under 6
10 Ceiling policy	March	1968-December 1969	Statutory	Zero norm, but $3\frac{1}{2}\%$ ceiling	productivity bargaining
11 Range policy	January	1970-June 1970	Statutory	2.5-4.5%	1 productivity bargaining

12 N-1 policy	October	1971-September 1972	Voluntary	1% less than previous settlements	4 pay structure reorganisation 5 exceptional market requirements
13 Freeze (Stage I)	November	1972-March 1973	Statutory	Standstill	—
14 12 month rule (Stage II)	April	1973-November 1973	Statutory	£1 per week + 4%	1 equal pay 2 reduced standard hours if in excess of 40 hours 3 improvements in holidays if less than 3 weeks
15 Partial indexation (Stage III)	November	1973-February 1974	Statutory	7% (or £2.25) plus partial indexation	1 flexibility margin of 1% of the total wage bill 2 productivity/efficiency agreements 3 unsocial hours
16 Social contract	July	1974-July 1975	Voluntary	compensation for price changes between main settlements	1 low pay 2 elimination of discrimination particularly as regards women
17 Social Contract (Phase I)	August	1975-July 1976	Voluntary, but sanctions against non-complying companies	£6 per week up to £8,500	Equal pay
18 Social Contract (Phase II)	August	1976-July 1977	Voluntary, but sanctions	5%, with min-£2.50 max-£4.00	—
19 Social Contract (Phase III)	August	1977-July 1978	Voluntary, but sanctions	10%	—
20 Social Contract (Phase IV)	August	1978-February 1979	Voluntary, sanctions abandoned	5%	—
21 Concordat	February	1979	Voluntary	none, but loose agreement to reduce inflation rate to 6% by early 1980s	—

*All workers were not automatically entitled to the 'norm'. Claims based on cost of living, profit trends, comparability criteria *inter al.* were to be de-emphasised.

Source: The Cases for and Against Incomes Policy—the Empirical Evidence—J. T. Addison & J. Burton Supplementary Booklet to Audio Learning Discussion ECA 044. Audio Learning Ltd. 1979, p 9.

2 Other government legislation

The Labour Governments of 1964–70 and 1975–79 in particular introduced several laws (apart from Statutory Prices and Incomes Policies) which directly or indirectly affected the determination of wage levels. The *Redundancy Payments Act* of 1965 insists that redundant workers receive compensation in line with their years of service. This affects contracts and conditions of work and puts firms into a cleft stick when faced with whether to make workers redundant or pay them an excessive wage – which is more expensive?

The *Equal Pay Act* (1970) and *Race Relations Act* (1976) aimed to improve the employment prospects and pay of disadvantaged groups – women and immigrants (and indeed British-born black people). Women's pay has gradually begun to catch up, as Table 3.1. illustrated. The *Employment Protection Act* (1975) includes clauses on lay-off pay, maternity pay and dismissal, which affect wage bargaining. The 1980 *Employment Act* repealed some of the Employment Protection Act and also discouraged closed shops, which may affect union power. Legislation concerning industrial action will be dealt with in the next chapter but anything which affects union powers or collective bargaining will have an influence on wage determination.

Thus, in the real world, there are many influences, notably government legislation and trade union action, which distort the labour market. Nevertheless, the basic elements in the marginal revenue product theory remain valid. Employers cannot for long afford to pay their employees more than the value of their employees' output, even though in the UK, like many other countries, 'Wages are usually determined by institutions, traditions and muscle'.[1]

Summary

1 An entrepreneur's demand for a factor of production is derived from the demand for the product which the factor helps to make.
2 An entrepreneur's demand for a factor depends on the value of the extra production contributed by that factor – its marginal revenue product.
3 In a perfectly competitive factor market the wage rate will remain constant, so the marginal wage (the addition to the wage bill incurred by employing one more unit of labour) will equal the wage rate. In an imperfect market, marginal wage will rise faster than the wage rate.
4 Employers will earn a surplus on the units of labour employed in equilibrium except when the factor market is perfect. Labour will also receive a surplus in an imperfect factor market.
5 Wage differentials in the real world are explained by factors concerning the job (eg dangers), the worker (eg skill, experience) and interferences in the market from trade unions and the government.

6   Unions can push up either wages or employment or perhaps both.
7   Prices and incomes policies interfere with free collective bargaining. They are used as part of a deflationary package or to assist the balance of payments, aiming to reduce production costs.
8   Prices are almost impossible to control; incomes control usually succeeds for a short time, but a 'catching-up' process often occurs when the policy ends.
9   Evasions and 'exceptional cases' reduce the effectiveness of incomes policies.
10 Attempts to use incomes policies to help the low-paid usually achieve only limited and temporary success.

Footnote

1 Economist: Schools Brief: 'The Market for Work', 30 October 1976.

24 Trade unions and labour relations

The functions of trade unions

Trade unions are a common target when blame is being apportioned for the UK's economic ills. Certainly, unions have many faults, but it is foolish to ascribe blame to them indiscriminately. The UK's strike record is variable, but by no means disastrous. Between 1969 and 1978 the UK lost through strikes, on average each year, 472 days per 1000 employees. Although figures for France (205 days), Japan (133), West Germany (53) and the Netherlands (36) were noticeably lower, many countries could produce higher annual losses. For instance, worse figures were produced in the USA (533 days), Austrialia (638), Eire (731), Canada (927) and Italy (1625). Table 24.1. shows the UK's figures for the period 1967-81. Large fluctuations can be seen; the years 1972 and 1979 stand out, with the highest number of days lost since the General Strike of 1926, but other years, like 1975 and 1976 show many fewer days lost. The number of stoppages in 1980 was the lowest since 1941. It is also worth noting that about 30,000 working days are lost each year because of illness and injury.

Trade unions are not solely concerned with industrial action over wage claims. A Royal Commission under Lord Donovan which had been set up to investigate unions issued its report in 1969, identifying these aims as being expressed by unions:

1 *Terms and condition of employment*

Wages and salaries, plus overtime, bonuses and other financial matters are clearly important ot unions, but many more factors are within their concern. Hours, holidays, pensions, physical working condition, safety, promotion prospects, dismissal and redundancy procedures, non-monetary advantages – all these are matters with which unions are concerned. Industrial actions, especially short-lived local stoppages are just as likely to occur over matters like tea breaks, shift work, staffing levels, dismissals or changes in job description as they are over wages issues.

Table 24.1 Industrial stoppages in the UK, 1967-81

	Number of stoppages	Number of working days lost
1967	2,116	2,783
1968	2,378	4,719
1969	3,116	6,925
1970	3,906	10,908
1971	2,228	13,589
1972	2,497	23,923
1973	2,873	7,145
1974	2,922	14,750
1975	2,282	5,914
1976	2,016	3,509
1977	2,703	10,378
1978	2,471	9,404
1979	2,080	29,474
1980	1,330	11,964
1981	1,280	4,196

Sources: Annual Abstract of Statistics, 1982 and Tree, N., 'The Year in Review 1980-81', Anforme Ltd., 1981, p 19, and 'The Year in Review 1981-82, p 24.

2 Job security and full employment

Unions are clearly concerned with keeping their members at work and the trade union movement as a whole places great priority on obtaining full employment nationally. Unions traditionally have placed employment above wages preferring short-time working to redundancies. Their policy was obviously coloured by memories of unemployment in the inter-war years. In the 1970s there seemed to be a harsher attitude for a time, wage rises being sought even at the expense of redundancies, but the increasing levels of unemployment in the late 1970s seemed to restore the full employment priority above large wage demands to some extent. Closed shops are, of course, a method by which unions try to maintain the employment of their members by keeping out non-members and also try to maintain wage levels by restricting the labour supply. Unions are also concerned closely with redundancy and dismissal terms and conditions in this context.

3 Improved social security

Unions are concerned to raise levels of social security, especially for the unemployed, low-paid and retired.

4 Industrial democracy and a voice in policy-making

Unions may seek greater control in the running of companies.

Worker-directors scarcely exist in the UK, unions tending to favour full nationalisation or, in a few cases, workers' co-operatives. Offers of appointing workers to the Board of Directors have usually been declined or regarded as a meaningless gesture which would place in an awkward position the worker appointed as director. Trade unions, of course, are responsible for providing most of the finances of the Labour Party and some unions sponsor Labour MP's. Thus, unions have a strong voice in policy-making at national level. The votes of the large unions dominate the Labour Party Conference and influence Party policy formulation, not only in the economic sphere but even in matters of Defence and Foreign Policy as well. There has been much debate concerning the power of unions in non-economic matters and their influence over the Labour Party and Labour Governments. It is generally thought that union pressure forced a Labour Government to drop an Industrial Relations Bill (and the Minister concerned) in 1969–70, for instance.

The structure of trade unions

In 1980 the trade union movement reached a peak of 12.2 million members, but the increasing unemployment caused some members not to pay their dues, so membership fell, for the first time since the War, between June 1979 and January 1982 by over a million. During this period employment in manufacturing fell by 1.3 million.

Although there are over 400 unions, the movement is dominated by six unions, which account for 50 per cent of the total membership. Table 24.2 shows the 'Top Ten' Unions. The general rise between 1970 and 1979 and subsequent dramatic fall can be seen. Also, the changes within the union movement are clear. Declining industries and unions of manual workers have lost members, while 'white collar' workers have increasingly become unionised, with the most spectacular rise being seen in the ASTMS, the Association of Scientific, Technical and Managerial Staffs. The smallest union in 1980, incidentally, was the Cloth Pressers with 30 members.

The largest unions tend to be relatively unskilled, manual and clerical, with the Engineers (AUEW) being by far the largest skilled workers' union.

About 200 unions, including the largest one are affiliated to the Trade Union Congress (TUC), an annual meeting first held in 1868. The TUC has a General Secretary and staff, but has little power over the member unions. The TUC is involved in negotiating with employers' organisations and government and its Secretary (Len Murray in recent years) is an influential figure (though several union secretaries, notably Clive Jenkins of ASTMS, are paid more).

Unions themselves have secretaries and staff, full-time except in the smaller unions. They hold their own conferences. The larger unions have regional, district and local officers. Yet much power is in the hands of the local branch and shop floor officials, the *shop stewards*. These people are often unpaid (though 4,000 were full-time in 1979 as opposed to only 1,000 in 1966) but work hard in recruiting, collecting dues, representing workers at shop floor level in negotiating with managerial staff, and liaising with union officials at higher levels. Shop stewards often lead short, unofficial strikes over local issues.

Each union has its own constitution. Some secretaries are elected for long periods; voting systems differ; some unions (like the miners) have strike ballots and have their votes counted by a neutral body. All the unions have their own system and structure and their own subscriptions.

Table 24.2 Trade union membership – the top ten (1981)

Union	Trade	Membership – thousands			
		1970	1979	1980	1981
TGWU	General	1,532	2,086	1,887	1,676
AUEW	Engineers	1,196	1,250	1,381	1,050
GMWU	Municipal Workers	804	967	915	866
NALGO	Local Government Officers	397	753	782	796
NUPE	Public Employees	305	691	699	704
ASTMS	Scientific, Technical, Managers	124	480	491	441
USDAW	Shop Workers	316	470	450	438
EETPU	Electricians	392	420	405	405
UCATT	Builders	227	349	312	299
NUM	Miners	297	289	257	245

Sources: *The Economist*, September 1981; *The Observer*, 4 April 1982.

The growth of the trade union movement

Trade unions grew in Britain slowly and despite setbacks. They were banned between 1799 and 1824 and even after that were often very restricted in what they were allowed to do. The skilled workers were the first to unionise, notably miners and engineers, and the mass of unskilled workers did not become unionised until the 1880s. Disputes and hard-won legislation gained unions legal status and protection for their officials and funds before the First World War, but the events of the 1920s hit the unions hard. The high unemployment of the interwar years and the failure of the General Strike in 1926 greatly reduced union powers and their membership halved between 1918 and 1939 from 8 million back to 4 million.

This early history still influences unions today. For instance, the desire of skilled workers to maintain differentials over the unskilled, demarcation disputes between unions, the desire to retain legal protection especially for hard-won rights such as picketing, all have their origins in the early years. Yet trade unions co-operated with the Labour Governments of 1945–51 which introduced socialist reforms such as nationalised industries and the National Health Service, and then shared in the recovery of prosperity in the 1950s. Only in the 1960s and 1970s did disputes become prominent again, partly because of squeezes imposed by Governments to cure the balance of payments deficit or inflation, and partly because unions at last began to realise their power in times of full employment. The inflation experienced in the 1970s certainly provoked unions into attempting to maintain their real incomes and the consequently large wage claims made the inflationary problem worse. Yet it was not only on the wages front where unions were active. The whole business of trade union rights came to the fore again.

The first significant event was the case *Rookes* vs *Barnard* in 1964 when a union official was successfully sued for damages after he had forced BOAC to operate a closed shop in the draughtsman's trade in 1956. The *Trades Disputes Act* (1965) granted immunity to union officials for actions performed while carrying out union policy. The most notorious episodes followed the passing of the *Industrial Relations Act* in 1971. This Act made contracts between employers and unions legally-binding, banned unofficial strikes and ordered unions to register with the Registrar of Trade Unions and Employers' Associations. Any union which did not register lost tax advantages and found that any industrial action it called was, by definition, unofficial and thus illegal. An Industrial Relations Court was set up to hear infringements of the Act. Compulsory strike ballots and cooling-off periods during disputes could also be enforced by the government.

Two years of conflict followed. The TUC suspended 32 unions for registering; strike ballots and cooling-off periods were enforced in a railway dispute, but only succeeded in strengthening the union's resolve; the AEU refused to answer a case in court, were fined for contempt and eventually had £100,000 sequestered from their funds by the Court; a bitter dispute in the docks about container cargoes led to arrests of union officials. With an incomes policy also in existence, bad relations between government and unions led to strikes, and the power cuts caused by miners' and electricity workers' actions resulted in a 3-day working week and an election in early 1974. The Government lost the election and the new Labour Government repealed the Industrial Relations Act. Union power was further strengthened by the *Trade Union and Labour Relations Act* which restored closed shops, where they were desired. The Act also set up the Arbitration, Conciliatory and Advisory Service (ACAS) to assist in settling disputes. The *Employment Protection Act* (1975) also aided unions by strengthening legislation concerning unfair dismissals.

Closed shops have always been a contentious issue. So has the related subject of recognition – ie the right of workers to join a union and have it recognised by employers as the organisation with which they must negotiate. The most notorious recognition issue in recent years was in 1976 at the film-processing firm of *Grunwick*, where the clerical union APEX claimed that the employer would not allow it to recruit and become recognised. The Appeal Court reject ACAS's report on the issue, thus reducing ACAS's power. The dispute lasted several months.

Another change of government in 1979 produced the *Employment Act* (1980) which weakened the closed shop and recognition legislation and declared *secondary picketing* illegal. Workers have long had the right to picket their places of employment during strikes in order to prevent people from going to work and discourage others from trading with the employers. Secondary picketing occurs when workers picket other establishments than those of their employer in order to make their strike more effective. For example, coal miners have picketed coke depots and electricity generating stations to prevent the distribution of coal stockpiles; steel workers in dispute with British Steel have picketed private stockists and distributors. It seemed inevitable that the secondary picketing legislation would be challenged sooner or later.

Criticisms of trade unions

Some of the criticism levelled against trade unions must now be examined.

1 *Inter-union disputes*

Unions are often not really fighting employers, but are in conflict with each other. Wage differentials, demarcation disputes (concerning which jobs are reserved to particular unions), comparability claims, closed shops, are all forms of inter-union rivalry. Strong unions, with large funds or in control of vital areas of the economy, like fuel and power, forge ahead of weaker ones. Part of the trouble lies in the fact that there are over 400 unions, a result of the haphazard growth of the union movement (there were 1360 unions in 1919). Disputes to maintain the differentials of craft unions are particularly common as the skilled workers fear losing their advantages to the mass unions. Many industries have several unions (nine in education; three in railways; more than a dozen at Ford's); few industries have just one union.

2 *Weakness of the TUC*

The TUC really has little power over its member unions, another symptom of the jealousies with which individual unions guard their powers.

3 *Weakness of union leaders*

Often, union leaders are thought to lack control over their members. Over 95 per cent of strikes are unofficial. Shop stewards seem to have more power than union leaders. The large strikes are almost invariably legal (ie officially backed by the Union), however. Only official strikers receive union strike pay assuming that the union has a strike fund.

4 *The unions have too much political influence*

Unions finance the Labour Party and carry much voting power. (The Conservative Party's finances come largely from contributions from industry, of course.) Members' contributions to union funds include a contribution to the Labour Party for those unions affiliated to the Party. It is possible to 'contract-out' of the political levy, however. In many unions few members contract-out. 97 per cent of the TGWU, 98 per cent of NUPE, 93 per cent of GMWU, 93 per cent of USDAW members contribute whereas only 32 per cent of ASTMS and 25 per cent of SOGAT members do. Some large white collar unions (eg NALGO, NUT, CPSU) do not affiliate to the Labour Party.

5 *Union dues are too low*

Being a full-time union official is not a popular job because pay is often low. Officials at regional level and below are often paid less than the workers they represent, so there is little incentive to leave the shop floor and become a paid official. Thus, extremists come to power sometimes because of little opposition for the posts. Apathy is one reason for this; only 3 or 4 per cent of members attend branch meetings; even leadership elections persuade only a minority to vote. Low dues are also to blame, though. No union had a contribution of as much as £1 per week in 1981. The National Graphical Association was highest at 82 pence; NUPE and USDAW were only 35 pence, the TGWU 38 pence, and the NUTGW just 30 pence. Few unions have very large funds and by no means all can provide strike pay.

6 *Restrictive practices*

Closed shops, overstaffing, demarcations are examples of restrictive practices which may reduce efficiency and prevent progress. Unions are likely to resist any moves which may cause unemployment, especially automation and changes in work practices. As in wage negotiations, union leaders see their job as representing *their* members, who elected them, and not to represent wider or national interests. Their members must come first. Thus, accusations of irresponsibility and selfishness are made, particularly by consumers whose interests may be harmed by higher prices, inefficiency or industrial action.

Trade unions will continue to be criticised and the battles to increase or reduce their powers will no doubt go on. There are many motes in the eyes of management, however, and unions cannot accept all the blame for the country's ills. Whatever legislation is passed, unions will not be absolished. Their existence and power must always be taken into account by governments and planners. Unions will not wither away and a revival in the UK economy would see a revival in their membership and potential strength. History shows that their powers are strengthened by the existence of full employment. Reducing union powers by reducing employment, however, makes little sense on any grounds, economic or otherwise. One move which might improve prospects would be a reduction of the fragmentation and divisions within the trade union sector.

Summary

1 Trade union exist to protect and advance the terms and conditions of employment of their members.

2 Unions have considerable political influence through industrial action and their influence in the Labour Party.

3 The history of the trade union movement goes a long way to explain some of their current problems, including differential and demarcation disputes, closed shops and recognition issues.

4 Trade unions have become powerful in the relatively prosperous years of post-war full employment and defeated the attempt to reduce their powers in the 1971 Industrial Relations Act.

5 The increase in unemployment has reduced union powers, but certain unions remain powerful, especially in the public sector.

25 Rent, interest and profits

The derivation of the demand for land and capital follows the same principles as the demand for labour. No unit of a factor of production should be employed if the value of its output is exceeded by the cost of employing it. Land, capital and enterprise do have some special features, however, which will be examined in this chapter.

Economic rent

In everyday language, rent is the money a person pays in order to use an asset belonging to someone else. Thus, tenants pay rent to landlords/landladies, consumers rent television sets or cars from retailers. In economics, however, rent is the income received by owners of land. Land is, of course, a natural resource. The unique factor concerning a natural resource compared with the other factors of production is that it has no supply price. Labour needs to be educated and trained, capital needs to be manufactured, but land has not incurred these costs. When settlers spread across uninhabited continents they settled on unowned free land; fishermen and hunters caught their fish or animals without having to pay anything to an owner; prospectors and miners did not have to pay an owner for the resources which they exploited. In their original state, natural resources had no owner and no supply price. Of course, nations, companies and individuals soon laid claim to these natural resources, so settlers and miners soon had to pay a rent to the land-owners, but originally *someone* had obtained the land free of charge merely by claiming it or settling on it. Thus, although there are now virtually no free natural resources in the world, except perhaps fish and minerals outside territorial waters (which partly explains why countries seek to extend their territorial waters), the concept of land having no original supply price is still used in economics.

The first owner of a natural resource, having obtained it free of charge, can make windfall profits from renting out the resource to other people. Thus, *all* income from the resource can be regarded as a surplus or profit. The UK, having been awarded by international law a large part of the North Sea's continental shelf, leases or rents to oil companies the rights to drill for oil there. All the rent received is a surplus. Similarly, when the USA laid claim to a large part of the interior of the North American continent and then leased or sold the land to settlers, all the income was a profit to the government. Because rent was regarded as a surplus, there has grown up in economics usage of the phrase *'economic rent'*, which means *'the surplus an owner of a factor of production receives in excess of that factor's supply price'*. Economic rent can accrue to any factor of production, not only land. Not all the income earned by other factors is economic rent, however, because these other factors have cost something to supply. In the modern world, not all the income received by land-owners is a surplus, of course, because few of today's land-owners are the original ones. Most natural resources have changed hands at some time, so the current owners have had to pay something for them. Some owners may well have improved the value of the land in their possession of course, for example by drainage, irrigation or fertilisation and have incurred costs in making these improvements. Other land may have appreciated in value in the owner's hands by sheer luck – previously unknown oil or mineral deposits may have been found, the development of modern communications may have made its site and location more valuable. Mussolini once contemptuously described Italy's North African Empire as 'a collection of deserts', never knowing that there were rich oil deposits in parts of it, from which great economic rent could have been earned.

How can the supply price of a factor of production be identified so that any economic rent can measured? Perhaps the easiest example is seen with the concept of normal and excess profits earned by the factor of production known as enterprise. In Chapter 1 (p 10) we found that normal profit was that profit which an entrepreneur wished to receive in order to stay in that occupation; if he received more, he was earning excess or supernormal profits; if he received less, he would not continue to operate. Thus, the level of *normal profit was his supply price; excess profits were his economic rent*. The actual level of normal profit is determined subjectively by the entrepreneur. In theory, it should equal the 'best earnings elsewhere' that the entrepreneur could receive. For example, if a shopkeeper knew she could get a job in a factory and earn £7,000 per year, the normal profits she wishes to receive from running her shop should be £7,000. Any profit below this would cause her to sell the shop and transfer to the factory job.[1] Thus, £7,000 is her supply price, or *transfer cost*. The supply price of a factor of production is known as its transfer cost or *transfer earnings*. Any excess earnings above this is economic rent.

Labour also follows this principle. A man's supply price when he offers himself for work is equal to the best he could earn elsewhere. In times of depression and unemployment, his transfer cost will be lower than in times of prosperity, because the opportunities of finding another job are not so good. Similarly, capital will be transferred

245

from one type of investment to another if the interest which could be earned elsewhere is more favourable. The 'best available elsewhere' is the transfer cost.

As always, things are not so simple in the real world. For a start, perfect knowledge does not exist. Neither worker, entrepreneur nor investor may know of better opportunities elsewhere. Alternatively they may not be able to take advantage of other opportunities; a worker may not be able to move house in order to get a better job, or may not wish to do so. Indeed, there may be many non-monetary advantages concerning a factor's present occupation. The shopkeeper may be satisfied with earnings below the level which she could receive in a factory because she places great value on being self-employed. An agricultural worker may accept comparatively low pay because he has a tied cottage, or he could not bear to work indoors in a more directly disciplined atmosphere. A teacher may value her holidays more than extra pay she might receive in a job involving longer hours of work. An investor may prefer (or need) to put his money into a savings account from which he can easily draw rather than earn higher interest from depositing his money for a longer period. Many of us might earn more abroad, but for a variety of reasons we would not dream of emigrating. Thus, in the real world, many factors may make the level of a factor's transfer earnings be lower than the simple 'best earnings elsewhere' rule. Notice in all this analysis yet another example of the principle of *opportunity cost*; an owner of a factor has many alternative decisions concerning possible employment for that factor.

For labour, in particular, economic rent may be very high if a worker has a skill which is in great demand. An outstanding sportsman or woman or entertainer might earn a huge income through their particular skill, but may have few qualifications or qualities which are of value in any other trade. When a professional sportsman retires his earnings often drop considerably as he has to take a much more menial job. He can no longer exercise his special '*rent of ability*'. 'Rent of ability' is, of course, surplus earnings above transfer cost which someone receives because of a special, even unique talent he or she possesses.

Economic rent earned temporarily is known as *quasi-rent*. There may be a temporary shortage of computer programmers or micro-chip designers, for example, when an economy first develops these industries. Many countries do not have sufficient engineers; the UK was short of dentists after the War. By elementary supply and demand principles the few people qualified to do these jobs could earn handsome rewards – until new men and women have been found or trained. Then, the windfall high earnings tend to fall.

Because economic rent is a surplus and, in a strict sense, unnecessary to its earner, perhaps it should be taxed? The earner would not leave his or her occupation if economic rent was lost, because he or she could not earn more elsewhere as long as transfer earnings were received. The taxes which perhaps come nearest to taxing rent in the UK are capital gains tax and development land tax.

The capital gains and development land taxes tax gains made when an article or an area of land appreciate in value while in someone's possession and are sold at a profit. Yet it is impossible accurately to tax rent, except by assuming transfer cost to be at an arbitrarily-decreed level. People only vaguely know what the level of their transfer earnings is, and would be reluctant to admit what it was, anyway. The non-monetary factors also make measurement difficult. So, although there is a case for taxing rent, it can hardly be done with any degree of accuracy.

Theory of the rate of interest

Liquidity preference

One of the functions of money is to act as a store of wealth (see Chapter 14, p 139); a person can decide to hold assets in a liquid form, or can hold them in the form of goods. Clearly, people will generally choose to do both; they will wish to hold some liquid assets and some goods. The desire to hold assets in a liquid form (ie in cash or in some easily cashable form, such as a bank deposit) rather than in goods is called *liquidity preference*, and a person's liquidity preference will vary from time to time. There are three motives for wishing to hold some assets in a liquid form:

1 *Transactions motive*

Everyone needs to hold some liquid assets in order to meet everyday purchasing requirements, to buy food, newspapers, petrol or whatever other goods and services enter normal expenditure patterns. Poorer people may need to hold nearly all their assets in this form, being unable to afford to save or invest. At certain times of the year (pre-Christmas shopping, January sales, summer holidays) most people will increase their liquidity preference above its normal level in order to meet above-average expenditure requirements. Other factors in the economic climate will affect liquidity preference under the transactions motive, such as an expectation of a rise in the inflation rate (people will wish to spend before the prices rise further), the availability of credit, and the availability of goods and services (eg rationing during war time means that people have little opportunity to spend money).

2 *Precautionary motive*

Most people try to hold some liquid assets in order to allow for unseen contingencies and emergencies. A consumer's car might break down, the house may need some repair work, an unexpected journey might need to be undertaken; many people will try to hold some cash or keep some money in a current account just in case some unforeseen expenditure is suddenly incurred. Indeed, most of us fall victim to the desire to buy something on impulse which we were not expecting to buy when we commenced our shopping expedition.

3 *Speculative motive*

The explanation of this motive is usually dealt with in connection with fixed interest bonds, rather than the more volatile ordinary shares.

Supposed a fixed interest security promised to pay the holder £5 per year. If the prevailing rate of interest in the market were 5 per cent, then the bond would be bought for £100 (£5 is 5 per cent of £100). If market rates fell to 4 per cent, then the bond price would move to a price that £5 is 4 per cent of – ie to £125. If market interest rates rose to 6 per cent, then the bond price would be £5 × $\frac{100}{6}$ = £83.33. The price of the bond moves *inversely* to the interest rates. A bond offering £5 per annum would be attractive if other investments only offered 4 per cent, so the rush to buy the bond would push its price up to £125. At that price, the income received (£5) is 4 per cent of the purchase price, so is in line with rewards offered on other investments. The process happens in reverse if market rates rise and the £5 bond becomes less attractive.

This process happens commonly in money markets; the prices of securities change until the rewards received all represent the same interest rate. A more attractive security has its price bid up until the reward is brought into line; a less attractive one's price falls until it becomes equally attractive. The same happens with ordinary shares. A struggling firm finds its share price falling; one paying high dividends finds its share price pushed-up.

It is not only interest rates which reflect the demand for securities, it is *expected* interest rates. If people expect interest rates to rise they will wish to sell the bond (ie demand cash), hoping to buy it back when the rate has risen and the bond price has fallen. Conversely, if rates are thought to be going to fall, there will be a rush to buy the bonds (ie there will be less demand for cash) so that they can be re-sold at a higher price when the rate has fallen. Clearly, the pressure either to sell or buy the bonds will, like all speculative pressures, help to cause the rates and prices to move in the anticipated directions. Notice that what is described is what people will try to do. They will only succeed in buying or selling if someone else expects the opposite trend and will sell when others are buying or vice versa. If everyone expects the same trend and acts in the same way, all that will happen is that interest rates and prices will move in opposite directions but no trade will take place until someone decides that it has gone far enough, anticipates a reversal of the trend in the near future and so acts against the general trend.

Diagram 25.1 shows a liquidity preference schedule and its relationship to interest rates. As interest rates fall, liquidity preference (the desire for liquid assets) rises and vice versa. The schedule never reaches the horizontal axis because at low interest rates *everyone* expects the next move in the rate to be upwards, so everyone demands cash. The speculative demand for liquid assets becomes perfectly elastic; everyone wants liquidity, no-one wants bonds. The area below this lowest-expected interest rate, OX, is called the *liquidity trap*. The schedule also never reaches the vertical axis. *Everyone* expects the rates to fall next, so everyone wants the bonds, not liquidity, but *some* cash will always be needed, for the transactions and precautionary motives.

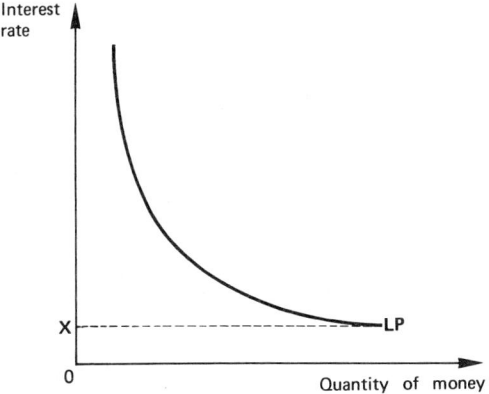

25.1 Liquidity – preference

Interest rates

At any moment in time the money supply (£M3, or whatever the official measurement is) is fixed. Thus, the quantity of money (Q_1) is perfectly inelastic in Diagram 25.2. The interaction of the money supply and the liquidity preference schedule determine the interest rate. The simple message of monetarism is clear. Reducing the money supply to Q_2 will raise interest rates and thus discourage the desire for liquidity and the desire to borrow; raising the money supply to Q_3 will reduce interest rates and increase the demand for liquid assets. The consequent fall or rise in the demand for liquid assets will influence spending levels and thus affect the levels of prices and economic activity.

The liquidity preference schedule can also change, of course. As interest rates have generally risen since the war, no-one would expect rates to fall below about 6 or 7 per cent per annum, whereas they use to fall to 3 per cent or even 2 per cent. Thus, the liquidity trap now exists below about 6 per cent, not 2 per cent; the liquidity preference schedule has moved upwards and to the right over time.

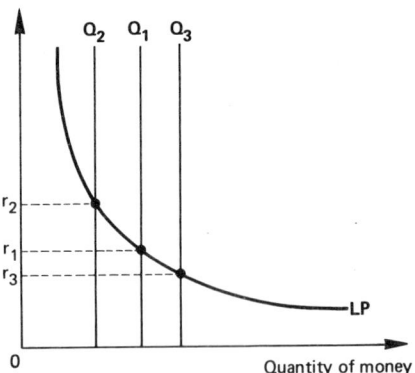

25.2 The determination of the rate of interest

Profits

There is little to say about profits at this stage. Normal profits are transfer earnings: excess profits are economic rent. Entrepreneurs, like any other factor of production, must 'earn their keep' according to the marginal revenue product theory.

Profits are also a signal to a firm indicating whether its policies are succeeding or not (except perhaps in nationalised industries, where profit maximisation is not the main aim). Yet profits may fall because of trends in the economy. Profits fell to less than 10 per cent of national income during the 1970s after being twice this figure in the 1960s. This was due to the rising share of wages in national income compounded by the slump in the economy and the accompanying fall in demand. Profits became squeezed as sales became difficult and wages and interest rates rose. For many entrepreneurs, the 'normal profit' level of profits was not reached, and contraction of the firm or even closure inevitably followed. Thus, profits are not wholly in the power of the entrepreneur – general economic trends will influence the situation. In a boom, profits in general will be high; in a slump, most firms will struggle. Yet profits are still a signal to a firm about its success or failure and Communist countries, who do not have a profit-based capitalist sector, may be missing a vital economic indicator from their system.

As Section three showed, monopolists are in a stronger position to earn excess profits, but *all* entrepreneurs in any type of competition seek to earn excess profits and all *can* earn them in the short-run. A self-employed entrepreneur's profits are difficult to measure if he or she provides most or all labour and capital. Some of the revenue should really be imputed as wages and interest; not all is truly 'profit'.

The part that is really wages, for example, could be calculated by setting-aside what would have to be paid to an employee to do the work instead of the entrepreneur. The main role of profit is as a reward for risk-taking, decision-making and possibly also innovation.

Profits is partly a cost ('normal profit') and partly a surplus ('excess profit'). Not all entrepreneurs can succeed in their efforts to maximise profits. Indeed, being an entrepreneur can be an unenviable, if challenging job. Pressures on the entrepreneur include consumers' demand, employees' wage claims and interest rates. In addition, general problems in the economy may thwart his efforts. The next section examines these general or 'macro-economic' problems, and looks at how the economy functions and how governments try to combat such problems as unemployment, inflation and slow growth.

Summary

1 Economic rent may be defined as that surplus a factor of production earns in excess of its transfer earnings.
2 Transfer earnings is that level of earnings a factor of production's owner wishes to receive in order to prevent the factor being transferred to other employment.
3 Transfer earnings are thus basically equal to the best earnings the factor could receive elsewhere, though the non-monetary advantages of a particular occupation may blur this slightly.
4 The desire to hold assets in a liquid form is known as liquidity preference.
5 Liquidity preference is governed by transactions, precautionary and speculative motives.
6 The interaction of the quantity of money and the liquidity preference schedule determine the level of the interest rate.
7 Normal profits are an entrepreneur's transfer earnings: excess profits are economic rent.

Footnote

1 The shopkeeper would also expect to receive some returns on the capital invested and the risks taken.

Section nine Macro economics

26 The circular flow of income

Macro economics

Macro-economics is concerned with the whole economy: problems such as unemployment, inflation and growth are macro-economic problems. In this section we shall be first examining the theories underlying macro-economics and then looking at real world problems and government policies to combat them.

In the 1980s we have a new situation in the Western World, especially in the UK, namely the simultaneous existence of both large-scale unemployment and inflation. Previously, it has been widely thought that these were opposite extremes. Inflation was thought to appear only when full employment existed, mainly because output could not keep up with demand; conversely, a slump or depression involving mass unemployment was associated with low and stagnant prices. It was thought that the economy moved naturally over a period of time from boom to slump and back again – a natural process, known as the *trade cycle* or *business cycle*. Diagram 26.1 shows this cycle. Over a period of time economic activity moves up and down. Full employment is seen to rise over time because of technological developments, the rise in the labour force and other factors raising the productive potential of the economy.

The situation of inflation and unemployment existing simultaneously, being new, needs special consideration and explanation. There is by no means universal agreement concerning either its cause or possible remedies. Thus, we shall have to consider the problems separately at first. Unemployment and the policies concerned with it will be considered first; then inflation will be dealt with; finally, an attempt will be made to get to grips with the strange new situation in the world in the 1980s.

Types of unemployment

In the UK, the unemployment statistics are obtained by identifying the number of people officially registered as seeking work – ie those drawing unemployment pay. The real number is larger. Many housewives and women at home would take a job, probably on a part-time basis, if one was available. Some people without jobs do not register as unemployed. Many young unemployed are on the Youth Opportunities Programme (see Chapter 4, p 55); others may have stayed in the education system. The complete number of those who might take work, if it is offered, is unknown.

As Chapter 4 showed (see pp 48-9) there are three types of unemployment for government to deal with, ignoring voluntary unemployment, whose hardships are presumably willingly accepted by those concerned.

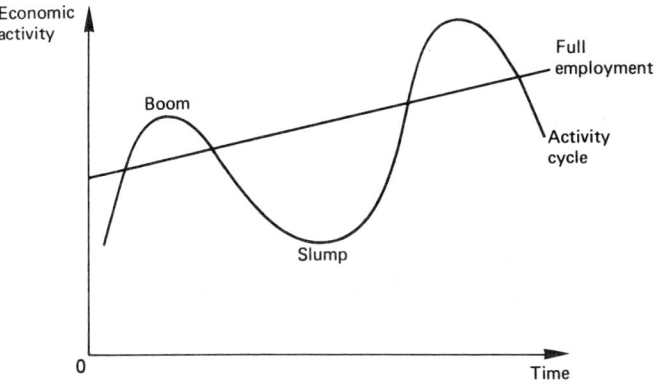

26.1 The trade or business cycle

1 *Frictional unemployment*

In the 1970's as many as 4 million people were moving between jobs and were temporarily unemployed each year. Seasonal unemployment could also come into this category, including residents of holiday resorts in the 'off-season', professional cricketers in the winter (footballers are paid in the summer), and construction workers in harsh winter weather. Frictional unemployment is temporary unemployment so it is not a permanent problem, but it can still be serious for some people. The winter unemployment rate in the fishing villages and holiday resorts of Devon and Cornwall can exceed 50 per cent, for example.

2 *Structural unemployment*

Structural unemployment is created when there are changes in the structure of industry in the economy, when some industries decline and others expand. Some workers in the declining industries find themselves unemployed for a long time, perhaps even permanently if they cannot move to expanding industries. The problem is more serious than frictional unemployment. In the UK structural unemployment has often been experienced on a regional basis because so many of the declining industries, like shipbuilding, textiles, steel and coal, have been heavily based in particular regions and not spread across the country, but structural unemployment does not *have* to be synonymous with regional. A decline in agriculture, education, clerical professions or many service trades and would affect a few people in many areas rather than many people in a few areas.

The methods of dealing with structural and particularly regional unemployment were discussed in Chapter 4. Specific micro-economic measures are required to help particular industries or areas.

3   General or cyclical unemployment

This is the type of unemployment with which macro-economics is concerned. Unemployment which is spread throughout many industries and areas requires action on a national or indeed international level. Almost invariably some areas will experience worse levels of unemployment than others, but a feature of general unemployment is that even areas of hitherto full employment will suffer some rise in unemployment although their problems may remain less severe than those in the traditionally troubled areas.

General unemployment is usually considered to be caused by a general lack of demand. Insufficient goods and services are being sold, so the derived demand for labour falls. Recent opinions suggest that there may be other causes, such as high wages pricing workers out of jobs because employers cannot afford to employ so many workers at the higher wage. This would accord with the marginal revenue product theory explained in Chapter 23 (pp 217–19); as wages rise, demand for labour falls. Yet high wages should bring high demand when the workers spend their earnings. There would seem to be evidence that high wages in the UK in the 1970s did help to raise unemployment. The unemployed people's spending power fell, thus counteracting the increased spending power of those still in work. As prices were rising, *real* spending rose little, in any case.

Other factors contributing to general unemployment include a fall in export demand, a rise in the demand for imports and a desire on the part of consumers to save a higher proportion of their income than they did before. All these trends have occurred in the UK in the 1970s and early 1980s.

The theories concerned with creating spending power in order to cure widespread unemployment are associated with the name of *John Maynard Keynes*, the famous UK economist of the inter-war years. It was Keynes who showed how to get an economy out of the slump of the 1930s. Rather accidentally, perhaps, the American President, FD Roosevelt, hit on the same ideas in his 'New Deal'. (Keynes and Roosevelt met only once, and their conversation was not particularly fruitful.) The next few chapters will be concerned with explaining Keynes's theories which aim to show how to reduce general unemployment and stimulate economic activity.

The circular flow of income

Diagram 26.2 is a simplified version of how the economy functions. Assume there are just two institutions in an economy, called *Households* and *firms*. All the members of households are consumers, so there is *consumption expenditure* (C) flowing from the households to the firms. Members of households work for firms in the form of labour, or they may provide land or capital, or they may even be entrepreneurs; for providing these factors of production, the household members receive *income* (Y). Most income earners will receive their rewards in the form of wages or salaries. Thus, there is a basic *circular flow* of money in the economy: firms pay incomes to householders, who then spend these incomes on goods and services produced by the firms.

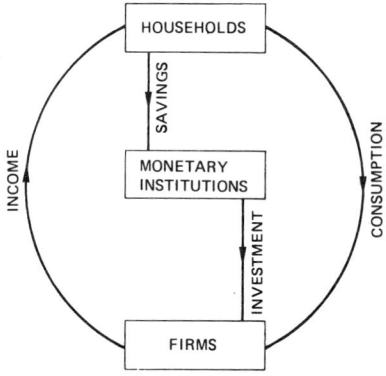

26.2 The circular flow

This circular flow is a gross over-simplification, however. Income earners may not wish to spend all their incomes; they may wish to save some in order to spend it in the future. Thus, all income earners have a 'propensity to consume' and a 'propensity to save'. If everybody's propensities to consume and save are added together, the economy's propensities to consume and save are obtained. The *average propensity to consume* is that fraction of income which the community spends, expressed as $\frac{C}{Y}$. The *average propensity to save* is that fraction of income which is saved, expressed as $\frac{S}{Y}$.

All income is either spent or saved. Spending (ie consumption) causes the money to continue flowing round the system. The firms receive the consumption expenditure and then pay it in the forms of wages, rent, interest and profits to factors of production, who thus receive income. As long as some income is spent money will continue to flow round the system. Any money saved will be a *leakage* or *withdrawal* from the system and will not stimulate the creation of further incomes and economic activity.

Firms are not wholly dependent on consumption, however. *Investment* (I) stimulates industrial activity as new machines are installed and new methods introduced. Banks, investment trusts and other institutions provide funds for industry in one form or another, thus creating Investment. Thus, output (Q) is stimulated by consumption and investment. Money received by the firms from output is paid to the factors of production in the form of income which, according to the appropriate propensities, is consumed or saved.

The real world contains more institutions than households and firms, however. The *government* plays a considerable part in the economy. The government (or, more accurately, the public sector) is an employer and thus pays its factors of production, creating incomes. The government is also a consumer, and buys from the private sector a vast array of goods and services from ships and aircraft to pencils and paperclips. Thus, the government pumps in money to the basic circular flow, stimulating output and income. In Diagram 26.3, all these various forms of government activity are summarised as *government spending* (G) and shown by a single arrow. In reality, there would be several arrows as the government directs money to both firms and households.

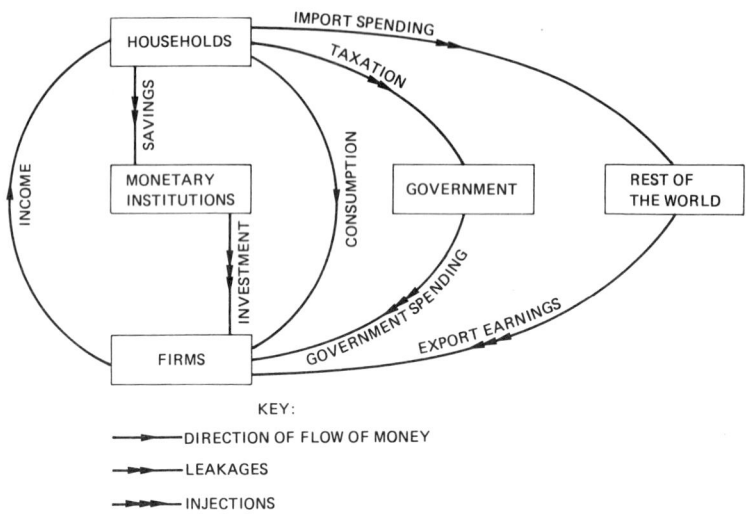

26.3 The complete circular flow

The government also withdraws money from the circular flow in the form of *taxation* (T). This is also show in Digram 26.3 as a single arrow, although in reality of course both firms and households pay taxes. Unless the government collects more in taxes than it injects in government spending, it will incur a deficit, financing this by borrowing (mainly by issuing gilt-edged securities). Therefore, governments are mainly stimulators of the economy rather than being an influence which reduces the circular flow.

The other real-world complication is the existence of the *Rest of the world*. The rest of the world buys *exports* (X) from the country in question and also sends it *imports* (M). Thus, exports as an injection which stimulate the circular flow; imports are a leakage or withdrawal.

Keynes's conclusions

Keynes's conclusions from analysis of this system were quite simple. If an economy is depressed, then economic activity can only be stimulated by *'priming the pump'*, which means injecting money into the system. The *injections* needed are investment, exports or government spending. All these will stimulate output and thus income. Receivers of incomes can do any of four things with it – spend it on home-produced goods, save it, pay tax or buy imports. Everyone has an average propensity to consume and save, and also average propensities to pay tax $(\frac{T}{Y})$ and to buy imports $(\frac{M}{Y})$

Not only do people have average propensities to do these things, they also have *marginal propensities*. For example, the marginal propensity to consume equals that fraction of a *rise* in income which is spent on home-produced goods. Similarly, the marginal propensities to save, pay tax and buy imports refer to those fractions of a *rise* in income which go to these respective leakages. In reality, it is difficult to distinguish between spending on home-produced goods and on imports, because there is an 'import content' in many goods manufactured here.

When an injection (I,X or G) raises output and then incomes, people will divert some of their extra income to the three leakages (S,M and T) but, according to the marginal propensity to consume, at least *some* of the rise in income will be spent on home-produced goods. This will stimulate further output and income, thus creating another 'round' of activity in the circular flow. So, to cure a depression or slump, injections should be pumped in (or leakages reduced, by discouraging savings and imports, and reducing taxes). This was Keynes's basic message.

In a depression, investment is difficult to stimulate, because economic prospects seem so poor that entrepreneurs are unwilling to risk borrowing, even though interest rates may be low. Raising exports is also difficult, because it needs foreign co-operation. If all countries are in a slump they are unlikely to want to raise imports (though, if they did, prosperity might eventually return to the world starting with the country whose exports and incomes had risen and who would therefore, via the marginal propensity to import, help other countries). In the 1930s a series of competitive devaluations, whereby each country tried to raise its exports, failed to achieve anything.

So, Keynes surmised, if investment and exports are difficult to stimulate, the government has a duty to stimulate the economy through its own spending. Similarly, people are reluctant to reduce savings in times of unemployment and depression. Imports are also difficult to reduce quickly. Thus, in order to stimulate consumption, the government should reduce taxes.

Keynes saw a key role, then, for the government. It should boost its spending and reduce taxes – ie *budget for a deficit*. This active *fiscal policy* was the key to stimulating the circular flow and recovering from a Slump. Before Keynes, theorists were trying opposite remedies. Incomes were *cut* in the 1930s because of an attempt to apply micro-economic analysis to macro-economics. The theory said that, to sell more chairs, the price of chairs should be cut (wages would be cut in order to reduce costs and therefore prices). This might work for a single industry, but *not* for the whole economy, because cutting *all* wages meant cutting consumers' spending power; people still could not buy, even at lower prices, because they could not afford to do so. Keynes discredited the micro/macro muddled thoughts and preached the revolutionary doctrine of *spending* your way out of a depression – budget deficits, printing money, fiduciary issues and other such heresies. Yet Keynes was correct. Whether reversing Keynes' policies to cure inflation in the 1970s or trying to apply them in the unique situation of the 1980s will work is less clear, however, as Chapter 29 will show. For curing a 1930s-type slump, however, Keynes found a solution.

There is a group of economists based on the University of Cambridge (the so-called '*Cambridge School*') who would advocate a further part for the government to play in curing the widespread unemployment in the UK. They support the introduction of protective tariffs or exchange controls in order to make British people buy British goods. They would back up their policy with Keynesian tax cuts in order to enlarge spending power and thus stimulate output and employment.

The history of protectionist measures in the 1930s makes sad reading. Retaliation and competitive devaluations defeated the aims of protectionism then and such results could occur again. Also there could be inflation resulting from shortages of goods if imports of some goods are banned or reduced. Nevertheless, calls for protectionism are increasing, especially from trade unions who are worried about unemployment among their members.

Summary

1 Macro-economics is concerned with problems of the whole economy, such as inflation and unemployment.
2 Inflation and unemployment have usually been opposite extremes, but exist simultaneously in the 1980s.
3 There are four types of unemployment: macro-economics is concerned with general unemployment.
4 There is a basic circular flow of income between households and firms. Injections (investment, exports and government spending) stimulate the flow; leakages (savings, imports and taxation) reduce it.
5 In a depression, Keynes proved that recovery is stimulated by increasing injections and reducing leakages, particularly using fiscal policy.
6 The Cambridge School of economists advocate import controls or exchange controls in order to restrict imports and revive consumption and output of home-produced goods.

27 National income accounts

The calculation of national income

National Income can be defined as:
'The total value of goods and services an economy produces in a given period'.

National income can be calculated by adding-up the total value of output, or by finding the total value of incomes received, or alternatively by totalling all the expenditure in an economy in the period in question. In theory, all income is received in the forms of wages, rent, interest or profits as a reward for contributing to output. All goods and services produced are sold, so output should also equal expenditure.

In the real world, matters are not as simple as this, and certain allowances have to be made. Table 27.1 shows a typical set of national income accounts and illustrates the modifications which have to be made in order to get the correct results.

Modifications to national income accounting

1 *International trade*
   Imports are part of consumption expenditure, but they are made abroad, so they do not form part of output, nor do they create income in the consuming country, so they have to be *subtracted* from total expenditure. Exports do contribute to both output and income, but do not form part of consumption expenditure in the country. Thus, in order to get the three columns to balance, exports are *added* to Total Expenditure.

2 *Indirect taxes and subsidies*
   Indirect taxes (ie taxes on goods and services) do appear in a country's expenditure column. If I buy a gallon of petrol, part of my consumption spending is the tax levied on petrol by the government and passed on to me by the oil company. The tax is not part of the cost of producing the good and the factors of production do not receive it, so it does not appear under the headings of output or income. Thus, indirect taxes are *subtracted* from total expenditure. Conversely, subsidies paid to the firms do accrue to the factors of production and do contribute to output,

Table 27.1 National income accounts 1980

Income	£m	Output	£m	Expenditure	£m
Income from employment	137,083	Agriculture, forestry, fishing	4,296	Consumption	135,403
Income from self-employment	18,394	Petroleum and natural gas	7,649	Government consumption	48,337
Gross trading profits of companies	24,979	Other mining and quarrying	3,222	Gross domestic capital formation	40,050
Gross trading surpluses of public corporations	6,185	Manufacturing	48,060	Value of physical increase in stocks and work in progress	− 3,596
Rent	13,231	Construction	13,025		
Imputed charge for consumption of non-traded capital	2,138	Gas, electricity, water	5,803	Total domestic expenditure	220,194
		Transport and communication	15,410	Exports	63,198
	202,010	Distribution	19,328		
Less Stock appreciation	− 6,477	Insurance, banking, finance etc	18,288	Total final expenditure	283,392
		Ownership of dwellings	11,996	*Less* imports	−57,832
Gross domestic product	195,533	Professional and scientific services	25,467		
Residual error	− 2,045	Miscellaneous services	18,734	GDP at market prices	225,560
		Public administration and defence	13,987	Net property income from abroad	− 38
GDP at factor cost	193,488		205,265		
Net property income from abroad	− 38	Adjustment for financial services	− 9,732	GNP at market prices	225,522
		Residual error	− 2,045	*Less* taxes on expenditure	−37,287
GNP at factor cost	193,450			Subsidies	5,215
Less capital consumption	−27,045	GDP at factor cost	193,488		
		Net property income from abroad	− 38	GNP at factor cost	193,450
Net national income	166,405			*Less* capital consumption	−27,045
		GNP at factor cost	193,450		
		Less capital consumption	−27,045	Net national expenditure	166,405
		Net national product	166,405		

Source: Annual Abstract of Statistics, HMSO 1982.

but they are not directly paid for by the consumer. Thus, subsidies are *added* to total expenditure in order to balance their inclusion in the output and income columns.

As a result of making these allowances for indirect taxes and subsidies, output is valued nor at *Market Prices* but at *'Factor Cost'*, ie at the true cost of the factors of production who have received wages, rent, interest and profits in return for their work.

3 *Transfer payments*

Transfer payments consist of incomes received other than as a reward for output, eg pensions, unemployment pay, social security. Clearly, these payments are incomes to the people who receive them, but they are not balanced by output, nor do consumers directly pay them. Therefore, transfer payments are *deducted* from total incomes. They are called transfer payments because they are sums of money transferred from one person to another via the government. For example, a coal miner pays income tax on his earnings and this tax revenue may be transferred to another person by the government in the form of a pension. Only one unit of work (the coal miner's) has been done, but two incomes have been received. So, the 'unearned' income must be deducted from total income.

4 *Double-counting*

Transfer payments are a form of double-counting (ie two incomes but only one amount of output). Another form of double-counting which must be avoided in national income accounting concerns output. For the purposes of calculating the value of output work done should only be counted once. A lumberjack is paid for cutting-down a tree; the timber mill which buys the fallen tree pays a price to the felling company which includes the cost of the lumberjack's labour; the furniture maker who buys the timber from the mill is paying a price which helps to cover the mill owner's costs of buying the tree, as well as paying for the process of turning the tree into processed timber. The consumer who buys the furniture is paying a price which also covers the sums paid by all the people involved along the whole manufacturing process from tree felling to furniture making. Yet the various pieces of work (felling, timber processing, furniture making) have each only been done once and each piece of work should only be included once in the accounts. Only the *'value-added'* at each stage of production should be counted for national income and output purposes; one piece of work should not be double-counted.

5 *Capital consumption*

Capital consumption or depreciation should be deducted from the national income statistics. Investment, or gross domestic capital formation is included in the expenditure column. It also generates both output and income, as circular flow analysis shows. Yet, each year, existing plant and machinery depreciates in value through increasing age and wear and tear. The true value of investment is gross investment *minus* depreciation of existing capital assets. In order to obtain the final figures for national income, depreciation of existing assets must be subtracted. Thus, in Table 27.1, £40,050m of new investment took place in 1980, but existing assets depreciated by £27,045m.

It is, of course, quite impossible to calculate capital depreciation absolutely accurately, so fixed tables exist to write off part of capital's value each year durings its life. Machinery, plant and vehicles, for example lose a little value each year from their original purchase price down to zero or (more probably) a nominal or scrap value at the end of the expected working life of the asset.

6 *Stock appreciation*

At any particular moment, goods have been made but not yet sold – ie they are in stock. These stocks, having been manufactured, appear in output and income, but not yet in expenditure, so they have to be added to Total Expenditure. Yet, because of inflation, stocks in hand may appear to be worth more than they were in the past – they have *appreciated* in value. Ford's may have 10,000 unsold cars worth £50m at the end of year 'x' and an identical 10,000 stock of cars worth £55m at the end of year 'x + 1', merely because the car prices have risen from £5,000 to £5,500 each. The increase or appreciation in the value of stocks due solely to inflation should be subtracted from the accounts. In 1980 stocks *fell* in value by £3,596m.

7 *Net property income from abroad*

There is a difference between gross *domestic* product (which is produced, earned and spent within a country) and gross *national* product (what the country has earned from both home and foreign sources). British companies and citizens have property abroad: foreigners own property here. The *net* property earnings must be added to the accounts in order to find gross national product, the total value of a country's earnings. In 1980, for the first time for decades, this was a negative item.

8 *Residual error*

Because of the vast sums involved and the huge number of institutions providing statistics complete accuracy is impossible so, as in the balance of payments statistics, an error occurs. The error for 1980 (£2045m) is, in fact, only about 1 per cent of the total figure, a remarkably small proportion.

To summarise the process shown in Table 26.1:

All *incomes* are added then stock appreciation deducted to find total income, which equals gross domestic product at factor cost. Net property income from abroad is added to find gross national product at factor cost.

The values (or 'value-added') of each industry's output are compiled to obtain gross domestic product at factor cost. Net property income from abroad will be added in order to obtain gross national product at factor cost.

All expenditure is computed, including investment and stocks. Exports are added and imports subtracted and then net property income from abroad is added. This gives gross national product at market price. To obtain gross national product at factor cost, indirect taxes must be subtracted and subsidies added.

If the value of capital consumption is deducted from gross national product at factor cost in each instance, *net* national product is found. This net national product is 'The national income' of the economy in that year.

Interpretation and uses of national income accounts

National income accounts are a major indicator of the growth of wealth and welfare in an economy. Trends in various categories can also be identified – for example, the rate of increase of consumption, whether wages are squeezing profits, whether services are growing faster than manufacturing.

There are two major questions to solve. If national income is rising, does that mean that economic welfare or the standard of living is rising? Secondly, can useful comparisons be made between countries by looking at their national income statistics? The following factors must be taken into consideration when looking at the national income accounts of a country.

1 *Price changes*

   Increases in the general price level will almost certainly increase the size of the figures in the accounts. Yet, in real terms, income, output and expenditure may not have risen. No extra output may be taking place; rising prices may be making the output worth more in money, although not in real terms. Allowance is made for stock appreciation, but little else is done to counteract the effects of inflation. Yet inflation can make the figures misleading. For example, incomes may rise 10 per cent in a year – but if prices have risen 12 per cent, then real incomes have fallen by 2 per cent in that period.

2 *Unpaid output*

   A great deal of work is done in the economy but does not appear in the statistics, particularly work done by housewives. Housekeeping allowances from husbands to their wives, even if they could be identified, would be regarded as transfer payments. If, for some reason, a large number of housewives stopped doing the family washing and took it to a launderette instead, or if 'do-it-yourself' husbands started to call in tradesmen to perform their household improvements, then it would appear that national output, income and expenditure had risen. In fact, no extra work would have been done; all that had happened would have been that certain work was now being paid for instead of being done by an unpaid agent in the home.

The so-called '*black economy*' is also relevant. A considerable amount of income, output and expenditure is not traced by the authorities. In order to avoid income tax or value added tax some people may provide services (eg plumbers, painters, private tutors) and be paid in cash, not declaring their complete income to the tax authorities. This tax evasion means that the work done and paid for is not included in the national income statistics. The size of the black economy is, of course, not known (otherwise it would be eliminated), but is quite considerable.

3 *Changes in population size*
Over a long period of time a change in population can mask some of the national income statistics. A country with a rapidly rising population may find that national income rises are scarcely keeping pace. If population rises 10 per cent over a period of years while national income rises 20 per cent, real national income per head has only risen by 10 per cent.

4 *Economic climate*
An unusual set of circumstances can distort the statistics. In war time, for example, output is very high – but production will be largely confined to goods essential for the war effort. Many goods may be unobtainable; rationing may restrict consumption; high incomes may be the result of long hours of work; women may have boosted the size of the workforce. The real standard of living and quality of life (eg leisure time and facilities, lack of stress and worry) may be falling.

5 *Distribution of income*
Even if national income is rising in real terms, not all the economy's inhabitants may benefit. National income accounts tell us little about the distribution of income. Some oil-producing sheikhdoms may have high national incomes, but most of the wealth may be concentrated in few hands and the bulk of the population may be relatively poor. Even in the UK, where income and wealth is more equally spread than in many countries, there are huge inequalities. 10 per cent of the population receive over 25 per cent of the total incomes in the country. With regard to wealth the picture is even more uneven. 10 per cent of the UK's population possess 60 per cent of the country's wealth – indeed the top 1 per cent have over 25 per cent of the wealth. The major form of wealth is, of course, property. Most people's major asset is their house. Most property, especially estates of land, is inherited.

The progressive system of taxation in the UK (the richer you are, the higher rates of tax you pay) has redressed the balance to some extent.

For example, on the eve of the First World War the top 10 per cent of the population possessed 92 per cent of the country's wealth, and the top 1 per cent around 69 per cent of the wealth. Yet incomes and more especially wealth are still unevenly distributed after taxes of various sorts have been paid. There is no wealth tax in the UK, but there is capital transfer tax, which taxes gifts, especially inheritances.

A device called a *Lorenz curve* can be used to show income or wealth distribution, as illustrated in Diagram 27.1. If wealth, for example, were completely equally distributed, the distribution would lie along the 45° line – 1 per cent of the population would own 1 per cent of the wealth, 20 per cent would own 20 per cent, 50 per cent would own 50 per cent and so on. With real world unequal distribution, things are different. In the UK 50 per cent of the population own only about 10 per cent of the wealth, so the Lorenz curve starts at a flat angle and becomes very steep as the last few per cent own a great deal of the wealth. After tax, wealth distribution will be slightly, but only slightly nearer to the 45° line.

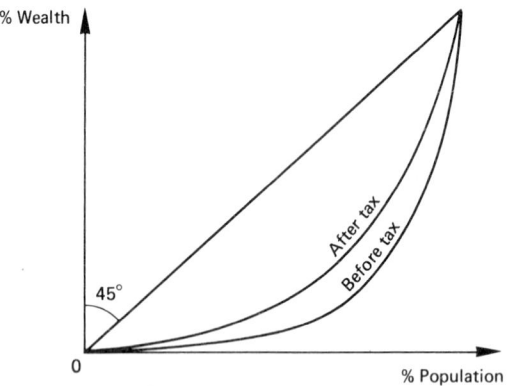

27.1 Wealth distribution – a Lorenz curve

International comparisons

Comparisons between countries are difficult to achieve. Production and consumption patterns are very different. In Scandinavian countries and Finland a great deal is spent on central heating and warm clothing in the harsh winters. In the Tropics, these items are scarcely produced or consumed at all. Sophisticated services (banking, hotels and restaurants) are produced and consumed at much lower levels in less developed countries. Living and working styles differ as does income distribution. The USA is a very rich country, but a Lorenz curve would show very unequal wealth and consumption patterns compared with other relatively rich countries like Sweden or Switzerland. National income per head is highest in Kuwait and other small oil-producing countries, but this does not necessarily mean that all or most of Kuwait's citizens are better-off than, say the UK's, or that Kuwait has a widely-based, thriving industrial sector or a wide range of goods and services available.

The use of different currencies and floating exchange rates also complicate the business of comparing different sets of national income accounts. Some common denominator of measurements needs to be found.

The relative rates of rise of national income in various countries and the changes in expenditure and output patterns can be deduced from national income comparisons, but a complete comparison between countries cannot be made.

Nevertheless, despite these limitations, national income accounting is a useful exercise. The effect of past policies and the need for policy changes can be seen, so the statistics are very important to planners and policy makers.

Next we must return to the theoretical world of the circular flow and examine in more detail the nature of the variables involved and how the process of pump-priming actually works.

Summary

1 National income consists of the total wealth produced, distributed and consumed in an economy in a given period.

2 When certain adjustments are made, national income can be calculated by adding-up either total incomes, total output or total expenditure.

3 National income accounts have limitations, but are a useful guide to trends in the economy.

28 The multiplier and the accelerator

Equilibrium in the economy

It will be remembered from Chapter 26 and the analysis of the circular flow that the value of output (Q) is derived from the revenue entrepreneurs receive from consumption (C), investment (I), exports (X) and government spending (G). Income (Y) is spent on home-produced goods (consumption (C)) or on imports (M) or is saved (S) or paid in taxation (T). Thus:

$$Q = C + I + X + G$$
$$Y = C + S + M + T$$

National income accounts show us that (if we make the appropriate adjustments described in Chapter 27) output equals income. Thus:

$$(C + I + X + G) = (C + S + M + T)$$

As consumption is common to both sides of the equation, then $(I + X + G) = (S + M + T)$. In other words, *injections* into the circular flow equal *leakages* or withdrawals from the circular flow. At this point an economy is in equilibrium. In this chapter we will examine the nature of each of the variables in the equations above – the injections, the leakages and consumption. We will also examine in detail exactly what happens when there is an injection into the economy and will illustrate the process in terms of both equations and diagrams.

Consumption and savings

We will start by simplifying our model to exclude government spending, taxation, imports and exports – ie we will examine a 'closed' economy with no foreign or government sectors. The role of the government and of trade will be introduced later.

In this simplified model, there is only one injection, investment, and one leakage, savings. Otherwise, all income is spent on home-produced goods. Both consumption and savings depend on income – without income there can be no spending or saving. Thus, consumption and savings are 'dependent variables' or are 'functions' of Income. They are shown diagrammatically in Diagram 28.1. This is known as a '45° Diagram' because, assuming the two axes are drawn to the same scale, along a line drawn at 45° from the origin, the variables on the vertical axis will equal those on the horizontal axis – ie consumption plus savings will equal income. Thus, at point X, consumption equals income. Therefore, savings will equal zero at this point, so the savings function will be at point Z on the horizontal axis.

To the right of point X, consumption is below the 45° line (ie is less than income), therefore savings will be positive. To the left of point X, consumption exceeds income, so savings must be negative. Why does this variation happen and in particular how can consumption exceed income to the left of point X?

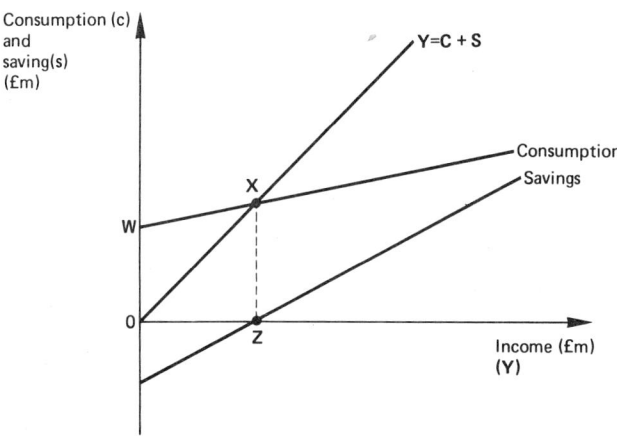

28.1 Consumption and savings functions

Consumption and savings are not constant functions of income because the average propensities to consume (APC) and save (APS) are not constant. As people become richer they spend a smaller fraction of their income. Poor people have to spend all or nearly all their incomes on food, clothing and shelter in order to survive. Richer people cannot only spend on a wider variety of goods (which poor people would regard as luxuries), they can also afford to *save* for future consumption.

At very low levels of income people may have to borrow, incur debts or spend from any meagre savings they may have in order to survive – ie they spend more than their current income or 'dissave'. Even people with no income need to consume, so consumption will exist even when income is zero. Thus, *some* element of consumption is partly independent of income. In Diagram 28.1, consumption is 0W at income 0, so 0W is that 'autonomous' element in consumption which is not a direct function of income.

Factors affecting the average propensities to consume and save in an economy include the income level and the distribution of income among the inhabitants. The economic climate is also important; in inflationary times, when prices are rising, money is losing its value so there is an incentive to spend; in depressions there is a higher propensity to save because of uncertain future prospects. The availability of goods and services is also important. In war time, with shortages and rationing, 'pent-up demand' exists; people cannot spend because the goods are just not available. The attractiveness of saving (eg the level of interest rates, particularly in comparison with the inflation rate) is a relevant factor, as is the prevailing social attitude to thrift. Victorian and Edwardian attitudes seemed to stress the alleged virtues of saving more than modern-day philosophies, which are influenced by inflation, which erodes the value of savings. War time propaganda also encouraged savings to help finance the war effort.

Investment

Investment falls into several categories. Industry invests in machinery, plant, equipment and vehicles; the government invests in public capital, such as roads, hospitals and schools, and private individuals invest in dwellings. All of these generate output and income, but the most productive type of investment is usually regarded as industrial investment in plant and machinery. This generates output and income and also serves to be part of technological growth and development in new productive processes.

Investment can be *autonomous* (ie completely independent from income levels) or can be a *function* of income. Diagram 28.2 shows the two types.

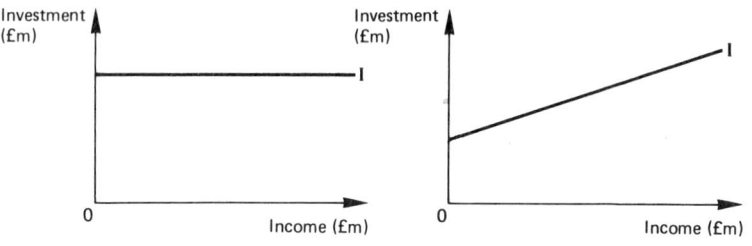

28.2a Autonomous   28.2b Dependant
Autonomous and dependant investment

Autonomous investment arises from inventions and innovations, which may occur at any time; regular replacement of worn-out capital; and a considerable part of public sector investment in essential things like schools and hospitals. Much investment depends on income, however. As demand for motor cars rises, for example, more machines are needed in the car industry. The capital goods industry is greatly affected by swings in demand for consumer goods. There is a *capital-output ratio* in all industries; 'x' machines are required to produce 'y' units of output. For every increase of 'y' units in output, 'x' new machines are required. Yet increases in demand for consumer goods produce a disproportionate increase in the demand for capital goods to make them. This exaggerated effect is called the *accelerator*, and is illustrated in Table 28.1.

Table 28.1 The accelerator

Year	Sales	Existing capital	Required capital	Replacement capital	New capital required	Total investment
1	£10,000	£20,000	£20,000	£2,000	–	£2,000
2	£12,000	£20,000	£24,000	£2,000	£4,000	£6,000
3	£14,000	£24,000	£28,000	£2,000	£6,000	£8,000
4	£15,000	£28,000	£30,000	£2,000	£4,000	£6,000
5	£14,000	£28,000	£28,000	£2,000	–	£2,000
6	£13,000	£28,000	£26,000	–	–	nil.

In Table 28.1 it is assumed that there is a capital-output ratio of 2:1 – £200 of machines are required to produce £100 of consumer goods. In Year 1, demand for consumer goods is £10,000, so £20,000 of machines are required. Let us assume that 10 per cent of the machinery is replaced each year because it has become worn-out. Thus, if sales remain at £10,000, £20,000 machines are required, so there will be a regular replacement of £2,000 of machines each year.

Suppose in Year 2 that final demand rises to £12,000. Now £24,000 of machines are needed; in addition to the £2,000 replacement of capital, restoring the stock to £20,000, £4,000 of new, extra machinery is required. Total investment in Year 2 is £6,000 instead of the usual £2,000. Thus, a rise of 20 per cent in demand for consumer goods has led to a rise of 300 per cent in the demand for machines.

If demand rises to £14,000 in Year 3, £28,000 of machines are needed. Only £24,000 exists, so £4,000 is needed as well as the regular £2,000 replacement. Demand has risen by about 16 per cent (from £12,000 to £14,000) but Demand for machines has remained at £6,000 – a rise of 0 per cent.

If demand rises to £15,000 in Year 4, £30,000 of machines are needed. The capital stock is £28,000, so only £2,000 *new* investment is needed in addition to the regular replacement of £2,000. Demand for the finished product has risen by about $6\frac{2}{3}$ per cent, but total demand for machines has *fallen* by 33 per cent (from £6,000 to £4,000). The relative decline in the capital goods industry has begun, when the increase in the demand for consumer goods has begun to slow down.

When demand actually falls, in Years 5 and 6, the demand for machinery falls even more quickly. Indeed, in Year 6, it is not even necessary to replace the usual £2,000 of depreciated machinery because there is surplus capacity.

Capital goods industries are, therefore, much more susceptible to trade cycle fluctuations than are consumer goods industries. The fluctuations would not be quite so pronounced in reality as in this example. Entrepreneurs would not install new machines unless they thought that the increase in demand was likely to be permanent. Also, firms would not suddenly dramatically decrease their capital stock unless demand was permanently falling; they would prefer to keep surplus capacity in case demand picked-up again. Firms also keep stocks of unsold goods in hand so that increases in demand can be met without having to install more machinery. So, in the real world, surplus capacity, short-time working, and building-up of stocks occur when demand falls; waiting-lists, overtime working and de-stocking occurs in the upswing of the trade cycle. All the time there is the likelihood of a technological breakthrough which will introduce new, more efficient machinery and methods.

Apart from that element of investment which is autonomous, most investment decisions are affected by the prospects of the income which the investment will bring in, and by the cost of the investment, particularly the interest rate to be paid on the funds borrowed to finance the investment.

As interest rates fall, investment should rise; investment projects do not require to be so profitable in order to pay the interest debts. With high interest rates, only very profitable investments can be undertaken. With any proposed investment, future demand, competition and price trends must be estimated. Calculations called *discounted cash flow* techniques must be undertaken to try to estimate the net revenues a project will bring in. In the public sector, social costs and benefits also may have to be included in these calculations.

Diagram 28.3 shows what Keynes called the '*marginal efficiency of capital*'. As interest rates fall, more investment is undertaken, because the 'marginal efficiency' or the extra returns gained from each unit of investment are more likely to be sufficient to pay the costs of the required interest rate. Clearly, in inflationary times, forecasting rates of return on investment over a period of future years is a very difficult exercise. Several investment decisions have gone very wrong, such as the Concorde aircraft project, which went ahead on the basis that over 120 aircraft would be sold. In fact, only 16 were built, of which 7 found buyers in the form of British Airways and Air France, both of whom were forced to buy by their governments.

The multiplier

Let us now examine the effects of an injection of investment. An injection of investment into the economy will generate output, incomes and employment. The extent to which extra income is generated depends upon a device known as the *multiplier*.

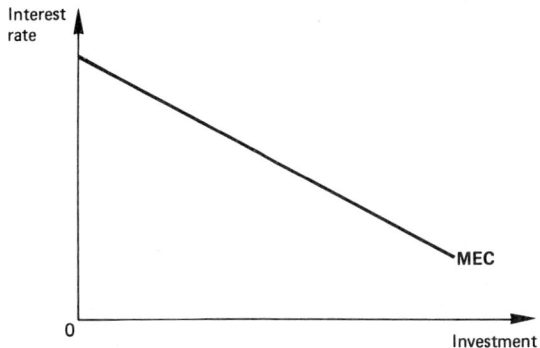

28.3 The marginal efficiency of capital

Let us assume that an economy is in equilibrium (savings equals investment) in the following circumstances:

Income	=	£100m
Consumption	=	£ 75m
Savings	=	£ 25m
Investment	=	£ 25m

Let us also assume that the average propensity to consume is ¾ and the average propensity to save is ¼. Over a small range of income, let us also assume that the marginal propensities to consume and save are identical to their respective average propensities.

Investment now rises by £20m. The immediate effect of this is to raise the incomes of the people who have received the investment by £20m. These people will wish to spend ¾ of their new income, ie £15m, and save ¼, which is £5m.

When this £15m is spent by the people concerned, the incomes of *other* people will rise by £15m, of course. The £15m is re-circulating round the circular flow; someone is spending it, someone else is receiving it as income. The recipients will, in their turn, spend ¾ of £15m, (ie £11¼m) and save ¼ of it is (£3¾m). And so the process goes on. Income rises by £15m + £11¼m etc. Savings rise by £5m + £3¾m etc.

The process only stops when income has risen by £80m, consumption by £60m and savings by £20m. At this point, ¾ of the extra income has been spent and ¼ saved, and investment equals savings. People are spending that fraction of income which they desire to spend and saving what they desire to save. The economy is in equilibrium.

This process can be explained in a formula:

$$\text{Rise in income} = \text{investment} \times \frac{1}{1 - \text{MPC}}$$

In this example, the rise in income = £20m × $\frac{1}{1-\frac{3}{4}}$

= £20m × $\frac{1}{\frac{1}{4}}$

= £20m × 4

= £80m

So, income has risen by £80m, consumption by £60m and Savings £20m. The expression $\frac{1}{1-\text{MPC}}$ is called *'The multiplier'*. In this case, the multiplier was 4. If the MPC had been $\frac{2}{3}$, the multiplier would have been $\frac{1}{1-\frac{2}{3}}$ or 3, If the MPC had been $\frac{5}{6}$, the multiplier would have been 6. This multiplier formula is identical to the creation of credit multiplier explained in Chapter 14 (pp 139-40).

If in our simple economy a government knows what the economy's MPC and MPS are (ie it knows the size of the multiplier), it can estimate the effects on income, consumption and savings of a proposed injection into the economy.

The multiplier effect can be shown on a 45° diagram, such as Diagram 28.4. The vertical axis measures expenditure (ie consumption plus investment) and the horizontal axis measures income. We are assuming, for simplicity, that investment is fixed or autonomous, so does not rise with Income.

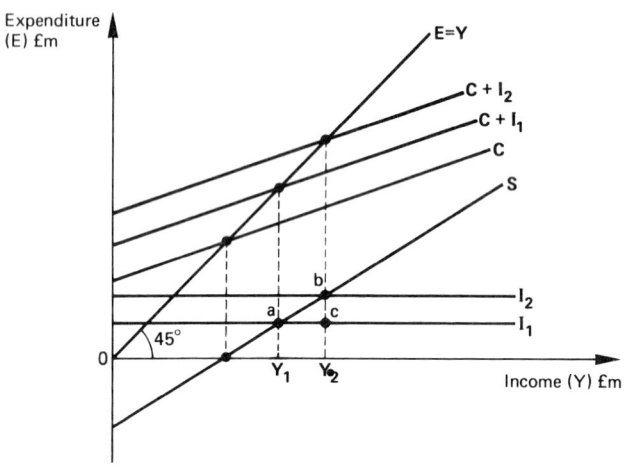

28.4 The multiplier

Original equilibrium is at income $0Y_1$: savings equals investment at point 'a', which means that income is $0Y_1$ and that consumption plus investment meets the 45° line at that income level. At that point, what people want to spend (C + I) equals income. As income equals output, desired spending exactly equals what the economy is producing. When investment rises to I_2, new equilibrium is found at $0Y_2$: investment equals savings at point 'b' and consumption plus investment meets the 45° line at income $0Y_2$. The extra income generated is:

$$\text{rise in investment} \times \frac{1}{1 - \text{MPC}} \text{ or rise in investment} \times \frac{1}{\text{MPS}}$$

MPS is the slope of the savings function between points a and b, which is $\frac{bc}{ac}$ - ie $\frac{\text{change in savings (bc)}}{\text{change in income (ac)}}$.

Thus, if an injection of investment takes place, new equilibrium is found by moving up the savings function to the new intersection of investment and savings.

The multiplier can work in reverse, of course. If original investment was I_2 and investment then fell to I_1, then equilibrium income would fall from $0Y_2$ to $0Y_1$ and both consumption and savings would fall by an amount determined by their marginal propensities.

Changes in the consumption and savings functions

It is quite possible that an economy might change its consumption and savings functions. Suppose consumers decided to spend more at all levels of Income (ie the APC rises). The APS would obviously fall, as APC and APS have to add up to 1. The effects are shown in Diagram 28.5: the APC rises so the consumption function C_2 rises parallel to C_1 and the Savings function S_2 falls parallel to S_1. (Notice, as always, that when the consumption function crosses the 45° line, savings are zero). The effect of greater consumption is, of course, to raise income from $0Y_1$ to $0Y_2$, because there is a new equilibrium at point b. Savings must equal investment in equilibrium and, because investment is unchanged, the level of savings must be unchanged. Consumption has risen, but savings is unchanged – though savings *as a fraction of income* (ie APS) is lower, because income has risen.

If consumers had wished to save more of their incomes (ie raise the APS), then Incomes would have fallen. In Diagram 28.5, imagine that C_2 and S_2 had been the original functions, with Income at $0Y_2$. A rise in APS would production functions S_1 and C_1, reducing both income (to $0Y_1$) and consumption – but leaving the level of Savings unchanged. Thus, an attempt to save more does *not* increase savings because investment has not changed, but it does reduce income (so that savings is now a larger fraction of income) and consumption. This so-called *paradox of thrift* (an attempt to save more does not increase savings) is even more clearly illustrated if we assume that some part of investment is a function of (ie varies with) income, as shown in Diagram 28.6. Here, a rise in APS not only reduces income, it also reduces savings! Because investment has fallen with income, the level of savings has also fallen, although of course savings is now a greater fraction of income at $0Y_2$ than at $0Y_1$.

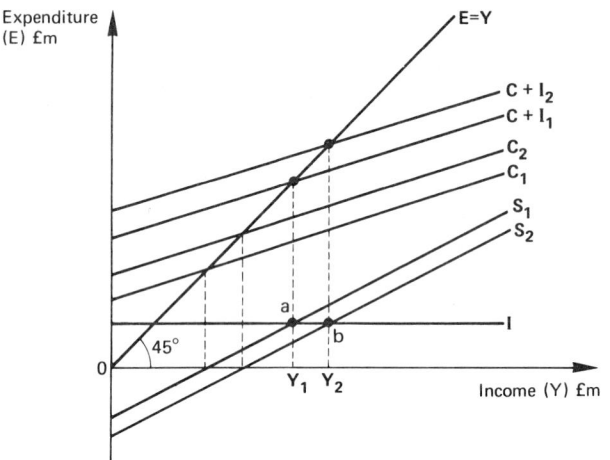

28.5 A rise in the average propensity to consume

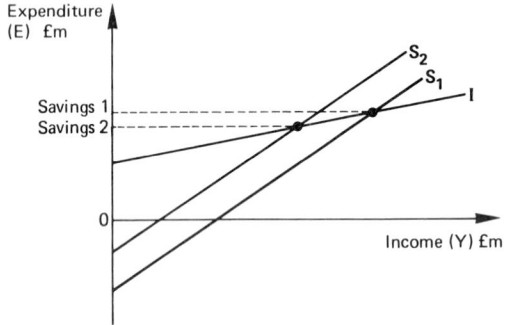

28.6 The paradox of thrift

It is, of course, possible that the *marginal* propensities to consume and save may change. For instance, in Diagram 28.7 the marginal propensity to consume at income levels beyond point x has risen, so the MPS has fallen beyond point y. The general effect is the same – to raise equilibrium income. An increase in MPS would reverse the process shown in Diagram 28.7.

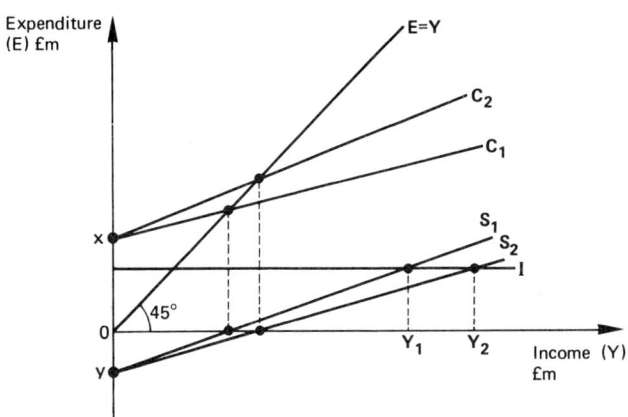

28.7 A change in the marginal propensities to consume and save

The trade multiplier

So far, we have confined our examples to a closed economy. Let us now add a new injection, exports, and a new leakage, imports. The economy has an average propensity to import (APS) which is that fraction of income spent on imports and a marginal propensity to import (MPM) which is that fraction of a rise in income spent on imports. Spending on imports is, of course, a form of consumption, so the basic theorem that all income is either spent or saved is still true, but unlike consumption of home-produced goods, consumption of imports is a leakage of money out of the system: it does not create output or income at home. Although there is an 'import content' in many goods made here making it difficult actually to identify and separate consumption on home-produced goods and on imports, we will assume that this can be done, and will define consumption as being purchases of domestically-produced goods and imports as being purchases of foreign-produced goods.

The effects on an economy or a rise in exports is the same as a rise in investment – income will rise. Suppose:

Income	= 3500m
Investment	= 500m
Exports	= 200m
APS = MPS	= 1/10
APM = MPM	= 1/10
APC = MPC	= 8/10
Savings	350m
Imports	350m
Consumption	2800m

The economy is in equilibrium, because injections (investment + exports) equal leakages (savings + imports) and people are spending, saving and importing exactly in accordance with their average propensities.

Now suppose exports rise by 100. The multiplier formula is:

$$\text{Change in income} = \text{Change in injection} \times \frac{1}{1-\text{MPC}}$$

The injection here is exports, so it is a *trade multiplier* which is taking place.

$$\begin{aligned}\text{Change in income} &= 100 \times \frac{1}{1 - 8/10} \\ &= 100 \times \frac{1}{2/10} \\ &= 100 \times \frac{10}{2} \\ &= 500.\end{aligned}$$

Income has risen by £500m to £4000m. Consumption will rise by $\frac{8}{10}$ of £500m (ie by £400m) and both savings and imports will rise by $\frac{1}{10}$ of £500m, or £50m each.

Investment (£500m) + exports (now £300m) equals £800m.

Savings + imports (now £400m each) equals £800m. Consumption is £3200m, which is $\frac{8}{10}$ of income. A new equilibrium exists. The trade multiplier is $\frac{1}{2/10}$ or 5. Diagram 28.8 illustrates what has happened. The export injection has raised imcome to $0Y_2$.

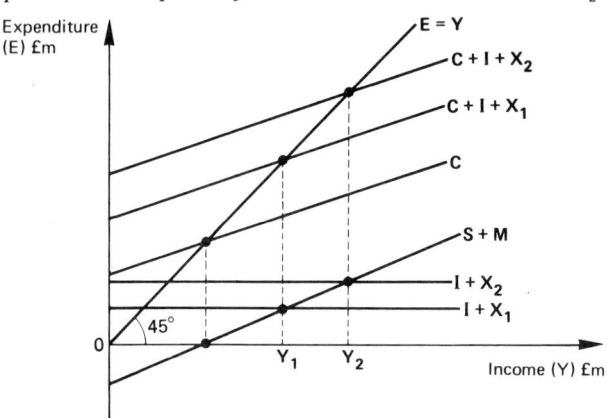

28.8 The trade multiplier

If a country wished to impose import restrictions this should raise its income, providing at least some of the money no longer spent on imports was spent on home-produced goods instead. If all the 'extra' money were saved, then the rise in one leakage (savings) would cancel the fall in the other (imports) and the situation with regard to income and consumption would remain unchanged. If some or all of the money withdrawn from imports is spent at home, though, income and consumption will rise. Suppose:

Income = £ 400m
Investment = £ 600m
Exports = £ 200m
APM = 1/10
APS = 1/10
APC = 4/5
Imports = £ 400m
Savings = £ 400m
Consumption = £3200m

Equilibrium therefore exists.

Now suppose import restrictions are imposed, so that APM falls to $\frac{1}{15}$, but APS remains $\frac{1}{10}$. APC will now be $\frac{5}{6}$.

So, Income will be $(600 + 200) \times \frac{1}{6}$

or 800×6
$= 4800m$

and consumption will be £4800m $\times \frac{5}{6}$ or £400m. Savings will be £480m and imports £320m.

Diagram 28.9 illustrates this. The leakage function (S + M) has fallen, so the consumption function has risen. Income has risen to $0Y_2$.

The trade multiplier can help spread economic activity or depression internationally. Suppose that the UK reduces its imports from Japan by £250m and suppose Japan's MPC is $\frac{4}{5}$. Japan's income will fall by

$250m \times \frac{1}{1 - 4/5}$

or $250m \times 5$
or $1250m$

If the UK had increased its imports from Japan by £250m, then Japan's income would have *risen* by £250m × 5 or £1250m. Thus trade stimulates economic activity and protectionism restricts it.

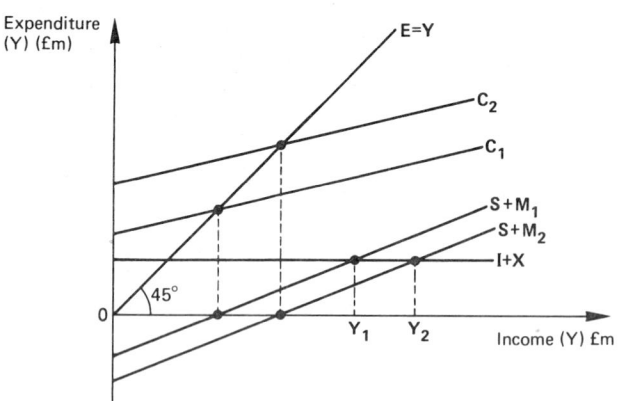

28.9 Import restrictions

The government multiplier

Now let us introduce the final injection, government spending, and the final leakage, taxation. The economy has an average tax rate or propensity to pay tax (APT) and a marginal tax rate or propensity to pay tax (MPT). A rise in government spending raises income. The full multiplier formula therefore is:

Rise in income = rise in investment, exports, or government spending $\times \dfrac{1}{1 - \text{MPC}}$

or = change in (I or X or G) = $\dfrac{1}{\text{MPS} + \text{MPM} + \text{MPT}}$

Thus, if the government pumps in £10m and the MPM $= \dfrac{1}{10}$, MPT $= \dfrac{1}{5}$ and MPS $= \dfrac{1}{10}$:

Rise in income = $10 \times \dfrac{1}{1 - 3/5}$ or $10 \times \dfrac{1}{1/10 + 1/10 + 1/5}$

= $10 \times \dfrac{1}{2/5}$

= £25m

Consumption will rise by £15m, taxes by £5m and imports and savings by £2½m each.

The Diagram 28.10 will resemble that for any injection. Income and consumption levels have risen.

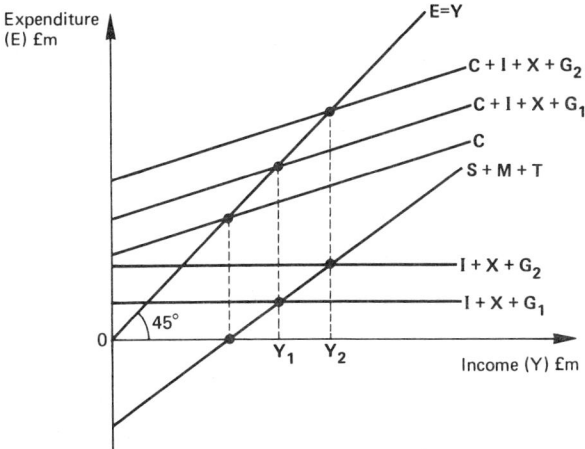

28.10 Government spending multiplier

Should taxes (APT) be changed, then the effect will be similar to those following a change in APS or APM. If taxes were reduced then, assuming at least *some* of the 'extra' money was spent on home-produced goods, incomes would rise.

Suppose people spent $\frac{2}{3}$ of their disposable income (ie income after tax) on home-produced goods and taxation was 25 per cent; consumption would then be $\frac{2}{3}(\frac{3}{4}Y)$ or $\frac{1}{2}Y$. If taxes fell to 10 per cent consumption would be $\frac{2}{3}(\frac{9}{10}Y)$ or $\frac{6}{10}Y$.

If injections totalled £24m, then with 25 per cent taxes, income would be £24m $\times \frac{1}{1-\frac{1}{2}}$, ie £24m $\times$ 2 or £48m. Consumption would be £24m. When taxes were reduced to 10 per cent, income would be £24m $\times \frac{1}{1-6/10}$ ie £24m $\times \frac{10}{4}$ or £60m. Consumption would rise to £36m. Again, the diagram would resemble that of a fall in savings or imports (Diagram 28.11). Income and consumption increase.

Inflationary and deflationary gaps

Both the multipliers and the 45° diagrams show the effects of changing injections and leakages. Incomes will change, therefore so will consumption, savings, imports and taxation. Injections will generate income and consumption and governments who know the size of the multiplier will be able to estimate the effects of injections. What is also important to know is the effect on *employment*. The 45° diagram can help here.

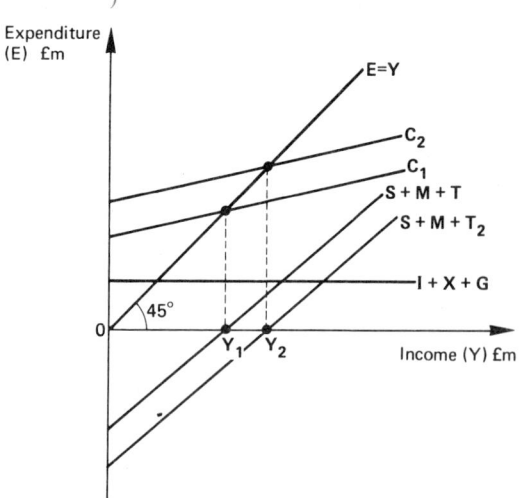

28.11 A reduction in taxes

Diagram 28.12 shows an economy in equilibrium at $0Y_1$, a level *below* full employment. Surplus capacity or a *'deflationary gap'* exists. Full employment is shown at 'FE', so there is surplus capacity of FE minus $0Y_1$. The 'C + injections' function cannot achieve full employment: it falls short by ab, which is the deflationary gap. Thus injections of 'injections 2' are needed to close this gap and achieve a new equilibrium at point a. Governments must try to estimate how much to inject in order to close this gap and achieve full employment.

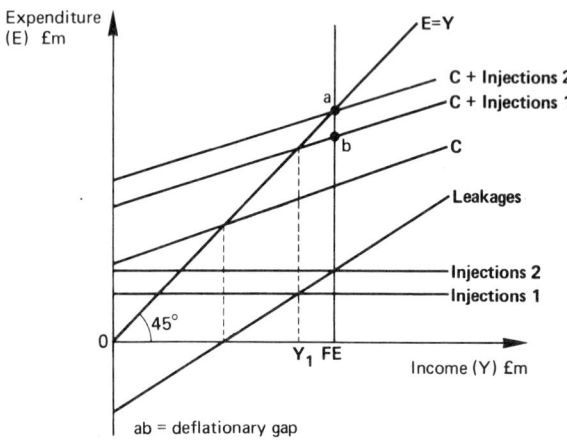

28.12 A deflationary gap eliminated by increasing injections

Alternatively, the government could reduce leakages again achieving equilibrium at the level of full employment, as illustrated in Diagram 28.13. Here, leakages are reduced (eg taxes remitted), so consumption rises; point a is reduced by 'C_2 + injections'.

The opposite of a deflationary gap is an *inflationary gap*. Here, the pressure of consumption + injections exceeds full employment: output cannot meet demand (ie point $0Y_1$ cannot be reached), so prices rise. In order to cure this, injections must be reduced (as in Diagram 28.14) to achieve a new equilibrium at point a or leakages raised (the reverse situation to Diagram 28.13).

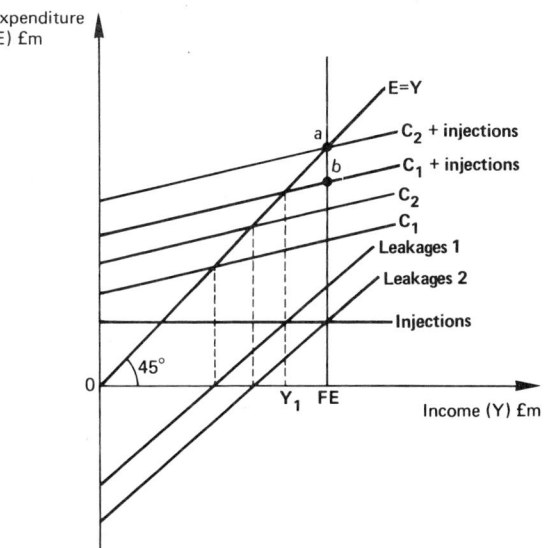

28.13 A deflationary gap eliminated by reducing leakages

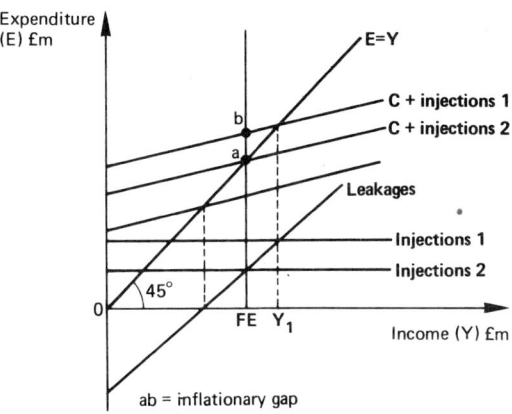

28.14 An inflationary gap eliminated by reducing injections

The economy is in equilibrium, not at full employment (which is what some economists used to think) but where injections equal leakages and where the levels of consumption, savings, imports and taxation exactly reflect the community's average propensity to do these things. If full employment is required, equilibrium must be moved there by manipulating injections or leakages. That was the message of Keynes.

The multiplier in the real world

What are the propensities in the real world? Diagram 28.15 shows the process. Suppose £100 of output is produced, generating £100 of income. The leakages at each stage are retained profits, taxes, savings and imports. Eventually, £31 is left as consumption of domestically-produced goods, and this sum re-enters the circular flow. Therefore, the APC is $\frac{31}{100}$, so the multiplier is $\frac{1}{1 - 31/100}$ or $\frac{1}{69/100}$, which equals approximately 1.45.

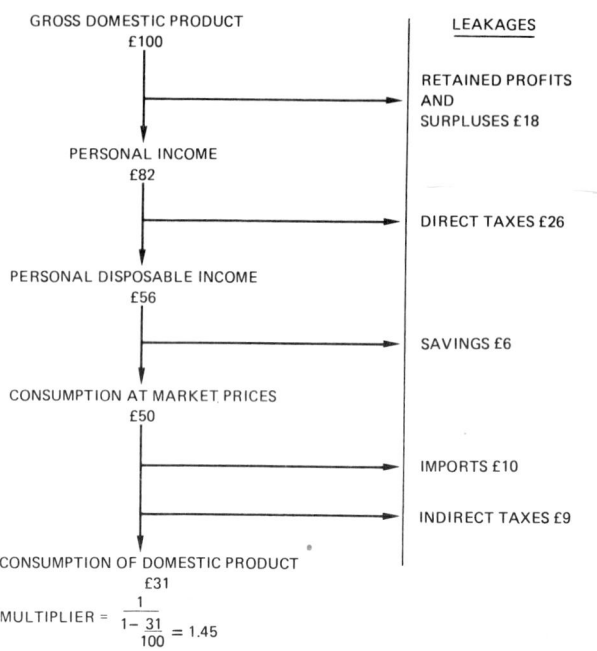

28.15 The multiplier in practice
 Source: M C Kennedy, 'The Economy as a Whole' in *The UK Economy*, ed A R Prest and D J Coppock, 8 ed, Weidenfeld and Nicolson, London, 1980, p 28.

So, in the UK, leakages are high, especially Taxes ($\frac{7}{20}$). The average propensity to import is also high by the standards of an industrial country. The average propensity to save is rather low, as perhaps would be expected in inflationary times. Yet the average propensity to save as a fraction of disposable income doubled during the 1970s, despite inflation. This is perhaps because people have an idea of a certain sum which they wish to keep in their bank account or other form of savings, regardless of the economic climate. This 'money illusion' tends to cause people to keep up the level of their savings even when savings are losing their value. Of course, unemployment has also risen, which would encourage people to save more according to the precautionary motive because they fear for their future position. Interest rates have also been high, encouraging people to save on deposit with various institutions.

Nevertheless, considering how inflationary the 1970s were, the average propensity to consume home-produced goods is lower than would be expected. The knotty problem of inflation and its ramifications will be examined in the next chapter.

Summary

1 An economy is in equilibrium when injections (investment, exports and government spending) equal leakages (savings, imports and taxation).
2 Consumption of home-produced goods, savings, imports and taxation are mainly functions of income, but some element of consumption is autonomous.
3 Investment contains both autonomous and functional elements. The accelerator measures the impact of changes in final demand on changes in demand for capital goods.
4 Investment decisions involve a comparison of the expected income from the project over its lifetime compared with its costs.
5 The multiplier measures the effects of an injection into the economy on the extra Income thereby generated. The multiplier formula is:

$$\text{change in income} = \text{new injection} \times \frac{1}{1 - \text{marginal propensity to consume}}$$

6 If equilibrium occurs at a level of economic activity which leaves resources unemployed, a deflationary gap exists. Conversely, an inflationary gap may exist when the economy can meet the demands placed on it by consumption plus injections. Keynes advocated the use of fiscal policy to eliminate these gaps and thus create equilibrium at full employment levels.

29 Inflation – causes and cures

Inflation

Inflation can be defined simply as a state of affairs where the general level of prices in an economy is rising continuously. To anyone born or coming to adulthood after the Second World War in the UK, inflation would seem to be a natural, apparently unavoidable phenomenon: each year prices rise and from the mid – 1970s into the 1980s, prices rose at annual rate of over 10 per cent. Thus, 100 per cent inflation occurred within six or seven years. Economic historians tell us, however, that inflation has *not* always existed. For example, 'Between the years 1400 and 1914 there was no effective inflation other than that which occurred roughly between 1500 and 1650 when substantial inflation resulted, firstly from Henry VIII's debasement of the coinage . . . . and secondly from the massive influx of gold and silver from the American colonies. Between 1650 and 1914 there was virtually no change in the price level, although certain episodes such as the Napoleonic Wars, brought about temporary fluctuations'.[1]

Massive inflation occurred during the two world wars, yet prices were stagnant or falling for much of the inter-war period. Steady price rises have occurred since 1945, however, and this 'creeping' inflation began to accelerate into annual double-figure rates in the 1970s. The big fear than was that '*hyper-inflation*' would occur – inflation would accelerate to hundreds of per cent per year. Several South American countries, such as Chile, Argentina and Brazil, have experienced this in recent years. Israel and Iceland have experienced annual rates in excess of 50 per cent. In the 1920s several currencies collapsed, notably that of Germany, where the inflation rate reached billions of per cent per annum. Small items, like bread and eggs, cost trillions of marks; people were paid daily, then hourly, and rushed to spend their money before prices rose further. A cup of coffee might cost 10 million marks when ordered, 20 million marks after being drunk. The currency became so worthless that it was no longer used and barter was re-introduced. A millionaire's savings were worth nothing (if they were in cash or bank deposit form).

The evils of hyper-inflation are clear: a currency becomes worthless; money savings are worthless; the marginal propensity to save dwindles to zero and the rush to spend accelerates the inflationary trend. The

UK has avoided hyper-inflation, yet the level between 10 per cent and 20 per cent which has come to dominate since the early 1970s is still regarded as harmful. Both the Labour Government (1974 - 79) and the Conservative Government which replaced it stated that curing inflation was their first priority in economic policy. Despite the fact that the standard of living is higher than it was in the 1930s and the country is more prosperous, and that this has been achieved during an era of inflation, official opinion is that inflation, or certainly inflation above a certain (though generally unspecified) annual rate is a bad thing and must be eradicated. Just what the unpleasant effects of inflation are will be examined shortly. First, we shall look at the possible causes of inflation. After that, we shall discuss the effects of inflation. Then, possible remedies will be examined. Finally, the condition of the Uk in the 1980s will be examined – an economy seemingly sufferings from simultaneous inflation and unemployment, a state of affairs sometimes called '*stagflation*'.

Possible causes of inflation

The word 'possible' may be used a great deal in this chapter, because the causes of and cures for inflation are a matter of fierce, even acrimonious debate between economists. There seem to be two main sets of protagonists – *Keynesians and Monetarists* and within the ranks of both group are many differences shades of opinion. As with much academic debate, the differences of opinion tend to be exaggerated and polarised positions become propounded. There are differencies but there are also points of agreement. Some discussion and evaluation of all this is necessary, of course, but first we must deal with the possible causes of and cures for inflation individually.

Table 29.1 should be of use throughout much of this chapter. It shows the annual percentage change in retail prices (the usual measure of inflation) and also shows either the levels or annual percentage changes in other variables which economists think are connected with or may even cause inflation. These variables are unemployment, wage rates, import prices, the money supply and the exchange rate of sterling.

1 *Cost push theories*
   One set of theories concerning the causes of inflation can be called 'cost-push' theories. Adherents of this body of opinion believe that inflation is caused by rises in the costs of production of goods and services – land, labour, capital and enterprise. Thus, prices can rise because entrepreneurs wish to pass on to the public increased costs which they have incurred, such as rents, interest rates, wages or raw materials. Alternatively, entrepreneurs may wish to increase their profit margin, so they raise their prices. This last possibility would not seem relevant to the UK's predicament,

except that the common agricultural policy of the EEC fixes food prices each year in order to guarantee farm incomes and profits. Profits, as a proportion of national income, have steadily fallen in the 1970s. Other costs have risen rapidly, however, as Table 29.1 shows. Wage rates rose at double figure level each year except one from 1970 to 1980 (regarding 1970's figure of 9.9 per cent as being double figures). Import prices rose at staggering levels in the mid-1970s (1973-74 was when the world oil price was quadrupled and the prices of many other raw materials and commodities soared). The exchange rate of the pound fell steadily from 1972 to 1977, exacerbating the rise in import prices. Interest rates rose to record levels in 1980-81. All these are costs of production to many firms, because they employ labour, import materials and borrow money. Thus, cost-push theorists believe that much of the UK's recent and current inflation is due to cost factors, particularly wages.

Table 29.1   Inflation, unemployment and related variables, 1955-1980

	Annual % change					
	retail prices	unemployment	wages rates	import prices	money stock (M3)[1]	exchange rate sterling[2]
1955	4.5	1.0	6.9	3.0		
1956	2.0	1.0	8.0	1.9		
1957	3.7	1.3	5.0	0.9		
1958	3.0	1.9	3.6	−7.2		
1959	0.6	2.0	2.6	−1.0		
1960	1.0	1.5	2.5	0		
1961	3.4	1.3	4.2	−2.0		
1962	2.6	1.8	3.6	−1.0		
1963	2.1	2.2	3.7	4.0		
1964	3.3	1.6	4.8	3.0	5.6	
1965	4.8	1.3	4.3	0.6	7.6	
1966	3.9	1.4	4.6	1.5	3.4	
1967	2.5	2.2	3.9	0.3	10.0	−14.3
1968	4.7	2.3	6.6	12.3	6.8	
1969	5.4	2.3	5.3	3.1	2.4	
1970	6.4	2.5	9.9	4.5	9.5	
1971	9.4	3.3	12.9	4.7	13.9	
1972	7.1	3.6	13.8	5.7	24.5	−4.8
1973	9.2	2.6	13.7	27.6	26.3	−9.3
1974	16.1	2.5	19.8	46.6	10.2	−3.1
1975	24.3	3.9	29.5	14.4	6.6	−7.7
1976	16.5	5.2	19.3	21.8	9.5	−15.3
1977	15.8	5.2	6.6	16.0	10.0	−5.0
1978	8.2	5.6	14.1	4.0	15.0	1.4
1979	13.4	5.3	14.9	10.4	12.6	7.6
1980	18.4	8.8 (December)	13.0	n.a.	18.6	12.1

1 Only officially measured since 1964.
2 Since sterling was floated (except for 1967 Devaluation).
Source: The UK Economy, A.R. Prest and D.J. Coppock (eds), 8th edition, Weidenfeld & Nicolson, p 45.

Wages are the main cost item in many industries, so rise in wages which are not backed by rises in productivity may lead to higher prices. Keynes advocated wage controls in his book 'How to Pay for the War' and incomes policies have become a firm plank of the policies advocated by post-war Keynesians.

Many economists do not blame cost factors for inflation: indeed, some say that wages do not initially cause inflation; workers only demand wage rises because prices are *already* rising. Wage claims are thus a defensive reaction to an existing inflation. Wage rises may perpetuate and perhaps accelerate inflation, but do not initially cause it. The evidence from Table 29.1 can be interpreted in several ways, unfortunately. Wages and prices tend to rise together from the late 1960s onwards. Both reached a peak in 1975. Wage-push theorists would point to the low figure for wage rises in 1977 (6.6 per cent) and the consequent reduction in the inflation rate in 1978. Opponents would reckon that wage rate figures follow-on from the previous year's price rise figures. The existence of incomes policies in 1966–69, 1972–74 and 1975–79 also complicates the issue by artificially supressing wages at times but allowing big rises in the brief 'policy-off' periods.

2 *Demand-pull theories*

Economists who dismiss or relegate in importance cost-push theories advocate instead demand-pull theories. As shown in the 45° Diagram (Chapter 28, pp 281–4) if the pressure of consumption plus injections is too great for output to keep pace, an inflationary gap occurs. There is 'too much money chasing too few goods', so prices rise. Either the average and marginal propensities to consume are too high, or else injections are too high. The main injection which is blamed is government spending; demand pull advocates say that rising costs are only a cause of inflation *if these costs are paid*. Thus, when oil prices quadrupled, inflation only occurred *because the oil was bought*; wage claims are only inflationary *because the employers pay up*. Thus, there must be a demand element present for inflation to occur. Entrepreneurs only pay the higher costs because they know they can pass the extra costs on to the consumer. If the consumer will not buy, there will be no derived demand for the factors of production. In 1980–81 oil producers failed in their attempt to raise prices, because demand for oil was falling. Trade unions found employers unwilling to pay higher wages because their sales were falling so they could not pass the higher costs to the public. Thus, without demand there can be no inflation. Inflation will be reduced by controlling demand.

Demand-pull theories tend to be associated with full employment, as the 45° Diagram shows. The economy just cannot produce enough. Thus, the 1980s phenomenon of inflation together with high unemployment raises difficulties for demand theorists.

Keynes, of course, advocated the use of fiscal policy to cure a depression or slump. Therefore post-war Keynesians decided that a reversal of Keynesian policies was the answer to inflation. Government spending should be reduced and taxation raised in order to control consumption and demand-pull pressure.

3 *Money supply theories*
Another group of theorists are the *Monetarists*, who follow the tenets of Professor Milton Friedman of Chicago University. Monetarists believe that inflation is caused entirely by governments allowing the money supply to rise too quickly. Monetarists base the policy on the quantity theory of money, outlined in Chapter 17 (pp 155-6). The quantity theory sees a close connection between the money supply and the overall price level. As the money supply rises, prices will rise. An increase in the velocity of circulation of money, which occurs when hyper-inflation is feared and people wish to exchange their money for goods quickly, increases the pressure on prices. Friedman has stated quite bluntly that 'Inflation . . . is and can be produced only by a more rapid increase in the quantity of money than in output'.[2] Yet although monetarists naturally stress monetary policy there is a fiscal element in their policies, because excessive Government Spending is regarded by monetarists as perhaps the main cause of excessive rises in the money supply.

Clearly, a rapidly-rising money supply is a feature of inflationary times. The fantastic rise in the printing of high-denomination banknotes in Germany in 1923 is a clear example. Over longer periods of time, discoveries of gold and silver, out of which currencies were minted, in the sixteenth century and the transport of these precious metals to Europe occurred at a time of rising prices. Similar gold discoveries and exploitation in the 1840s (in California and Australia) and the 1890s (in Alaska and South Africa) also accompanied inflation in Europe. Monetarists would say that these events caused the inflation. Non-monetarists would argue that inflation is caused by other factors and that the rise in the money supply was a *result*, not a cause of that inflation. Table 29.1 shows a huge rise in the money supply in 1970-73 and again in 1978-80, and it also shows high inflation in these times. The Table also shows a high rate of rise of wage rates and import prices. Non-monetarists would argue that it was cost features like wages and import prices which caused the inflation; the money supply then went up *only in order to service the inflation*. As Manser states clearly 'the history of recent times demonstrates that the demand for money overwhelmingly arises out of rising costs rather than out of excess activity'. [3] The money suppply rose only to provide the resources necessary to pay these extra costs.

There are, therefore, conflicting theories about the cause of inflation. Excess demand, high wages, interest rates, rising import prices, government budget deficits, a supply of money which exceeds output – all these have been put forward as causes. One factor on which general agreement can be found, however, is that inflation is very difficult to reverse or eliminate once it is under way because of people's *expectations*. Because we live in inflationary times, we *expect* inflation. Thus, we tend to demand high wages to protect ourselves against expected future inflation; we tend to have a high propensity to consume because money loses its value if it is saved. Our actions are determined by our expectations, which are influenced by our experiences. Only when inflation has fallen do we expect it to fall. Thus, 'once generated the inflationary spiral is largely expectational'.[4] Governments have to produce results in order to influence our behaviour – but our behaviour tends to obstruct their attempts to produce results! Friedman approved of the Conservative Government's actions on assuming power in 1979 when it announced money supply and PSBR targets for the following five years, each year's targets being less than the previous year's. This action was intended to affect people's expectations about future inflation. Unfortunately, it is easier to announce targets than to fulfil them, and the targets have not all been met. In 1980 and 1981 the Government also issued index-linked securities and savings bonds – an action which perhaps assumed that inflation would *not* fall. Consumers' expectations may have been affected by this indexation.

Yet economic climates *do* change. In the 1960s no-one would have expected unemployment to soar from less than 1 million to more than 3 million by 1982, which is what happened. Now that unemployment *has* risen and seems not to be a short-lived phenomenon, people's experience of it will affect their expectations and therefore their actions.

It is necessary, of course, to consider the various anti-inflationary policies which have been suggested, but first we must be clear just *why* it seems to be important to reduce or even eliminate it. What problems does inflation actually cause?

The problems created by a high rate of inflation

1 *Some sectors of the population are hard-hit*
The effects of inflation are somewhat arbitrary. Workers in strong trade unions or in vital industries (eg gas, electricity, coal, oil) tend to be granted wage rises which at least keep up with inflation. People in weak unions or not in unions at all, or workers with no industrial 'muscle' (eg nurses) tend not to keep pace. Pensioners, the unemployed and others reliant on state aid are especialy vulnerable, especially in the short-run.

These problems have been overcome to some extent by indexation. Many workers had their wages and salaries indexed in Phase 3 of Mr Heath's Incomes Policy in 1973–74. Tax allowances are automatically indexed in the Annual Budget (the so-called 'Rooker-Wise' Amendment). Other state aid such as pensions and supplementary benefits have also entered the field of indexation. Undoubtedly, however, price rises do lead to higher wage claims and a *wage-price spiral* tends to occur with everyone trying to catch up, keep up or get ahead, and thus accelerating the process.

2 *The balance of payments may deteriorate*
High prices can handicap exports (unless foreigners' demand is very inelastic) and also lead to greater penetration by cheaper imports. A rise in the average propensity to import instead of to consume home-produced goods will reduce inflationary pressure, of course, but can ruin the balance of payments.

This can be counteracted to some extent in the era of floating exchange rates if a government allows its exchange rate to fall. This stimulates exports and reduces imports – but can worsen inflation because of the rising price of imports which devaluation or downward floating produces. A government is not entirely the master of its exchange rate, however, as Chapter 21 explained (pp 196–200). Speculation, interest rates at home and abroad, political rumour and a host of other factors determine exchange rates. Since the mid–1970s the UK has rather lost control over its exchange rate. The 'coming on tap' of North Sea Oil helped to make sterling a strong currency and it began to appreciate, thus reducing the UK's competitiveness. The rapid rise in wages from 1975 accompanied by sterling's rise from 1978 produced a loss of competitiveness estimated at 55 per cent by the middle of 1981.

3 *Investment and growth can be discouraged*
Evidence on the effects on growth is not conclusive. Between 1967 and 1977 Brazil and Israel experienced very high inflation rates, but had high growth; USA and Switzerland had low inflation and low growth, Belgium, Germany and Austria had low inflation and high growth. Investment and growth may be deterred by inflation if full employment exists and the anticipated profits are high. It is more likely that some *anti-*inflationary policies (eg high interest rates) have deterred investment and growth.

4 *Profits and capital gains can be distorted*
Some anomalies have occurred in the taxation system because inflation appears to make profits and capital gains higher than they really are. For example, a firm may increase its profits by 10 per cent in a year, so pays more tax, but if inflation has been running at 10 per cent in that year, real profits have not risen. After the increased tax, they have fallen, in fact. These problems are not insurmountable, as indexation can again be used. Capital gains were indexed in the 1982 Budget, for example, so that only real rather than nominal gains were taxed.

5 *Inflation may generate unemployment*
As the next section will show, most anti-inflationary policies tend to raise unemployment, but it now seems possible that inflation itself may cause unemployment. Entrepreneurs are no longer so willing to pass higher costs on to the consumer in a competitive situation, especially if foreign competitors do not have to pay

them. Thus, there is a search to reduce average costs, to become more efficient and competitive. So, for example, if unions press for a rise in wages the employer may give way, but may seek to reduce the size of the work force. If 10 per cent rise is granted but the labour force is reduced by 10 per cent, the employer can prevent the wage bill from rising. Workers may be pricing themselves (or their colleagues, or potential new recruits to the labour force) out of a job. Table 29.1 shows the rise in unemployment in the 1970s, an era of high inflation – but was this because of inflation or the results of anti-inflationary policies? The evidence again is not conclusive.

Inflation certainly produces problems, but many countries and people have prospered in post-war inflationary times. What is important is not so much just the existence of inflation, but the *rate* and volatility of it. Hyper-inflation is clearly a very serious blow to an economy, but the low rates of less than 5 per cent experienced before 1970 did not seem to create serious problems. It is when inflation gets above rival countries' rates that some problems come, initially to the balance of payments.

Some economists see an important distinction between anticipated and unanticipated rates of inflation. Anticipated rates can perhaps be coped with via indexation, exchange rate manipulations, spending plans, wage controls and so on, but unanticipated rates do create distortions, instability and even panic. Thus, a steady rate of inflation may be as acceptable (and more attainable) than a zero rate. The expectations thesis is, of course, of great relevance to these theories, as it stresses that people can cope with expected events but not an unstable situation. Indeed, if inflation suddenly *falls*, distortion can occur. For example, what happens to government bonds? Debt interest payments would become an unnecessarily large burden to a government which had contracted to pay high annual interest rates.

Reducing inflation would not necessarily cure all the UK's problems. Indeed, at least one economist has questioned whether the 'enormous costs' to the community involved in reducing inflation are worthwhile and suggests that there is a 'dreadful prospect that, granted success against inflation . . . the underlying problems of the British economy would remain much as they were, almost unaffected by what the Government would regard as a tremendous achievement'.[5] Nevertheless, governments will still regard the reduction or control of inflation as a key policy so it is now time to look in detail at the various policies which have been tried or suggested.

Controlling inflation – Keynes or Friedman?

The methods which a government chooses in order to try to reduce or eradicate inflation depend, of course, on the view it takes of the causes. There are at least four main sets of policies which can be used – fiscal policy, as advocated by Keynes, monetary policy, as advocated by Friedman and the monetarists, incomes policy, as advocated by modern Keynesians and manipulation of the exchange rate, favoured by some people from both schools of thought. Exchange rate proponents and the Cambridge economists in particular see their policies as being useful in counteracting other British problems (especially unemployment) in addition to inflation.

1 *Fiscal policy*

   Fiscal or budgetary policy was explained in Chapter 28. In order to reduce inflation, government spending should be cut and taxation raised. Thus, less money would be pumped into the economy while more would be taken out. By reducing national income, consumption will fall (unless consumers raise their average propensity to consume in order to compensate) and demand-pull pressure will fall. Both the multiplier and the 45° diagram would enable the government in theory to estimate the effects of such a policy.

   Although Monetarists descry the value of fiscal policy as a stabiliser of economic activity, they agree upon the restriction of government spending as an anti-inflationary policy. Indeed, strict control over public spending was a central plank in the policy of the basically Monetarist-influenced Conservative Government which assumed power in 1979. Fiscal policy in more general terms, especially the use of taxation, has been widely used in the UK since 1945, either to cure inflation or improve the balance of payments. The main aim has always been to reduce consumption.

Problems and criticisms of fiscal policy

a) In practice, governments have found control of public spending to be difficult to achieve. Governments are committed to so many items of expenditure (eg Education, National Health Service, Pensions and Social Security) that reducing them is difficult. Should roads be left in disrepair, council houses not built, unemployment pay reduced, defence spending cut? The public sector has continuously assumed a bigger role in the UK as it has expanded (eg National Health Service, nationalised industries, regional aid) and consequently its expenditure programmes are difficult to cut.

b) On the taxation side, no government retains popularity (and therefore power) if it continually raises taxes to what the voters regard as unacceptable levels. Since 1970 taxes have rarely met expenditure requirements anyway, so budgetary deficits occur which are financed by the PSBR. There are also a considerable differences involved by the raising of different taxes. There are two types of tax – *direct* and *indirect*. The main form of direct tax in the UK is income tax. The main indirect tax is value added tax (VAT). Indirect taxes, like VAT, or excise duties on alcohol, tobacco and oil, are levied on firms who pass them on to the consumer; the consumer pays them, but in an indirect manner via a producer or supplier of the goods.

The main revenue-raiser in the UK's tax system is income tax, which contributes over 40 per cent of total reveune. Income tax is progressive – the more you earn, the higher rate you pay. The basic rate in 1982 was 30 per cent, the top rate 60 per cent. When the Conservatives came to power in 1979 they abolished the top rates above 60 per cent and therefore gave tax relief to the relatively rich. The rich are the main savers, so the idea was to encourage savings and investment in order to raise growth. If tax relief had been given to poorer people, the main effect would have been to raise consumption, as the poor have a higher marginal propensity to consume (and import) and a lower marginal propensity to save.

Indirect taxes tend to be at a flat rate, like VAT which was raised from 8 per cent to 15 per cent in 1979. These taxes are regressive; all people pay at the same rate, so the taxes bear most heavily on the relatively poor. The tax element on a gallon of petrol (about £1 in 1982) is a greater proportion of a poor person's disposable income than a rich person's. Thus, raising indirect taxes directly deters consumption. Although this is the aim of anti-inflationary policy, a strange anomaly exists. Raising indirect taxes directly raises prices, which might seem a strange way of trying to reduce prices! A brief survey of the UK tax system appears in Appendix 1 to this chapter.

c) Fiscal policy is also a rather crude weapon inasmuch as it is difficult to go in for *fine tuning*. Until the mid-1970s the UK economy had both low inflation and low unemployment: if a government wanted to reduce inflation when it rose to 4 per cent or 5 per cent per annum, or increase employment if the jobless total rose too much over ½ million, it had to 'fine tune' the economy. These small adjustments were difficult to estimate in advance and 'overkill' often resulted, the economy being pushed too far in the required direction. Time-lags also occur, as it takes a whole financial year for the results of an income tax change, for example, to have full effect. As it takes some time to recognize that a trend is in existence in the economy, most policies start late – they are a cure rather than preventative medicine. If there is then a time-lag before policies have full effect, the whole process may be very slow to work – indeed they may come to work just when the trade cycle is changing anyway, so they may then be the wrong policies. Monetarists in particular say that trying to regulate the economy via fiscal policy, especially if fine tuning is required, just does not work. It is too crude and slow-working a weapon.

2 *Incomes policy*

Incomes policy was dealt with in Chapter 23 (pp 228-34). It is an attempt to restrict the rate of income rises, especially wages. Usually, an attempt has to be made to control prices directly as well, in order to get trade unions to accept wage restrictions. The UK has had four official Incomes policies since the War, plus several voluntary or unofficial ones (see Table 23.4). Income policy can be used to restrict consumption, but is usually advocated by those who blame wage costs for inflation – ie cost-push theorists.

Incomes policy was given a boost in 1958 when Professor AW Phillips produced his famous scatter diagram relating the annual rate of change of money wages to the rate of unemployment. Information from the years 1861–1957 showed a close relationship in most years between these two variables, as shown in Diagram 29.1. When there was little or no unemployment wage rises rose considerably; higher unemployment led to lower wage rises and indeed in the 1920s in particular to wage cuts. Thus, post-war full employment was bound to lead to high wages (employers had no alternative but to pay up, because there was no surplus labour to employ and little danger of unemployment for the workers). Thus, to reduce the rate of wage rises, unemployment was needed or, if this was politically unacceptable, wages must be controlled in order both to preserve employment and also to prevent wage-cost inflation.

Unfortunately, in the 1970s the *Phillips curve* no longer seemed valid. Years occurred where high wages and high unemployment co-existed. Were there just 'rogue' years (several had occurred between 1861 and 1957) or was there a new trend? Had the Phillips curve moved 'north-east' proving the *more* unemployment was needed in order to reduce wages than had previously been thought? Or was the Phillips curve relationship no longer valid?

The Monetarist School came up with an explanation which said that there was a *vertical* Phillips curve occurring at what they said was the '*natural*' rate of unemployment. Just what the 'natural' rate of unemployment is has not been clear. Estimates of 3 per cent for the UK, 6 per cent for the USA and, most recently 1.4 million (about 5 per cent) in the UK, have been made. Presumably it may vary over a long period of time. Whatever its actual level, the 'natural' rate is defined as that level of unemployment which is created by market forces and cannot be reduced without creating inflationary pressures.

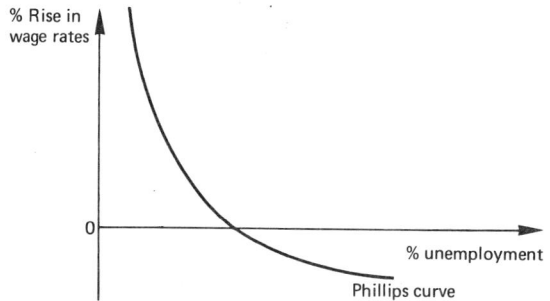

29.1 The Phillips curve

Diagram 29.2, the 'natural' rate as at point U_1. Expected price changes are zero. If the government raises the money supply by 4 per cent, demand rises, so more people are employed to make the extra goods. Unemployment falls to U_2 at point A. But wage inflation of 4 per cent has also occurred by now, raising prices by 4 per cent, so people are no better off. The newly-employed realise that they are no better off, so they give up their jobs and unemployment rises to U_1 again but at point B. If the government meanwhile pumps in another 4 per cent of money, unemployment falls to U_2 again, but at point C, as we are now on a different Phillips curve. So the process goes on: Philips curves appear moving 'north-east', but unemployment remains in the long-run at U_1 where the longer-run Phillips curve becomes vertical. All the time wages and prices are rising. Thus, to reduce inflation, the money supply should be reduced. Monetarists therefore explain inflation in monetary terms, giving wage rises a subsidiary role. They claims that it is impossible to try to reduce unemployment below its 'natural' rate – the only result is inflation.

This thesis is still the subject of debate. After all, the apparently 'natural' unemployment rate in the UK was below 4 per cent (ie 1 million) from 1946 to 1975. Unemployment of less than 2 per cent failed to generate inflation. Is it now to be considered to be higher, and if so, why? Can governments and electorates tolerate permanent unemployment of 6 per cent or 8 per cent if that is the natural rate now? These problems have yet to be resolved.

More important, perhaps, is this. If high wages and unemployment are co-existing, can unemployment reduce the rate of growth of wage rates any longer, or do wage rises merely mean that some people are dismissed while others receive the benefit of the higher wages? In any case, does the Phillips curve really help to prove that full employment and high wages cause inflation and that income policies are necessary to cure the situation?

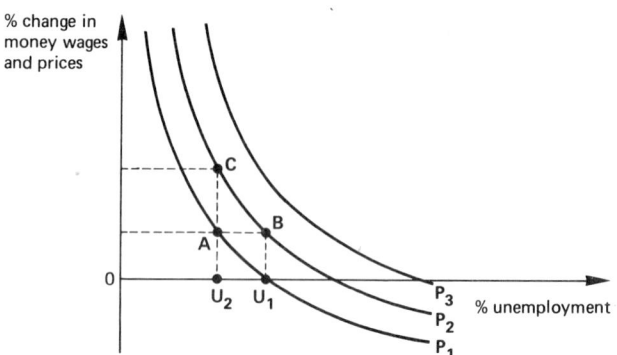

29.2 The vertical Phillips curve

The debate about incomes policies rages fiercely. Many of the points made in Chapter 23 are the subject of discussion, for example concerning whether income policies can be made to work or are easily evaded and whether huge wage claims occur when the policy comes to an end. The main point of discussion, of course, is whether they are a correct and relevant policy. Another glance at Table 29.1 shows that when incomes policy was enforced in 1966–67 and 1975–79, inflation did fall, but the direction of causality between wages and prices has not been proved to all economists' satisfaction. Did the wage control lead to lower inflation, or lower inflation lead to lower wage claims?

This section has appeared to ask more questions than it has answered because the whole subject is one of great controversy. Yet as Table 23.4 showed, most post-war governments have had official or unofficial incomes policies. Some authorities are sure that incomes control holds the key to inflation – 'without a reform of the system of pay bargaining, the economics profession may have to admit that it simply does not have a politically workable curve for inflation to offer'.[6] Others see wage rises as the way in which inflation is perpetuated rather than initiated. Nevertheless, most economists now seem to be coming to accept *some* role for wage control in a counter-inflationary policy. There is also the possibility that wage control may help reduce unemployment by preventing workers from gaining wage rises which cause employers to compensate by reducing the work force.

One form of incomes policy which is gaining popularity is indexation of wages, first tried by the Conservative Government in Phase 3 of its 1972-74 policy. Indexation guarantees that employees will receive compensatory rises when the cost of living goes up without their having to resort to wage claims or industrial action. Indeed, indexation has spread to savings with issues of index-linked securities and savings bonds. Indexation certainly protects some people from inflation, but it tends to suggest that the authorities anticipate the continuation of inflation which, if one gives credence to the expectations theories, means that ordinary people will also expect it to continue and will act accordingly to try to protect themselves. By raising wages when prices rise, indexation may also perpetuate inflationary pressure.

3 *Monetary Policy*

Monetarism stresses that inflation is entirely a monetary phenomenon caused when the growth of the money supply exceeds the growth of output of goods and services. Thus, the remedy is clear – the money supply must be reduced until it grows only in line with the expansion of output. Monetarists do not believe that fine tuning is possible. Friedman himself has stated that 'In the present state of our knowledge we cannot hope to use monetary policy as a precision instrument to offset other short-run forces making for instability'.[7] Thus, starting from a position of inflation, monetarists believe that the only course of action is to reduce the rate of growth of the money supply steadily until it is in line with output. If targets are announced (as the Conservative Government in 1979 laid down targets for £M3 and the PSBR for the following give years, each year's target being slightly more stringent than the previous year's) and are achieved, inflation will be brought under control, aided by the consequent changes in people's expectations which the announcing of targets should produce. Most monetarists see no quick solution to inflation, even through the use of monetary policy. A sharp contraction of the money supply would greatly increase unemployment in the short-run, which might be politically unacceptable. Some increase in unemployment is regarded as inevitable in the short-run, even with gradualist monetarism, although monetarists tend to believe that this is mainly because unemployment has been allowed to get below its 'natural' rate. The long-run effect would be to move down the vertical Phillips Curve at the 'natural' unemployment rate.

Monetarists regard their policies as preventive medicine as well as a cure. Once inflation has been mastered they believe that it can be prevented from recurring by keeping money supply growth in line with the growth of output – a steady, controlled expansion. Monetarism is a 'laissez faire' doctrine of non-intervention; governments cannot achieve much success by counter-cyclical meddling with the economy, so they should not try.

The mechanisms of monetary policy were outlined in Chapter 17. Altering interest rates is a well-known mechanism. Raising interest rates should deter borrowing and thus reduce demand-pull pressures. Control of printing and of the monetary base on which credit is created is also advocated. Monetarists blame governments for the excessive rate of growth of the money supply. They say that the public's demand for money is a fairly stable factor and thus it is government spending which raises the money supply and even 'crowds out' private investment from the market. Competition and Credit Control (1971) and the subsequent rapid rise in money supply which led to inflation, speculation and the secondary banking crash (see Chapter 17, pp 160-3 and Table 29.1) was a classic mistake in the eyes of the monetarists.

Problems and criticisms of monetary policy

a) As Chapter 17 showed, there is a great deal of difficulty both in defining and controlling money. Friedman, in his television series 'Free to Choose' and his book of the same name said that the fact that every country had a different definition of money was 'a smokescreen' and that a country should just decide upon its definition and control it. Yet sterling M3 may not be the best definition of the money supply, hence the discussion about PSL_2, a wider definition, or monetary base control, a narrower one (see pp 154-5). Some critics are quite clear: 'The selected variable, Sterling M3, has turned out to be one that the Government is not in a position to control with any precision'.[8] Because of disintermediation (the ability of borrowers to find sources outside the Bank of England's direct control) and the attraction of hot money by high interest rates, tight money policy does not always succeed. Targets are not easily or quickly reached and technical distortions arise – eg if the Bank of England sells securities to that private sector money supply falls: if the banks buy them money supply rises (see p 158). It is worth noting that a country with a successful post-war economic record has rarely met its money supply targets, namely Japan.

b) Restricting the money supply creates unemployment (as does raising taxes, of course). This unemployment is largely funded by the State so that, as the UK found when unemployment soared in 1979-81, doubling to 3 million in little over 18 months, government spending on unemployment pay, the Youth Opportunities Programme and other measures of relief also rose sharply. Thus, fiscal policy was counteracting monetary policy and the government could not prevent this without seemingly impossible and unacceptable public sector spending cuts in other fields like health, education and defence.

c) Prices and wages do not seem to fall when restrictions are imposed; instead, unemployment rises rapidly. Some firms stay in business, some workers stay in work; prices are high enough to ensure profits and wage rises for these people. Other firms go out of business or reduce their workforce. Thus, the unemployed bear the burden on behalf of the community. Fiscal policy would produce similar results, but juggling with different taxes might spread the burden more evenly. Incomes policy might help to preserve employment, as might exchange rate variations or import controls.
d) Many critics wonder whether monetary policy by itself is, in fact, sufficient to cure inflation and whether laissez-faire policies are possible in the complicated modern economic world. Some counter-cyclical policies (even if fine tuning is impossible), control of wages or imports or manipulation of the exchange rate may be necessary, even if only to back up monetary policy.
e) There is little evidence that government spending does 'crowd out' private investment. If business prospects are good, private sector investment does seem to occur. Investment abroad occurs because prospects seem better there rather than because the public sector has monopolised investment opportunities here.
f) Monetarists believe that the private sector's demand for money is stable over quite long periods of time. Therefore, they say, the supply of money will only rise if the government pushes more money into the economy. This will *create* extra spending and therefore demand-pull inflation, Expectations-led wage claims and so on. The causal relationship *could* be the other way round, however, an increased average propensity to consume or a desire for higher real wages, or a need to pay higher prices for imported materials *could* have come first and the money supply then have risen, either through government-sanctioned printing or by more credit creation, in order to finance this extra demand for money. The causal relationship has not been established beyond all dispute: nor has the assertion that the private sector's demand for money is stable.

4 *Exchange rate manipulation*
Some economists believe in the use of the exchange rate to avoid 'importing' inflation. For example, appreciation of the exchange rate will reduce import prices and avoid repetition of the situation of the mid-1970s when oil and commodity prices boomed at the same time as sterling's value was falling. Yet appreciation of the currency can badly harm the balance of payments. Depreciation of the currency can improve the balance of payments and stimulate both output and employment, but it raises import prices and may thus be inflationary. The price of exports would fall, however, so that foreigners' demand could be maintained and the effects of inflation on exports nullified. Some economists regard deprecia-

tion of the currency as a 'soft option' and somewhat irresponsibile, allowing governments to avoid tackling inflation, but others regard it as a valuable weapon in coping with inflationary pressure without resorting to harsh domestic restrictive policies. The main danger of the policy would seem to be its effects on import prices and thus on living costs, hence leading to wage pressure.

Conclusions

It is probably unwise to believe that any single policy will reduce inflation; most governments have resorted to a mixture of fiscal, monetary, incomes and exchange rate policies. Most enthusiasts for fiscal policy see a place for interest rate management or incomes policy: many monetarists seem to accept that wage rises contribute to inflation even if they do not originally cause it. What must be done is both to reduce people's *expectations* of inflation in order to reduce their high average propensity to consume, and at the same time to raise output so that excess demand does not arise. Expectations can only be reduced if some reduction of inflation seems likely – a vicious circle. From 1979 onwards inflation was only reduced (albeit slowly) at the expense of a huge rise in unemployment. This has given the UK, in common with some other countries, a peculiar problem – simultaneous inflation and high unemployment, sometimes called '*stagflation*'. This situation must now be examined.

Stagflation

According to the implications of both the Phillips curve and more clearly the 45° Diagram, inflation occurs at or above full employment, so how can it occur with a double-figure unemployment percentage figure? Several reasons have been suggested:

1 It is the *counter-inflationary policies* which have caused unemployment, even though they are only achieving slow success in reducing inflation. The public sector spending cuts and monetary squeeze have led to a reduction in demand and led to a fall in profits and a rise in bankruptcies.

2 Unions have resisted wage cuts, but because of the fall in demand, some workers have lost their jobs while those remaining at work have continued to enjoy high wages.

3 *Automation* is raising the natural rate of unemployment. Certain jobs no longer exist because machines can do them instead. New technology has permanently ended certain jobs, especially manual ones. Nearly 1½ million male jobs were lost between 1966 and 1976: employment in manufacturing fell from 8.2 million to 6.3 million between 1960 and 1980. The public sector (mainly services and administration) grew for much of this period, but public spending cuts have reduced this compensatory process.

4   Appreciation of sterling's exchange rate because of the oil boom and rising interest rates has led to uncompetitiveness and speeded the de-industrialisation process. Unfortunately, oil has not created the jobs to replace those lost in other industries. 'De-industrialisation appears to be a new name for the old British problem of uncompetitive manufacturing . . . exacerbated by the appreciation of sterling'.[9] In other words, the UK's industry's deep-seated problems of delivery dates, quality and reputation still exist. After all, sterling may have appreciated in the later 1970s, but by 1982 it was still below its official 1972 level, so the overall trend of the 1970s should have helped industry. Unfortunately, the rise in domestic Average Costs of production has outweighed this advantage.

5   Higher redundancy payments, unemployment pay and early retirement compensation have discouraged people from needing a job quite so much as in the past. Although this has been suggested, there seems little positive evidence to support it. There is similarly little evidence confirming the 'crowding-out' thesis, which states that the public sector has prevented job-creating private investment from taking place.

6   The world slump in demand, especially for vital articles like steel, has hit the UK as well as other countries.

The huge rise in oil prices during the 1970s hit many countries hard, particularly underdeveloped ones with small reserves of foreign exchange. The oil bill is so high that countries cannot afford to spend money on other goods and services, or on investment projects. Thus, the demand for manufactures and machinery has fallen, hitting countries like the UK.

If some or all these factors have contributed to the rise in unemployment in the UK, then why has inflation not abated? We are back to the argument about the causes of inflation in the UK in the 1970s. Was it the rapid rise in the money supply, the sharp rises in wages or the fall in sterling's exchange rate? Undoubtedly inflationary pressures increased dramatically in the UK in the 1970s; the rise in the money supply either caused this or was a reaction to it; whatever the truth, inflationary pressures increased at a time when the oil price rise pushed much of the world into a slump. Domestic demand was fuelled in the UK, but much of it was dissipated in price rises and not in rises in output.

This co-existence of inflation and unemployment seems almost impossible to solve. Is the real underlying problem still inflation and it is unemployment which is the 'accident' which is happening temporarily as a result of anti-inflationary policies? On the other hand, is the real problem that of unemployment as the UK and the world in general enter a slump, and inflation is merely the 'accident', caused by some lingering effects of the inflationary factors of the 1970s? It is important to know, but the evidence is far from conclusive. Towards the end of 1982 inflation fell to single figures, with unemployment still rising. Thus a more 'orthodox' slump was beginning to replace stagflation as deflationary policies began to bite severely.

Policy measures to cure 'stagflation' must appear contradictory. Stimulating demand and employment could worsen inflation. Counter-inflationary squeezes certainly create unemployment. At the same time, the government has to avoid balance of payments crises (see Chapter 30, pp 318-9). If the UK economy was restored to full employment with a high level of demand, some economists have estimated that the high average propensity to import would lead to a current account deficit of £8bn - including the oil surplus!

Both Conservative and Labour Governments have put countering inflation as their chief priority. Yet, is 3 million unemployed a price worth paying? It is possible that owing unemployment may become the chief priority. Mr T Barker examined ten possible policies for relieving unemployment in an article in January 1982.[10] He found that direct employment subsidies, raising government spending, abolishing the national insurance surcharge which employers have to pay and reducing taxes all would raise the PSBR considerably. Devaluation and trade controls would provoke retaliation and would be inflationary and lead to shortages of some goods. Barker concludes that 'incomes policies are outstanding in that they combine increases in employment with reductions in the PSBR and reductions in the rate of inflation without great costs to the balance of payments'.[11] Not all economists would agree.

Thus it seems that, whether countering inflation remains the first priority, or reduction unemployment replaces it, there are no easy or quick cures for either problem. Priming the pump may have been the policy for the 1930s; it does not seem that it is the policy for the 1980s. It may also be true that, like previous Prime Ministers, 'Mrs. Thatcher's policies are not based on a consensus among economists in Britain'.[12] Unfortunately, a consensus does not exist. The situation is a new one and a new Keynes is needed to solve it.

Summary

1 Inflation occurs when the general level of prices is rising.
2 Inflation has occurred in the UK since the economy revived from the slump in the 1930s, but it did not seem to be a serious problem until it rapidly accelerated in the 1970s, bringing fears of hyper-inflation.
3 Economists disagree about the causes of inflation, but it may be due to rising costs (especially wages), excess demand or an excessive supply of money.

4 Once inflation takes a hold, people come to expect it to continue. Therefore they act to protect themselves by seeking 'inflation-proof' wage rises and raising their average propensity to consume. This perpetuates the inflationary process.

5 Inflation hits the unemployed or those who cannot easily gain income rises, and discourages savings, but these effects can be mitigated by indexation of social security, pensions, wages and some forms of savings.

6 Inflation can harm the balance of payments, but devaluation can help to offset this.

7 Despite inflation, the UK and its inhabitants have prospered since the War. Anticipated inflation or a low rate of inflation may not be harmful, but unanticipated sudden changes or very high levels of inflation may cause problems which are difficult to cope with in the short-run.

8 It is possible that inflation has accelerated unemployment because costs have risen but demand has not; thus employers have reduced their workforce.

9 Economists cannot agree about how to cure inflation. Fiscal policy, monetary policy, incomes policy, and exchange rate depreciation have all been advocated.

10 Fiscal and monetary restrictions tend to cause unemployment to a greater extent than the other counter-inflationary policies.

11 The Phillips curve relationship between wages, prices and employment is not longer so clear. There is some debate about whether there is a 'natural rate' of unemployment.

12 'Fine tuning' seems impossible to achieve and there is considerable debate about whether and to what extent governments should try to intervene in the economy to counteract cyclical trends.

13 There seems more agreement now about the need to control public spending and wages, and there is an increasing tendency to advocate exchange rate changes as a weapon against inflation.

14 The co-existence of inflation and unemployment may be connected (eg high wages may be contributing to unemployment) or may be coincidental (eg technology may be causing unemployment).

15 The problems of unemployment and the 'de-industrialisation' of the UK may supplant inflation as being the chief economic problem of the UK in the 1980s.

16 There seems to be no simple solution which will overcome 'stagflation'. Monetarists suggest keeping the money supply growth in line with the rise in output and accepting a 'natural rate' of unemployment: Keynesians suggest incomes policy: the Cambridge School advocate trade controls: others suggest exchange rate depreciation. None of these policies can guarantee to solve the problem of restoring full employment without accelerating inflation.

Footnotes

1. W.A.P. Manser, 'The Monetary Year', National Westminster Bank Review, May 1981, p. 45.
2. M. Friedman: 'The Counter-Revolution in Monetary Theory', Occasional Paper 33, London, Institute of Economic Affairs, 1970.
3. Manser, op cit, p 47.
4. P. Andrews and G. Evans: Inflation and the Phillips Curve, Stirling Economics Teaching Papers, University of Stirling. June 1980 p. 9.
5. R. Bootle: How Important is it to Defeat Inflation? – The Evidence, Three Banks Review, December 1981, p 46.
6. F. Cairncross and P. Keeley: The Guardian Guide to the Economy, Methuen, London 1981, p.16.
7. M. Friedman: Monetary Theory and Policy p. 144 quoted in 'Inflation' R. Ball and P. Doyle. Penguin 1969 pp 136–145.
8. RCO Matthews and J.F. Sargent: Macro-Economic policy in the UK: Is There an Alternative? Midland Bank Review, Autumn 1981, p. 9
9. Cairncross and Keeley, op cit, p 58.
10. Long-Term Recovery: A Return to Full Employment?, T. Barker, Lloyds Bank Review, January 1982.
11. Ibid., p. 34.
12. C.F. Pratten: Mrs Thatcher's Economic Experiment. Lloyds Bank Review. January 1982 p. 38

Appendix

The UK's taxation system

The aims of taxation

Taxes can be levied for the following reasons:

1 To raise money to finance essential public sector spending.
2 To redistribute wealth from one sector of the economy to another.
3 To deter consumption of a particular product.
4 To be a weapon of fiscal policy used in Keynesian counter-cyclical policy to ameliorate inflation.

The UK taxation system

These are the principal taxes.
1 *Income tax*
   This tax is levied directly on incomes. It is paid by about 25 million people. The tax starts (1982) at 30 per cent, then rises by progressive stages to 60 per cent. After the 1982 Budget, the higher bands of tax, started at £12,800 pa. 1½ million people paid at the higher rates. There is also a surcharge on investment income.
   Each taxpayer has an allowance of tax-free income which varies according to whether he is single or married, and several other expenses are allowed as tax-free income (eg single parent, dependant relative, old age pensioners' earnings allowance). By the *Rooker-Wise Amendment* (1977), the personal allowances for single and married people is indexed to the cost of living.
2 *Value-added tax*
   VAT was introduced in April 1973 as part of the terms of the UK joining the Common Market. It started at 10 per cent, was reduced to 8 per cent in 1975 and raised to 15 per cent in 1979. It is, from the consumer's point of view, a purchase tax levied on most goods and services. Some products are exempt (eg postage, education, funeral services, insurance, land transactions) and others are liable to tax but zero-rated for the time being (eg food, books and newspapers, exports, public transport, drugs and medicines, children's clothes).
   From the point of view of producers, VAT is paid on the 'value-added' by them; they can reclaim tax paid on the materials or

products when they receive them. Table 29.2 illustrates the working of such a tax, assuming a VAT rate of 10%. The Table assumes that a felling company sells some timber to a timber mill for £20 + £ VAT. The timber mill processes the timber and sells it to a chair manufacturer for £40 + £4 VAT. Yet the 'value-added' bu the timber mill is only £20 (£40 minus £20, the tax-free purchase price), so the tax liability is only 10 per cent of the £20 value-added, ie £2. The timber mill can claim £2 tax credit because of the tax it paid to the felling company for its work. The process continues until the retailer sells to the consumer. Each person in the process can claim VAT credit on what he paid so that the tax is only levied on the value-added at each stage. The only person who cannot reclaim tax is the consumer, who pays (in this case) 10 per cent of the final price.

Table 29.2 The operation of a value-added tax rate of 10 per cent

	Purchase price to seller (£)					
	excluding VAT	including VAT	Selling price (excluding VAT)	VAT liability	VAT credit	VAT paid
Felling company sells to Timbermill	0	0	20	2	0	2
Timbermill sells to Chair manufacturer	20	22	40	4	2	2
Chair manufacturer sells to wholesaler	40	44	50	5	4	1
Wholesaler sells to retailer	50	55	60	6	5	1
Retailer sells to consumer	60	66	70	7	6	1

Thus, consumer pays £77.

3 *Petroleum revenue tax*
This tax is due to bring in a great deal of revenue in the 1980s. It is a tax at 75 per cent of petroleum revenue levied on oil companies. None was collected until 1978/79, though the oil companies paid 12½ per cent royalties and Corporation Tax (and still pay these). The companies can claim allowances on capital expenditure and operating costs.

4 *Corporation tax*
This tax is a tax on profits and is levied on companies at a rate of 52 per cent for profits over £130,000 or 40 per cent for small companies and building societies. The lower limit of liability is £90,000.

5 *Customs and excise*
These are duties on imports and on tobacco, oil, alcohol and some other products. Oil also has VAT and excise duties levied on it.

6 *Capital gains tax*
This is a tax levied on a gain a person makes when he sells something at a higher price than he paid for it. Gains up to £5,000 (1982) are exempt, then tax is paid at 30 per cent. Exemptions include a person's principal residence, car, National Savings

Certificates, life insurance, capital gain on land transactions and betting winnings. *Development land tax; betting and gaming taxes* cover these last two activities.

Capital gains became index-linked in 1982. Even so, over 90 per cent of personal savings were in the form of Life Assurance, Pension Funds and Residences in the 1970s – all exempt from the tax.

7 *Capital transfer tax*

This tax replaced estate duty in 1974. Estate duty could be evaded if a person gave away their wealth seven years before their death. Capital transfer tax is levied on gifts. Donors are taxed on gifts made throughout their lifetime above a total of £55,000 (1982). Gifts to spouses are exempt as are gifts to charity and marriage gifts to a certain limit. The tax is higher on money transferred at death, ranging (1982) from 30 per cent to 75 per cent as opposed to a range of 15 per cent to 50 per cent for gifts made earlier. Index-linking was introduced in 1982.

8 *Rates*

Rates are paid to local authorities by householders and occupants of business property. Each property is given a rateable value equivalent to its annual rental value, then each local council levies a rate at a percentage of the rateable value. By 1982 most properties were paying rates levied at over 100 per cent of the rateable value after rises of 91 per cent in 1978–1981. Rates provide only 25 per cent of local government revenue (although the amount varies dramatically from county to county), the rest coming from Government grants, revenue (from rents on council property, car parks, municipal sports centres etc) and borrowing.

9 *National insurance*

Although national insurance contributions by both employers and employees are not taxes, they are regarded as the equivalent of taxes by the payers, because they are compulsory deductions from earnings. They go to fund sickness and accident pay.

Table 29.3 gives an example of the proportions of revenue raised by taxation in the UK and of how the public sector spends the tax revenue. There is, of course, a deficiency – the *Public Sector Borrowing Requirement* (PSBR), which is mainly financed by the issuing of gilt-edged securities.

Criticisms of the UK tax system

1 The tax system is complicated and costly to administer (the UK has as many tax collectors as the USA). Yet there is evasion, especially of VAT and Capital Transfer Tax, mainly because of untraceable cash transfers and unrecorded transactions.

2 The '*poverty trap*' exists at low levels of income. People can receive state aid via various forms of social security and still earn

enough to pay income tax. An income rise raises tax liability, but *loses* the right to receive social security. This is the equivalent of a marginal tax rate near to or even fractionally above 100 per cent. A person can actually be worse off if he or she receives an income rise which takes him or her out of this 'overlap' area where he or she pays tax but receives social security.

Table 29.3 Public finance – 1981/82 estimates

Income	£bn	Expenditure	£bn
Income tax	28.2	Social security	30.3
National insurance	16.4	Education and science	14.1
VAT	12.6	National health service	13.4
Rates	10.3	Defence	12.3
North Sea oil taxes	5.9	Housing and environment	10.4
Oil duties	4.8	Law and order	4.4
Corporation tax (excluding north sea oil)	4.0	Transport	3.7
		Industry	2.5
National insurance surcharge	3.8	Employment	2.4
Other taxes	12.5	Nationalised industries	2.4
	98.5	Overseas aid	2.0
		Agriculture, fish, food, forestry	1.5
Interest and dividends	4.0	Energy	0.4
Local authority housing rents	3.2	Trade	0.2
Other	0.7	Other	3.0
	106.4		103.0
		Contingency reserve	2.5
		Allowance for underspending	−0.9
		Special sales of assets	−0.2
			104.4
		Debt interest	12.8
			117.0

PSBR   £10.6bn

Source: Economic Progress Report, September 1981

Schemes have been proposed, but never implemented, to integrate tax and social security into one system. This would involve a *negative income tax*, as illustrated in Table 29.4. A person with no income would have a tax liability of minus £3,000 – and would receive £3,000 from the State. At income £2,000 he or she would receive £2,000; at £4,000 he or she would receive £1,000; at £6,000 he or she would neither receive nor pay money; at £8,000 he or she would pay £1,000. There is no poverty trap; there is always an incentive to raise one's income.

Table 29.4 A negative income tax system

Income (£)	Tax paid (£)	Income after tax (£)
0	−3,000	3,000
2,000	−2,000	4,000
4,000	−1,000	5,000
6,000	0	6,000
8,000	1,000	7,000
10,000	2,000	8,000

4 The *Meade Report* (1978) suggested a revolutionary system – switching from income tax to a progressive universal expenditure tax. Normally, expenditure taxes like VAT are thought to be regressive – they hit the poor hardest. Indirect taxes took up 24.3 per cent of the disposable income of the average family in 1980, but only 21.9 per cent of the top 20 per cent of households, for instance. Meade recommended this his tax would be progressive – the more you spend, the more tax you pay. There would appear to be assessment and collection problems, but the aim is to encourage savings and investment but tax spending. Income tax does not distinguish between what people wish to do with their incomes.

5 The UK has no wealth tax, which many countries do. Capital transfer tax is too easily evaded and there is little other tax on wealth, as opposed to income. The arguments against wealth taxes are on the grounds of disincentives and the problems of assessment and collection. Meade strongly argued for a progressive annual wealth tax, however, on the grounds of equity.

6 Many anomalies exist in the tax system, eg 'perks' like company cars, which avoid an employee receiving extra taxable income, and exemptions from various taxes, especially for house-owners. It is true to say, of course, that *all* tax systems have anomalies in them. Tax systems are complicated in order to try to avoid evasions and to be fair, but this causes anomalies and loopholes.

7 There are insufficient taxes in the UK which 'make the users pay'. For example, there are few tolls on motorways, bridges and roads, compared with European countries. In many cases the taxpayer gets little benefit from the way his or her taxes are used – eg an aged house-owner's rates go to finance schools and colleges in the area.

Conclusion

There are many changes in the tax system each year in the budget, but few of the changes amount to a radical reform. There seems little prospect of a real reduction in taxes because of the difficulty of cutting public spending. If one tax is cut, another seems to have to rise in order to compensate (eg the cuts in income tax in 1979 coincided with rises in VAT and national insurance). Taxation often redistributes income, but the burden of taxes is rarely reduced.

30 Economic growth and the clash of macro-economic targets

Economic growth

Economic growth involves *enlarging the productive potential* of an economy and thus *increasing real income* per head. In the short-run, an important economic problem is to use resources fully and efficiently in order to ensure maximum benefit to the community. In the long-run, the quantity and quality of the resources can be increased and improved. Output can be increased and this growth would lead to higher standards of living. Diagramatically, we are back to Diagrams 1.1 and 1.2 (pp 11 and 12). Growth will extend the production-possibility frontier of an economy, so that point Z in Diagram 1.2 can be obtained. Thus, in Diagram 30.1, growth will push the production possibility frontier from AB to CD. Exactly where a country will produce along CD is a matter for its government to decide. The nearer to point C, the great is the opportunity-cost of sacrificed consumption. Yet an increase in the stock of capital goods is generally regarded as being essential in ensuring the continuation of economic growth. A country with a high growth rate is more likely to be following growth path 1 than growth path 2.

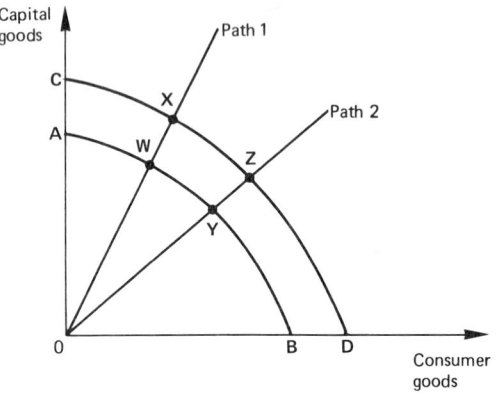

30.1 Economic growth

Factors affecting economic growth

1 *Investment*

As stated in the previous paragraph, an increase in the capital stock is essential for economic growth to take place. The agricultural sector in underdeveloped countried benefits greatly when the first tractors or seed drills or ploughs are brought in. Mechanical excavators dramatically improved the road construction and civil engineering industries. Machines, as Chapter 1 showed, have advantages over labour in terms of the scale of production they can perform.

It is not only the *quantity* of investment which is important, however. The *quality* must be continually improved. Thus, better machines are required, not just more machines. Invention and innovation, research and development are essential in order to obtain *technological advance*. Jet-engined aircraft are more efficient than turbo-prop engines; computers have replaced adding machines; micro-chips have supplanted transistors (which had themselves replaced valves). Rapid technological advances may well cause unemployment, at least in the short-run. The worst thing to do in an underdeveloped country would be to introduce sophisticated agricultural machinery which would replace the labour force; what is needed is tools which the peasants can work with, not machines to replace them. Nevertheless increased technology and new processes are essential in order to ensure growth.

2 *Labour*

Despite the obvious advantages of machines, labour is still essential to economic growth. Western European countries developed rapidly in the 1950s and 1960s, yet they needed to import labour in order to help to achieve this; they had insufficient labour of their own.

To-day, shortage of labour is only a problem in a few countries, notably the oil-rich Middle Eastern countries with great wealth but tiny populations. Yet is is not only the *quantity* of labour which is important; its *quality* is also vital. Mobility, education, vocational training, even the health, diet and living conditions of the workforce are important considerations. The ability to produce technologists, computer programmers, and indeed skilled managers is essential. Many countries, including even the U.K. in some respects, are held back by their inability to produce adequate numbers of appropriately skilled workers to keep up with advancing technology. As always, development in management techniques must not be forgotten.

3 *Consumption* – but not at the expense of investment

Simple multiplier theory shows that investment creates income and this in turn, via the marginal propensity to consume, produces increased consumption. This stimulates further output and, via the accelerator, more investment. Consumption is a vital element. There is no point in inventing and developing new technology unless there is going to be a demand for it. The Concorde aircraft project is a notorious example of a technological development for which insufficient demand existed. There is inadequate information as to whether a Channel tunnel would be a worthwhile project. Chelsea Football Club have built a superb new grandstand – which remains largely empty at each home match. A large, predictable and standardised demand is necessary for an investment project to be economically viable. The demand can exist abroad, of course. The Arab oil-producing countries consume only a tiny fraction of the oil they produce, but overseas demand makes production worthwhile and export-led growth occurs via the trade multiplier (Chapter 28, pp 277–80). The wealth of prospective consumers is as important as the number of them. The 250 million consumers of the European Community form a richer and more attractive market to most industrial producers than do the 900 million people of China, for instance.

The social attitudes of consumers are also important. Contraceptives cannot be sold openly in most Roman Catholic countries; perfume and lipstick would find virtually no market in strict Moslem areas; tinned beef could not be sold in India. The products developed must find suitable markets. Demand must exist or be created. Consumption must *not* be allowed to squeeze out Investment, however. One of the UK's problems have been a very high average propensity to consume and a low propensity to save. Money has been spent on consumer goods instead of being invested in growth-creating new projects.

4 *Government policies*

Governments have a part to play in the growth process, either in providing investment themselves (NB the Government multiplier, Chapter 28, pp 280–1), or in providing a stable and encouraging political and economic climate. Support for research and development and technical and managerial training is just as important as more general subsidies, grants and creation of employment.

Economic stability is clearly advantageous; volatile interest rates, exchange rates or taxation policies can discourage investment because of uncertainty concerning costs, markets and retention of profits. Political stability is also important. Countries which are liable to revolutions, or which may default on loans cannot attract foreign investment, or even retain investment from domestic sources. Stable dictatorships may possibly attract more investors than unstable democracies, in fact.

The costs of economic growth

Economic growth can have unfortunate side effects on various groups of people in the economy. Indeed, some economists, notably the American, JK Galbraith, are very critical of the perpetual pursuit of higher growth rates and higher living standards. Among the costs of economic growth are these.

1 *Social costs*

The community may suffer harm to their environment brought about by a new project. *Pollution* of all types – noise, visual, noxious fumes, discharge of waste material into the atmosphere or into rivers, traffic congestion – all these can affect people living near some industrial project. The firms responsible, of course, do not pay these costs; they do not appear on their balance sheets as accounting costs. Yet the community suffers.

Some of these costs really do cause mental or physical suffering or death. People who live in certain areas of London and near the famous 'Spaghetti Junction' motorway convergence in the Midlands have been found to have dangerous levels of lead poisoning, which causes brain damage, caused by vehicle exhaust fumes. The incidence of mental stress is high near Heathrow Airport because of noise and fear of accidents. There are even fears that earth's climate may be being changed by the discharge of various fumes which affect the upper atmosphere.

Some costs can be measured, for example, the decline in property values or cost of double-glazing for people living near airports or motorways. Other costs cannot be so easily measured, notably visual damage to landscapes, destruction of river and canal recreational amentities caused by discharge of factory waste, time lost through traffic congestion. Only rarely are firms made to compensate, though oil companies now often agree to restore the environment of rural areas after burying their pipelines. Environmentalists do sometimes win. For example some Scottish lochs were preserved from being oil-platform building sites, mineral mining in the Lake District has been prevented and only limited oil exploration in the Southern countries of England has been permitted. Clean air acts, banning of night flights, regulations concerning noise and lead in petrol have also occurred to reduce social costs.

Projects do produce social benefits, however, which are equally difficult to measure. Road, rail and air projects save time, congestion and often lives, for example. Many public projects are subject to *cost benefit analysis* (CBA), which 'tries to estimate the costs and benefits at market prices of all the unmarketed consequences of a project, and to give an estimate of its net social benefit when these are combined with the marketed consequences'.[1] CBA attempts to measure social costs and benefits and add them to the private or marketed costs and benefits.

CBA was first used with regard to the Ml motorway plan in 1960 and has subsequently most frequently been used for public projects in the field of transport, including a new 'third' London Airport, the Victoria Underground line and motorway planning. The Victoria Line investigation, incidentally, showed that most benefits would accrue not to the users but to people continuing to use surface transport, because traffic congestion would be greatly reduced. The most detailed report was that of the *Roskill Commission* on the proposed new site for an airport. The Government of the day (1971) overruled the Commission's recommendation, as it has done in other cases, including a rare example from outside the transport field, the decision to re-locate the Covent Garden fruit and vegetable market in 1974. CBA studies cannot be enforced in the private sector, so some form of more direct and specific regulation has usually to be applied in order to restrict the harmful effects of private sector investment projects.

2   *Unemployment*
Rapid technological development may be thought to cause unemployment as machines take over jobs previously done by labour. There are many examples of this in economic history, such as handloom weavers losing their jobs to weaving machines, firemen being displaced by diesel engines on the railways, and stock control clerks being replaced by computers. This unemployment has tended to be temporary, however. New jobs have been created in new industries as aggregate demand (consumption, investment, exports and government spending) rises and creates derived demand for labour in expanding new industries. In the nineteenth and early twentieth centuries in Britain, people moved from the primary to the secondary sectors. Now, as employment falls in the secondary (manufacturing) sector. the tertiary sector (services) is expanding. Government policies can help, of course, via direct government spending, tax remissions to stimulate demand, or devaluation to encourage exports. For the community, any employment created by technological change is probably temporary, but for some individuals, who cannot move or learn new skills, it may be permanent. On the macro-economic scale, however, technology creates as many jobs as it eliminates. Studies on the effects of the introduction of computers, for example, prove this.

Unemployment is a waste of resources and a social evil. Although science fiction writers may sometimes visualise a future utopia in which machines work and people live a life of leisure, most contemporary observation seems to suggest that people need the self-respect and dignity of work. Perhaps a future world where no-one works may be different, but the present situation where most people find work, but a minority do not, is undesirable on economic and social grounds. Not the least of the problems

created is the rise in crime in areas of high unemployment.
3 *Exhaustion of finite reserves*
Economic growth uses the world's resources, notably of fuel and minerals. These resources cannot be replaced and thus, logically, will eventually be exhausted. Oil, coal and minerals are finite in supply; they will not last for ever. Hopefully, technology will be able to harness the virtually inexhaustible supplies of solar, wind or water power, or may find safer ways of developing nuclear power, but these possibilities are long-term. There is a danger of some resources, notably oil, being exhausted in the short-run, with harmful consequences to a world reliant on them and unable to sustain its standard of living without them.
4 *Widening the gap between rich and poor*
Undoubtedly the gap between industrialised countries and underdeveloped countries is widening. Technology and investment grows faster in the industrialised world leading to an uneven spread of wealth and resources. The only solution would seem to be if the developed world directed resources to the underdeveloped, and there is no authority to enforce this.

The UK's growth rate

The growth rate of the UK since 1945 has been disappointing. In the the 1950s the rate was 2½ per cent per annum, compared with an OECD average of 4 per cent: in the 1960s the UK's figure was 3½ per cent per annum compared with OECD,s 5½ per cent; in the 1970s it was 2 per cent compared with 3½ per cent. By the end of the 1970s, the slump in the UK had led to annual *falls* in output and low investment figures. Reasons for this modest performance include the following:

1 *Lack of savings and investment and too high a propensity to consume*
In Diagram 30.1 the UK's expansion path has been Path 2 rather than Path 1. There has been a great desire for consumption goods and people have not been willing to forego this in return for promises of greater wealth in the future. More than half the research investment in the UK is by 10 companies in 3 industries – aerospace, electronics and chemicals. In the 1960s and 1970s only 17.8 per cent and 18.7 per cent respectively of GDP was invested compared with OECD averages of 20.8 per cent and 22.2 per cent and Japan's steady figure of 30 per cent. Unfortunately, some projects which have been pursued, notably Concorde and the Advanced Gas Cooled Reactor, have not done well.
2 *Growth of non-productive sectors of the economy*
The biggest growth sectors of the economy have been in services

and public administration. Productivity improvements are possible in services, but not to the extent that they are in manufacturing, where output can be more clearly quantified.

3 *Priority has been given to other targets*
The next section will deal in detail with this, but suffice to say that UK governments since 1945 have had problems of balance of payments and exchange rates, inflation and more recently unemployment to tackle. These have seemed to be urgent; growth can always be postponed; it is less urgent and counts for less in the game of vote-winning. Counter-inflationary squeezes, of course, deter investment, usually because interest rates rise, and thus deter growth.

4 *Labour and training problems*
The workforce in the UK has been reluctant to accept new developments and practices if they threaten employment. To quote just two examples from British Rail in 1982, train drivers rejected flexible working hours, a scheme which threatened to do away with some jobs, and railwaymen refused to accept new electric trains on the Bedford-St Pancras line because they would require a single operator. Trade unions have been reluctant to abandon old working practices including demarcation, closed shops, unwillingness to accept re-training qualifications awarded by Skill Centres and overstaffing. The working population has been both geographically and occupationally immobile. Yet one can understand people's fear of unemployment.

The education system has also been criticised for failing to keep pace with new technology and for inadequate vocational training. The proportion of teenagers who leave school at 16 and who enter relatively unskilled jobs is high compared with most other industrial countries, notably West Germany, where part-time education and vocational training is undergone by the majority of recent school leavers.

The clash of macro-economic targets

There are four targets which governments seek to achieve in the Macro-Economic sphere:
1   full employment
2   control of inflationary pressure
3   balance of payments equilibrium
4   economic growth.

A fifth policy objective, redistribution of income and wealth, may also exist, but is not really a macro-economic target in the sense of the other four.

The first task of a government is to decide on its priorities. In the UK in the 1950s and 1960s balance of payments problems seemed paramount. In the 1970s inflation was the major problem. In the

1980s reducing unemployment could be the primary task. Economic growth, always seemingly postponable, usually seems to bring up the rear – which possibly explains many of the UK's post-war problems?

The second problem for a government is that policies to tackle one problem may worsen another. Some countries, like Japan and West Germany, have achieved considerable success in all four fields, in the 1950s and 1960s at least. The UK has been unable to achieve all four targets simultaneously. Indeed, in the late 1970s, all four went wrong – an equally unusual achievement! Usually, the UK alleviates one problem but worsens another.

For example, measures to reduce inflation usually raise unemployment. Higher interest rates, money supply squeezes and higher taxes deter both investment and consumption, and therefore reduce the demand for labour. Conversely, 'pump-priming' policies to create more jobs may increase inflationary pressures.

High interest rates and slack demand deter growth. Depreciation of the exchange rate helps exports, output and jobs but is inflationary. Appreciation of the exchange rate deters exports, employment and growth but reduces inflationary pressure. Import controls may help output, employment, and growth but could cause shortages and raise prices. Incomes policies may reduce inflationary and preserve jobs, but reduce spending power. There is no single set of policies which can solve all the problems. Governments have to decide to cure most urgent problems while realising that others are being accumulated as a result of their policies.

The UK in the 1980s

The 1970s saw five unstable factors appear in the world economic sphere, none of which helped the UK. *Exchange rates*, previous virtually fixed under the Bretton Woods system, were floated. *Inflation*, not a serious problem in the 1950s and 1960s in the industrialised world accelerated. *Oil prices* rose 400 per cent in a few weeks in 1973–74 and rose sharply again in 1979–80. The oil problem caused *very uneven balance of payments* figures, with the UK moving sharply and hugely into deficit and back into surplus, and countries like Japan beginning to suffer deficits. Partly because of oil and exchange rates, *interest rates* also became very volatile and generally higher in the UK and the Western world. All these trends made the world's economic problems even more difficult to solve.

For the UK, oil exploitation seemed to relegate the balance of payments in order of priorities. The UK entered the 1980s with surpluses. Yet, oil had pushed up sterling. The rest of the industrial structure suffered. The UK's surpluses were due to oil; the 'non-oil' sector was really in huge deficit.

The UK entered the 1980s with double-figure inflation, which even massive unemployment was slow to reduce. Then, of course, unemployment exceeded 3 million in early 1982, having doubled in less than two years. The UK's growth rate was zero.

So, what were the prospects for the 1980s? The only macro-economic target being achieved was the balance of payments, and even this was miseading because of oil's overwhelming contribution. No magic solution seemed at hand. Oil was creating as many problems as it solved. Inflation though falling by 1982 was still a problem, unemployment seemed intractable. Yet the UK was still a wealthy, industrialised, relatively stable country. It must not be forgotten that underdeveloped countries' problems were far greater than those of the UK. No-one was actually starving in the UK.

Economics will continue to search for the solutions and will continue to disagree. Governments will still wrestle with their priorities in terms of the problems to solve. Some of the problems may seem dismal but the excitement of seeking solutions to them makes economics anything but the 'dismal science'.

Summary

1 Economic growth is concerned with enlarging the productive potential of an economy and increasing the level of real income.
2 The keys to economic growth are technological development and increased investment.
3 An adequate and well-trained labour supply is also required. Education and training must keep pace with technology.
4 Consumption is a stimulus to output, employment and growth. Investment projects are wasteful if there is inadequate demand for the products in question.
5 Political stability is an aid to encouraging investment.
6 Growth can have disadvantages to the community in the form of social costs, notably pollution. Cost-benefit analysis aims to measure and possibly prevent some of these costs.
7 Economic growth may cause unemployment and will also accelerate the exhaustion of finite resources.
8 The UK's growth rate has been disappointing, partly because of inadequate investment, immobility of labour and educational conservatism.
9 There are four macro-economic targets for a government to achieve – full employment, control of inflation, balance of payments equilibrium and economic growth.
10 Policies to achieve one target often have harmful effects on others. Growth usually seems to have the lowest priority.
11 Economies become particularly unstable in the 1970s, with oil prices much to blame.
12 Unemployment may surpass inflation as the UK's major problem

in the 1980s. Oil production is proving a mixed blessing and major macro-economic problems seem destined to remain.

Footnote

1 What About Welfare?, Economist, Schools Brief, 18 December 1976, p 65.

Bibliography

The aim in presenting this bibliography is to present a short-list of books and articles which a student pursuing an 'A' level or equivalent course can find useful and comprehensible. There are many textbooks available on economic theory. This bibliography presents a list of concise specialist books and recent articles on some of the subjects relating to the real world which are accessible to the average student at this level.

1   *General*
The following are regular publications, giving recent facts, figures and opinions.

British Economic Survey (Oxford University Press, twice a year) *The Treasury*, Economic Progress Report (HMSO, monthly) *Tree, N.*, The Year in Review (Anforme Ltd., annually).

In addition, the following is published every other year:

Prest, A.R. and Coppock, D.J. (eds), *The UK Economy, A Manual of Applied Economics*, Weidenfeld and Nicholson, 8th ed., 1980.

Also of value are:

NIESR, *UK Economy*, Heinemann Educational Books, 2nd ed., 1979
Cairncross, F. and Keeley.P., The Guardian Guide to the Economy, Methuen, 1981
Maunder, P. (ed), The British Economy in the 1970s, Heinemann Educational Books, 1980.

For statistics, the most accessible single source is:

Annual Abstract of Statistics (HMSO, annually).
2   *Population*
Williams R.M., *British Population*, Heinemann Education Books, 2nd ed., 1978
Mallier T. and Rosser, M., *The Changing Role of Women in the British Economy*, National Westminster Bank Quarterly Review, November, 1979.
3   *Structural and regional unemployment*
Lee, D., *Regional Planning and the Location of Industry*, Heinemann Educational Books, 2nd ed., 1979.
Button, K. and Gillingwater, D., *Case Studies in Regional Economics*, Heinemann Educational Books, 1976.
Myers, D., 'The Youth Opportunities Programme,' Economics Summer, 1981.
4   *Monopoly and restrictive practices*
Pass, C. and Sparkes,J., *Monopoly*, Heinemann Educational Books, 3rd ed., 1975.
Hunter, A. (ed), *Monopoly and Competition*, Penguin, 1969.
Blois, K. et al., Case Studies in Competition Policy, Heinemann Educational Books, 1976.
5   *Competition*
Maunder, P.J. et al., *Case Studies in the Competitive Process*, Heinemann Educational Books, 1976.
6   *Nationalised industries*
Reid, G.L. and Allen, K., *Nationalised Industries*, Penguin, 1970. Barker, P.J. and Button, K.J., *Case Studies in Cost Benefit Analysis*, Heinemann Educational Books, 1976.
Lipton, M., 'The Government and the Nationalised Industries', Lloyds Bank Review, April 1976.
Redwood, W.R., 'What is Nationalisation For?'. Lloyds Bank Review, July 1976.
Robson, W.A. 'The Control of Nationalised Industries', National Westminster Bank Quarterly Review, November 1977.
Lumley, S., 'New Ways of Financing Nationalised Industries', Lloyds Bank Review, July 1981.
7   *The monetary system and monetary policy*
Anthony, V., *Banks and Markets*, Heinemann Educational Books, 3rd ed., 1979.
Bain, A.D., *Control of the Money Supply*, Penguin, 1970.
Bank Information Service, Monetary

Control in Britain 1971-1981
Congdon, T., 'The Monetary Base Dilemma', National Westminster Quarterly Review, August 1980.
Lewis, M.K., 'Understanding the Monetary Control Debate', Economics, Autumn 1981.
Tew, B., 'The Implementation of Monetary Policy in Post-War Britain', Midland Bank Review, Spring 1981.
Wilkinson, M., 'U.K. Monetary Policy 1979-1981: Policy, Events and Mechanisms of Control', Economics, Spring 1982.

8 *International economics*

Llewellyn, D. et al., *Case Studies in International Economics*, Heinemann Educational Books, 1977.
Bird, G, 'International Monetary Developments in the 1970s', Economics, Spring 1980.
Unattributed: 'The E.E.C. Budget and the U.K.', Midland Bank Review, Summer 1980.
Lewis, D., *Britain and the E.E.C.*, Heinemann Educational Books, 1978.
Swann, D., *Economics of the Common Market*, Penguin, 4th ed., 1978.
Davies, B., The U.K. and the World Monetary System, Heinemann Educational Books, 2nd ed., 1978.
Davies. B., 'Order and Disorder in International Monetary Arrangements-A Perspective of the 1970s', Economics, Spring 1980.
Unattributed: 'A Return to Bretton Woods?', Midland Bank Review, April 1981.

9 *Incomes policy*

Blackaby, F. (ed), *An Incomes Policy for Britain*, Heinemann Educational Books, 1972.
Unattributed: 'A Future for Incomes Policy?', Midland Bank Review, Winter 1980.
Williamson, H., *Trade Unions*, Heinemann Educational Books, 5th ed., 1979.
Chater, R.E.J. et al (ed), *Incomes Policy*, O.U.P. 1981.

10 *Macro-economic theory*

Stanlake, G.F., *Macro-Economics: An Introduction*, Longman, 2nd ed., 1979.

11 *Inflation*

Ball, P. and Doyle, R.J. (eds), *Inflation*, Penguin, 1969
Jackson, D. et al., *Do Trade Unions Cause Inflation?*, C.U.P. 1975.
Congden, T., Monetarism, Centre for Policy Studies 1978.
Trevithick, J., *Inflation*, Pelican, 2nd ed., 1980.
Stewart, M., *Keynes and After*, Penguin, 1970.
Andrews, P. and Evans, G., 'Inflation and the Phillips Curve', Stirling University Teaching Papers, No. 9, 1980.
Vane, H. and Thompson, J., 'Monetarism and Government Intervention', Economics, Summer 1980.
Lomax, D., 'Monetary Policy', National Westminster Quarterly Review, November 1980.
Matthews R.C.O and Sargent, J.R., 'Macro-economic Policy in the U.K. – Is There an Alternative?'. Midland Bank Review, April 1981.
Preston, M., 'The Integration of Monetary, Fiscal and Incomes Policy', Lloyds Bank Review, July 1981.
Manser, W.A.P., 'The Monetary Year', National Westminster Quarterly Review, May 1981.
Snowdon, B., 'Phillips Curve or Trade-Off Curve?', Economics, Winter 1981.
Bootle, R., 'How Important is it to Defeat Inflation?', Three Banks Review, December 1981.
Pratten, C.F., 'Mrs Thatcher's Economic Experiment', Lloyds Bank Review, January 1982.
Higham, D. and Tomlinson, J., 'Why Do Governments Worry about Inflation?', National Westminster Quarterly Review, May 1982.

12 *Unemployment*

Barker, T., 'Long-Term Recovery: A Return to Full Employment?', Lloyds Bank Review, January 1982.
Shackleton, J., 'Economists and Unemployment', National Westminster Quarterly Review, February 1982.

Index

Abyssinia, 181
Accelerator, 271-2
Acceptance Houses - see Merchants Banks
Advanced Gas-Cooled Reactor, 317
Advertising, 3, 120
Advisory, Conciliation and Arbitration Service (ACAS), 240
Arbitrage, 196
ASTMS, 238, 242
Atomic Energy Authority, 128, 133
AUEW, 238-40 passim
Automation, 302

Babcock and Willcox, 115
Balance of payments, Chapter 20 passim
 and inflation, 292; and monetary policy, 156; methods of curing deficit, 190-2; structure, 184-9; UK's post-war history, 192-5, 209, 214, 319; (See also Exports, Imports)
Bank Charter Act (1844), 142
Banking Act (1979), 152, 161
Bank of England, Chapter 15 passim
 and finance for industry, 27; as nationalised industry, 128, 133, 142; functions, 142-5; history, 142; monetary policy weapons, 157-9, 300; (see also Monetary Policy, Minimum Lending Rate)
Banks, Clearing see Banks, Commercial
Banks, commercial, Chapter 15 passim;
 asset structure, 146-8; debt, 139; deposits, creation, 139-40; functions, 145-6: lending to industry, 27, 145-6; mergers, 115; (see also Monetary policy)
Banks, foreign, 48, 151-3
Banks, saving, 152, 153
Banks, secondary, 161
Barter, 3, 138
Betting and gaming tax, 309
Bills of exchange, 146-9, 152
 (see also Treasury bills, Commercial bills, Local Authority bills)
Birth rate, 40
Black economy, 265
Black market, 102
Bretton Woods system, 199-202
 collapse, 202; subsequent events, 202-4; (see also IMF)
British Aerospace, 24, 25, 127
British Airports Authority, 133
British Airways, 13, 107, 109, 133, 134, 136, 186
BBC, 24, 107
British Caledonian Airways, 109
British Gas, 107, 110, 133, 136
British Leyland, 24, 28, 39, 98, 126-7, 133, 134
 (see also British Motor Corporation, Leyland)
British Match Corporation, 110
British Motor Corporation, 110, 115
British National Oil Corporation (BNOC), 109, 127, 128, 133
 (see also North Sea Oil)
British Overseas Airways Corporation (BOAC), 239
British Oxygen Company, 107, 110
British Rail, 13, 107, 132, 133, 178, 318
British Shipbuilders, 53, 55, 98, 133, 136, 178
British Steel Corporation, 133, 136, 181
British Telecommunications, 133
British Waterways Board, 133
Budget line, 74
 (see also Demand)
Budgets, annual 18
 (see also Fiscal policy, Taxation, Government expenditure)
Building societies, 152-3
Bullion market, 48
Business cycle, (trade cycle) 252
Business Start-up Scheme, 18

Cable and wireless, 127, 130, 133
Cadbury's, 110
Capital, 9-10, 13
 as factor of production, 9-10; circulating, 10; fixed, 10; (see also Investment)
Capitalism, 10-11
Capital gains tax, 308-9
Capital transfer tax, 309
Cartels, 117-18
Cambridge school, 194, 258
CCC, see Competition and Credit Control
Cedar Holdings, 161
CEGB, 133
Central Bank, see Bank of England
Centralised economies, 10-11
Certificates of deposit, 146-9, 163
Chelsea FC, 314
Circular flow, 255-8
Clearing banks, see Banks, commercial
Closed shops, 39, 225, 242
Cobweb theorem, 91-2
Collective bargaining, Chapter 24 passim
Commercial banks, see Banks, commercial
Commercial bills, 146-9
 (see also Bills of exchange)
Common Agricultural Policy (CAP), 53, 207, 210-2, 215
 (see also EEC)
Commonwealth preference, 177
Companies, 23-4, 27, 29
Comparabilities Commission, 231
Comparative advantage, law of, 172-8
Competition, see Imperfect competition, Perfect competition, Oligopoly

324

Competition and Credit Control (CCC) (1971), 160-3, 300
  (see also Monetary policy)
Competitions Act (1980), 116
Concentration ratio, 112
Concorde, 7, 272
Confederation of British Industry (CBI), 168
Conglomerates, 110
Conspicuous consumption, see Veblen effect
Consumers' surplus, 70
Consumption
  and growth, 313-4; average and marginal propensities, 255-6, 272-82 passim; function, 268-70, 272-6
Co-operative societies, 24
Corporation tax, 308
Corset – see Supplementary deposits
Cost-benefit analysis, 5, 315-6
Costs, Chapters 10, 11, 12 passim
  comparative, 172-8; in imperfect competition, 120-2; in monopoly, 110-4, 128-30; in perfect competition, 122-4; opportunity cost, 4, 10, 40, 246; production 58-61; social, 59, 315-6
Council of Europe, 206
Courtaulds, 112
Covent Garden Market, 316
Coventry, 48
CPSU, 242
Cross-elasticity of demand, 84-5
Crown agents, 133

DanAir Ltd, 109
Death rate, 41
Debentures, 25
Deficiency payments, 211-12
Deflationary gap, 281-4
Deflationary policies, 190, 294-304
Demand, Chapters 6, 7 passim
  Individual:
  factors influencing, 68-9; Giffen goods, 71, 76-8; indifference curves, 72-8; inferior goods, 74; utility, 69-72
  Market:
  changes in, 83-6, 90-6; composite, 96; cross-elasticity, 84-5, 94-5; derived, 96, 217; income elasticity, 84; joint, 94-5; in monopoly, imperfect competition, 104-6; in perfect competition, 122-4; origin of demand curve, 79; perverse, 85-6; price-elasticity, 80-3, 93, 98-100, 181; tastes, 85
Devaluation, 191-2, 196, 201, 301-2
Development areas, 52-3, 56
Development Land tax, 309
Diminishing marginal productivity, law of, 69-72
Diminishing marginal rate of substitution, 73
Diminishing returns, law of, 13-14
Discounted cash flow, 272
Discount houses, 150-1, 153
Diseconomies of scale, 15-17
Disintermediation, 160
Distribution of Industry Act (1945), 52
Division of labour, 31-4
Docks Board, 133
Domestic Credit Expansion (DCE), 159-60
Donovan Report, 236-8
Driving and Vehicle Licensing Centre (DVLC), 55
Dumping, 180
Duopoly, 107

Economic rent – see Rent
Economics, Introduction passim

forecasting, 7; macro, Section 9, passim; models, 7; micro sections, 1, 2, 3, 4, passim; normative, 4-5; positive, 4-5; sphere, 3-4; systems, 10-11; task of economists, 4-5; techniques, 5-7
Economies of scale, 14-17
EEC – see European Economic Community
EETPU, 239
Eisenhower, DD, 208
Elasticity of demand, 80-3, 86-7, 93, 98-100, 191
Elasticity of substitution, 19
Elasticity of supply, 62-4, 93-4, 98-100
Electricity Council, 136
Emigration, 41-2
Employment Act (1980), 234, 241
Employment Protection Act (1975), 234, 240
Engel, E, 87, 169
Enterprise, 10
  (see also, Entrepreneur, Profits)
Enterprise zones, 53
Entrepreneur, 10, 12
  (see also Enterprise, Profits)
Envelope curve, 65
Equal Pay Act (1970), 38, 234
Equilibrium, Chapters 10, 11, 12 passim
Equi-marginal returns, law of, 71
Equipment Leasing Association, 29
Equities – see Shares
Equity capital for industry, 27
Eurocurrencies, 151-2
European Community – see European Economic Community
European Currency Unit (ECU), 203-4
European Economic Community (EEC), Chapter 22 passim
  budget, 212; common agricultural policy, 53, 100, 207, 210-12, 215; ECSC, 206-7; Ewatom, 206; evolution, 206-7; investment bank, 208; membership, 206; organs, 107-208; population movement, 42; regional fund, 53, 208, 213; social fund, 53, 208; treaties of association, 207; UK and 50, 193-4, 208-10, 212-5
European Ferries Ltd, 115
European Monetary System (EMS), 199, 203-4, 207, 214
Exchange rates, Chapter 21 passim
  determination, 196-9; fixed and fluctuating, 198, 319; systems, 199-200
Excise duties, 97, 308
Exports; as injections into circular flow, 257; invisible, Chapter 20 passim; multiplier – see Trade multiplier; (see also International trade) visible, Chapter 20 passim
Export Credit Guarantee Department, 179

Factors of production, 9-10, Section 8 passim
Factoring, 29
Fair Trading Act (1973), 119
FEOGA see EEC, Common Agricultural Policy
Ferranti, 127
Finance corporation for industry, 27
Finance for industry, 27
Finance houses, 152-3
Fine tuning, 295
Firm
  definition, 13; finance, 25-9; types, 22-5
Fiscal policy, 258, 289, 294-6
  (see also Budgets, Keynes, JM)
Ford Motor Company, 13
Foreign exchange market, 48, 196
Franchises, 109, 128
Friedman, M, 291-2, 300

325

(see also Monetary policy)
Funding, 158

Galbraith, JK, 5, 315
GATT, 178, 182
Gearing, 26
General Strike (1926), 239
Giffen goods, 71, 76-8
GMWU, 239, 242
Gold exchange standard, 201
  (see also Bretton Woods system, IMF)
Gold standard, 200
Government expenditure
  and growth, 314; as injection into circular flow, 256; industrial aid, 27-8; nationalised industries, 28, Chapter 13 passim; unemployment, 28, 51-7; (see also Fiscal policy, Keynes, JM)
Government intervention in free market, 97
  price control, 101-3; public goods, 103; rationing, 101; subsidies, 98; taxation, 97-100
Government training centres – see Skill centres
Green currencies, 212
Growth, Chapter 30 passim
  costs of, 315-7; definition, 312; deflationary policies and, 292; UK growth rate, 317-8, 320
Grunwick, 240-1

Hawthorne experiments, 6, 45
Healey, D, 229
Heath, E, 210, 231, 281-2
Hebrides, 50
Herbert, Alfred Ltd, 127
Herbert Committee, 132
Herbert Morris Ltd, 115
High Wycombe, 48
Hire-purchase, 29, 159
Hoffman La Roche, 112-3
Hong Kong and Shanghai Bank, 115
House of Fraser, 115

IATA, 117
IBA, 107
ICI, 13, 16, 24
Immigration, 6, 41-2
Immigration Acts, 41
Imperfect competition, Chapter 12 passim, 107-8, 120-1, 124
Imports, Chapter 20 passim
  as leakage from circular flow, 257-8, 277-80; UK and EEC, 208-9; (see also International trade)
Income elasticity of demand, 34
Income tax, 97, 295, 307, 310-1
Incomes policies, 228-34, 296-9
Index numbers, Chapter 18 passim
  calculation, 166-8; indexation, 231; industrial production, 167, 170; problems, 170; retail prices, 168-70; tax and price, 170
Industrial and Commercial Finance Corporation (ICFC), 27
Industrial development certificates, 53
Industrial Relations Act (1971), 240
Industrial relations couet, 240
Industrial reorganisation corporation, 116
Industrial Training Boards, 54, 56
Industry – see Production
Inferior goods, 74
Inflation, 6, Chapter 29 passim
  control, 294-302; cost push, 287-9; definition, 286; demand pull, 289; growth, 319; hyper, 156, 186, 293; inflation gaps, 281-4;
problems, 291-3; (see also Fiscal policy, Monetary policy)
INMOS, 28, 109
Inputs – see Factors of production
Integration, 110
Interest, 9-10, 319
  theory of, 247-50; (see also Liquidity-Preference)
Intermediate areas, 52-3, 56
International Monetary Fund (IMF), 190, 193, 199, 200-4
International trade, Chapter 19 passim
  free trade and protection, 177-82; in national income, 260-1; quotas, 178; tariffs, 177-8, 181; terms of trade, 182; (see also Exports, Imports)
International Trade Organisation (1947), 182
Investment, 256
  and growth, 313; as injection into circular flow, 256; autonomous and dependent, 270-2; forms, 270; (see also Accelerator, Marginal efficiency of capital, Multiplier, Interest)
Investment trusts, 152-3
Invisible trade, 184-9
Iso-cost curves, 19-21
Isoquants, 19-21
Issuing houses, 23

J-curve, 191
Jenkins, R, 208
Job Centres, 34, 54

Kelloggs, 112
Kennedy Round, 182
Keynes, J M (Lord), 5, 254
  Keynes Plan, 201; Keynesian Policies, 281-4, 287, 299; (see also Fiscal policy)
Kirkby Manufacturing and Engineering, 24-5
Korean war, 193

Labour, 9, Chapter 23 passim
  and growth, 313; demand, 217-9; supply, 34-9, 94, 219-21
Laker Airways, 117
Land, 9, 244-6
  (see also Rent)
Leasing, 29
Leyland, 110, 138
  (see also British Leyland)
Licensed deposit-takers, 152
Liquidity, 138
Liquidity-preference, 249
Liquidity trap, 249
Limited liability, 23
Lloyds Shipping Insurance, 48
Loan guarantee scheme, 18
Local authority bills, 152
Location of industry, 46-8
Location of offices bureau, 56
Lome Convention, 207
Lonhro, 115
London Passenger Transport Board, 24
Lorenz curve, 266
Luddite riots, 34
Luton, 48

McIntosh Report, 134
Macro-economics, Section 9 passim
Malthus, Rev T, 44
Manpower Services Commission, 55-6
Marginal efficiency of capital, 272
Marginal revenue product theory, 217-9
  (see also Wages)

Market, 3, Chapters 8, 9 passim
  Foreign exchange market, 48, 196; Market demand, Chapter 7 passim; structures 106-8
Marshall aid, 193, 201, 207
Marshall-Lerner criterion, 191, 193
Mars Ltd, 23
Meade Report, 311
Merchant Banks, 151-3
Mergers, 110, 115-6
Micro-economics, Sections 1, 2, 3, 4 passim
Migration, 41-2
Minimum lending rate, 150, 158, 161
  (see also Bank of England, Monetary policy)
Mixed economy, 11
Monetarism, 156, 287, 296, 299-301
  (see also Friedman, M, Monetary policy)
Monetary base control, 163
Monetary compensation amounts, 212
Monetary policy
  aims, 155-7, 299-300; competition and credit control, 160-3; mechanisms, 157-9; 1981 changes, 163-4; problems, 300-301; (see also Friedman, M, Monetarism)
Money, Chapter 14 passim
  at call, 146, 147, 150; definitions, 137; Eurocurrencies, 151-3; forms, 137-9; functions, 138-9; hot, 163; money supply multiplier, 140, 158; quantity theory, 155-6; secondary money markets, 151-3; supply, 154-5, 162
Monopolies and Mergers Commission, 114-6, 128
Monopoly, Chapter 11 passim
  and competition, 124; criticisms, 111; definition, 106-7; discriminating, 112; equilibrium, 110-111; sources 109-10
Monopsony, 118, 221
Moral suasion, 157
Multiplier, Chapter 28 passim
  calculation, 272-5; government, 280-2; real world, 284-5; trade (export), 277-80
Murray, L, 238
Mussolini, B, 245

NALGO, 239, 242
National Bus Company, 128, 133
National Coal Board, 132, 133
National Economic Development Organization, 134
National Enterprise Board, 28, 116, 126-7, 133
National Freight Corporation, 127, 130, 133
National Health Service, 3, 11, 126, 239
National Income Accounts, Chapter 27 passim
  calculation, 260-4; uses, 264-7
National Insurance, 309
Nationalised industries, 11, 24, 104, 109, Chapter 13 passim
  criticisms, 130-5; investment policy, 128-30; motives, 127-8; pricing policy, 128-30; (see also Public corporations)
National Loans Fund, 130, 132
National Savings Certificates, 157
National Water Council, 133
NATO, 206
New towns, 53
New Towns Act (1946), 52
North Sea Oil, 7, 9, 51, 193-4, 214
  (see also British National Oil Corporation)
Norton Villiers Triumph Meriden Co-operative, 24
NRDC, 133
NUM, 239
NUPE, 239, 242

NUT, 242
NUTGWU, 242

OEEC, 206
OECD - see OEEC
Oligopoly, 107-8, 116-7
Open market operations, 144, 158
Opportunity cost, 4, 10, 40, 246
Ordinary shares, 25-6
Organisation of Petroleum Exporting Countries (OPEC), 117, 162, 189, 193, 197, 203
Output - see Production

Paradox of thrift, 275-7
Partnership, 22
Patents, 109
Pay Board, 231
Pension funds, 152-3
Perfect competition, 108, 121-5, Chapter 12 passim
  in factor market, 219-21
Petroleum revenue tax, 308
Phillips curve, 296-9
Picketing, 239, 241
Population, 40-4
Post Office, 55, 132, 133
Precautionary motive, 247-9
Preference shares, 25-6
Pressed steel, 110, 115
Price elasticity of demand, 80-3, 86-7, 93, 98-100, 191
Prices, Chapters 8, 9 passim
  determination, 89; discriminatory and differential, 110-11, 129; function, 89; marginal cost price, 60-1, 128-30; price control, 101-3
Prices and Incomes Board, 231
Prices and Incomes Policy, 228-34, 296-9, 304
Prices Commission, 231
Proctor and Gamble, 107
Production, Section 1 passim
  average and marginal, 13-14; equilibrium, 104-6; factors of, 9-10; large-scale, 14-17; optimum, 14, 19-21, 60; production-possibility frontiers, 11, 12, 173-7, 312; shutdown point 60-1; small-scale 17-18
Profit, 3, 10, Section 4 passim
  and inflation, 282; excess, 10, 245, 250-1; normal, 10, 245, 250-1; retained, 27, 29
Psychology, 2, 3
Public corporations, 24
  (see also Nationalised industries)
Public Sector Borrowing Requirement (PSBR), 157, 159, 291, 304, 309
Purchasing power parity theory, 196

Quantity theory of money, 155-6
Quasi-rent, 146
Queueing, 102

Rank Xerox, 112
Rates, 309
Rationing, 101
Reading, 48
Redundancy Payments Act (1965), 234
Regional policy, 51-7
Re-intermediation, 162
Rent, 9, 244-7
Resale Price Maintenance (RPM), 119
Restrictive practices, 118-9, 128
Restrictive Practices Court, 118
Retail Prices Index, 168-70, 228
Revenue, Chapters 11, 12 passim
Rhodesia, 181

327

Rights issues, 24, 27
Rolls Royce, 13, 28, 39, 126–7
Rome, Treaty of, 206–8
 (see also European Economic Community)
Rooker-Wise Amendment, 291, 307
Rookes v. *Barnard* (1964), 240
Roosevelt, F D, 254
Roskill Commission, 5, 316
Round-tripping, 161
Royal Bank of Scotland, 115

Sampling, 165–6
Sanctions, 181
Savings, 268–84 passim
 function, 268–70, 272–6; propensity, 256–8, 272–82
Schweppes, 110
Scottish Newspaper Enterprises, 24
Sealink, 115
Secondary money markets, 151–2
Securities, 25
Selective credit controls, 159
Self-financing, 27
Shares, 23–7
Shaw, G B, 1
Short-time working compensation scheme, 156
Skill centres, 54, 318
Skilled workers' mobility experiment, 54
Smith, A, 34
Smithsonian Agreement, 193, 202
Snake in the tunnel, 203
Social benefit, 100, 130
 (see also Cost-benefit analysis)
Social contract, 233
Social cost, 59, 100, 130, 315
 (see also Cost-benefit analysis)
Sociology, 2, 3
SOGAT, 242
Sole proprietor, 22
Special Areas Act (1934), 52
Special deposits, 158–60
Special development areas, 52–3, 56
Special drawing rights, 189, 202–3
Speculative motive, 248–9
Stagflation, 287, 302–4
Standard Charter Bank, 115
Sterling balances, 192–3
Stock appreciation, 263
Stock Exchange (Stock Market), 23, 24, 48
Stocks
 convertible, 157; debentures, 25; gilt-edged, 25, 157–8, 248–9; index-linked, 157; partly-paid, 157
Subsidies, 98–100
Substitution, electricity of, 19
Sunday Times, 115
Supersnake – see European monetary system
Supplementary deposits, 160–3
Supply, Chapter 5 passim
 calculation of schedule, 61–2; changes in, 90–6; elasticity, 62–4, 93–4, 98–100; joint, 66, 94; labour, curve of 94; long-run, 64–6

Taxation, 307–11
 as leakage from circular flow, 256–58; criticisms, 309–11; in national income accounts, 260–1; UK system, 307–9; on goods, 97–100, 307–9
Tax and price index, 170
TGWU, 39, 239, 242
Thatcher, M, 304
Times Newspapers, 115
T I Raleigh, 116
Totalisator Betting Levy Board, 24
Town Development Act (1952), 52
Trade bills – see Commercial bills
Trade cycle, 252
Trades unions, 6, 39, 224, Chapter 24 passim
 and Labour Party, 238, 242; criticisms, 241–8; dues, 242; functions, 236–8; growth, 239–41; structure, 238–41; TUC, 238, 241
Trade Unions and Labour Relations Act (1974), 240
Trades Disputes Act (1965), 240
Training Opportunities Programme (TOP's), 54
Transactions motive, 247–9
Transfer cost, 245
Transfer earnings – see Transfer cost
Transfer payments, 261–2
Transport Act (1968), 128
Treasury bills, 147–9
Two-tier guild system, 202

UCATT, 239
Unemployment, 39, 156
 and growth, 316; and inflation, 292; frictional, 49, 253; general, 49, 254; regional, 49–57; structural, 48–50, 253–4; voluntary, 48
Unilever, 16, 107
Unit Trusts, 152–3
USA, 35, 141
USDAW, 239, 242
Utility, 68
 Law of diminishing marginal utility, 69–70; Law of equi-marginal returns, 71–2; (see also Demand)

Value-added tax (VAT), 97, 295, 307–8
Veblen effect, 69, 71, 86
Venture capital scheme, 18
Victoria line, 316
Visible trade, 184–5, 208–10
 (see also International trade)

Wages, 8, Chapter 23 passim
 and government, 227–34; differentials, 222; drift, 227; in UK, 221–33; marginal revenue product theory, 217–19; national minimum wage, 227; (see also Incomes policy)
Western Electric Company, 6
White Plan, 201
Wilkinson Sword, 110
Wilson Committee, 27
Wilson, Sir H, 27, 210
Witney, 48

Youth Opportunities Programme (YOP), 55–6, 300
Youth Training Scheme (YTS), 55